Praise for *"No Equal Justice"*:
The Legacy of Civil Rights Icon George W. Crockett Jr.

"George Crockett is an inspiration for freedom fighters everywhere, and it's an honor to carry on his legacy of working for the people in Congress. A true people's lawyer, his life serves as a model of courageous, unflinching advocacy, and it's long past due that new generations learn about his pioneering civil rights and social justice work."

—Congresswoman Rashida Tlaib

"In 1949, George W. Crockett Jr., as a Black lawyer, was one of five who defended the constitutional rights of the leaders of the United States Communist Party. This criminal trial, then America's longest and most important, ended with contempt citations—Crockett served four months in a segregated Kentucky prison. Later, in 1952, he and his partner, Ernie Goodman, represented most of those called before the House Un-American Activities Committee in Detroit, including future mayor Coleman A. Young. Early on a Saturday morning, in 1969, Crockett, while a Detroit Recorder's Court judge, went to Detroit Police Headquarters with writs of habeas corpus and began arraignments freeing most of the 142 men, women, and children illegally arrested after a shoot-out at the New Bethel Baptist Church. After I became a lawyer in 1970, I practiced law before this brilliant and ethical jurist. He respected the civil liberties of everyone regardless of race, religion, or political affiliations. He became my mentor and I managed his 1980 campaign for the U.S. Congress. This superb and long-overdue book is for young and older readers of law, history, and biography. It instructs on what was and how a determined person can make positive differences in the lives of others. It is a quintessential must-read."

—Dennis Archer, Mayor of Detroit (1994–2001), Michigan Supreme Court Justice (1986–90), President National Bar Association (1983–84), and President American Bar Association (2003–4)

"*'No Equal Justice': The Legacy of Civil Rights Icon George W. Crockett Jr.* makes abundantly clear that this dedicated life led by George Crockett Jr. must not be forgotten lest we forget our own history and disregard the road map George Crockett's life is in this struggle for justice. While George Crockett's life could stand for how elusive justice can be and how history repeats itself, Professors Littlejohn and Hammer successfully make the case for how we must stay encouraged in the struggle, and how we can draw inspiration from the giant warrior that George Crockett was. These authors bring George Crockett Jr. back to life—to educate and inspire a new generation of social activists, judges, and all who are invested in eradicating racism from our institutions, hearts, minds, streets, and courtrooms. I commend 'No Equal Justice' to anyone who must be encouraged, strong, and courageous."

—Judge Victoria A. Roberts, United States District Court, Eastern District of Michigan and 62nd President of the State Bar of Michigan (1996–97)

"George Crockett was a man of extraordinary courage, character, and conscience. Unwavering and impactful in his efforts to create a more just America—and to end apartheid in South Africa—his life set a standard to which persons of conscience should aspire. This book shows what it means to be a person of principle and consequence, and should be read by all who wish to better understand the searing battles that led to the rights to which Blacks have access today."

—Randall Robinson, lawyer, author, human rights activist, and founder of TransAfrica

"George W. Crockett Jr., who represented my father and Coleman Young during the Red Scare hearings in Detroit, was a hero in my family, but more important was a vital and underappreciated figure in the fight for social and racial justice in America. I am thrilled that his courageous story is finally being told."

—David Maraniss, Pulitzer Prize–winning author of *A Good American Family: The Red Scare and My Father*

"The authors . . . make Crockett's story accessible for any reader, not just for lawyers and intellectuals, and it is because his life and career had such an impact on the social and political struggles of his time that it is an important story for us all."

—National Lawyers Guild

"No Equal Justice"

Great Lakes Books Series

Editor

Thomas Klug
Sterling Heights, Michigan

African American Life Series

Editor

Melba Joyce Boyd
Department of Africana Studies, Wayne State University

A complete listing of the books in these series
can be found online at wsupress.wayne.edu.

"No Equal JUSTICE"

The Legacy of Civil Rights Icon George W. Crockett Jr.

Edward J. Littlejohn and Peter J. Hammer

Wayne State University Press
Detroit

ISBN 9780814350584 (paperback)
ISBN 9780814348765 (hardcover)
ISBN 9780814348772 (ebook)

Library of Congress Control Number: 2021943633

On cover: Republic of New Africa members detained at the New Bethel Baptist Church, March 28–29, 1969. Courtesy of Valerie and Carolyn Baker and the General Baker Institute. Cover design by Will Brown.

Wayne State University Press rests on Waawiyaataanong, also referred to as Detroit, the ancestral and contemporary homeland of the Three Fires Confederacy. These sovereign lands were granted by the Ojibwe, Odawa, Potawatomi, and Wyandot Nations, in 1807, through the Treaty of Detroit. Wayne State University Press affirms Indigenous sovereignty and honors all tribes with a connection to Detroit. With our Native neighbors, the press works to advance educational equity and promote a better future for the earth and all people.

Wayne State University Press
Leonard N. Simons Building
4809 Woodward Avenue
Detroit, Michigan 48201-1309

Visit us online at wsupress.wayne.edu.

Gerry M. Doot
November 1, 1956–September 15, 1998
Lawyer, CPA, research assistant, friend, and ardent
admirer of George W. Crockett Jr.

Contents

Congressman George W. Crockett Jr.

Acknowledgments

Three of the best lawyers ever to work in Detroit were Maurice Sugar, Ernest (Ernie) Goodman, and George W. Crockett Jr. It is impossible to tell the story of one without including important parts of the lives of the others. Fortunately, there are good biographies of Sugar and Goodman: Christopher H. Johnson, *Maurice Sugar: Law, Labor, and the Left in Detroit, 1912–1950* (1988), and Steve Babson, Dave Riddle, and David Elsila, *The Color of Law: Ernie Goodman, Detroit, and the Struggle for Labor and Civil Rights* (2010). This book completes the trilogy.

Writing this biography has been a labor of love, but it has also been a labor spanning multiple decades. Edward Littlejohn conceived the project as early as 1990. Sadly, Maurice Sugar passed away in 1974, but both George Crockett and Ernie Goodman were available and willing participants for the work. Crockett and Goodman made their personal records, legal files, and photograph collections available to Littlejohn. They also spent many hours in interviews and conversations, discussing their cases and personal histories, making invaluable contributions to this book.

We are also indebted to Tom Lonergan for generously sharing transcripts of his earlier interviews with Crockett, "It's in the Constitution" (1993), and William "Bill" Bryce for permission to use the videotapes of Goodman, "Counsel for the Common People," which he produced while at the Wayne State University College of Urban, Labor, and Metropolitan Affairs. Those tapes and transcripts, along with the Littlejohn interviews, transcripts, and voluminous related documents, are housed in the Walter P. Reuther Library of Labor and Urban Affairs.

As with many endeavors, life events and other demands eclipsed the work with the manuscript about two-thirds complete. This is where Peter Hammer came in. In the course of collaborating on other projects, Littlejohn suggested a joint effort to finish the Crockett biography. It was a brilliant idea, bringing together the founding director of the Damon J. Keith Collection of African American Legal History with the founding director of the Damon J. Keith Center for Civil Rights to tell the story of George Crockett.

The narrative that follows is cast heavily from Crockett's and, where appropriate, Goodman's own words and represents their personal recollections of historical events. Thus, in addition to giving unique and insightful meanings to the cases and events that have been known primarily from impersonal court opinions and public and other records, their words personify their clients as well as the humanity that motivated both as lawyers. This is particularly significant with respect to the Battle of Foley Square. Littlejohn conducted the central interviews with Crockett in 1993 by mail, by telephone, and in person, which included a "working" week with Crockett at his cottage on the Chesapeake Bay in Maryland. While Crockett had given many interviews about Foley Square, there has not been, beyond brief quotes and comments, any major explication of his opinions and views about what remains one of the United States' most important and controversial cases. Of the lawyers who appeared on both sides of the Foley Square trial, Crockett at that time was the sole survivor. As such, detailed commentaries by him are valuable additions to the volumes that have been written about the case. This is particularly true because Crockett's role in most existing accounts is often flattened and two-dimensional. We seek to remedy this omission. Crockett's personal comments include little-known connections with the case by Black leaders like Charles Hamilton Houston, Walter White, Paul Robeson, and Thurgood Marshall and provide a different view of these significant events.

At the outset, both Crockett and Goodman expressed concerns that the work not be too academic. Crockett recalled a Yiddish expression: "Shrieb as de kinder zol keinein farstehen"—"Write so that the children can understand it." Goodman insisted that we write "so that it can be read and understood by ordinary people who might want to know something about George and me." To the extent academics can, we tried.

Special acknowledgment is also owed to Littlejohn's former research assistant Gerry M. Doot. After graduating from Wayne State University Law School, Gerry continued to work as his assistant, proofreader, and editor for the early stages of the project. Her uncommon devotion also followed the deep respect and admiration she developed for George W. Crockett Jr. and Ernest Goodman. Regrettably, she passed away before the work was completed. Gerry and her contributions are profoundly missed.

We are also grateful for Dr. Louis Jones, field archivist for the Walter P. Reuther Library at Wayne State University, for his major contributions to the project and his assistance in curating the Littlejohn Collection of African American Legal History, from which many of the primary sources for this biography are derived. Additional thanks are owed to the reference librarians at the Arthur Neef Law Library at Wayne State University Law School and to our anonymous reviewers for a number of thoughtful and constructive suggestions on how to strengthen the narrative.

Finally, we want to express our gratitude for the Crockett family for their assistance and support, particularly Dr. Ethelene Crockett Jones and Kyra Hicks.

Introduction

We live in a time when virtually everyone has an opinion but few have deeply held principles. Even among the principled, not many have the courage to take serious risks in support of their convictions. This was not always the case. There was a time, not long ago, when giants walked in our midst. George W. Crockett Jr. (1909–1997) was one such giant.

Two key principles drove Crockett's life. First was an unshakable commitment to racial justice, what we call today an unapologetic antiracist agenda. The second, paradoxically, was a belief in the power of law and the Constitution. This was not the Constitution revered and applied by white judges. It was the latent power of a Constitution that only Black judges and other judges of color could see, understand, and wield. It was the United States' real, but unrealized, Constitution.

Crockett's own words are the best means to introduce him to a new generation.

> Racism pervades every area and facet of American life. It is a characteristic of American life; and hence, it is a characteristic of American law.[1]
>
> To deny that racism exists throughout our judicial system is to be oblivious to the most fundamental truths about twentieth-century America.[2]
>
> Racism has been an integral part of American law since the first Negro slaves arrived in Virginia in 1619. A new nation, which bore witness to the world in 1776 that all men are created equal, experienced neither logical nor moral difficulty when, eleven years later, it adopted a constitution that sanctioned human slavery and decreed that a person held in bondage should be counted as three-fifths of a person.[3]
>
> Racism is evident in our courts whenever and wherever a black litigant is involved. It is indigenous to the law as applied to blacks

1

whether the proceeding is in Michigan or Mississippi, in a federal
or a state tribunal, or in a court of civil or criminal jurisdiction.[4]

There is no equal justice for black people today; there never has
been. To our everlasting shame, the quality of justice in America
has always been and is now directly related to the color of one's
skin as well as to the size of one's pocketbook.[5]

The reasonable doubt that is usually interposed to save the life and
liberty of a white person charged with a crime seldom has any
force or effect when a colored person is accused of a crime.[6]

How do you change the mores of the police officer on the street or
the sergeant at the precinct station who still believes that black
people have no rights that white people are bound to respect?
How do you change the thinking of a black nationalist whose
despair has turned into a bitter hatred of all white people?[7]

Although the Constitution was written two centuries ago, it has no
life or meaning for black Americans until the people breathe life
into it by living it—and that has been the struggle of the twentieth
century.[8]

We live in a multiracial, unjust world. Its problems cannot be corrected by men who don't understand what it is to grow up powerless and oppressed. Until the status quo is changed to reflect and
use the diversity as well as the knowledge we could have available
to us, we won't solve anything.[9]

I refuse to allow myself to forget the fact that I am a black judge.
Once I do that, I think I'm lost.[10]

George W. Crockett Jr. was born in 1909 in the Jim Crow South of
Jacksonville, Florida. His early life was defined by segregation, but he found
strength and guidance within the Black community. Crockett had a formative experience in high school that he shared repeatedly throughout his life
as a tribute to his mother and his teachers. He wanted to participate in an
interschool debate competition addressing the postemancipation constitutional amendments.[11] The top prize was a substantial $200 scholarship,
but the speech coach told him that two students had already been chosen.
His mother would have nothing to do with it, instructing her son that as
long as there was a higher authority for appeal, all was not lost. Crockett

took his case to the principal, who agreed that the school representatives should be chosen by competition. He went on to win the intraschool competition, the interschool contest, and the $200 scholarship that enabled him to attend Morehouse College.

This important lesson was taught within the confines of segregated space. Crockett learned his values, sense of self, and sense of fairness from his family, his teachers, and the broader Black community. His principles were shaped by being raised within a Black southern tradition that emphasized race pride and self-respect by consciously countering pervasive narratives of racial inferiority. As he grew older, he took these lessons into more dangerous white spaces. In the white world, not all of his victories would be as easy as his high school speech competition, and not all authority figures would be as fair or as trustworthy as his high school principal.

In 1948–49, approaching his fortieth birthday, Crockett found himself the only Black lawyer on the defense team of the most important political trial in U.S. history, *United States v. Dennis*.[12] In a period of increasing national hysteria, following the rise of McCarthyism and the communist Red Scare, the Department of Justice arrested and placed on trial the entire top leadership of the United States Communist Party.[13] Party leaders were charged with violating the Smith Act's prohibition against *teaching* or *advocating* the overthrow of the government by force. The controversial trial was followed internationally and resulted in several U.S. Supreme Court landmark decisions, notably *Dennis v. United States* (1951). For Crockett, the defense was about protecting the First Amendment's guarantee of free speech. All the prosecutors, the jury, and the rest of the country could see, however, was red. After the longest criminal trial in history to that date, all defendants were convicted.

For the defense lawyers, however, the trial was not over. Judge Harold R. Medina had what he termed some "unfinished business." In an unprecedented decision, without a hearing, he summarily sentenced the defense attorneys to prison for contempt of court. Additional Supreme Court landmark decisions resulted, for example, *Sacher v. United States* (1953).[14] Crockett served four months in jail. In essence, he was imprisoned for doing his job as a lawyer, after already suffering tremendous personal and professional backlash for defending the rights of the politically unpopular defendants.

For a man who believed deeply in the rule of law, this was Kafkaesque. What happens when everything you hold true is turned upside down? There was no due process, no impartial adjudicator, and no rule of law. This extra-legal punishment was inflicted on some of the only lawyers in the country willing to step forward to defend communists. Demonstrating the contempt that bar associations had for lawyers who defended "Reds," Crockett and his colleagues soon faced disbarment proceedings. In defending himself in front of his colleagues at the Michigan bar, he struggled to reassert his own fundamental identity. "I am first and foremost a lawyer proud of his profession; second, a Negro deeply conscious of the wrongs done his people; and third, an unrelenting champion of the civil liberties of all people regardless of race, religion or political affiliations."[15]

———————————

Two decades later, in 1969 Detroit, Judge George Crockett would be wearing the judicial robes, but the challenges were no less daunting. At 5 a.m. on a Saturday morning, Crockett heard a knock on his door. Standing there was a Black state representative and a community leader, Reverend C. L. Franklin, father of the music superstar Aretha Franklin. The Republic of New Africa, a Black separatist group, had been holding its convention at Reverend Franklin's New Bethel Baptist Church when an altercation with police occurred, leaving one officer dead and one wounded. The police stormed the church, arresting 142 people, including women and children. The arrestees were detained en masse in a police garage.

Many people feared that the event would spark another riot in Detroit, a city still on edge after its 1967 Rebellion. Getting dressed and armed only with a writ of habeas corpus, Judge Crockett went straight to the police station to hold court on that Saturday morning. Crockett's actions set off a firestorm that received national attention and resulted in efforts to impeach him. The "New Bethel Incident" and the confrontations around Judge Crockett that followed became bellwether events for the emergence of Black political power in a racially divided Detroit.

Crockett had an amazing range of achievements. He graduated from Morehouse College and, in 1934, was the sole Black student to graduate in his class from the University of Michigan Law School. He was the first Black lawyer to work at the U.S. Department of Labor, rising to a level from which he could advance no further because it would involve supervising white attorneys. He left the Department of Labor in 1943 to become the first hearing examiner for the newly created Fair Employment Practices Commission. Crockett was recruited by the United Auto Workers union (UAW) and rose to be executive director of its Fair Practices Committee, fighting racial discrimination in the industry and the union. It was at the UAW where he met Maurice Sugar and Ernest (Ernie) Goodman, UAW general counsel and associate general counsel, respectively. It was also in Detroit that Crockett became active in the National Lawyers Guild (NLG), one of the few integrated bar associations in the country.

After a meteoric rise in the legal profession, Crockett faced a major fall. As part of a long and calculated rise to power, Walter Reuther purged from the union those who were communists, those he thought were communists, and those who were too sympathetic to their cause. Sugar, Goodman, and Crockett, among numerous others, all received the axe. Maurice Sugar remained a lifetime friend and mentor. Crockett would describe Sugar as his father "in the law." It was Crockett's connection to Sugar that led him to become part of the defense team in *United States v. Dennis*. Returning to Detroit after the trial in 1950, Goodman and Crockett founded the nation's first racially integrated law firm, Goodman, Crockett, Eden & Robb.[16] Before 1950, no law firm had accepted the obvious risks associated with an integrated practice; for almost two decades thereafter, law partnerships in the United States remained segregated.[17]

Goodman, Crockett, and other NLG attorneys fought for the rights of the politically oppressed throughout the turmoil of the Red Scare in the 1950s before pivoting to take on the Black struggle for civil rights in the 1960s. Crockett went to Jackson, Mississippi, in 1964 to spearhead the NLG's efforts to provide legal support for civil rights workers during what was known as the Mississippi Summer Project.

In 1966, Crockett was elected to the Detroit Recorder's Court, the court that heard the city's criminal cases. As a jurist who provided equal justice in his courtroom and demanded honesty from both defendants and the police, he was both revered and reviled. From the bench, Judge Crockett protected constitutional rights, fought against police brutality, demanded reasonable bail for detainees during the 1967 Rebellion, and weathered tremendous political backlash for ensuring the release of more than a hundred citizens wrongly arrested in the New Bethel Incident. As a judge on the Recorder's Court, Crockett was in the middle of Detroit politics as the city transitioned from a majority-white city to a majority-Black city. In 1974, the same year that Coleman A. Young became Detroit's first Black mayor, George Crockett was elected Chief Judge of the Recorder's Court, a position he held until his retirement from the bench in 1978.

Crockett did not remain retired long. In 1980, he was elected to Congress and served until 1990. In Congress, he took his fight for civil rights global and became an outspoken member of the House Foreign Affairs Committee. Crockett was active in the anti-apartheid movement in South Africa and in efforts to free Nelson Mandela. In a reprise of his struggles during the Red Scare, he stridently opposed many of the Reagan administration's policies in Third World countries. He led an unsuccessful federal lawsuit that sought to keep U.S. troops out of El Salvador. He fought against the U.S. invasions of Grenada and Panama, aid to the Nicaraguan contras, and U.S. arms sales in the Middle East.

Crockett's life intersects a remarkable range of episodes in U.S. history. As a young lawyer, he was a child of the New Deal. At the UAW, he was steeped in the labor movement at a pivotal transition point when Walter Reuther seized control and expelled anyone he thought might be too radical. Crockett was on the front lines fighting political oppression during the Red Scare. In the summer of 1964, George Crockett advised James Chaney, Michael Schwerner, and Andrew Goodman on their fateful trip to investigate a church burning in Philadelphia, Mississippi. It was a trip from which the three civil rights martyrs never returned. As a Recorder's Court judge in Detroit, he was in the center of the racial struggles, police brutality, and urban unrest that defined U.S. cities in the 1960s and 1970s.

Throughout this long journey, Crockett was the steady rock that others relied on. From the outside, he could appear formal, austere, and unflappable. Internally, even when facing controversy, he maintained a deep sense of calm that came from the confidence of doing what he knew was right. He developed a unified rights-based philosophy in his youth that guided him the rest of his life. This grounding gave him a strong sense of self that enabled him to navigate a segregated world and face tremendous physical danger and violence, all while being able to envision strategic action for social change leading to what he hoped would be a better future.

This is the story of a singular lawyer who practiced the ideals of his profession with a fierce and uncommon dedication.

1

The Early Years

Influences and Michigan Law

The story of George W. Crockett Jr. is a true American story, beginning in slavery and ending in an ongoing struggle for freedom. He was shaped and nurtured by a critical range of segregated Black institutions: his family, the church, and a budding Black civil society. The importance of family is illustrated by the care Crockett devoted to researching, writing, and preserving the family history. The Crockett family history includes this dedication: "This Family History is dedicated to all who came before us, whose courage and experiences we celebrate." Acknowledging the many ways that racism erases personal identities and individual identities, the history begins, "As far as we have been able to ascertain . . ."[1]

This is the Crockett family story. Sidney Weatherly (Crockett's great-great-grandfather) was brought to the United States as a slave in about 1778 to the city of Salisbury, on the Eastern Shore of Maryland. Sadly, many details are simply unknown. No one knows the place or date of Sidney's birth or death, the name of his wife, or the number of children they had. It is known that Weatherly was the name of his slave master.[2]

Charles (Weatherly) Crockett (Crockett's great-grandfather), son of Sidney Weatherly, was born a slave in or around Salisbury in 1803. He lived 105 years, passing in Laurel, Delaware, in 1908 or 1909.[3] How Charles got from Salisbury to Laurel is a matter of some mystery. The Crockett family history reports, "After the Emancipation Proclamation following the Civil War, Charles crossed over from Maryland into Delaware, dropping his slave name Weatherly, and took the name Crockett. He settled on a farm in the

7

vicinity of Spring Hill Church near Laurel, Delaware."[4] The history also states that "John Crockett [Crockett's grandfather], the son of Charles and Anna Wales Crockett, was born on February 12, 1863 at Laurel, Delaware."[5]

The Emancipation Proclamation did not apply to Maryland or Delaware. Slavery did not legally end in these states until 1865. In what the historian Barbara Jeanne Fields terms the "middle ground" of Maryland, such technicalities made little difference. "Neither the preliminary Proclamation nor the final one on January 1 embraced Maryland. But to the slaves, who cared nothing for the reasons of state that exempted their owners from the edict of freedom, that hardly mattered."[6] Fields notes, however, what a weighty and dangerous decision self-emancipation was. It appears that Charles escaped from Maryland to Delaware (also a slave state) with his pregnant wife sometime after the Emancipation Proclamation was announced on September 22, 1862, and the birth of their son, John, on the twelfth of February. In other words, John was apparently born free through an act of self-emancipation. The mystery only deepens when one realizes that Laurel is only fifteen miles north of Salisbury. They did not escape very far.

One wonders why the act of escaping from slavery during the Civil War is not stated more directly or even celebrated in Crockett family lore. As we will see, George Crockett Jr. was meticulous about details. He did not make mistakes or tolerate omissions. Interestingly, he drops a hint as to the likely truth in the family history. The history reproduces an article from the *Washington Post Magazine* titled "Maryland's Eastern Shore: Tracing the Underground Railroad." In 1860, Maryland had eighty-four thousand free Blacks and a slave population of eighty-seven thousand persons. The article asserts that there were many opportunities for slaves to escape: "The town of Easton (Maryland) harbored a sizable community of Quakers, the white linchpins of the Underground Railroad, and Quakers operated a string of safe houses in Delaware, along the Railroad's route to Philadelphia."[7] Whether via the Underground Railroad or through a series of personal contacts and relationships spanning the fifteen miles, the Crockett family made it to Laurel, Delaware, which became and remains the family's spiritual home.[8]

There is something fitting about Maryland being the place of the Crockett family origin, the same state that birthed Frederick Douglass.

Douglass was a fierce advocate for racial justice and the power that a properly interpreted antislavery Constitution could deploy. These are values George Jr. would embrace his whole life.

John Crockett, George's grandfather, married Minnie Conway of nearby Bethel, Delaware. John and Minnie had seven children; all died in infancy save two—George William Crockett (George Jr.'s father) and Elizabeth Crockett Thorgood (George Jr.'s aunt).[9] George Sr. was born March 20, 1883, in Seaford, Delaware. His sister Elizabeth was born February 17, 1892. The Crockett family's sojourn from slavery continued farther and farther north. John moved his family to Camden, New Jersey, to perfect the trade of cement layer and to provide a better education for his children.[10]

Unfortunately, fate intervened: "George Sr. terminated his public schooling at the high school level when his father's broken leg made it necessary that he go to work in a garment factory to support the family."[11] He was so employed when he met Minnie Amelia Jenkins in 1904, his future wife and George Jr.'s mother.

Minnie Amelia Jenkins's father, Moses Frazier Jenkins, was born a slave in 1861. "It is believed that his birthplace was located between the towns of Starke and Waldo, some 60 miles southwest of Jacksonville [Florida]."[12] The details of George Sr. and Minnie's courtship, marriage, and early years are told in their own words in a news article commemorating their fiftieth wedding anniversary.[13] Minnie was born in Georgetown, South Carolina, in 1883. "When she was about 14, her mother died and she was adopted by her cousins Dr. and Mrs. H. T. Johnson and went to live with them in Camden, N.J."[14] This is where the couple met in 1904.

What is meant by Minnie being "adopted" is unclear because sometime later her father, Moses Jenkins, traveled to Camden to take her back with him to South Carolina. George Sr. told Moses that he and Minnie wanted to be married. Moses told George that he would have to come to South Carolina for her when they were ready.[15] In the meantime, Minnie taught high school in Georgetown for about two years, when, true to his word, George Sr. "traveled to Georgetown to find this young lady," and the couple were married.[16]

A serious question for the couple was where they would live. Escaping slavery, the Crockett family, starting in Maryland, traveled north for relatively more safety and better educational opportunities. Now, George Sr.'s heart had taken him to South Carolina and was about to lead him even farther south. Around the time of the wedding, Moses Jenkins sold his two farms in South Carolina and bought two other farms in Waldo, Florida, near where he had been born. The newlyweds moved with him in 1906, but the rural farm town proved more than George Sr. could handle. "After arriving there I didn't like the conditions, so we came to Jacksonville."[17]

George William Crockett Jr. was born in 1909, in Jacksonville, Florida. Not surprisingly, George Jr. was greatly influenced by his parents. "My mother was small in stature, but she was strong-willed and pugnacious; she never took anything lying down. My father, who was six feet tall, was a community leader. He was the head of the Black Elks in Florida, a leader in the Black Masons, as well as the Baptist church."[18] George Sr. subsequently became an ordained minister. During his later years, he was the pastor of Jacksonville's Harmony Baptist Church.

By standards in the Black community, the Crockett family would have been considered middle, if not upper-middle, class. The Crockett household was full of activity, including the union and civil rights work that would become so important to George Jr. George Sr. was employed, full-time, by the Atlantic Coast Railroad as a skilled carpenter, repairing and building railroad boxcars. He was also a member of the Black Carpenters Union.[19] Prior to the marriage in 1906, Minnie Crockett was a licensed public school teacher in South Carolina. Described as vivacious and bright, she, like her husband, was an active leader in their church and in Jacksonville's Black community.[20] She remained committed to education and civil rights. Minnie Crockett was a personal friend of Mary McLeod Bethune and was president of the Jacksonville Bethune-Cookman Circle.[21] She was well known for poetry recitals, which were described as dramatic. Her love of family and her devotion to church are shown in excerpts from her poem "Our Children":

> *They are dear to us, our children three; all loving, kind and free*
> *The eldest one, a gentle girl, who to us is a precious pearl*
> *The next, a noble boy who is his parents' hope and joy*
> *Bearing his father's name as thus he travels on to fame*
> *'Tis of John F. that we speak with gentle disposition sweet*
> *He is called the "Mother's Child," for he is ever ready with*
>   *a smile*

Dear God, bless these children three, and may they ever cling
to thee
'Til this fleeting life is o'er, then live with Thee for ever more.[22]

George Jr. had an older sister and a younger brother. Alzeda Crockett, two years his elder, was born on October 9, 1907. Demonstrating the family's unusual commitment to education, she went on to graduate from Fisk University, the first college graduate in the Crockett family, and studied at the Juilliard School of Music. Later she would become dean of women at Bethune-Cookman College in Daytona Beach, Florida.[23] John Frazier Crockett was born on January 8, 1912. He would graduate from the Tuskegee Institute and work in Jacksonville as a railroad and shipyard worker, staying close to home to support his parents.[24]

Family support was accompanied by some level of family pressure to succeed and to make a difference in society. Moreover, there were basic norms of behavior enforced by family elders, like grandfather Moses Jenkins. George Jr. recalled that his grandfather "was a stickler on children showing respect to their elders." When George Jr. was about eight, he addressed his Uncle Rufin by his first name within hearing range of his grandfather. Moses Jenkins quickly admonished young George to "'put a handle on it,' which meant using either 'Uncle' or 'Mister' as appropriate adult titles."[25] Sadly, George Jr. would lose both of his paternal grandparents relatively early in his life. Grandfather John Crockett moved back to Laurel, Delaware, from Camden, New Jersey, by July 1910. He died in the nationwide influenza epidemic of 1917.[26] Grandmother Minnie Conway Crockett died two years later in June 1919, also in Laurel.[27]

George Sr. and Minnie Crockett had high expectations for their children. Minnie would often state, "My philosophy is that children should be ahead of their parents, should climb a step higher and make a contribution to the family and to society."[28] Similar inspiration came from George Sr. Even after receiving a call to the ministry, he continued working with the railroad, conducting his pastoral duties evenings and Sundays. "It was an example to the children that their daddy could do all this."[29]

George Jr. recalled that the Blacks who were considered upper class in Jacksonville during his youth were doctors, teachers, and mail carriers. These careers had their attractions for George, but he also enjoyed working with his hands, like his father. He became a skilled carpenter, and carpentry became a lifelong hobby. At one point, when he became disillusioned with practicing law, he seriously considered carpentry as a new career.

Growing up in the Deep South, Crockett was well aware of the Jim Crow laws that segregated the races. "Before I could read, I knew what it meant.... Every black kid was told by his parents at a very early age ...what discrimination was all about."[30] Nevertheless, he did not share these experiences with his own children. His youngest daughter, Ethelene, reflected, "I never once heard my father mention anything about experiences with segregation, discrimination, intimidation as a child growing up in Jacksonville."[31] That said, she recalled that even during her childhood when her family visited her grandparents in Jacksonville in the very house her father had grown up in, they "never saw white people."[32] Ethelene characterized her grandfather George Sr. as a "strong disciplinarian" who was extremely protective of the family. She recounted, "He told me to go with the girl who lived across the street that was about my age and to stick with her and don't go anywhere she didn't go and listen to everything she told me to do."[33]

Ethelene described her grandmother in very different terms: "From the way my father talked about his mother, I think she shaped him more than anybody else. She was all about 'do the right thing' and 'look out for your fellow man.' My grandfather was all about protecting yourself and protecting your family. But my grandmother was about taking care of community, taking care of family, not going with the crowd, but being true to yourself."[34]

Crockett's first experiences in the North came through his father's work with the railroad as travel passes were provided for the family. In the summer, they would go to Philadelphia or to Delaware, where the Crockett family had settled after slavery. These visits maintained connections with the important family network still centered in Laurel and provided Crockett a set of social perspectives that complemented those he found in Jacksonville. In the North, Crockett also witnessed considerable discrimination against Blacks. In contrasting the racism in the North versus that in the South, he noted,

[In] my lifetime discrimination was never as bad in the North as it was in the South. And yet there were some good things that characterized discrimination in the South that did not characterize discrimination in the North. In the South you "knew your place" and you didn't face embarrassments and mortification because you knew not to put yourself in that position. In the North, they professed to be open and to admit you and so forth, only to find when you tried to exercise that, that it wasn't true. In other words, there was hypocrisy that you experienced in the North that you didn't experience in the South.

The white man in the South just didn't have a damn thing for you to do as a class. On an individual basis, if he liked you, he would prefer you over some white person that he disliked. It was just that kind of relationship.

And that I think more than anything else explains why desegregation has proceeded far more rapidly, comparatively speaking, in the South than it has in the North. It's astounding what has happened in the South. But I don't see anything astounding about what has happened in the North since the civil rights revolution.[35]

Later, during his college years, Crockett would continue to return to the North for summer employment. He also received his introduction to labor unions. During the summers of 1928 and 1929, he worked as a waiter on boats running out of New York and joined the International Stewards and Cooks Union. He recalled that in the Deep South during his childhood, Blacks were barred from the white trade unions. The Black workers who were organized belonged to loosely organized, uninfluential Jim Crow unions. Crockett also remembered the skepticism that existed in the northern Black communities toward the trade union movement. Some of the leading Black organizations were "concerned about getting support from the white community and that really meant getting support from the white corporate community. Blacks were warned about 'getting mixed up' with those radicals in the trade union movement": "Of course, my own feelings were opposed to all of that."[36]

Jacksonville and the state of Florida had their own complicated history of racism and segregation. In the Pulitzer Prize–winning book *The Warmth of Other Suns*, Isabel Wilkerson details the life of George Swanson Starling, nine years younger than Crockett, providing a window into some of the horrors of growing up Black in rural Florida. Starling was lucky to escape north with his life.[37] The history of Jacksonville is no less steeped in racism, but urban life was different from rural life. Moreover, Jacksonville was a seat of substantial Black power in the Reconstruction Era and retained a residual of strong, if segregated, Black institutions, even as Reconstruction waned and Jim Crow bore greater and greater oppressive weight throughout the state.[38] In 1900, Jacksonville was a majority-Black city with a total population of 28,429 people, 57 percent Black and 42 percent white. By 1910, four years after the Crocketts arrived, the total population had grown to 57,699, and the racial composition was nearly a 50–50 split. Thereafter, Jacksonville became a majority-white city.[39] Ironically, Crockett was born in a majority-Black city that became majority white and would later work in Detroit, a majority-white city that became majority Black.

One of the residual Reconstruction Era institutions in Jacksonville was Edwin M. Stanton High School, named after General Stanton, Abraham Lincoln's secretary of war during the Civil War. Although it has gone through many iterations, Stanton High School was originally founded in 1868 with money from the Freedman's Bureau.[40] James Weldon Johnson, one of Black Jacksonville's brightest native sons, was a graduate of Stanton High School and served as its principal (1894–1902) before going on to serve as executive secretary of the National Association for the Advancement of Colored People (NAACP).[41]

Johnson was born in Jacksonville in 1871 and died in 1938. He bemoaned the fall of Jacksonville from its Reconstruction strength to its Jim Crow oppression and shame: "When I was growing up, most of the policemen were Negroes; several members of the city Council were Negroes; one or two justices of the peace.... Many of the best stalls in the city market were owned by Negroes.... Jacksonville is today a one hundred percent Cracker town."[42] Johnson was not the only hometown hero. The labor leader and civil rights activist A. Philip Randolph (1889–1979) lived in Jacksonville from his early childhood. The inspiration for young people like Johnson and Randolph, and to a lesser extent Crockett, who grew up witnessing the legacies of Reconstruction cannot be underestimated. "Randolph recalled that his father's stories of the revolutionary Black heroes and the positive legacy of Reconstruction taught him to stand up for his rights at an early age."[43] Growing up in a world with even living memories of Blacks in positions of authority gave them a different vision of what was possible.

One can imagine how Jacksonville heroes like Johnson and Randolph helped shape Crockett's worldview. Like twin engines on a plane, Johnson fueled the belief in racial justice and civil rights, while Randolph fueled the belief in economic justice, particularly through empowering workers.

Crockett attended Stanton High School, where he developed a fascination with and love for the Constitution early in life. As detailed in the introduction, through the strength of his mother, he learned the significance of pressing the right to appeal when he was excluded from participating in an oration competition. From the Stanton High School principal, he learned the importance of that appeal being made to an independent, objective, and impartial decision-maker. Through his own passion and skill, he won the speech competition touting the importance of the Thirteenth, Fourteenth, and Fifteenth Amendments, resulting in a $200 scholarship. This scholarship allowed him to attend yet another premier but segregated institution, Morehouse College in Atlanta. While there, he took additional courses in constitutional law, so that when he entered the University of Michigan Law School, he "was pretty much steeped in civil rights and civil liberties and had a love for constitutional law."[44] This early training guided him throughout his life.

While Crockett was a student at Morehouse, his rebelliousness and his willingness to challenge the status quo and powerful authorities surfaced. He organized and became president of the first student government at Morehouse. He did so despite the substantial opposition of the college president. This may not sound very radical now, but at that time, opposition to student organizing was strong among Black colleges that were tightly operated by powerful administrators; Crockett remembered that only Howard and Fisk universities had student governments before Morehouse. Even years later, Crockett noted with pride, "Fortunately, it [the student government] is still in existence."[45] Student governance reflects a deep belief in democratic principles, deliberative processes, and checks and balances. This is just as important in institutions controlled by powerful Black officials as it is in those controlled by powerful white officials.

While at college, Crockett further refined his talent for public speaking. "I went to Morehouse ... with the intention of being a dentist, ... but I'm afraid I wasn't too good in organic chemistry."[46] He excelled, however, in debating and the research required for debate competition. He became president of the debating society and was captain of the debating team in his sophomore, junior, and senior years. The orderly process by which Crockett chose law over dentistry manifested the reputation he would later earn as a meticulously careful lawyer and judge: "One evening, I went over to one of the classrooms and cleaned off two sections of the blackboard and at the top of one section I put dentistry and at the top of the other one, I put law and wrote down the pros and cons for each one, sat back and looked at them and made a deliberate, informed decision that I wanted to be a lawyer. And from that time on, everything I did was pointed in that direction."[47]

Initially, Crockett's sights were set on Harvard Law School, but the $500 annual tuition was an insurmountable barrier. He became interested in the University of Michigan Law School after he read a *New York Times* article about a wealthy Michigan alumnus named William W. Cook who had donated funds to build a legal-research building on campus.[48] Crockett's decision to attend law school in Ann Arbor was cemented when he learned the annual tuition for out-of-state students was only $150.

In 1931, Crockett arrived in Ann Arbor. It was not just a change in weather from Jacksonville that awaited him. He was familiar with the North, having spent substantial time with family in Delaware and on boats running out of New York, but Ann Arbor was different. Segregation is an evil in and of itself, but segregation can also afford shelter and opportunity. Crockett was nurtured, supported, and strengthened at Stanton High School and Morehouse College. This training gave him the armor he would need to take on the hostile white environment he found at the University of Michigan in the absence of substantial Black support.

Crockett's educational preparation was essential, but this was not enough. He also needed the support of family. The love of his parents was unquestioned, but that would not pay the bills. Other assets of the extended Crockett family were needed. George Sr.'s sister, Elizabeth Crockett Thorgood, and her husband had no children. They viewed their nephews and niece very much as their own. Aunt Elizabeth lived in New York for several years and was employed as a housekeeper for a wealthy couple.[49] She agreed to provide George Jr. with a "stipend" to help pay his tuition and living expenses for his ambitious goal of becoming a lawyer. Her only conditions were that George Jr. focus on his studies and not marry until he had graduated.[50]

With enough money to pay his tuition and the commitment from Aunt Elizabeth to send money every month for room and board, Crockett started law school. It was not surprising that he was one of only two Black students among three hundred in the first-year class. Because their last names were at opposite ends of the alphabet, they were placed in different first-year sections. Crockett, who grew up completely separated from white people, recalled his feelings of isolation and psychological pressure:

And here you are surrounded by a sea of whiteness. It's a hell of a psychological situation, because every time the professor calls on you, you feel that you've got the weight of the whole black race on your shoulders. And are they going to conclude now, that this proves the inferiority concept—he can't even answer the question— that kind of thing.

It can be an incentive, also, to study like hell the night before, to read the footnotes to the cases so that no matter which way the professor came, you at least could answer intelligently even if you couldn't give him the answer that he wanted. . . .

Anyway, it wasn't the most comfortable situation. You would meet your professors on the Diagonal, for example, and they would look the other way. . . .

Also, you miss having the companionship of students as far as talking and exchanging ideas, which is very important if you're studying law because it enables you to refine your own thinking.[51]

The burdens of race were compounded by the daily struggle for bare essentials. Crockett waited tables at a white fraternity house each evening. He worked out of necessity, despite a warning he received from Paul A. Leidy, secretary of the law school, that accompanied his notice of admission: "I notice in your previous correspondence with [Dean] Bates that you suggest deferring payment of part of your tuition. This would suggest a financial situation that you may possibly be planning to remedy by doing outside work during the school year. . . . It is only fair to warn you that only the exceptional student can afford to devote much time to outside work if he is carrying the full course."[52] One benefit of waiting tables was that it guaranteed at least one good meal a day from the fraternity kitchen. Crockett acquired the habit, which continued after law school, of not eating breakfast. If he became hungry studying late at night, his usual fare was peanut butter and jelly sandwiches and the milk given to him by the mother of a friend, who was the cook at another fraternity house.

Crockett had become accustomed to the warmth, closeness, and comradery of smart fellow students at Morehouse. Nevertheless, he overcame the isolation, segregation, and psychological burdens he encountered in Ann Arbor and completed law school with an excellent academic record.

Two incidents with law professors forecasted for Crockett the difficulties to be anticipated in the legal profession. The first involved a conversation he had with a professor who, of all his professors, "was pretty friendly."[53]

"As the colloquy unfolded," he asked me, "How did you do in exams?" I said, "Well, I took a course in domestic relations, I didn't do too well in that; as a matter of fact, I think I made a C. But, on the other hand, I took public utilities and I got an A and I took bills and notes and I got an A."

He said, "Well, you see now, the course . . ." and this might have been a racist statement, though I didn't consider it such, "See, the course in which you should have made the A was domestic relations, divorces, and so forth. That's where you are going to have the cases when you get out."[54]

The second incident occurred during his final year and involved the law school dean. The dean offered to write recommendations for seniors who deserved them, in his opinion, based on their academic credentials. Crockett requested a recommendation. While the dean expressed his pleasure at being able to provide a letter of recommendation, he noted the lack of opportunities for Blacks in the profession. He suggested that Crockett consider the Department of Justice in Washington or teaching law as a career, and he advised him that the Black law school at Howard University might have an open teaching position. The dean, who was acquainted with Howard's dean, the legendary Charles H. Houston, offered to assist. The situation was not lost on Crockett, who recognized the underlying racism: "He has it within his power to name me to the faculty right then to teach law, but he wasn't thinking about me teaching law at the University of Michigan or teaching at a predominantly white law school. He was thinking about the one black law school in the country."[55]

In any event, the dean sent a letter to Dean Houston on Crockett's behalf. The reply from Houston, which Michigan's dean showed Crockett, had historical importance:

Well, the letter said, in effect, I want to thank you for bringing Mr. Crockett's record to my attention. Unfortunately, we don't have any vacancy on the faculty now because we've just taken a very brilliant young man who graduated from Harvard. His name was William Hastie. Well, that should strike a familiar note to you. Bill Hastie was one of our outstanding black legal giants.

He was the first black federal judge. He was the first black governor of the Virgin Islands. He was the first black circuit court judge. He was judge of the United States Circuit Court for the Third Circuit in Philadelphia and was the first black to become the chief judge of a federal court—the United States Circuit Court in Philadelphia. He also became Dean of Howard's Law School, and he was the black aide de camp, I think it was called, to the secretary of war during World War II. And he resigned in protest because of continued segregation in the United States Armed Forces.

He and I became very good friends and then in subsequent years, we used to reminisce and sort of smile about how he went to Howard to teach and deprived me of an opportunity to become a law school professor.[56]

While at the University of Michigan, Crockett met his future wife, Ethelene Jones, whom he described as "wonderful wife and mother." Ethelene, who came from a poor pastor's family in Jackson, Michigan, was attending Michigan on a one-year scholarship she had earned from a Black sorority, Alpha Kappa Alpha, by virtue of an outstanding high school academic record. Although Ethelene had to leave Michigan after a year, her determination to succeed would prove to be the equal of George's. From an early age, Ethelene wanted to be a doctor.[57] She and George were married by her father, Reverend James E. Jones, on January 1, 1934, in Jackson, Michigan.

Although the wedding took place while he had one more semester of law school, there is no record of Aunt Elizabeth making any objection.

While Crockett reports that he started law school as one of two Black students, in June 1934, he was the only Black student to graduate in his University of Michigan Law School class. The fate of his former Black colleague is unknown.

2

Toward a Radical Law Practice

After graduating in 1934, Crockett returned to Florida. While he may have been a graduate of one of the premier law schools in the country, he was still Black. This fact was impressed upon him after he registered to take the bar. Officials would not permit him to sit for the bar like a prospective white lawyer: "The Florida bar examination was given in the chamber of the Florida State Senate and heaven forbid that a Black man should sit in a white senator's seat in the Senate chamber. So instead, they put up a temporary table just outside the door of the chamber in the corridor and put a chair there. That is where the one Black applicant [Crockett] took the Bar examination in December, 1934."[1]

When Crockett was asked if such blatant racism deleteriously affected his exam performance, he replied in a manner reminiscent of his listing the pros and cons of becoming a lawyer or a dentist on the blackboard at Morehouse College: "I don't get hung up on problems like that under those circumstances. I have a one track mind. If I am to fight that kind of racism, I must get myself in a position to do it. So don't worry about it, you subject yourself to it; just don't forget about it. Concentrate on getting admitted to the Bar. Then you can raise hell about that kind of condition. You can help prevent it from happening to subsequent candidates."[2] Crockett took the bar, passed, and was admitted to practice in Florida.

Well aware of the stringent racial barriers in his home state, Crockett decided not to establish a practice there. "I couldn't accept what I would have to do, even as a lawyer to get along, so I decided to go to a border state like West Virginia."[3] With a $150 loan from the University of Michigan Law

School, he set up a solo legal practice in Fairmont, West Virginia.[4] However, Crockett was unable to bypass the realities of being a Black attorney in 1935: "Practicing law by myself and surviving on the few cases brought to me by the local blacks—whites would never come to a black lawyer—was no way to make a living."[5] Crockett grossed $19 during his first month in practice.[6]

Undaunted by his limited resources and by his status as the only Black lawyer in the northern part of the state, Crockett began to challenge local segregation laws. Soon after arriving in West Virginia, he organized and was the first president of the Tri-County Chapter of the NAACP in northern West Virginia, which is still in existence.[7] When the mayor of Fairmont announced plans to build a segregated municipal swimming pool, Crockett garnered the support of the new NAACP chapter and instigated a protest over the use of public funds for a segregated facility. With advice from Howard Law School dean Charles Houston, who was then general counsel for the NAACP, Crockett's threat of a lawsuit successfully prevented the swimming pool from being built.[8]

Arriving in West Virginia a Republican, Crockett tried to get involved in Republican politics. In 1936, he ran for a position on the party's county executive committee. "George W. Crockett, Jr., progressive young Negro lawyer of this city, has announced his candidacy for the committeeman on the Republican county executive committee to represent the seventh ward of the city of Fairmont. It is believed that this is the first time a Negro has sought office for this ward."[9] His bid was not successful. On the news clipping in his scrapbook announcing his run, he wrote, "My first try for public office. I lost!"[10]

Crockett became disillusioned with the Republican Party. The July 29, 1938, edition of the *Fairmont (WV) Times* printed a lengthy story covering Crockett's decision to switch from the Republican to the Democratic Party. He declared that the "Democratic party has done more for America in six short years, what the Republican party could not do in six generations."[11] The article provides an important window into Crockett's political thinking. First and most important, he is focused on racial justice—antilynching legislation. Noting how the Republicans filibustered recent efforts to pass antilynching laws, he observed, "This, to me, is an indication of a clear lack of sincerity on the part of the Republican party that for 60 years has done lip service to the slogan—'friend of the Negro.'"[12] Second, Crockett stressed issues of economic justice and labor rights. "It cannot be truthfully denied that the present leadership of the Republican party is definitely anti-labor. The overwhelming majority of Negroes belong to the labor class and their sympathies naturally are with organized labor."[13] Third, in place and priority, was support for New Deal legislation: "The Negro press and the bulk of the national organizations among Negroes are solidly behind the New Deal. The reason is obvious—the Democratic party has undergone a decided reorganization and rejuvenation, so much so that today it represents the liberal element of America, while the Republican party continues to represent and be led by reactionary conservatives."[14] Crockett predicted that this would be a permanent shift: "I personally take pride in this realignment of the Negro vote, and now that I am convinced that it is permanent and not merely of political expediency, I gladly join them, determined that we shall do everything possible to keep our friends in power and hasten the coming of this brighter order."[15]

Crockett became active in the Democratic Party and its political campaigns in West Virginia.[16] He became a Black political spokesperson throughout the state, and during the elections of 1938, he supported the Democratic senatorial candidate Matthew M. Neely. Crockett's switch of political parties and his support of Neely received wide publicity in West Virginia newspapers and was credited with garnering the decisive Black vote for Neely.[17] His legal career in West Virginia ended in 1939, when as a reward for his political work, he was appointed as the U.S. Labor Department's first Black assistant attorney.

The Move to Washington: The Fair Employment Practices Committee's First Black Lawyer

In retrospect, the importance of Crockett's appointment as a Black government assistant attorney in 1939 was quite remarkable. Crockett recalled the attention it garnered: "The leading black newspaper, the *Pittsburgh Courier*, carried a front-page story about my appointment to the Department of Labor. Subsequently, *Life* magazine carried a whole spread on outstanding blacks in the federal government, along with my picture and about ten others. We were the ten top blacks in the federal government."[18]

The government appointment also gave the Crockett family a stability
it previously lacked and needed. George's annual salary of $2,400, which he
regarded as "excellent," was ample to support the family, which had grown
to three children, and allowed Ethelene to complete her premedical studies
at Howard University.[19] Because of her superior academic record, Ethelene
was awarded a medical school scholarship, and three years later, she graduated at the top of her Howard University Medical School class.[20]

While working at the Department of Labor, Crockett began what was
to become an important and consistent aspect of his legal career: scholarly research and writing. He published two articles in the *Michigan Law
Review* on the federal Wage and Hour Act, the first in 1941, "Jurisdiction
of Employee Suits under the Fair Labor Standards Act," and the second in
1944, "Reinstatement of Employees under the Fair Labor Standards Act."[21]
Crockett recalled that his articles were the first full-length articles in the
Michigan Law Review by a Black author. Many other publications followed.[22]

Crockett's work at the Department of Labor involved the struggles and
problems of organized labor and soon earned him several promotions. He
advanced from assistant to associate attorney, then to full attorney, and
finally to senior attorney. When he reached the senior level, he was told
that he would receive no additional promotions. The next higher level was
principal attorney. This position required supervising a unit of lawyers, all
of whom were white. "Upon being told that I'd reached the end of the
promotion line, I began looking around for some other agency that would
interest me."[23]

In 1943, President Roosevelt, by executive order, created a second,
reorganized Fair Employment Practices Committee (FEPC), which was
fashioned after the National Labor Relations Board (NLRB) but lacked
the NLRB's enforcement powers.[24] Blazing yet another trail, Crockett was
hired as the FEPC's first hearing examiner.

The FEPC's purpose was to investigate complaints and to formulate
policies intended to eliminate discrimination within the workplace.[25]
Although it could issue cease-and-desist orders, conduct hearings, and certify its findings to the president, it lacked enforcement powers and the
authority to compel disclosures of fact and cooperation by companies
under investigation.[26] The FEPC's lack of enforcement authority was
greatly limited. Crockett explained,

FEPC was the result of agitation led by A. Philip Randolph. And, as a compromise to prevent a march on Washington by blacks, Roosevelt agreed to issue an executive order creating a commission to advise, primarily with respect to race relations, as a part of the war effort. That's how Roosevelt's FEPC came into existence. And blacks began to complain because it had no teeth; it had no enforcement powers.

Roosevelt issued a second executive order revising FEPC and creating a format by which it could conduct hearings. . . . It still had no authority to compel testimony. . . . So what I was complaining about was this lack of authority to compel disclosure and cooperation.[27]

Despite these structural limitations, FEPC did have significant victories. Even given serious wartime labor shortages, the Philadelphia Transit Company refused to hire Black motormen and conductors. Crockett was sent as the FEPC hearing examiner to investigate. The violations were clear, as was the recalcitrance of the organization. Crockett drafted a proposed opinion and cease-and-desist order and sent it to the FEPC.[28] The committee adopted the opinion and issued the order. The workers at the Philadelphia Transit Company defied the FEPC directive and went on strike rather than comply. The lack of a formal enforcement mechanism was not an obstacle in this case. President Roosevelt sent in federal troops to take over the operation of Philadelphia's street railway system until Black motormen and conductors were hired. In the wake of the controversy, Crockett became known as "the black man's champion" at the FEPC.[29]

A complaint similar to that in Philadelphia was filed alleging discrimination against Blacks in the hiring of motormen and conductors on Detroit's streetcars. The FEPC sent Crockett to investigate. Crockett was also instructed to meet with R. J. Thomas, president of the UAW, to seek the UAW's support for proposed legislation to make the FEPC a permanent agency with stronger enforcement powers.

Crockett's eventual meeting with Thomas was so totally implausible that it seemed predestined:

I visited Thomas's office and waited in the anteroom until I could wait no longer without missing my train back to Washington, so I left. I was traveling by Pullman, which was rather unusual in those days. You seldom saw a black traveling Pullman unless he was a government employee. While seated in the Pullman car, another black passenger came through and, of course, he spoke to me and I spoke to him. We began chatting. We spoke about the war, about discrimination in the army, the difficulty blacks were experiencing getting decent jobs in war industries, and so forth. While this conversation was going on, I noticed just across the aisle a white man who seemed to be very much interested in what we were saying. When we would smile about something, or find something amusing, he sort of found it amusing also. And when we were very, very serious you could see him with a very serious look on his face.

When the conversation ended and my companion left, the white fella across the aisle turned to me and said, "Pardon me, but I couldn't help but overhear your conversation and I gather that you are with FEPC in Washington." I said, "Yes, that's right." He said, "Well, I'd like for you to say hello to my good friend Frank Hooks, who was the former congressman from our Upper Peninsula in Michigan." I said, "Oh, yes, I know Frank and I'll be glad to say hello for you, but who is sending hello?" He said, "I'm R. J. Thomas of the Autoworkers."

Well, you can imagine my reaction. I said, "You know, I sat in your outer office for at least an hour this afternoon waiting to talk to you." He said, "Really? Let's talk now. Come on over." So I moved across the aisle and we talked for two or three hours about discrimination in war industries, about FEPC, about the trade union movement, and about blacks in the trade union movement.[30]

The UAW was one of the most important unions in the country. Its principal leaders consisted of President Thomas, Secretary-Treasurer George F. Addes, and General Counsel Maurice Sugar. Sugar would end up having a great impact on Crockett. Sugar was a legendary lawyer in national fights for labor and civil rights. He helped found the National Lawyers Guild in 1936. He was the UAW lawyer during the 1936–37 General Motors Flint sit-down strike and helped draft the UAW constitution in 1939, before becoming its general counsel. Sugar maintained his own law firm, farming out work to a loose association of lawyers. Most significantly, Sugar started assigning UAW work to a young Ernest (Ernie) Goodman in 1935. Goodman joined the Sugar firm in 1939 and later became a lifelong friend and partner of Crockett.

Before Crockett's 1943 train ride with R. J. Thomas was over, they had reviewed the struggles that were going on in the UAW.

> He told me that at the Buffalo convention in 1943 he had made a commitment to bring on board some top black person who would be able to not only advise the union concerning fair employment practices but also prepare a program for the union to follow to improve the lot of minorities in the UAW.
>
> When I got back to Washington, I gave Frank Hooks the message from R. J. Thomas and also told him about our discussion, at which point Frank said, "Well, R. J. was talking to the very man he should have on his staff to do that job. Do you have any objection if I suggest to him that perhaps he should employ you?" I said, "Well, I'll think about it." Later on, I told him, no, I had no objection, and evidently he made the recommendation to R. J. Thomas, and Thomas asked me to come to Detroit for an interview.[31]

The position was offered to Crockett. He accepted and prepared for the move to Detroit and the awesome task of combating discrimination in the UAW locals, as well as in the UAW plants.

The Move to Detroit: Auto Workers and the UAW

In the early 1940s, racial conditions in Detroit were abysmal.[32] Racial tensions had worsened with the advent of World War II and the ensuing labor shortages that resulted in the migration of both Black and white workers from the South. On June 20, 1943, one of the United States' most devastating and horror-filled race riots broke out in Detroit. Tellingly, the rioting did not spread to the plants. Years later, Maurice Sugar recalled the comparative calm within the plants in the midst of the violence that occurred in the city: "To me, there was one welcome ray of light in this dark situation. While sporadic conflicts and attacks were going on in various parts of the city, thousands of black and white workers continued to work side by side in the plants where the automobile workers were organized, without a single incident to reflect the terror which prevailed elsewhere. How proud I felt of these men, who indirectly, through their union, were my clients."[33]

While there may have been no fighting in the plants during the riots, race relations within the UAW were far from ideal.[34] The UAW leadership, however, particularly R. J. Thomas and George Addes, with support from Detroit's leftist community, took strong positions on racial equality and denounced discrimination.[35] At the UAW-CIO's eighth annual convention in 1943, it adopted a Minority Rights Resolution that reiterated the union's firm opposition to any form of racial discrimination and its pledge to fight for the social, political, and industrial rights of minorities.[36]

Soon after the 1943 riot, the UAW leadership was challenged on its commitment to racial equality over the issue of job assignments. Traditionally, Blacks were assigned the most menial tasks in the auto plants. As more work was transferred to defense-related jobs that required higher-level skills, companies were pressured to include Black workers in these jobs.[37] As a result, some changes in the traditional job assignments did occur, and these, combined with the wartime labor shortage and the UAW's antidiscrimination policy, created new and better jobs for Black workers.[38]

Black advancement, however, provoked bitter resentment among whites. White "hate strikes" and Black walkouts followed the transfer and promotion of Black workers. A strike that occurred during the fall of 1944 particularly illustrated the tension among UAW workers and the intensity of their feelings over job assignments. When four Blacks were upgraded from unskilled jobs to metal polishing at Packard Motors, thirty-nine thousand white workers walked out in protest.[39] The plant was completely closed, and the union leadership was unable to end the plant walkout, in which a majority of its members participated. The walkout eventually ended, but only after the transfer of the Black workers was suspended. To protest the union's capitulation, angry Black workers staged their own walkout but returned to work after UAW officials promised "to rectify the situation."[40] By late 1944, racial tensions among workers were being exacerbated by the fear that the end of war production would mean heightened competition for a reduced number of peacetime jobs.

The story of the UAW leadership struggle told here focuses primarily on the issue that immediately crossed Crockett's desk: racial justice. Within the UAW, factions formed over the issue of racial discrimination. George Addes, secretary-treasurer, and his group supported a plan for developing an internal minority-affairs department, headed by a Black member, who would also be a member of the international executive board. Walter Reuther, then head of the General Motors Department of the UAW, opposed Addes's plan. R. J. Thomas, UAW president, was in the middle but leaning toward opposition. As a compromise, Thomas agreed to find a top-level Black, skilled in race relations, to work on the international staff.[41]

Consequently, a plan written by Crockett and Maurice Sugar to create the Fair Practices Committee (FPC) was approved by the UAW's international executive board, and George W. Crockett was named to organize and direct it. Crockett, as executive director of the FPC, reported directly to Thomas. He was expected to advise top union officials on race relations, increase the number of Blacks on the international staff, and establish a grievance system for resolving racial incidents.[42]

In 1944, Black involvement in union affairs was minimal. Very few Blacks had leadership roles at the locals, and only eight Blacks worked on the international union staff.[43] Black input increased substantially with Crockett's hiring. A caucus of Black UAW members met periodically to discuss problems and to decide the group's position.[44] Crockett, as the FPC's executive director, attended the international executive board meetings and often was able to present important caucus views along with his FPC reports.

Under Crockett's direction, the FPC successfully resolved many discrimination complaints ranging from getting Black workers admitted to a southern local by threatening charter revocation to forcing northern locals to end their sponsorship of social affairs that barred Blacks.[45] Through his work in attacking racism in the UAW as well as in the auto plants, Crockett became identified with George Addes's "left-wing" caucus in the union.

The Addes group frequently clashed on internal matters with Reuther's "right-wing" group. Crockett's relationship with Reuther eroded irreparably over the issue of the nondiscrimination clause.[46] While UAW officials sought to strengthen antidiscrimination clauses in their contracts, employers strongly resisted pledging to eliminate racial bias in the hiring of Black workers.[47] The General Motors Corporation (GMC) was exceptionally obdurate about signing any nondiscrimination clause. Because a majority of Black autoworkers worked at GMC and "most of the discrimination was in General Motors plants," Crockett was insistent that the GMC labor contract include a nondiscrimination provision.[48] Crockett also believed that Walter Reuther, who was head of the General Motors Department of UAW, should be more aggressive in addressing the GMC nondiscrimination contract problem.

Personal animosity between Crockett and Reuther heightened during the 1946 UAW strike at General Motors. Reuther assured Crockett that he would not call off the strike until the proposed nondiscrimination clause was included in the contract. The collective bargaining agreements between the UAW and Ford, Chrysler, and Kaiser-Frasier already contained the clause. General Motors was steadfast in its refusal, stating, as Crockett recalled, "We will in the future, as we have in the past, follow a policy of nondiscrimination."[49] Reuther subsequently reneged on his assurances to Crockett and settled the strike without the contract's nondiscrimination provision. Crockett was angry: "I never forgave him, and he knew I never forgave him, and that was the basis of the big split between Walter Reuther and me."[50]

In retrospect, Crockett believed the Fair Practices Committee was effective.[51] "I felt that on the whole, the UAW-FPC was really doing a good job. And the proof of that was the fact that other international CIO unions copied what we were doing."[52]

Sugar, Goodman, and Crockett Get Thrown Out of the UAW

Obviously, the larger battle for UAW leadership was much broader than issues of nondiscrimination. Reuther's rise to power within the UAW widened the gulf between his group and the Addes faction, which included Sugar. Sugar fervently opposed Reuther and his politics within the UAW. He deeply mistrusted Reuther and knew that if Reuther gained control of the board, he would eliminate Sugar's position and those of other staff members, including Crockett at Fair Employment.[53] Reuther's tactics inside the UAW presaged the growing authoritarian and antidemocratic practices that would soon characterize the Red Scare nationally. As early as the UAW convention in 1940, Reuther was railing against communism and chiding his opponent's failure to condemn communism. By 1946, Reuther, in violation of an international board ruling on red-baiting, declared that "10% of the Union who are Reds" would be eliminated.[54] This was about much more than exclusionary name calling. It was about how the community (union) was defined, who was or was not included, and what deliberative practices were used to make decisions and resolve conflicts. Sugar adamantly opposed Reuther's red-baiting tactics, and the tensions between them mounted. Reuther, in solidifying his power within the UAW, assailed the Addes faction as "pinko sympathizers" and formed alliances with such groups as the Association of Catholic Trade Unionists and with followers of Max Shachtman, who was described as an eccentric "Trotskyite."[55]

The Addes caucus responded in kind. Reuther was disparaged as a capitalist and "a power-hungry opportunist with little concern for the true interests of the workers."[56] Sugar, with an uncharacteristic naiveté, assumed that morality and justice would prevail and eventually Reuther would be deposed. But this was about power and not morality. As the postwar Red Scare swept the country, the leftist-liberal alliance within the labor movement weakened, and it became clear that Sugar and Addes's other allies, including Crockett, would soon be forced out of the UAW by Reuther.

Crockett's life illustrates an uncanny tendency to intersect important national issues at critical historical points. His time at the UAW during its fights over leadership and direction would prove no exception. When he accepted his position, he probably had only a faint understanding of the maelstrom of conflicts that boiled beneath. The broader fight for UAW leadership was for the heart, soul, and future direction of the union. Crockett aligned himself with the Thomas-Addes-Sugar faction that hired him, in part because of their deep commitments to racial justice, in part because his own progressive vision of economic justice fit more comfortably with theirs, and in part because of his commitment to open deliberative processes for resolving conflict. Crockett developed this latter concern in more detail later, as a primary justification for free speech and the First Amendment in his defense of the Michigan Six. Each of these rationales gave Crockett plenty of justification for supporting his allies and opposing Walter Reuther.

There is no doubt that there were members of the Communist Party in the UAW. There were other union members who were sympathetic to their cause. There was a broader coalition of groups with complementary objectives supporting the Addes faction. Crockett was never a member of the Communist Party, but he had no qualms about working with its members for common objectives of racial and economic justice. At the same time, Crockett had no patience for those, like Reuther, who were not deeply committed to the cause of racial justice. He also had no patience for the practice of red-baiting. These issues would follow Crockett throughout his career. At one point, he penned a reply to comparable allegations: "I am not a 'communist'; but that is NOT the issue."[57] He probably would have made a similar response while at the UAW.

The beginning of the end started in 1946, when Reuther narrowly won the UAW presidency over Thomas in a hotly contested election. At the convention, Crockett was trying to make the Fair Employment Practices Committee more permanent by turning it into a "department" rather than just a "committee." The Reuther faction used it as an opportunity to sideline Crockett. They supported the effort but added an amendment that stated only a UAW member could serve as the department's director.[58] Since Crockett was not an actual union member, he could no longer head the program he helped found and develop. At this point, Crockett became Addes's administrative assistant, before taking a leave of absence from the UAW to work at Sugar's law firm.

In early 1947, Sugar was still the UAW general counsel, and Crockett aspired to return to run the UAW Fair Employment Practices Department, if the Addes faction could regain control at that year's November convention. To regain his position, he would have to become a union member. So, while practicing law during the week, Crockett worked as a janitor at an auto garage on Saturdays until he had enough hours to join the UAW Garage and Mechanics Local.[59]

Crockett was once again engaging in the private practice of law. Ironically, while at the UAW, he had limited interactions with Sugar. Crockett recalled that they were introduced at the first international board meeting he attended as the head of the FPC. He has a vivid recollection of his first personal conversation with Sugar: "We were concerned about discrimination in bowling alleys. We had UAW integrated bowling teams, and those teams were having difficulty finding a place where they could play as a team because of discrimination around Detroit. And we decided to make an issue of that and take it up with the American Bowling Alley Association. I went to speak to Maurice about what kind of legal action we could bring."[60] As their conversation about bowling neared its end, Crockett decided to raise another issue that had been troubling him: the lack of Black attorneys on Sugar's staff:

> I said to him, "Look, one thing I find rather difficult to understand, judging from what I've heard about you in the Detroit area. Your thinking is right as far as race relations are concerned; you worked with Clarence Darrow in the Sweet case involving Dr. Sweet, the black [physician] who bought a house in a white neighborhood and then his white neighbors tried to run him out with force of arms. Here you have what amounts to a law firm even though it's just an association of lawyers, but there are about ten or twelve of you, and I don't see a single black lawyer up here." He said, "Well, maybe it's because I haven't found the right one." I said, "Well, that shouldn't handicap you; you're looking at the right one now." He said, "Oh no. R. J. Thomas told me that he was bringing in this brilliant young black lawyer from Washington up here and for me to keep my hands off him. So, no chance."
>
> I learned afterward that he had indeed interviewed two or three black lawyers around Detroit but had decided that none of them would fit in. There was one fella, I think LeBron Simmons, who was identified with liberal causes around here, but I don't think he ever worked for Sugar. I think I was the first one.[61]

Once Crockett was ensconced in Sugar's Cadillac Tower offices, he and Goodman soon established what was to become a close, lifelong friendship. They first met, Goodman remembered, at a public meeting in Detroit in 1944, where Crockett spoke: "I recollect that I was deeply impressed by his fluency as a speaker, the clarity with which he expressed his views, his avoidance of typical cliches and superficialities, and the compelling logic of his theme—that racial discrimination and segregation must be eradicated from our society."[62] No doubt, neither realized at the outset of their professional association that so much of their legal careers would be jointly consumed attempting to realize Crockett's invocation.

Sadly, Crockett faced the same intense discrimination suffered by every other Black lawyer in Detroit. He was the first Black lawyer in the Cadillac Tower.[63] Lawyers' offices in downtown Detroit were rigidly segregated. Prior to 1955, when the Black attorneys S. Allen Early and Ralph J. Osborne signed an office lease with the National Bank Building (now the First National Building), no Black lawyer had been a lessee in any major office building west of Woodward Avenue.[64] The exclusion of Blacks from Detroit's more prestigious buildings concentrated Black lawyers' offices in downtown Detroit's east-side fringe, near the Gratiot and Broadway Avenues area.

Furthermore, with Crockett present, the firm's members could not eat together in most downtown Detroit restaurants and hotels. They, too, were segregated. The restaurant on the first floor of the Cadillac Tower Building was no exception.[65] "Often we ate in the cafeteria at the [Black] Lucy Thurman Branch of the YWCA. It was not easy being a black lawyer in downtown Detroit."[66] Eventually the restaurant in the building made an exception for Crockett as the attorneys "rais[ed] so much hell about it."[67] Goodman recalled that at other restaurants, they would sometimes call the police and file formal complaints when service was refused. A session or two with the prosecuting attorney usually led to a deal with the restaurant owner, who agreed not to discriminate in the future. Goodman readily acknowledges, however, that filing individual complaints for such a limited result was hardly worth the effort because discrimination was so widespread in downtown Detroit.[68]

The Addes faction did not regain control at the UAW's November 1947 convention, and Crockett, now a UAW member, would never return to the UAW in any capacity, let alone to head the Fair Employment Practices Department. It was inevitable that Sugar would be fired as general counsel once Reuther also gained control of the UAW international executive board. His firing was anticipated. Totally unexpected, however, were the scathing indictments Reuther made about Sugar and his lawyers. The attacks were so petty and mean-spirited that they created a hostile and permanent rift between the Reuther camp and Sugar, his associates, and Detroit's leftist community.[69]

"Sugar's lawyers" were characterized as ineffective, tainted, and disliked in the Detroit courts because of their political leanings.[70] Reuther's charges were obviously false as, in fact, the legal staff had an admirable record in Detroit, notwithstanding the fact that many of their cases were difficult and controversial. This was particularly true with regard to Goodman and Crockett. Goodman had already had two U.S. Supreme Court victories.[71] He and Crockett would have more to follow. "Judges may have disliked them, but … Sugar and his associates knew the law."[72] Crockett, in turn, was one of the most successful Black lawyers in the country.

The fights within the UAW and Reuther's personal attacks took their toll on everyone. Goodman recalled, "When Reuther cleared house, he cleaned our house pretty thoroughly. Nobody who he supported or who supported him thereafter sent any legal work to us, as a matter of fact they made sure that none came to us as far as they could. So things changed very quickly. A large number of the lawyers in the office just left because they knew there was no work for them, and they had to make a living."[73] The heaviest price, however, was paid by Sugar: "Sugar could not reverse a process that made him an actual liability to anyone associated with him. The pain of it would drive him away from the office, to long trips north, away from the city and into the country."[74] A tired Sugar ultimately left the active practice of law.[75]

Sugar sold his furniture and equipment to the associates who had decided to remain in the Cadillac Tower office: Ernie Goodman, George Crockett, Mort Eden, and Dean Robb. The newly independent lawyers shared space but practiced individually. To earn their livings, they each handled a variety of cases, but they also maintained their shared interests in civil rights cases, as well as political and social causes. These associations became the foundation of an incipient partnership whose legal existence would abide three additional years of enormously difficult struggle, financial as well as political.

In the meantime, Crockett was considering a range of other professional options. He was called to an interview in Washington, DC, for possible appointment as the United States District Attorney for the Virgin Islands:

I went to Washington and spoke to the official in charge. He was concerned about my connections in UAW and I refused to do any red-baiting. He suggested Negroes were more inclined to follow the communist line than others. I told him I would say nothing on the matter. As far as Blacks are concerned, we don't care who helps us so long as we are helped. It doesn't make any difference to us whether you call them a communist, whether they are communists, or anything else. If they are going our way, welcome to the fight. I knew then I would not be U.S. District Attorney in the Virgin Islands.[76]

When Crockett was asked whether he was afraid that being so outspoken might jeopardize his future career, he responded, "No. You develop a certain amount of self-confidence. You have studied and burned the midnight oil. So you have a sense of your own competence and are prepared to say, 'If I can't make it here, I can make it over there; so why should I be unfaithful to my beliefs and principles just to get this job?'"[77]

There was one unexpected consequence of Crockett's frankness and his willingness to speak his mind. It would not be known until years later, when documents were made public, but his interview for the U.S. Attorney for the Virgin Islands triggered the opening of an FBI file.[78] The FBI would keep Crockett under steady surveillance for decades and would actively seek to undermine his career from that point forward.

Crockett returned from Washington and continued his private law practice. Sugar took a hiatus from Detroit to spend a year in New York. The year 1948 found Sugar consulting with the team of lawyers in the great communist conspiracy trial, *United States v. Dennis*.[79] This would have life-changing implications for Crockett. By the end of 1948, again through his "Sugar connection," Crockett would be at the center of one of the United States' most celebrated and controversial political trials. Ironically, Crockett's experience of a red purge inside the UAW had prepared him for the dynamics he would now see at a national level.

3

The Great Communist Conspiracy Trial

Battle of Foley Square

You who believe in the maintenance of our fundamental Constitutional rights will remember the rare and shameful occasions in American history when our government has seen fit to ignore the Constitution, to suppress unorthodox ideas.... The most recent attempt was at Foley Square where eleven men were convicted—not for specific acts of violence, but for the teaching of ideas.

—O. John Rogge, former U.S. Assistant Attorney General, introduction to *The Communist Trial: An American Crossroads* by George Marion (1950)

The Smith Act prosecution of the Communist Party leadership in 1949 marked the most blatant political trial in American history, a trial of the Party's purposes, ideology, and organization, as well as of its leaders. The indictments in July 1948 reflected a growing national demand to counter the expanding international menace of Communism and signaled a national commitment to destroy domestic Communism.

—Stanley Kutler, "'Kill the Lawyers': Guilt by Representation," in *The American Inquisition* (1982)

The "Battle of Foley Square": Background and Actors

The Battle Begins

At 10:30 a.m. on January 7, 1949, with a robust "All Rise!" Fred Loeffelman, a court crier for the U.S. courthouse on New York's Foley Square, opened a criminal trial that *Life* magazine described as the "longest, most noisy, most controversial in U.S. history."[1] As the court clerk William J. Borman shouted, "Hear ye, hear ye," the sixty-one-year-old federal district judge Harold R. Medina, trim, erect, bespectacled, and neatly mustached, entered the high-ceilinged, darkly paneled courtroom 110, mounted the judge's bench, and sat in his large leather-backed chair. Shortly thereafter, Medina began his first big case.

The trial, which became known as the "Battle of Foley Square," lasted nine months and consumed 21,157 pages of text in twenty-eight volumes of transcripts and over one thousand exhibits, at a total cost to the government and the defense of over $1.5 million.[2] Press coverage was the largest in the United States since the Lindbergh kidnapping trial in 1935. Half of the courtroom's 140 seats were reserved for the press. Its daily coverage amassed billions of words. The trial was also the most picketed in U.S. history. On opening day, the City of New York assigned four hundred police officers to the courthouse, more than for any trial in Foley Square history. Because of the pickets, which occasionally numbered in the several thousands, the U.S. House of Representatives passed a bill outlawing picketing at federal trials.[3]

It is difficult to imagine anyone getting a fair trial in this environment. Crockett argued a defense motion before Judge Medina seeking to have the police officers removed from outside the courthouse. As he would throughout the trial, Crockett centered his analysis on race: there was no difference, he argued, between the atmosphere surrounding this trial and the infamous Scottsboro trial of 1931, when nine young Black men in Alabama were falsely accused of raping two white women. "I know exactly what happens when a trial is held under conditions resembling mob conditions," Crockett said. "I am convinced, and I think the court should be convinced, that the mob is no less a mob merely because it is clothed in a uniform and has a pistol on the side."[4] It is worth noting that the Communist Party was critical in helping mount the defense in the Scottsboro case, when other groups were unwilling to defend the rights of African Americans. The defense motion was denied, and the tension exhibited between Crockett and Medina would foreshadow clashes to come.

Over seventy years later, it is impossible to recapture the near-hysterical fears over the "Red menace" that converged on the Foley Square defendants and their lawyers. As the Soviet Union expanded its spheres of influence in an intensifying Cold War, anticommunism became a powerful force in U.S. politics. Communists controlled mainland China; the Soviet Union commanded a growing nuclear arsenal; and Wisconsin senator Joseph McCarthy, who galvanized and frightened the nation, declared that many "card-carrying" communists worked in the U.S. State Department. In 1950, Alger Hiss, a State Department official and accused Soviet spy, was convicted of perjury after his testimony during a congressional investigation. Also in 1950, while the Foley Square appeals were pending, the United States went to war against communist North Korea.

The events of the day, at home and abroad, created a context of hatred and fear that the defendants and their lawyers had to confront as they prepared the defense. At the outset, it was clear that the task was formidable, even if the trial was meticulously fair, virtually impossible if it were not. In and around the courtroom, the charged atmosphere underscored the enormity of the issues at stake for the country as well as the defendants. As *Life* magazine noted, it "was more than a big trial. It was one of the most important cases, and might become the most significant in U.S. history."[5] The case, without doubt, was destined to reach the U.S. Supreme Court.

The U.S. government, by charging the entire top leadership of the Communist Party with secretly advocating its overthrow, raised enormous issues of law, politics, and philosophy. Overriding the case's jurisprudence, however, was one extraordinarily pragmatic question: "What *are* the means a democracy can use to protect its existence?"[6]

The troubling law "made" by the Foley trial has fortunately faded from U.S. jurisprudence. Ironically, the case's most important legacy is its lessons about the *means* that can be used to purge those who threaten a democratic government. The details that follow, particularly Crockett's observations about them, address many of the disturbing questions that still persist over the Foley Square trial: Did the enormity of the perceived threat to democracy cause the U.S. system of justice to break down? Was the trial "tainted" at the outset with a purposely manipulated jury? Was Judge Medina improperly "prosecutorial" and a participant in an unstated conspiracy with the government to convict the defendants at all costs? Was a trial record created to justify contempt of court findings against lawyers who were, in fact, diligently defending clients against biased rulings by the court? Did the press abandon its obligation to inform the public and instead galvanize an entire nation against the defendants and their lawyers because the ideas they expressed and defended were unpopular? And, ultimately, did the Supreme Court itself fall victim to the perceived threats to the very fabric of democracy and place in jeopardy democracy's most treasured right, freedom of speech?[7]

Whatever one may conclude from Crockett's retrospectives of the communist trial, he and his attorney colleagues paid dearly for their principles in representing the truly least among us. Notwithstanding the legal profession's venerable tradition that every person is entitled to fair and vigorous representation, the lawyers were branded with their clients' beliefs and associations. In 1948, communists were so despised that it was widely believed, even by leaders in government and within the legal profession itself, that only fellow travelers or other communists would defend them.

The Attorney General, the Indictments, and Justice Clark

The indictments against the country's top communist leaders were the culmination of massive government efforts calculated to crush the U.S. Communist Party. The FBI and the Justice Department had been building a case against the party for several years. By 1947, the government's brief against the communists comprised over eighteen hundred pages and eight hundred exhibits.[8]

By 1948, Cold War hysteria and the government's ongoing "spy" hearings had enveloped partisan politics at the highest levels. The Republicans, their members on the House Un-American Activities Committee, and anti-administration Democrats sought the political rewards from seizing the anticommunist initiative. After learning of the Justice Department's brief, Republicans accused the Democrats of laxity toward communists and their sympathizers and pressured U.S. Attorney General Tom C. Clark to start prosecutions. The Democrats, however, had already developed a strategy. Their plan called for the arrest of communists across the country before the 1948 national elections. The effort was to be spearheaded by the Justice Department and the nation's chief law enforcement officer, Clark.[9]

Clark had established anticommunist credentials. In a well-known 1949 *Look* magazine article, he recounted his and the Department of Justice's successes in prosecuting and deporting communists and declared,

"Communism is on its way out in this country with a one-way ticket."[10] Clark also attacked lawyers who represented communists. In speeches and in print, he urged that the right to practice law should be denied not only to communists but also to those "lawyers who are not probably card-carrying Communists, but who act like Communists and carry out Communist missions in offensives against the dignity and order of our courts."[11] While stating that he did not believe in "purges," Clark, in a 1946 speech before the Chicago Bar Association, urged bar associations to "take those too brilliant brothers of ours to the legal woodshed for a definite and well-deserved admonition."[12] Clark was appointed associate justice of the Supreme Court while the Foley Square trial was in progress.

On July 20, 1948, a true bill was returned by a federal grand jury against twelve leaders of the national Communist Party for violations of what was commonly known as the Smith Act.[13] The act, which became law in 1940, made it a crime to teach and advocate the overthrow of the government by force or to belong to a group that advocated such overthrow. The indictments numbered twelve paragraphs and charged two types of Smith Act violations: *conspiracy* to teach and advocate the overthrow of the U.S. government by force and violence[14] and *membership* in the U.S. Communist Party, a group committed to the purposes alleged in the conspiracy count.[15] The Smith Act "was the first American Law since the Alien and Sedition Acts of 1798 to make the spreading of ideas a crime, regardless of whether action followed advocacy."[16]

U.S. Attorney for the Southern District of New York City John F. X. McGohey was the lead government prosecutor. He was assisted by U.S. Attorneys Frank H. Gordon, Irving S. Shapiro, and Edward C. Wallace. McGohey, similar to Clark, ostensibly benefited from his association with the Foley Square trial. Shortly after it ended, he was appointed to a federal district judgeship.

Before Foley Square, the government had invoked the Smith Act only twice. The first was a successful prosecution of a group of Minneapolis "Trotskyites." The second trial, against alleged fascist sympathizers, ended in a mistrial when the trial judge died of a heart attack. The death of this judge, which many observers attributed to acrimonious and provocative tactics by the defense lawyers, was to affect deeply Judge Medina's conduct of the Foley Square trial and his treatment of the defense lawyers.

Judge Harold R. Medina

Medina, the son of a wealthy Mexican immigrant father and an American mother of Dutch ancestry, received his early education at Public School 44 in Brooklyn. He completed high school at the private Holbrook Military Academy in Ossining, New York, where he excelled academically. Medina graduated from Princeton University in 1909 with honors and a Phi Beta Kappa key, and in 1912, he finished Columbia University Law School at the top of his class. He entered private practice in New York City and soon became well known in the bar when he established the very popular *infra diq* bar review course, an enterprise he was to conduct for the next twenty-nine years. In addition to his full-time law practice and the demanding bar review course, an extraordinarily energetic Medina began teaching morning law courses at Columbia University Law School in 1915. Ten years later, after publishing seven books and many legal articles, Medina, still in private practice and with the bar review business, was named Associate Professor of Law at Columbia, a post he held until 1940.[17] With his enormous drive, it is not surprising that Medina was described as "excessively aggressive" and an "insufferable egoist—qualities that later emerged in the Foley Square trial."[18]

On the other hand, Medina's simultaneous, long-term careers as successful lawyer, bar review entrepreneur, and law professor gave him the experience, legal knowledge, and professorial credentials that garnered wide support from the legal fraternity for his appointment to the important and demanding judgeship in the U.S. District Court for the Southern District of New York. Following a fiercely competitive selection process, Medina was nominated by President Harry S. Truman. On July 18, 1947, he was confirmed by a unanimous U.S. Senate.

Although Medina was a relatively new judge, the abilities that placed him on the bench plus his obvious physical strength and stamina caused Chief Judge John C. Knox to select him for the trial that was expected to be uncommonly arduous and lengthy.[19] Judge Knox's assessment was confirmed by the sensational trial that followed—the longest and most publicized criminal jury trial in U.S. legal history at that time.

Medina studied the records of the 1944 mass Smith Act trial of thirty-one fascists in Washington, DC, during which Judge Edward C. Eicher died, allegedly from the "strain put on him by the excesses [of] the defendants and some of their lawyers."[20] The trial, which was described as "one of the most bizarre episodes in American courtroom history," lasted nearly eight months as the defendants and their lawyers persisted in objecting to virtually any evidence offered by the prosecution and "insulted and harassed" Judge Eicher.[21]

Medina steeled himself against a repeat of Judge Eicher's fate. He resolved to stay fit, exercise, take a short nap daily, control his anger, and avoid gavel-pounding.[22]

The Defendants and Their Lawyers

The defendants were the top leaders of the national Communist Party. Twelve were indicted, but the party's national chairman, William Z. Foster, was seriously ill and was granted a separate trial. The remaining eleven were Eugene Dennis, who as the national general secretary was the most important of the defendants;[23] Carl Winter, the Michigan state chairman and former education director of the Ohio Communist Party; Robert Thompson, the New York chairman who had fought with the Abraham Lincoln Brigade during the Spanish Civil War and with the U.S. Army in World War II, earning a Distinguished Service Cross; John Gates, editor of the *Daily Worker*, party propagandist, and former head of the Young Communist League; Henry Winston, national organization secretary and former head of the Youth Communist League who had studied at Moscow's Lenin Institute; John B. Williamson, the party's national labor secretary who at the time of trial was facing deportation proceedings; Benjamin J. Davis Jr., a Harvard Law School graduate, communist member of the New York City Council, chairman of the party's legislative committee, and secretary of the *Daily Worker*; Jacob Stachel, the party's education director, who was born in a section of Poland that became part of the Soviet Union and who was also defending deportation proceedings; Irving Potash, Russian-born vice president of the International Fur and Leather Workers Union, who was on bail in a deportation case and who had been convicted previously for criminal anarchy and conspiracy to obstruct justice; Gilbert Green, the Illinois party chairman and former New York chairman and secretary of the Young Communist League; and Gus Hall, the Ohio chairman, who had also attended the Lenin Institute in Moscow. Winston, who was born in Mississippi, and

Davis, a native of Alabama, were Black. Gates, Winston, and Green were sentenced for contempt during the trial.[24]

The five lawyers on the defense team brought different levels of experience and legal skills to the trial. They, with the exception of Louis McCabe, an established criminal lawyer from Philadelphia, were primarily labor attorneys. All five were members of the National Lawyers Guild and had long associations with leftist causes.

Harry Sacher, of New York, functioned as the lead attorney for the defense. Sacher had previously represented communists, primarily in deportation cases, and among the unions he had represented were the Transport Workers Union and the Fur Workers Union.[25] Abraham J. Isserman, of New Jersey, was well known for his civil liberties work. Previously, he had represented Gerhart Eisler, a communist who jumped bail and fled the country. Isserman had been a member of the American Civil Liberties Union National Board but left after the ACLU decision in 1940 to expel communists.[26] Richard Gladstein, from California, was the team's most experienced trial lawyer and was known for his successful defense in the 1930s and 1940s of the prominent labor leader Harry Bridges.[27] McCabe had been Eugene Dennis's lawyer during his recent conviction for contempt of Congress.[28] He began the Foley Square trial representing Dennis, but after the jury was impaneled, Dennis elected to represent himself.

There is one lawyer seldom listed on the roster of Foley Square attorneys: Maurice Sugar. Sugar, who had been barred from practice in the federal courts, was participating early in the case and sat at the defense table as "advisory counsel." Sugar had been convicted in 1917 under the Federal Espionage Act for failing to register for the draft in World War I and for advocating draft resistance. He served a one-year sentence in the Detroit House of Correction and was subsequently disbarred for standing up for his political convictions. In 1923, Sugar was reinstated to the Michigan bar but was never readmitted to federal practice.[29]

Crockett Joins the Defense Team

Crockett was the last lawyer to join the defense team. Once again it was the "Sugar connection" that irreversibly altered his life. The Communist Party wanted to have an integrated defense team and therefore needed a

Black lawyer.[30] On Sugar's recommendation, the Communist Party wanted Crockett on board.

In October 1948, Crockett, while painting his living room, received a long-distance call from Maurice Sugar in New York. The offer to join the communist conspiracy trial defense—the United States' "hottest" case—was totally unexpected. Crockett described it "like a 'bolt out of the blue.'" Apparently, Crockett had known one of the defendants, Ben Davis, very casually from his Morehouse days. "Ben had been a high school student at Morehouse, but he didn't go to college at Morehouse. He went to Amherst instead. His father was head of the Black masons of Georgia, and so it was a very well-to-do family. Ben would come home in the summertime, and there were occasions when I saw him playing tennis on the campus at Morehouse dressed in his whites and was pointed out to me as the son of Ben Davis Sr."[31]

Sugar asked Crockett if he would be interested in coming to New York as one of the defense lawyers.

As of that time, I knew practically nothing about the trial beyond the fact that Sugar was not in the office and that he'd gone to New York to assist with this big case. After some discussion, I asked him to give me time to consider it. My reluctance to go into the trial was not over the fear of being stigmatized. I was asking myself, "Are you ready professionally to take on that kind of a defense? Are you a good enough lawyer?" That's what it amounted to. My recollection is that I made that protestation to Sugar, and, of course, as expected, I received his assurance. He said, "Hell, I wouldn't have recommended you if I didn't think you were good enough."[32]

When Crockett got off the phone, his friend Bill Beckham just happened to stop by. Beckham was the father of William Beckham Jr., who later became deputy mayor of Detroit in the Coleman A. Young administration.

Beckham was administrative assistant to Walter Reuther. Notwithstanding that Walter Reuther and I didn't have anything to do with each other, this didn't affect my relationship with many other people in the UAW. So on this Sunday night, Beckham stopped by my house, and I told him about the telephone call I just received. He said, "Well, I can tell you one thing: if you go to New York and accept that assignment, you can just about pass up your usefulness as far as the black struggle is concerned because you will be labeled." I had to consider that also.[33]

Like most important decisions in his life, Crockett carefully weighed the pros and cons. There were many reasons to accept the offer.

First, because I certainly had read and knew something about the ethics code and that no lawyer should decline a case because of reasons personal to himself, or words to that effect. That was one reason. The second reason was my high respect and high regard for Maurice Sugar. I knew that Maurice would not recommend that I get into anything that he thought would be detrimental to me. But I also knew that the fact that he recommended me was sort of a single honor, that he thought that I was good enough. Those were the two primary considerations: the obligation of a lawyer and Sugar. And the third one was a commitment to constitutional freedoms. He told me what the case generally was about and what the basic defense was: free speech.[34]

Indeed, the case would go down as "one of the seminal free speech trials of twentieth-century American History."[35]

There were also some serious downsides. There would be a heavy price to pay for any lawyer willing to represent the Communist Party.

I had to balance my reasons against the fact that I was going to be labeled—no question about that. I was still trying to build a law practice, which at that time I was a long ways from doing. Two years after leaving the UAW, I had practically no practice of my own. I had small children, and I knew they were going to be taunted: "Your dad is a communist," that kind of thing. My wife was building a medical practice, and I knew she, too, would suffer. In fact, as a result of me taking the case, she was later denied admission to the staff at Women's Hospital in Detroit, and they made no bones

of the fact that she was denied because her husband was a "red."
And in those days, if you were a practicing physician, you needed
some recognized hospital where you could take your patients. Otherwise, you had to take them to one of those two or three all-black
hospitals that they had then in Detroit. They were very inadequate
as far as equipment is concerned. Those were some of the factors
that went into the picture, before I accepted.[36]

Crockett's decision to join the defense team at Foley Square was so
momentous that other family members have their own recollections. His
wife, Dr. Ethelene Crockett, recounted, "He was up on a ladder painting our
ceiling. The telephone rang and George just listened to the caller for a long
time. Then he told me what it was all about and I asked him if he intended
to take the case. He said he wanted to think about it for a while, so he went
upstairs and reread the Smith Act and the U.S. Constitution. He came
downstairs after a while and said he was leaving for New York. I remember
his words: 'If they can do this to people because they are Communists,
how long will it be before they do the same thing to people just because
they're black?'"[37] The decision to take the case was one thing; how to communicate it to the family and get family support was another. Crockett's
youngest daughter, Ethelene, recalled that all major decisions were made
by the family as a whole. Her father provided the background of the case
and the particular difficulties people accused of communism had finding a
lawyer. "We took a family vote and voted that, yes, he should do it."[38]

Crockett's son, George III, shares his own traumatic memories of his
father's departure: "On the day before he was to leave to New York for the
Carl Winter Trial . . . I stuck an icepick in my eye and the doctors told him
my eye would have to be removed. My father told me he would not go to New
York, that he would stay with me for the operation if I wanted him to. Then
he explained to me what the trial was about, what the issues were, what was
at stake. I only saw him cry twice. That was one of those times."[39] With the
family's blessing, including that of George III, Crockett went to New York.

Crockett agreed to join the team even though he knew he probably
had less actual trial experience than any of the other lawyers and even
though he had no background or familiarity with the Communist Party's
philosophy.

I didn't dream of what I was going into. I didn't know one thing about Marxism. I don't think I'd even heard the word "Leninism" then. I knew that there was a guy named Karl Marx who had written an important book on communism. You couldn't possibly get a minor in economics at Morehouse, as I did, without knowing that there was a book called *Das Kapital*. But I had never read it or the *Communist Manifesto*. I had heard the words, something about, "You have nothing to lose. . . . Workers of the world, unite. You have nothing to lose but your chains." I knew I'd heard that, but I couldn't tell you that I knew that it came from the *Communist Manifesto*. . . . How many people did I know, who I knew at that time, were members of the Communist Party? Only one. The defendant Ben Davis.[40]

Crockett would soon learn that he was not the first Black lawyer to work on the case.

After I got to New York, I discovered I was, in fact, replacing a black lawyer who was in the case and had left. I'd come across one of the briefs that had been filed in one of the pretrial motions, and to my pleasant surprise, the lawyer was the legendary Charlie H. Houston, the former dean of Howard University Law School and who we usually referred to as the father of civil rights attorneys. He was the architect of *Brown v. Board of Education*. Well, he had been in the case. It was a big honor for me, following Charlie. I don't to this day know why Charlie did not stay in the case. I suspect that it was a matter of money. We didn't get the kind of fees that even civil rights lawyers would've charged in a trial of that magnitude.[41]

When Crockett had been looking for an academic job upon graduating in 1934, Charles Hamilton Houston was the person to whom the dean of the University of Michigan Law School had sent a letter of recommendation. It remains unclear why Houston left the Foley Square team. It may have been an issue of money, as speculated by Crockett. It may have been his ongoing health issues. Houston would die of a heart attack at age fifty-four just a year and a half after Crockett received his call from Sugar. Crockett's later interactions with Thurgood Marshall and the NAACP might also suggest that too close of an association with the Communist Party was too threatening, even for some of the nation's leading champions of civil rights.

Crockett, as was his nature, acted out of principle, neglecting even to inquire about financial matters.

> Money wasn't even discussed before I agreed to enter the case. I didn't even inquire what the compensation was going to be until I got to New York. The national party was paying our fees. I don't even remember what it was, but I seem to recall that it was something like maybe $1,000 a month. I'm not sure if it was that much. I had to pay my own living expenses, but we didn't have any office expenses or office overhead. The party took two floors in a small building down on Broadway, just below Canal Street, and that's where we had the office of defense counsel. So that's how I, a relatively unknown black lawyer from Detroit, became involved in one of this country's greatest cases. And, notwithstanding what happened to me, I never, for even a single moment, regretted my decision.[42]

Pretrial Strategies: Motions and Maneuverings

Crockett was now part of the case, but he came late to the party. Many important strategic decisions had already been made, and he had to play catch-up. Crockett's clients, at least nominally, were Jacob Stachel and Carl Winter. "As far as the defendants were concerned, they were represented by a battery of five lawyers. No one actually had a personal lawyer, but where it was necessary to have an individual client, then we made that distribution. So that when I filed my appearance in court, I'm appearing—and Judge Medina understood this—I'm appearing as counsel for Jack Stachel and Carl Winter."[43] Jack Stachel was from New York. Carl Winter was from Detroit. Crockett had actually met Winter once before the trial, during the Progressive Party campaign in 1948. At a symposium held in Detroit, each of the political parties was asked to send a representative, and Carl Winter spoke as a representative of the Communist Party and Crockett spoke as a representative of the Progressive Party. Harry Sacher, on the other hand, was appearing as counsel for Davis and Winston, the two Black defendants in the case.

Crockett was not shy about expressing his opinions about his fellow lawyers: "There was Harry Sacher, who was the more fiery one of the team; Richard Gladstein from San Francisco, who was personal attorney for Harry Bridges and also attorney for the longshoremen's union; Abraham Isserman by all odds was the best in terms of knowledge of law, as well as experience; Lou McCabe was the oldest member of the group, and he commuted over from Philadelphia each day for the trial. By and large, he was in court with us every day, but there were some days when he didn't show."[44]

Lawyers are supposed to represent the interests of their clients. This creates problems in such a politically charged environment. Early strategic decisions between the lawyers and their clients had significant and, at least from Crockett's perspective, detrimental consequences for the trial.

Initially, the lawyers made a fundamental decision that was the basis of most of the difficulties we had in the Foley Square trial. That basic decision was allowing the clients to work out among themselves the theory of the defense and then give that theory to us to somehow transform it into criminal jurisprudence and present it to the court. That was a very major mistake. We didn't control our clients, and, therefore, we didn't control the case as lawyers should. Our clients decided that this really was a repetition of what they always referred to as the Dimitrov trial in Germany, following the burning of the Reichstag (Georgi Dimitrov's defense during the Reichstag Fire Trial in 1934).

That approach was basically this: This is a political trial; it's a political attack on the Communist Party and on the political theories of the Communist Party, which are grounded in the teachings of Karl Marx and Lenin. Therefore, every decision in the course of presenting the defense had to be geared to the notion that we are repudiating the government's efforts to condemn and to outlaw our political theories. . . . By insisting on making rote Marxist-Leninist responses to our questions rather than using the language we wanted, they didn't give the jury much to help their case.[45]

Crockett would learn from this experience and try to apply lessons from Foley Square to Smith Act cases that he and Ernie Goodman would later defend in Michigan. "Now the reason I say I think it's wrong, . . . you don't have lawyers who are competent to do it. You got someone like George Crockett, who doesn't know a damn thing about Marxist/Leninist theory."[46]

At the end of the day, however, the lawyer's job is to provide counsel. Given that this really was a political trial where traditional legal principles were being turned upside down, it is difficult to stand in too harsh a judgment of the defendants' or their lawyers' strategic decisions. "Actually, there was nothing we could do about that because your clients are determined that's the way it's going to be, even if they martyr themselves, and maybe they preferred to martyr themselves, I don't know. But these were high-ranking, top-echelon leaders in the national party, and they were committed to their cause—no question about that. But it was very frustrating for the lawyers. Perhaps they should have represented themselves."[47]

Sadly, even when the lawyers were clearly in control in the pretrial setting and the defense had both the law and the facts on their side, it made very little difference. Politics, not law, would determine the outcome of this case. The primary defense arguments were simple and direct: the indictments charged no crimes. Rather, the indictments made criminal the defendants' constitutional rights to meet, speak, teach, and advocate from books and other publications, fundamental rights, the defense argued, that Congress could not proscribe through the Smith Act or otherwise. These were clear constitutional freedoms. Rather than vindication, these arguments generated judicial derision. From the outset and throughout the trial, the defense lawyers' vigorous attacks on the indictments, as well as on the Smith Act itself, put them on a collision course with Judge Medina.

Medina heard and denied more than a dozen hotly contested pretrial defense motions, including one that he disqualify himself for bias. Ironically, the bitter hostility that developed early between the defense lawyers and Medina over his rulings, particularly over the admissibility of evidence, catapulted Medina into immediate and lasting national prominence.[48] This was a no-win scenario for the defendants and their lawyers.

Challenging the Jury: The Trial within a Trial

Much of the trial preparation had already been done, and almost all of the pretrial motions had been made, heard, and denied before Crockett arrived in New York.[49] Two important stages of the proceeding remained in which Crockett would actively participate. The first was a substantive challenge to the entire jury-selection process. This challenge can be viewed as a "trial within the trial," taking months and raising a number of significant factual and legal issues.[50] The challenge to jury selection would be a prelude to the trial in chief, in which the government would have to prove the alleged Smith Act violations of a Communist Party criminal conspiracy.

Crockett recalled, "The first thing that we addressed after I became involved was the jury challenge. Our basic contention was that the panel of jurors was put together in a fashion intentionally calculated to exclude blacks, workers, and generally members of minority groups, but primarily blacks and workers." This was a lengthy legal proceeding. "Just the trial of the jury challenge took three months—three months in court every day. So that gives you some idea of what an important aspect of Foley Square was represented by the jury challenge. And that's where the basis was set for the antagonism between Judge Medina and defense counsel because that was really a knock-down, drag-out struggle."[51]

The defense team raised problems with the jury-selection process for the entire Southern District of New York. One issue was the intimate relationship between the federal court and many large corporate employers in the district.

> We argued that the panel of jurors in the federal court was made up of the wealthy and the influential in the Southern District of New York. And we undertook to prove that by pointing out that it was a system designed by Chief Judge Knox and the leading corporations in the Southern District, public utilities like Consolidated Edison, the power company, and so forth. A deal had been worked out between Chief Judge Knox and these corporations under the terms of which the corporations agreed to facilitate service by their employees on federal juries and to do this by guaranteeing these prospective jurors, in addition to the meager compensation that they would be entitled to as jurors, their compensation

as employees of the corporation. This was the policy that was in effect, established by Judge Knox, and it was referred to as the "blue-ribbon system" of selecting jurors.[52]

An additional problem was the conscious manipulation of the geographic segregation of the Southern District to influence the racial composition of the jury.

The other complement to this system was that there existed in New York what was called an address-telephone directory so that telephones were listed by the address and not by the name of the person. Therefore, by looking at the address-telephone, you could be assured of getting people who lived in a particular section of the city. And to that extent, you could exclude Harlem and some of the other areas from which you felt that the jurors would be the least desirable.

Now, how do you prove this? We attempted to prove it by creating charts with little pins that we stuck in each point where a juror came from for the panel that was going to try this case. Based on that, we could show that you only had three or four people that you were calling in for jury duty from Harlem. The court could judicially notice that Harlem was virtually 100 percent black. So we went to Harlem to find out who lived at these places where we stuck the pins. And we found that invariably it was a white store owner who was living in an apartment above his or her store.[53]

The facts would show a level of intentional discrimination that went well beyond the geographic manipulation of jurors.

Another complement to this scheme was to interview the prospective jurors. Based on that interview, you determine who is black and who is not black. And if he or she was black, put a little C on the card to indicate that is a black brother or sister. Then when you get ready to get your jury panel together, reach over in the cards that have Cs on them to control how many black prospective jurors you're going to put in this pile. You may decide you only want, in a panel of fifty prospective jurors, two or three blacks. But no one, you think, can come in and argue that you have intentionally excluded blacks just because the actual trial jury turns out to be twelve whites. You show that in the crowd from which they were selected, you did have some blacks in there. It was a well-thought-out scheme. They did the same thing with workers—they just didn't draw prospective jurors from working-class neighborhoods, and we were able to show that by the charts that we made.[54]

The life of George Crockett demonstrates time and time again that truth is often stranger than fiction. In sorting out the names of African Americans on the cards, Crockett discovered the name of the executive secretary of the NAACP and resident of Harlem, Walter White.

In going through these cards of prospective jurors, I came across one that had the name Walter White on it; the card called for the prospective juror to indicate his or her employment, and it said, "Executive Secretary NAACP." I knew of Walter White. I don't think I'd ever met Walter White at that time, and I knew that he was so fair that you couldn't tell Walter White from a white person. But they had a C on his card. So, in the course of the challenge, when we put the jury clerk on the stand, I inquired of him what the C on the card meant, and he looked at me as much to say, "You should know. That means colored." Of course, I'm feigning shock that in a federal court you are maintaining a discriminatory record by dividing American citizens into black and white. And of course the judge looks down at me as much as to say, "Come on, come on, go to the next question," that kind of thing.

So then I asked the witness, "How did you know that this person whom you interviewed—you did interview him?" "Yes." "How did you know he was colored?" He said, "You can look at his employment." At first you said, "You can look at him," and that's when I pointed out that Walter White just couldn't be distinguished from a white person. I probably offered to call Walter White as a witness in the case. We did everything that occurred to us to win this case, so it would not have been an unusual move to subpoena

Walter White to come in to testify—not to testify, just to present himself, that's all. So the fact that I told him that Walter White could not be distinguished from a white person led him to give me the obvious answer. He looked at his employment; his employment said that he was executive director of the NAACP, and the witness at least knew that NAACP meant National Association for the Advancement of Colored People. So this chap must be colored. He put a C up there.

That was really all I needed from the clerk. It was the basis for our argument and support for our contention that all they did was to put in a few token names they thought were residents up in Harlem, and then it turns out that the bulk of those whose names you put in there were really white....

It was also during this period that we indicated that we might call Chief Judge Knox himself to inquire about how he went about putting together this blue-ribbon panel, and that created a feeling of unease as far as Judge Medina was concerned. There was legal merit to our jury challenge. It posed a danger to all working-class people in the Southern District and a danger certainly for all blacks and other minorities. You would expect the Communist Party to be conscious of that and to make that kind of argument. That's part of what they meant by this is a political case and we made a political defense.[55]

Not every exchange between Medina and the defense attorneys was confrontational. Crockett, while arguing that over three hundred thousand Blacks had been excluded from jury selection in New York's Southern District, was moved to tears. The next day, his apology to Judge Medina for the "emotional outburst" resulted in the following lighter moment:

"You certainly wept, and wept profusely," returned Judge Harold R. Medina. "I make no objection to it but it is generally better for counsel to refrain from weeping in the courtroom."

"Thank you," said Crockett. "I appreciate your permission to weep."

"In moderation, of course," Medina cautioned.[56]

The lawyers for the Foley Square defendants were pulling out all the stops. During the course of the jury challenge, Crockett sought the assistance of the NAACP, which was headquartered in New York. Crockett arranged a meeting with Thurgood Marshall, who at the time headed the NAACP Legal Defense Fund and was the civil rights organization's chief legal counsel. Their meeting was a major disappointment; it also demonstrated how the "practical politics" of anticommunist hysteria influenced even the strongest defenders of civil rights.

It occurred to me—and I suppose it occurred to the other counsel, but I don't think they suggested it to me—that it would be helpful to the jury challenge if we could get the NAACP to file an amicus brief. After all, they had been the foremost proponents in raising the issue of discrimination in jury selection and jury service under the Constitution. So why shouldn't they? Secondly, here was their own executive director, Walter White, who has a C on his card. Why shouldn't they be interested in that? So I decided that I was going to speak to Thurgood Marshall about it.

At the time, the NAACP was having its convention in Detroit, and I made a special trip back to Detroit to speak to Thurgood. I went up to his room, which was in the Cadillac Hotel, as it was called then. I not only spoke to him about it but also took along the exhibits, the picture showing the pins I mentioned before and what few jurors we had from Harlem, and how those few were located in the commercial district of Harlem and so forth. When I pointed out the juror cards, I had a photostat copy of Walter White's card with the C on it. Then I asked him to file an amicus brief on the question of racial discrimination. His answer was, "You guys have got a case, no question about it. But if the NAACP filed a brief, the NAACP would be labeled as supporting communists and communism, and we can't afford that."

Their fundraising would be affected. So Thurgood told me, "Frankly, I'm not prepared to recommend that a brief be filed." I hate to say it, but Thurgood dropped in my estimation then, and his subsequent achievements, which were many and which were great, didn't restore that. No. Because I felt that it was the "nitty gritty." That's where you either said I stand for something or you don't stand for it. It didn't mean that you had to make the final decision, but you could at least recommend it to your board and let them decide whether the organization wanted to do it. He refused to do even that.[57]

Crockett felt himself increasingly isolated, not just in the legal community but within the Black community, even among those who were committed to fighting for civil rights.

In the end, the efforts to challenge the jury-selection process failed. "It was a foregone conclusion that the jury challenge would be denied. It was really a foregone conclusion that everything the defendants asked for, if there was any basis for denying it, was going to be denied. Medina demonstrated that from the beginning."[58]

Whether as a matter of fate or as a result of the intense scrutiny the jury-selection process was put under, the jury actually selected to hear the case was surprisingly diverse.[59] The jury consisted of the following members: "Mrs. Thelma Dial, Negro housewife and part time dressmaker, foreman; Russell Janney, theatrical producer; Mrs. Ida F. Howell, Negro beautician; Miss Kathryn K. Dunn, unemployed former clerical worker; George L. Smith, Negro salesman; Mrs. Lillian Berliner, housewife; Patricia S. Reynolds, retired beer salesman; Henry E. Allen, unemployed industrial engineer; Mrs. Lillian Schlesinger, widow and department store clerk; James F. Smyth, telephone wireman and assembler; Mrs. Carrie L. Robinson, widow; and Mrs. Gertrude Corwin, housewife." The *Christian Science Monitor* noted that the list of jurors "reads like a small United Nations."[60]

The Case in Chief: Proving the Communist Criminal Conspiracy

With the jury selected, the substantive portion of the government's case was about to begin. The trial, however, was already well off the rails. Foley Square had become ground zero for U.S. anticommunist hysteria. But the primary reason for the unfolding travesty was the very nature of the government's indictment. It was the United States, not the defendants, that made this a political trial. The defendants were not being tried for wrongful *deeds* but for wrongful *beliefs*. This was a trial in defiance of core protections of the First Amendment and the country's commitment to civil liberties.

The defendants also wanted this to be a political trial for their own reasons, and their attorneys had lost substantial control over the process. In addition, two of the lead defense lawyers, Sacher and Gladstein, were competing with each other to appear the most prominent lawyer on the team, which Crockett called a "two-ring circus."[61] All the while, the media was whipping the trial into an often one-sided frenzy, covering the best show in town.

Overseeing the proceedings and failing to exercise any sense of balance was Judge Medina. Despite whatever significant legal skills the judge brought to the task, he also brought a set of personal eccentricities. These seemed to become more pronounced as the trial progressed. He was concerned about his own health beyond the point of paranoia. After studying the Smith Act trial of the fascists, in which the presiding judge had died in the middle of the trial, Medina feared for his own life, perhaps sincerely but without objective verification. "The judge even thought the communists had planted 'hypnotists' in the courtroom and he 'consciously forced himself to keep his eyes moving so that he wouldn't let himself be placed in trance.'"[62] In addition to health concerns, Medina brought a healthy dose of narcissism. He loved the attention he was getting from a fawning public and an attentive media.

In the midst of these swirling forces, the substantive portion of the trial was set to begin. The lawyers made their opening statement. Against all odds, Crockett tried mightily to recenter the trial where history will vindicate that it should have begun and ended, on principles of free speech and the First Amendment.

> Mr. Crockett: May it please the Court, members of the jury . . . I think that before the case is over you will say that it has been the most unusual experience "in my lifetime," because in this case we are really not trying facts, we are really not trying men, we are trying ideas, we are trying a basic philosophy in which men believe. You are being called upon as a cross-section of the American public to determine whether or not these defendants are entitled to hold the beliefs which they believe. . . .
>
> . . . Suppose we turn now to find out what it is that they are charged with. I recall that in making his opening statement the

United States Attorney read to you the Smith Act and the Court has instructed you that that is a part of the law in this case. There is another law that I should like to read to you at this time, and I think you will recognize it. It also has pertinence in this case. It says:

"Congress shall make no law abridging the freedom of speech or of the press or the right of the people peaceably to assemble and to petition the government for a redress of grievances."

That, I think you will recognize, is the First Amendment to the United States Constitution. That is the law on which we rely as justification for everything that my clients have done or have said or have influenced others to do or to say.[63]

The defense lawyers made sure that the jury was well aware of one other fact: the government had the burden of proof. It was the government's responsibility to prove all elements of the Smith Act violations beyond a reasonable doubt. The indictment charged that the defendants' advocacy of "Marxism-Leninism" constituted knowing and willful violations of the Smith Act, because the term's real meaning was the overthrow of the government by force and violence. Accordingly, establishing what "Marxism-Leninism" actually meant to the defendants was essential for the prosecution. Here, a clear double standard emerged. Judge Medina allowed the government to prove this critical aspect of the case by having its witnesses testify that the defendants' use of Marxist-Leninist principles was, in fact, criminal but refused to permit the defendants themselves to testify on the very same subject—their *own* understandings of communist doctrine.

On March 24, 1949, the government called its first witness, Louis F. Budenz.[64] Budenz had been a high-ranking member of the Communist Party and the editor of the official Communist Party newspaper, the *Daily Worker*, for many years. He later broke away from the party. Lead prosecutor McGohey asked him to interpret the first sentence of the Constitution of the Communist Party of the United States of America (CPUSA): "[CPUSA] is the political party of the American working class, basing itself upon the principles of scientific socialism, Marxism-Leninism." Budenz testified as to what "Marxism-Leninism" meant: "socialism can only be attained by the violent shattering of the capitalist state, and setting up of a dictatorship of the proletariat by force and violence in place of that state. In the United States this would mean that the [CPUSA] is basically committed to the overthrow of the Government of the United States as set up by the Constitution of the United States."[65]

An even more significant aspect of Budenz's testimony was his claim that the defendants used euphemistic language to disguise words with criminal meanings. This practice, which Budenz called "Aesopian language," was introduced to the jury.[66] It allowed members of the jury, if they believed that communists used Aesopian language, to find, through Budenz's translations of otherwise innocuous and lawful passages, that the defendants had the knowledge and intent needed to violate the Smith Act.

By means of that ingenious process of "interpretation," the prosecution was able to read into books, newspapers, periodicals, and all publications of the defendants—however lawful and proper the contents might be and no matter how explicitly they reiterated the defendants' attachment to the principles of the Constitution of the United States—hidden and unexpressed doctrine allegedly known only to the initiated and secretly instructing that the reader's duty was to destroy the government by force and violence. Thus, Budenz's testimony that communists mean something different from what they say, if believed, led to the negation of much of the defendants' evidence as to what they did in fact teach and say. Judge Medina on a number of occasions reinforced Budenz's testimony by stating in the presence of the jury that he too found that the defendants applied peculiar meanings to common words.[67]

Crockett recounted,

> Budenz referred to the fables of Aesop, and if you remember the fables of Aesop, the cardinal principle was whatever is said really means just the opposite. And he drew this jury into accepting that as the basic interpretation of all communist literature: they never mean exactly what they say. There's a hidden meaning, and you've got to be able to look behind and see that hidden meaning—even in the written text in the book!

That was called later in the trial "Aesopian language." That's how they got the excerpts in. The government prosecutor, for example, would have a witness identify himself and how long he was a member of the Communist Party, what his background was, how much reading he had done on Marxist and Leninist literature, and so forth. Then he would identify a book and its author, for example, *State and Revolution* written by Lenin. And then, the government would eventually direct his attention to particular passages that they have already decided that they could interpret as advocating force and violence. And then they will ask him, "What is the meaning of that passage?"

Immediately, we would be on our feet objecting like I don't know what, that it is for the individual who reads the book to determine his understanding of what the meaning of the passage is, and he would determine it in the context of the whole book or the whole chapter. We had good law in our favor, too, such as the *Schneiderman* case. But here they were asking the guy to take one sentence and tell you what that sentence is supposed to mean for everybody in the organization, and he's just not competent to do it. And then you hear Medina say, "Overruled. Proceed."[68]

Crockett was referring to *Schneiderman v. United States*,[69] in which the U.S. Supreme Court, after considering *The Communist Manifesto*, *State and Revolution*, and *Foundations of Leninism*, all introduced by the government, wrote,

Political writings are often over-exaggerated polemics bearing the imprint of the period and the place in which written. Philosophies cannot generally be studied in vacuo. Meaning may be wholly distorted by lifting sentences out of context, instead of construing them as part of an organic whole.

. . . A tenable conclusion from the foregoing is that the Party in 1927 desired to achieve its purpose by peaceful and democratic means, and as a theoretical matter justified the use of force and violence only as a method of preventing an attempted forcible counter-overthrow once the Party had obtained control in a peaceful manner, or as a method of last resort to enforce the majority will if at some indefinite future time because of peculiar circumstances constitutional or peaceful channels were no longer open.[70]

The practical difference is that *Schneiderman* was decided in 1943, and it was now 1949. The national mood of communist hysteria had changed "politics as usual" that dramatically in six short years. At least for purposes of Foley Square, *Schneiderman* was no longer good law.

> The whole thing came out of this one witness's [Budenz's] mouth, as there was nothing in the Communist Party literature that said when reading communist doctrine, you should apply the Aesopian principle to it. Nothing that I know of said that, not in literature. . . . Now that's what the government's "stool pigeons" would testify to, and Medina would allow it. He would say that the witness is entitled to give his own opinion or interpretation of what it is he read, and he is also entitled to testify whether or not any of the others associated with him shared his opinion and interpretation. And any others would mean the entire membership of the Communist Party.[71]

Government witnesses were permitted to testify to any Aesopian interpretation they pleased, but the defendants themselves were not permitted to answer the exact same questions in light of their own interpretation. Recall prosecutor McGohey's question to Budenz about the meaning of "Marxism-Leninism" as used in the first sentence of the Communist Party's constitution. When defense lawyers were presenting their rebuttal case, they called defendant Robert G. Thompson as a witness and asked him the exact same question. Remarkably, the judge did not permit him to answer, even though this was the central issue in the criminal case. The exchange would be comical if the lives of the defendants and the founding legal principles of the country were not at stake. Defense lawyer Gladstein asked,

Q. Will you state to this jury what is Marxism-Leninism?
Mr. McGohey [prosecutor]: Objection.
The Court: Sustained.

Mr. Gladstein: May I call Your Honor's attention to the state of
the record—

The Court: No, I don't want to hear any argument about it.

Mr. Gladstein: But, Your Honor—

The Court: I will hear what this witness directed to be taught,
resolutions that he voted for setting up the schools and what
was to be taught in the schools, and when the time comes, if it
does, for him to testify what he taught and in particular schools,
within certain limitations I will permit. I do not conceive the
question before us to be one which makes that question relevant.

Mr. Gladstein: Would Your Honor notice that in the record Your
Honor permitted the witness Budenz to be asked precisely that
question and to give an answer to it?

The Court: You know, I just told you I didn't desire to hear
argument but you wanted to get that point in and so again you
have become contemptuous. Go ahead.

Mr. Gladstein: May I ask the witness the very same question that
Mr. McGohey asked, Your Honor?

The Court: I tell you Mr. Gladstein, again, I do not desire to hear
argument.

Mr. Gladstein: I do not want to argue but I am asking permission—

The Court: No, you are arguing and you are again contemptuous.[72]
(11,818–19)

Mr. Gladstein proceeded to ask the question in exactly the same words
used by McGohey in questioning Budenz.

Q. I will read the testimony in the record at p. 1808:
I will read that sentence to you again. "The Communist
Party of the United States is the political party of the American
working class, basing itself upon the principles of scientific
socialism, Marxism-Leninism." What did you, in connection
with these other Communists that you were working with there,
understand that to mean?—

Mr. McGohey: Objection.

Q. I put to you that question and I ask you to answer it.

The Court: Is there objection?

Mr. McGohey: There is, Your Honor.

The Court: Sustained.

Q. Will you tell the jury what, as you understand it, Mr. Thompson, is the historic meaning of Marxism-Leninism? (11,821)

The language of this question was a repetition of Budenz's testimony in which he described what he called "the historic meaning of Marxism-Leninism." The defendant Thompson was being asked to refute the prosecution's evidence.

Mr. McGohey: Objection.

The Court: Sustained. Better get down to cases, Mr. Gladstein....

Q. I am reading from page 1132, a portion of Mr. McGohey's opening statement to the jury "that reconstituted, they went back to the old Communist Party organized to establish Socialism in the United States according to the Marxist-Leninist teaching. That teaching is—as we shall show—that Socialism can only be established by the violent overthrow and destruction of our constitutional form of government through the smashing of the State government and the setting up of the dictatorship of the proletariat by violent and forceful seizure of power under the leadership of the Communist Party."

I ask you whether that statement is a correct statement of the teachings which Mr. McGohey called the Marxist-Leninist teaching.

Mr. McGohey: Objection.

The Court: I will allow it.

A. It is not.

Q. Now, will you state what are the teachings of Marxism-Leninism?

Mr. McGohey: Objection.

The Court: Sustained. (11,823–24)[73]

On the key issue of the meaning of "Marxism-Leninism," the issue for which the defendants were being prosecuted, they remarkably were not permitted to speak.

Ironically, on a range of other issues, including the identity of other participants in meetings or other members of the Communist Party, defendants *were compelled to speak* on pain of being found in contempt of court. This is true even though naming such names would put the lives and livelihoods of those persons at risk.[74] Crockett recalled,

> Not only did we have a serious problem overcoming the Aesopian theory once it was allowed in, a second major problem we had with putting our clients on the stand had to do with the "labeling" of third parties as communist and the devastating effect that had at the time. Every defendant who took the stand could expect to end up in jail for contempt because the routine was to try to get that defendant to identify somebody who was not a participant in the trial as a member of the Communist Party, and the defendants steadfastly refused to do that. And if they refused to answer the question, Medina, with a wave of a hand: "Take 'em away. Contempt of court until such time as they are prepared to answer the question." It started off with Gates, who, if I remember correctly, was the first defense witness. He ended up in jail.[75]

Judge Medina's Growing Bias against the Defense

In addition to problems of bias, Judge Medina was frequently discourteous to the defense lawyers in the jury's presence. He appeared to reserve his most barbed shafts for defense counsel George W. Crockett Jr., the only Negro attorney in the case. Although he attacked all defense attorneys, his comments addressed to Mr. Crockett had a special character.

> Well, how any sane person can think otherwise is difficult for me to see. (2825)

> Well, that is the most ridiculous thing I have ever heard, Mr. Crockett. I wish you wouldn't do that. There is just no sense in that at all. (3323)

> Well, I am afraid that you understand things in a different sense from what they were said. (10,014)

Well, that sounds crazy. You always seem to do that. (10,038)

Mr. Sacher, what is it you desire to say that Mr. Crockett was not competent to take care? (9865)

The Court: Is that all you are going to say? You don't touch the subject at issue and under discussion at all. I suppose that is because Mr. Dennis is standing.
Mr. Crockett: I believe I did, and may I add that no one need speak for me in court. I believe I am competent to speak for myself. . . .
The Court: You want to talk some more, Mr. Crockett? (1575)

Oh, my, Mr. Crockett. You have something to add. (7275)

Get down to business, Mr. Crockett. (12,133)

Why don't you get down to work, Mr. Crockett, instead of all this fooling around, repetition. (12,262)

No, Mr. Crockett, you seem so consistently to misunderstand me. (13,897)

I wonder if it is possible for me to impress upon you. . . . Now, I beg of you to try to absorb that thought. (12,321–22)[76]

Tellingly, Crockett never felt he was being singled out by Medina because of racial discrimination or prejudice:

I was a victim of his anticommunist prejudice, no question about that. All of us were. From my point of view, Medina made it very clear at the very beginning of the trial that he was going to do a job on these defendants, and before the trial was over, he made it clear that he was going to do a job on the lawyers. As a matter of fact, on one occasion, my now-deceased wife reminded me that I actually wrote to her that this is a case where the defendants just might be found not guilty and their lawyers sent to jail [*laughs*]. The defendants had benefit of a jury; we didn't.[77]

In addition to Medina's demonstrable partisanship for the prosecution,[78] antagonism toward the defense attorneys,[79] and rulings on evidence that obviously favored the prosecution,[80] he protected witnesses for the government and harassed and badgered those for the defense.[81] Medina ultimately issued a ruling that effectively "gagged" the defense attorneys. This "rule," as Crockett would describe it, followed the unsuccessful but rancorous jury challenge by the defense that lasted nearly three months. After this experience, on April 4, 1949, while the prosecution's first witness was on the stand, Judge Medina announced that thereafter no legal arguments could be made or legal grounds given when objections were made or motions offered without permission from the court.[82] This gag rule, which Medina used throughout the course of the trial to silence *only* the defense lawyers, was an obvious departure from established trial procedure. It prevented the defense from establishing many bases for appellate review, and, ultimately, it spawned numerous and vigorous objections from Crockett and his colleagues that Medina would later use as a basis for their punishment.

Crockett recalled,

Medina said, "If one of you lawyers or one of you defendants makes an objection I will assume that objection is on behalf of all of you, and therefore it's not necessary for all of you to argue the objection. In addition to that, for purposes of appeal, I will assume and give you the benefit of any argument that you could make in support of that objection. I will just assume that you have made that argument and I have ruled on it, and if my ruling is that it's overruled, then it means I have overruled you on that point. And you can rely on that in going upstairs that you did raise the point and you did get a ruling on it."

That was the framework in which we had to try the Foley Square case. And that's the basis for much of the contempt citations. One of the contempt citations against me was that I persisted in arguing after the court had said he didn't want to hear any more argument. Well, as I just told you, he wouldn't hear any arguments. But I can't think of anything that's more normal to a lawyer in the course of a trial than not only to say, "Your Honor, I object," and then go on and give the argument in support of your objection.

Medina's position was, at most, all you say is "I object." Then he said, "You can assume that I know the basis for your objection. I know enough law to know every possible argument you can give for every possible objection." So at the conclusion of the trial, he went back through the record and picked out instances when I allegedly argued in violation of his affirmation not to argue, and he sentenced me to four months in prison for that.

And in the same situation on behalf of the prosecution, he would let them get the argument in, make whatever statements they wanted to make, rule on it, typically favorable to the prosecution. And when the defense would raise almost an identical argument or something very similar, he would give an adverse ruling or an opposite ruling or would not tolerate the defense doing it.[83]

It did not take long until everyone in the courtroom could predict the pattern of the judge's rulings. Crockett described one example of how the disparate treatment by Medina became so pervasive and obvious that courtroom spectators, including members of the press, began to anticipate his rulings and became sideline participants in them:

> Medina was so prejudiced that he would rule in favor of the government, and then when in a similar position, calling for a similar ruling for defense counsel, he would rule just the opposite. One of the citations of contempt against me grew out of that kind of situation.
>
> The prosecution had announced that it was going to rest. Abe Isserman and I were not in court at that time; we were at the office preparing for our opening statements at the beginning of the defense when we get word that the prosecution has rested.[84] So we immediately jumped in a cab, rushed to court, and asked for a continuance at least until the next morning to begin the defense.

Medina said no. We persisted, and finally, I got up and said something to the effect, "This ruling on the part of Your Honor is characteristic of rulings that have occurred throughout this trial. And it exhibits so much prejudice and bias that it really has been noticed by the audience itself." I said, "Now sitting here, with the audience right behind me, when the prosecution makes an objection, before the court can rule, I hear the audience back here saying, 'Sustained.' But when one of us makes an objection, again, before the court can rule, I hear the audience back here saying, 'Overruled.' Now that, I submit, is an indication of bias and prejudice on the part of this court."[85]

These were not isolated incidents.

There was limited seating capacity in this courtroom even though it was perhaps the largest courtroom in the federal courthouse at Foley Square. So it had been decided at the beginning, in the interest of fairness, that one side of the courtroom would be for prosecution and the other side would be for defense. And tickets would be given out so that the only way you could get into that courtroom as a spectator would be to have a pass. Well, you can imagine what happened. The prosecution side was always overflowing—a shortage of passes. But who the hell wants to have a pass [*laughs*] from a defendant, a communist, and sit on his side of the courtroom. So Medina decided that he couldn't waste all of that space on the defense side, so he reserved the seats up front just behind defense counsel for members of the press and for special friends of the court. His wife was always sitting in one of those seats just behind us. And it was from that group, including reporters, that I would get this chorus: "Sustained." "Overruled."[86]

Medina did not treat the prosecution in a similar manner.

Medina, of course, treated the prosecutors differently. McGohey, who was the U.S. Attorney, was a gentleman all the way through. He went out of his way to give the impression of being sort of a straight-backed, upright. . . . But he had some little bastards who were his assistants, a fellow named Gordon, particularly. You could always count on him to make some snide crack or remark and never get an upbraiding from Medina because of it. We might call attention to it, and Medina would smile and say, "Gentlemen, gentlemen, let's get on with the trial. Let's forget about these little things." But he never gave a direct reprimand to the prosecution.[87]

The Media's Role

It was not just the judge and the prosecution that were out of control. The courtroom behavior of the defendants and their lawyers received much media attention. This coverage incited charges from the Left that the press, with the obvious exception of the *Daily Worker*, was stridently biased against the defense. There were few reliable sources of information. One of these, the National Non-Partisan Committee to Defend the 12 Communist Leaders, published a report titled *Due Process in a Political Trial: The Record vs. the Press, in the Foley Square Trial of the 12 Communist Leaders*. While styled as nonpartisan, the organization included among its officers prominent members from the Left, such as Paul Robeson, cochair, and Howard Fast, treasurer. Despite these clear allegiances, it is difficult to argue with the report's principal conclusions. After reviewing more than thirteen thousand pages of the trial record, the group concluded in the report that the press was hostile to the defense and that its reporting was neither fair nor objective.[88]

As the trial began, a 1949 *Look* magazine article written about U.S. Attorney General Tom C. Clark helped introduce the Foley Square defendants to the U.S. public. It contained pictures of six of the indicted communist leaders. Characteristic of the press's general treatment of the defendants, these pictures were, in fact, police "mug shots." They portrayed the defendants with "booking" plates over their upper torsos, with the notations "FBI-NYC," followed by identification numbers.[89] As the trial concluded, *Life* published an article on the trial and its outcome that, similar to hundreds of other news stories written during the trial,[90] was patently anti-defense.[91] The following passages are illustrative:

The defense attorneys, buzzing among themselves and watching, hawklike, for a chance to jump up and disrupt the court's procedure.

They ... tried, with taunts and inflammatory outbursts, to throw the courtroom into confusion and the case into mistrial. . . . Judge Medina remained calm, refusing to be goaded.

The Communists responded with more oratory, more courtroom antics. . . . Pointedly, impartially, Judge Medina gave the case to the jury.

Head Red Eugene Dennis, [and] his battery of lawyers . . . tried to show ... they now abhorred violence as a reformed drunk abhors the bottle.

Defense lawyers, aimed at provoking a mistrial . . . yammering at the judge.[92]

Crockett does not recall a single instance when he thought a "mainstream" reporter actually analyzed an important issue associated with the case, including why the defense attorneys constantly confronted Judge Medina, and reported it fairly. Crockett attributes some of the biased press coverage directly to Judge Medina, who Crockett charges held secret "press conferences" for his favorite reporter at the *New York Times*.

It was my feeling, and I think it was the feeling of my fellow counsel, that Medina himself was a part of this media attack on the lawyers and on the defendants. Each morning he would religiously call a recess in the trial just before the deadline for the *New York Times* reporter to get his copy in for the evening edition. Not only would he call a recess, but the reporter would then get up and go back to Medina's chambers to talk with the judge—obviously about what of significance happened in the course of the trial that morning. And we could always tell what the story was going to be in the *New York Times* that evening.

As far as I know, he only met with the *Times* reporter. He didn't have what you might call a press conference as such. The door was just open for this reporter.[93]

The name Russell Porter appears on the byline on virtually all of the *New York Times* stories of the trial.

Medina's use of the press deeply troubled Crockett.

It is most unusual, to say the least, for a sitting judge in an ongoing case to be communicating on a daily basis with the press. To me, it was a clear and serious violation of judicial ethics. We never challenged what was going on as it wouldn't have accomplished much, because no reporter worth his salt would be stupid enough to quote a sitting judge in the course of a trial. But that doesn't keep the judge from planting the seed with the understanding that it's you, the reporter, who is saying this, not me, the judge. The reporter never wrote the story, "I had a meeting in the chambers with the judge this morning, and he told me so-and-so." He just wrote stories that, purportedly, covered the trial.

All the press coverage was unfavorable to the defense. No question about that. The only newspaper whose comments favored the defendants was the *Daily Worker*, that's all—everybody else was unfavorable and that was nationwide.[94]

The media was the only window the rest of country had to try to understand what was going on inside the courtroom.

The Peekskill Riots and Paul Robeson on the Witness Stand

The Congress for Civil Rights organized a fundraising concert for the Foley Square defendants in Peekskill, New York, on August 27, 1949. The concert featured the legendary Black lawyer, actor, singer, and activist Paul Robeson. In the hysteria of the trial, tensions ran high, but no one anticipated the violence that broke out. On the evening of the concert, the event was shut down before it even started by waves of attacks by anticommunist vigilantes.

Organizers regrouped and planned a second concert for September 4. With a defensive perimeter in place, Robeson performed an abbreviated concert. The violence this time took place as concertgoers left. Departing cars were forced to run a miles-long gauntlet where right-wing vigilantes attacked passengers and threw rocks through windshields. The folk singer Pete Seeger performed that evening; he described the terror he felt leaving Peekskill: "People threw stones with the intent to kill. At my own family. I had two little babies in the car."[95] Like every other aspect of the Battle of Foley Square, the Peekskill Riots became a national scandal. Judge Medina, on the other hand, saw the Peekskill concert and its disruption as a communist plot to delay or "break up" the trial.[96]

The FBI was in on the Foley Square action as well. The FBI conducted surveillance of the defendants and their lawyers, including defense conferences and trial strategy sessions, as well as the lawyers' private lives.[97] In one FBI report, Crockett was described this way: "Dresses neatly; air of confidence; tendency to assume poses."[98] While Crockett and the other defense lawyers knew they were being watched, they did not realize how extensively the FBI had penetrated their security.[99]

We assumed that there was a security problem. This was during the McCarthy period, when everything was being "bugged." We had our own security detail working with us to check periodically the telephones that were available to us to see if any "bugs" had been actually put on the physical equipment, that kind of thing. We always followed the policy of assuming that any telephone or any living quarters or certainly any office that was available to anybody connected with the defense in this trial was compromised. So we didn't say anything that we didn't expect to hear again in the course of the trial.[100]

Crockett's description of a surreptitious meeting with Paul Robeson reveals the precautions they took to keep their trial plans secret from the government.

Paul Robeson, the great actor/singer, was to be a defense witness. It was decided, even though he was being called as what amounted to a character witness for Ben Davis, that I would be the one to examine him and not the lawyer who was representing Ben, Harry Sacher. All right, since I'm to be the one to examine Paul, obviously I must meet, talk with him, find out what his testimony is going to be, or suggest to him what manner of testimony we would like to obtain from him. Now where do I meet with him? Any place Paul was likely to be, customarily, would be bugged. This is after Peekskill.

So we finally pick out the home of one of Paul's friends up in Harlem, and that's where we went to have our conference. I can see Paul now, that big frame, stretched full length on the lounge in the living room and me in a chair asking him questions, and he's smiling and giving me the answers and that kind of thing. This is after both of us talked lawyer's talk [Robeson was also an attorney] about Medina and the trial and the objections that are being made and what objections we can anticipate and so forth.[101]

Unfortunately, the defendants' tendency to seek sensational events and dictate the strategies to their lawyers again produced counterproductive results.

I put Paul on the witness stand, but he wasn't permitted to say anything. I didn't get to first base except for his name and who he was, and then Medina wanted to know for what purpose this witness was being called. I think he probably wanted to know, "Is this one of your expert witnesses on Marxism-Leninism?" It would be just like Medina to ask a question like that in the course of the trial. I'm sure he made some snide remark at that point, and I told him that Mr. Robeson was being called as a character witness. "Character witness for whom?" I said, "For Mr. Davis." "Is Mr. Davis going to testify in this case?" "Your Honor, I don't know. I can't tell you that. I don't represent Mr. Davis." "Well, I don't think Mr. Robeson can testify as a character witness for a defendant who is not gonna take the witness stand, Mr. Crockett, so unless you can assure me"—and I'm paraphrasing now; obviously I can't quote the record, but this is the substance—"unless you can assure me that Mr. Davis is going to testify, I'm afraid we will have to dispense with Mr. Robeson's testimony unless and until such time as Mr. Davis does testify." Now, Medina was right; that was good law, no question about that.

This was a part of the defense strategy that I said earlier was all wet. It's true you want to make it a political trial, but then you handicap your lawyers. We know what the rules of evidence are and what we can do and cannot do, and I can tell you as a lawyer there's no point in putting a Paul Robeson on the stand as a character witness unless we were prepared to either assure the court that the person whose character you're trying to bolster is going to testify or put that person on first to testify. But the clients said, "No, no, no, we want the favorable publicity that's going to come from having the famous Paul Robeson appear for the defense."[102]

As a result, Robeson's involvement, which was certain to attract international attention, was reduced to a cameo appearance.

Crockett Tests the Legal Waters at the Supreme Court

Toward the end of the trial, Crockett had an opportunity to argue a related case to the U.S. Supreme Court. The case, which Crockett called "Dennis One," involved the appeal of the Foley Square defendant Eugene Dennis's earlier conviction for contempt of Congress. Crockett argued the case on November 7, 1949, while the Foley Square trial was in progress. The fate of this case suggested how hostile and unwelcoming the appellate courts would probably be for the Foley Square defendants and their lawyers.

It was my practice during the recesses of the trial in New York to walk up and down the corridor outside the courtroom. Eugene Dennis had a habit of doing the same thing. And one day he and I were walking together. Gene was a very taciturn person; he didn't do much talking. Out of the blue, he wanted to know if I would represent him by arguing his appeal in the United States Supreme Court. I was shocked. Every lawyer's ambition is one day to stand before the highest tribunal in the country and present an argument, and here's Gene asking me if I would go down to Washington and argue his case for the United States Supreme Court.[103]

"Dennis One" had all of the political intrigue of the nation's anti-communist hysteria and the subsequent bending of legal norms as was happening in Foley Square.[104]

His case was for contempt of Congress. He had been subpoenaed to appear before the House Un-American Activities Committee at a hearing in Washington. In the course of that hearing, he had been asked some questions that he either refused to answer or claimed the privilege against self-incrimination. I can't tell you right now what those questions were, but I'm sure they were related to the membership of some people other than himself in the Communist Party. Well, he declined to answer the questions, and then the issue arose whether or not he would be cited for contempt before the Congress of the United States.

There was quite a bit of discussion on the floor of the House of Representatives that time because some members of the House felt that [Attorney General] Clark was dragging his feet on bringing contempt charges against Gene Dennis because he was head of the Communist Party. They were very strong in their feelings on that score, and it was even suggested that maybe they should institute impeachment proceedings against Clark to speed up this process. Dennis was literally the head of the U.S. Communist Party. The chairman of the party was more or less titular. The chief executive officer of the party was the national secretary.[105]

This was the same Attorney General Clark who had admonished lawyers for daring to represent members of the Communist Party. As Crockett tells the story more than four decades later, he speaks of Clark with obvious disdain.

Clark meanwhile had written some very—I call them scurrilous—but very strong magazine articles condemning lawyers who represented members of the Communist Party and saying that they should be taken to the woodshed, which was his way of saying that they should be disbarred. . . . Additionally, he had authored the Attorney General's List, as it was called, in which he deliberately characterized certain organizations as communist front organizations. One of the badges of condemnation would be for your organization or your committee or your group to be on the Attorney General's List. That was Clark's list.

Eventually Clark did institute criminal proceedings for contempt of Congress against Gene Dennis, and the case came to trial in Washington, and he was convicted.[106]

Dennis's appeal focused on loyalty oaths for federal employees in Washington, DC. If one had taken a loyalty oath, how could one be a fair juror in a trial of Communist Party leaders?

The big issue raised on his appeal was that he couldn't possibly get a fair trial in Washington because a jury in Washington would necessarily include employees of the federal government, and employees of the federal government were subject to loyalty oaths. Therefore, any employee of the federal government who served on a jury trying the head man of the Communist Party and who dared to acquit him would be suspect and would likely lose his or her job. That was a kind of pressure that no reasonable juror could be expected to resist. Therefore, Dennis argued that he could not get a fair trial under those circumstances. That was the argument I presented to the United States Supreme Court.[107]

But there was another legal issue important to Crockett: inherent conflicts of interest on the part of Tom Clark, who had been appointed to the Supreme Court on August 24, 1949.

Would he sit in this *Dennis* case in view of all that he'd written about lawyers and communists and so forth and in view of the fact that he'd been the architect of the Attorney General's List and in view of the fact that he'd been threatened with impeachment by members of the House of Representatives? Wouldn't it be more appropriate for him to disqualify himself and step down? Well, when the case was called for argument, Clark showed no disposition whatever to excuse himself and get up and leave the bench. He just sat there.

Clark, if I remember correctly, was sitting in the last seat to the right of the Chief Justice, and right next to him was Justice Jackson. Jackson literally turned his back on Clark the whole time the argument was going on because Jackson and, I think, certain other members of the Court felt that this was really unconscionable. For a guy who was the Attorney General at the time the prosecution was started and who had vocalized so much anticommunism to be sitting in judgment on the chief executive officer of the Communist Party was clearly outrageous.[108]

But how do you get a justice of the Supreme Court to recuse himself?

When I got back to New York, it occurred to me, "Why don't you give him a little push?" But how can you do that without being in contempt? Certainly you don't have a press conference and say he should disqualify himself. How do you do it? Eventually, it occurred to me to write something that you might call a suggestion—a Suggestion of Disqualification. So that's what I did. It was easy to do because all I had to do was go back and recite the different things that he had done that indicated his anticommunist bias.

So I wrote a motion that I had never heard of—a Suggestion of Disqualification. I sent it down to a lawyer friend of mine in Washington for filing. He took it over and gave it to the clerk of the Supreme Court. He said the clerk turned a half dozen different colors when he saw what that document was, but he accepted and filed it. There were sufficient copies to go to each justice of the Supreme Court. Within a matter of a few days, as I recall—I don't know, it may have been more than a week—I get word that Mr. Justice Clark has disqualified himself in the *Dennis* case. That, as far as I've been able to ascertain, is the first time that anyone ever, in effect, asked a Supreme Court justice to step down because of a claim of prejudice and bias and prevailed on the request—a remarkable piece of history, I think.[109]

Even with Clark disqualifying himself, the Supreme Court ruled against Dennis. This was a shot across the bow and a strong indication that the Foley Square defendants would face an uphill battle in the appellate courts, regardless of the merits of their legal claims.

Medina's Complaints about His Health

Many of the defense lawyers' confrontations with Medina were legitimate efforts to protect defendants against the judge's biased rulings. In response, Medina, who was fit and had assertively controlled the trial throughout, complained frequently on the record that the defense lawyers were adversely affecting his health. With all of the controversy and high political stakes surrounding the case, Medina had a tendency to want to make the case all about him.

You have my nerves so frayed here with all this dispute and argument that I do not know how I am going to carry on this trial month after month. (2502)

In fact, I have been meditating for some time about having some kind of a little recess of two or three days because I have been getting myself in such a state of fatigue that I really am beginning to get worried. (2564)

Usually I enjoy discussion by lawyers, but I found in this case that it got absolutely intolerable and such a burden that I never could physically continue through to the end of the trial if I permitted it to continue. (3252)

This continuous wrangling has worn me so that I do not see how I am ever going to conclude this trial. There must be some stop to it. This continual going back, reading this little thing, reading that little thing, every trivial item must be argued at length—now, it is grievously wearing to me and it must be stopped. (3966)

Well, you keep digging at me, you and your colleagues. It is digging here and digging there. I suppose it is to wear me down and it does wear me down. (4110)

I am not going to try to wear myself down on you anymore but I hope you will go on with your next question. (6441)

We are getting back to where we were a month or two ago. I don't want that business to get a real good start because it pretty nearly got me out of business the last time, and I don't want to go through that again. Now I have had enough of an ordeal on this trial without you men getting up and badgering me the way you have been doing. (9096)

I wish to state on the record that I am physically and mentally incapable of going through very much more of this wrangling and argument and I shall have to do something about it if it is continued and counsel refuses to obey my admonition. It is more than any human being can stand. (10,785)[110]

The jury, undoubtedly, viewed the defense lawyers as responsible for Medina's complaints of ill health. These complaints, which amounted to deliberate attempts to subvert justice by attacking a federal judge, must also have given credence to the charge that the defendants intended to undermine the government of the United States.

Medina was assigned around-the-clock protection by the New York Police Department and the FBI. The judge began to regard the defendants and their supporters as "dangerous, well-organized revolutionaries."[111] He was convinced that everything done by the defense was for two overriding reasons: to spread communist propaganda and to disrupt the trial by any means possible.[112] He conducted himself and the trial accordingly. He was not an impartial arbiter. Medina had become an adversary.[113]

As the trial neared its conclusion, the question of how ordinary jurors could overcome and defy an atmosphere of inflamed public opinion and hysteria created by the press and the government had become moot. No one, including Crockett and the entire defense team, expected anything but guilty verdicts. Making and preserving a record for appeals had become paramount for the lawyers, and they sustained a determined defense to the trial's end.

Crockett Sums Up: "Freedom Is Everybody's Job"

Crockett's summation to the jury took over three hours and filled 145 pages of the trial transcript.[114] As he began, Crockett told the jury of his devotion to the Constitution, the importance of their verdict, and his belief that "freedom is indivisible."

> May it please the Court, ladies and gentlemen of the jury:
> This is the moment which to me is the highlight in my life. I have the feeling that I have lived for this moment when an opportunity will be given me to tell you how much the Constitution means not only to me but to these eleven men who are on trial here.
> . . . In riding the subways here in New York I have noticed a sign, a sign that says, "Freedom is everybody's job."
> Freedom is indivisible. We cannot deny freedom of speech to Communists and at the same time preserve freedom for Jews or for Catholics or for Negroes or for persons of foreign ancestry. You cannot outlaw the Communist Party because of its political theories without creating a most dangerous precedent, a precedent that may in the future be used to outlaw the religious organization or the political organization or the inter-racial organization to which you or I might belong.
> Once we in America forget that freedom is everybody's business, once we accept the fascist theory that Communists have no rights or that all Communists should be sent to Russia or put in concentration camps, once we begin thinking and speaking in those terms we descend to the very depths of Hitlerism.
> I can recall and I am sure you can recall also that three years before Hitler came to power remarks similar to those I have mentioned were being made in Germany about Communists and about Jews. And all of us know what happened then. First came

the Reichstag trial of the Communists and the outlawing of their party. Then came the pogrom against the Jews and the concentration camps, and then—and then came the banishment of everyone who disagreed with the Nazi ideology.

You have the power by your verdict to forestall that chain of events here.[115]

Much of Crockett's lengthy closing dealt with what he called "a peripheral issue in this case ... the Negro question."[116] Two prosecution witnesses had testified that Blacks' grievances were exploited by the Communist Party for political gain.[117] Crockett responded to the charge, which he said made him "boil with resentment."

That in this day and time anyone can think that Negroes are so immature, so childish, so inclined to, shall I say, be a good boy, when they are far above 40 years of age, that they can believe that any organization whether it is the Communist Party or any other organization can treat the Negroes in America as so many pawns to try to use for whatever purposes they see fit to use them.

The whole notion of using Negroes is part and parcel of that white supremacy which seemingly is running roughshod over this country, not only in the South but in recent weeks right here in the North.

... So far as the Communist Party is concerned it is probably more accurate to say that Negroes have used the Communist Party. It is the one party in which they feel free to speak and to act like Americans. It is the only party that seemingly cares about the plight of Negroes in this country.

... The Communist Party moreover has used the Negro question in the trade union movement. It was not until recent years that Negroes were accepted on an equal level with whites in the trade union movement, not until the CIO came into existence. And it was the Communist Party that instituted that practice, and it has accounted for more Negroes being employed, more Negroes being upgraded, more Negroes getting wage increases than any other one organization in this country.

... We Negroes, regardless of our economic or educational status, are still second class citizens. The best evidence of that in
this case is the fact that in this day and time it is still considered
unusual that I, a Negro, should be representing two white defendants in a Federal Court. And of course, you and I know that it
is the general practice in our American courts not to have Negro
lawyers in important cases like this. You don't see a Negro lawyer
at the prosecution's table and there is a very obvious reason why
you don't see one. It is not the practice of the Democratic Party
to employ Negroes as United States attorneys. Because we have
allowed this pattern of Negro discrimination to become fixed in
our American way of life, that very pattern has been made the basis
for anti-Semitism, for prejudice against Catholics, Mexicans and
other minorities, and other prejudices which you know exist in
large sections of our land.

Our aim in life should be to make democracy ring out for all
the people of this country, not for just a few.

If, therefore, the program and activities of the Communist
Party on the Negro question as set forth in its 1945 resolution
and constitution constituted "utilizing the grievances of Negroes,"
as the prosecution contends, then this country needs a great deal
more of that, not only by the Communists but by everyone else
and by every other organization that calls itself an American
organization.[118]

Crockett castigated the FBI, the American government, and both the
Democrats and Republicans for refusing to protect the civil rights of Black
citizens—rights that the Communist Party advocated.

But it does not seem to me that an FBI that is omnipotent enough
to find an error of fact in the certified copy of Mr. Winston's
birth certificate; or to know precisely where Mr. Winter was living in Los Angeles on a given date five or six years ago; or that
Mr. Davis' application for a driver's license contained an erroneous
answer—it seems to me that an FBI sufficiently competent to fer-
ret out details about Communists should be able to find evidence

sufficient to support a conviction of at least one lyncher. And yet the records show that never in the history of Mr. J. Edgar Hoover's FBI have they been able to locate, identify and convict a single member of a lynch mob. And this includes their so-called investigation of the brutal slaying of those four Negroes in open daylight in Monroe, Georgia in 1946, as well as many other instances of mob violence in which they have been called in to investigate.

. . . This system of prosecuting the victims and exonerating the perpetrators of fascism reflects the demagogy on the part of the administration and on the part of this prosecution. The demagogy which all of us know and see in the shameless desertion of the Civil Rights program in Congress, the promotion to our Supreme Court of the chief architect of the denial of civil rights to the people; and the voting of additional public funds to that thought control agency under the domination of the poll-taxer Rankin for the purpose of continuing this notorious work of denying civil rights to the American people. These administration acts, together with this trial, have subverted our constitutional safeguards and made of the First Amendment, the 13th Amendment and the 14th and 15th Amendments to our Constitution so much Aesopian language.

. . . This is an attempt to illegalize the party that has fought against the whole system of force and violence practiced upon Negroes.

This is an attempt to outlaw the party that leads the fight against those Jim Crow curtains in our railroad dining cars which set aside Negroes as untouchables. This is an attempt to outlaw the Party that leads the fight against those who would confine Negro children to the tubercular slum areas of our city. This is an attempt to outlaw the party that leads the fight against those who would keep the Negro "in his place."

And finally, and most important of all, this is the persecution of a party which in the 30 years of its history has acted as the conscience of America. For make no mistake, to the extent that the Republican Party or the Democratic Party or any of the other political groups in this country have advanced the cause of democracy, it has only been because of the prodding by the small group

of conscientious democratic citizens of this nation who find themselves members of the Communist Party. To that extent, the Communist Party is in truth and in fact the conscience of America.
America needs this party of protest.[119]

Although the verdicts were anticipated, the swiftness with which they
came was surprising. After the longest criminal trial in the country's history, the jury deliberated less than seven hours before it found all of the
defendants guilty as charged. Judge Medina immediately polled the jurors
and, thereafter, politely discharged them with the customary expressions
of appreciation. He then announced, "Now I turn to some unfinished
business."[120]

4

Aftermath of United States v. Dennis

Medina's Unfinished Business

On October 14, 1949, at 11:35 a.m., immediately after Judge Medina thanked and dismissed the jury, he turned in his chair. He looked toward the defense lawyers and announced, "Now I turn to some unfinished business. The following will kindly rise."[1] Crockett remembered that the judge spoke softly, almost matter-of-factly, as he unfolded one of the most controversial episodes in U.S. legal history.[2] The names of the five defense lawyers and defendant Eugene Dennis, who represented himself in the trial, were called. They stood, and Medina began reading from a prepared document—a certificate of contempt. Medina's conclusions in the contempt certificate were uncannily similar to his long-held views of the defense lawyers' conduct in the 1944 Smith Act trial of the fascists—a trial that he believed took the life of Judge Edward C. Eicher.[3]

"Before the trial had progressed very far," he stated that he had concluded that the Foley Square defense lawyers and defendant Dennis "deliberately entered into . . . a cold and calculating" conspiracy. This conspiracy, he charged, was formed for the purposes of (1) causing "delay and confusion as to make it impossible to go on with the trial," (2) "provoking incidents" to cause a mistrial, and (3) impairing the judge's "health so that the trial could not continue."[4] These acts, Medina found, were willful and intended to sabotage the federal judiciary and, as such, constituted misconduct so grave "as to make the mere imposition of fines a futile gesture and a wholly insufficient punishment."[5]

Medina read only a portion of his lengthy certificate of contempt, which contained forty specifications against the five lawyers and Dennis. The conspiracy charge in Specification 1, however, was critical. Medina stated that, without the conspiracy, he "would have overlooked or at most merely reprimanded counsel for conduct which appeared to be the result of the heat of controversy or of that zeal in the defense of a client ... which might understandably have caused one to overstep the bounds of strict propriety."[6] By charging a conspiracy,[7] Medina was able to deflect the contempt proceeding from specific acts contained in the trial record that he, himself, deemed "harmless" to a sinister and illegal but totally unsubstantiated, unseen, and unchallenged out-of-court agreement.[8]

All the lawyers were found guilty of Specification 1—the conspiracy count. Medina then followed with the contempt specifications. Prison sentences were imposed *concurrently* for *each* contempt count: Sacher, twenty-three counts, six months for each; Gladstein, eighteen counts, six months for each; McCabe, six counts, thirty days for each; Isserman, seven counts, four months for each; Dennis, five counts, six months for each; and Crockett, nine counts and four months for each.[9]

While the defense lawyers had actually expected some kind of contempt action as Medina had frequently threatened it, Crockett recalled being surprised nonetheless:

We didn't expect it the way it came down. We had no hearing, no trial, no jury, nothing. He summarily cited five lawyers for contempt and sentenced us to prison. We were shocked, stunned by the sentences, period. Even if he had said ten days, I would have been shocked by the notion of going to jail. It never occurred to me that George Crockett, an attorney at law, a graduate of Morehouse College and the University of Michigan, would go to jail.

At the time, you got no hearing or a jury trial, just the judge certifying the conduct happened in his presence and that it was contemptuous. The sentence follows—that's all. Changes in contempt law came after our case. We argued before the Supreme Court that we were entitled to a hearing and jury, but the Court wasn't prepared to make changes in the law at that time, at least not in our case, even though two of us got sentences of six months. The judge didn't even have to ask you if you had anything to say before sentence was imposed. Medina did, however, after we requested, allow us to speak before he dispatched us to prison.[10]

Crockett spoke after Isserman, Sacher, and Gladstein. In his unprepared statement to the court, he called his contempt citation a "badge of honor." He spoke also of the future and of ultimate vindication.

Mr. Crockett: May I be heard, with the Court's permission?
The Court: Yes.
Mr. Crockett: Long prior to today Your Honor saw fit to adjudge
me in contempt, which I believe was the first adjudication of
contempt that had been made in the course of the trial. Today
additional adjudications have been made. As a lawyer, I shall
of course take whatever course of action is open to me to
remove from my record that any Court has found my conduct
inconsistent with the best conduct to be expected from a
member of the American bar. Nevertheless, in this particular
instance I regard it as a badge of honor to be adjudicated in
contempt for vigorously prosecuting what I believe to be the
proper conception of the American Constitution, and I say
again that if I were offered the opportunity to participate in
another trial like this I would fight it just as vigorously as I
have tried to fight at this time.

It so happens that because of conditions in America, I of
course look upon many problems different from the way my
associates, perhaps the Court, would look upon them: I have
to look upon them not only as a lawyer but also as a member
of a minority group. For the first time in the fifteen years
that I have been practicing law I have had an opportunity to
practice law as an American lawyer and not as a Negro lawyer.
I have enjoyed that brief trip into the realm of freedom, as far
as the practice of law in America is concerned. I have enjoyed
it so much that I intend to continue that way. I am aware, of
course, that this is an important case. I am also aware that this
is not the end of this case. There have been similar instances

in history, especially in connection with trials under the Alien
and Sedition Laws, and judges have seen fit to imprison
attorneys because the attorneys had disagreed with the judge's
conception of the law, but history revealed that the attorneys in
those cases were correct.[11]

Of the nine contempt citations against him, Crockett considers one
particularly grating. When retelling the story in 1993, however, he was able
to laugh repeatedly.

Gates was on the stand. He had declined to identify some person as a member of the Communist Party, and Medina summarily
cited him for contempt. I don't know whether it so shocked the
defendants or what or took them by surprise, but they all stood up.
I didn't stand up. I kept telling my client, who was looking down
at me, "Why don't you sit down?" And he said, "Why don't you
stand up?" The other lawyers stood up, but I didn't. Even though
I never stood, Medina still cited me for contempt—for failing to
control my client—four months. The lawyers who stood were also
cited—for failure to control their clients. Anyone who represented
a member of the Communist Party in a Smith Act trial soon
learned that lawyers don't control their clients.[12]

A second citation against him, Crockett believes, illustrates the judge's
predisposition to punish the defense lawyers.

I had my client, Carl Winter, on the stand. When I had finished
my direct examination, the government, on cross, had a document
they wanted put into evidence—a California marriage license. The
government wanted to use it to show that he was in California at a
certain time as, I believe, they had a witness who would testify he
attended a party meeting about then.

My client called me to confer with him while on the witness stand. He objected strongly to the document's introduction because it would show on its face that his daughter, who was
then about five years old, was born out of wedlock. I approached

the bench and told Medina about our concern. Believe it or not, Medina agreed. He said he would only let in the part that showed Winter's address and the date. I said, "Fine, Your Honor," and went back to my seat.

Medina then picked up the document and proceeded to read the very part that I had objected to and that he said would not be admitted. I stood and objected very strongly. I can still recall his looking down at me over the rim of his glasses: "Mr. Crockett, did I do something in error?" I responded, and this is a direct quote:

"Your Honor seemingly unintentionally read into the record the very portion of that document that you said you were excluding."

"Mr. Crockett, seemingly unintentional?"

"Yes, Your Honor."

"That's contemptuous conduct, Mr. Crockett."

I didn't say anything more, but for saying "seemingly unintentional," he gave me four months in prison.[13]

A third citation against him, Crockett believes, typifies the unfairness of all the contempt specifications against him and the punishments imposed. On this occasion, Crockett, with the court's permission, was attempting to establish, through the testimony of a community leader, the fact that Negroes were excluded from jury service.

The Court: Have you some case, Mr. Crockett, to cite to me where the Supreme Court held that it was all right to ask a politician or Congressman a blanket question about the literacy of all the people in his district or the intelligence of all the people in his district? Have you such a case?

Mr. Crockett: I want first of all to object to the Court's characterization of Congressman Marcantonio as a politician.

The Court: Yes, and you will just answer as you did the last time.

Mr. Crockett: I wish also to object to your statement with reference to my own conduct. I think the record will show that on each occasion I have given the Court an answer when I was asked to give an answer.

The Court: I think not.

Mr. Crockett: Now in this case Your Honor is requesting that I refer you to some cases.

The Court: That is right.

Mr. Crockett: That is what I want to do.

The Court: Go ahead and do it.

Mr. Crockett: The case of *Patton vs. Mississippi* is one.

The Court: Wait a minute, *Penn vs. Mississippi?*

Mr. Crockett: *Patton vs. Mississippi.*

The Court: What is the citation? And for once give me the official citation.

Mr. Crockett: If Your Honor prefers, I will prepare a list of these cases and give it to you in the morning.

The Court: No. I will check this one right now and we will see if there is anything in there on the subject.

Mr. Crockett: *Patton vs. Mississippi* is 332 U.S. 463.

The Court: Now, if you will just sit down and let me look at this book. *(Reading.)* Well, I find absolutely nothing in that opinion which even remotely touches the subject under discussion. So we will proceed now without any further argument, please.

Mr. Crockett: I should like merely to request permission to give the Court a memorandum, Your Honor.

The Court: Well, if you are going on, Mr. Crockett, you are doing it in defiance of my request to you.

Mr. Crockett: I am not arguing; I am merely trying to get permission to submit a memorandum—

The Court: You are talking. Go, keep it up.[14]

Crockett's case was relevant. In *Patton v. Mississippi* (1947), a Black man was indicted for murder by an all-white grand jury and convicted by an all-white petit jury in a county with a substantial Black population and where no Black had served on a grand or petit criminal court jury in the county for thirty years. The Court held that these facts created a strong presumption that Blacks were systematically excluded from jury service because of race, and it became the state's duty to justify such exclusion as having been brought about for some reason other than racial discrimination.

This conduct was found contemptuous, not when it occurred but several months later, and for it, Crockett received a four-month prison term. Medina's rulings created profound difficulties for Crockett and his colleagues as they contemplated their appeals and confronted the reality of actually going to prison.

> Our contempt sentences were to run concurrently. Therefore, in order to escape prison, I had to get reversals on each of nine citations of contempt.[15] Conspiracy was the basic charge of contempt that Medina found against all of us. If this conspiracy ruling was affirmed, it would be exceedingly difficult to distinguish it from the way lawyers cooperate, even in a civil case. They compare notes, have meetings to plan strategies, arguments, and who is going to take this position and who is going to take that one, and so forth. Medina's ruling was extremely dangerous for all lawyers. There was absolutely no desire among defense lawyers to delay or drag out the trial. We all wanted to get it over and get back to our law practices as soon as we could.[16]

Free from the rigors of the country's longest trial, Crockett looked toward home and to relative safety and comfort with his family and friends. New threats loomed, however. Attorney General Tom C. Clark's call for bar associations to "purge" the lawyers who represented communists had not been unheeded. In addition to Crockett's fighting for his freedom, he, like his trial brethren in other jurisdictions, returned to Michigan only to find that his career and his very livelihood were in grave jeopardy.

Foreboding Homecoming

As news of the trial verdicts and the lawyers' contempt sentences made headlines across the country,[17] Crockett's office associates in Detroit reacted quickly. The day after the trial ended, Ernie Goodman dispatched a telegram to Crockett:

October 15, 1949

Mr. Geo. W. Crockett, Jr.
Office of Defense Counsel
401 Broadway
New York, N.Y.

READ OF YOUR SO-CALLED CONTEMPT. WE ARE SURE YOU WILL CONTINUE
TO PRESERVE YOUR INDEPENDENCE AS A LAWYER DESPITE UNJUSTIFIED
EFFORTS TO SILENCE YOU. WE STAND WARMLY BESIDE YOU.
         HARRY ANBENDER, MORTON EDEN, JACK TUCKER, JEROME KELMAN, N. L.
SMOKLER, DON LORIA, BENJAMIN SAFIR, BENJAMIN MARCUS, ERNEST GOOD-
MAN, MIN C. TURNER, PHYLLIS A. SUGAR, ELLA MARCUS, MARIJANA RELICH.[18]

Two days later, Crockett responded with a handwritten letter. Damage to
his reputation and beginning his defense were his primary concerns:

Monday
10/17/49

Please express to the office my sincere thanks for the telegram.
It really was not necessary since if I am sure of anything it is the
loyalty of those of you with whom I work.

I am aware of the newspaper job that is being done on me and
other defense counsel back in our respective communities. It is all
part of the pattern of terrorism that has been associated with this
trial from its inception. If the people could only read the record
in this case the whole conspiracy of the press would be exposed. To
that end I am enclosing (or rather sending) to you several copies of a
pamphlet giving actual reprints of the record and showing the biased,
prejudiced and unjudicial conduct and attitude which the judge
exhibited toward us from the beginning. I suggest that this pamphlet
be placed in the hands of individuals whose opinions mean a great
deal and who may be able to interpret our position to others.

One more word: I hope that those who have known me in the
profession will remember the Crockett they knew there. I assure

them that, not withstanding what they may have read in the press, I am the same Crockett. A bit more mature, yes; but the same courteous and conscientious upholder of the traditions of the bar that I always have tried to be.

> Best wishes to you and all of my friends.
> Sincerely,
> Crockett.[19]

The pamphlet Crockett described was the same *Due Process in a Political Trial: The Record vs. the Press* discussed earlier, put together by the National Non-Partisan Committee to Defend the 12 Communist Leaders. It is a document written by lawyers, for lawyers. Organized by various themes, the document systematically reproduces portions of the trial transcript that contradict dominant media themes.[20]

Leftist lawyers in Detroit had for years honed their skills organizing publicity and community support as standard, essential tactics for defending unpopular causes. On October 26, 1949, Goodman wrote to Crockett to tell him that a campaign to influence members of the Michigan bar was already under way:

October 26, 1949

Mr. Geo. W. Crockett, Jr.
401 Broadway, Suite 1608
New York, N.Y.

Dear George:

We are considering the possibility of mailing copies of the pamphlet "Due Process in a Political Trial" to all or most of the members of the Bar of Michigan. Can you find out how much it would cost to print 3000 or 6000? Also, whether there is to be an early revision of the pamphlet making it worthwhile for us to wait. Unless such a revision is completed quickly, we will probably want to send out the old pamphlet. Please let me know as soon as possible.

We are having a pheasant dinner at our house Friday night. Will you be in town early enough to come? If so, you are invited, but let me know in advance.

Sincerely,
Ernest Goodman[21]

The next day, Crockett telegraphed an answer:

ERNEST GOODMAN=

3220 BARLUM TOWER DET=

UNDERSTAND PAMPHLET ALREADY SENT TO EACH MICHIGAN BAR ASSO-
CIATION AND TO EACH MEMBER OF GUILD REVISION READY NEXT WEEK
APPROXIMATE COST INCLUDING MAILING IS 20 CENTS BE HOME SATURDAY

GEORGE W. CROCKETT JUNIOR[22]

Meanwhile, Judge Medina had become an instant national hero. His contempt judgments against "obstreperous, overzealous defense lawyers" were acclaimed in wire service reports.[23] Of his new iconic status and the thousands of supporting letters he received, Medina commented, "Everyone seems to have gone crazy."[24] On the other hand, with the exception of the National Lawyers Guild, the *Daily Worker*,[25] and some of the Black weekly papers,[26] Crockett and the defense team garnered little national support. Goodman remembered the homecoming, the work that lay ahead, and the effect the Battle of Foley Square had on George.

In the first place, we knew that the case was to be appealed—the contempt part of it, and that it was going to be a lot of work in connection with the argument . . . and that it would go to the U.S. Supreme Court.

. . . So, it wasn't as if he was coming home in order to go to prison. He was coming home to appeal his whole case, and there was going to be a lot of support for George. We wanted to help in any way we could and get as much public support as possible. But,

of course, as far as George himself was concerned, the fact that he
was sentenced to prison at all deeply affected him. . . . He was a
black lawyer, one of a few black lawyers period, and he had been
rising constantly in the profession. He had held important positions that made him nationally prominent and widely respected.
His family was a middle-class family that felt it important that
they should have a good reputation—and George did personally
have a very good reputation all his life, and there was a strong family feeling that each knew that the others would lead a good and
proper life. . . . But George, in particular, because of his background,
felt that they were leading a good life in the way they worked and
helped others. To be sentenced to a federal penitentiary for being
a lawyer, which was an important goal in itself, was very disheartening for him. He never figured that if you were held in contempt
that a lawyer would be thrown in jail for it or that it would happen
the way it did. When it was dropped on him, it was just terrible for
him to find himself involved in something of this sort.[27]

Despite Goodman's encouraging words, the future of Goodman's own
legal practice was a matter of some doubt. Babson, Riddle, and Elsila
describe the bleak state of affairs for Goodman, Crockett, and other remain-
ders of the Sugar firm when Crockett returned to Detroit:

Sugar himself was gone, semiretired to Northern Michigan and
only passing through on the way to somewhere else. He had spent
much of the last year in New York City advising Crockett and other
members of the defense team in the first Smith Act trial of the
Communist Party leaders. . . . Sugar's office overlooking Cadillac
Square now had the still air of a neglected storeroom; Crockett's
office was also deserted, a mounting pile of unopened mail spill-
ing across the desk. Neighboring offices were empty or little used.
Their occupants were drifting away, foraging for clients further and
further from the barren ground left by the Red Scare and the wid-
ening boycott of Sugar's firm.[28]

Such was the state of affairs as 1949 became 1950.

The Dennis *Lawyers' First Appeal:* Sacher v. United States

By today's standards, the contempt appeals were decided very quickly. Oral arguments in *Sacher v. United States* were heard before the United States Court of Appeals for the Second Circuit on February 6, 1950, and a decision was issued on April 5, 1950.[29]

The panel of federal circuit judges, Augustus N. Hand, Jerome Frank, and Charles Clark, were experienced, highly respected, and scholarly. Judges Frank and Clark were regarded as liberals, particularly Frank, who, in the 1930s, had been a prominent New Dealer. Any elation the petitioners may have had with a seemingly favorable draw of judges was short-lived. In a 2–1 decision, the court upheld the contempt sentences, even though it reversed Judge Medina's crucial conspiracy ruling.

The judges wrote separately. Clark dissented on all counts. Only he addressed directly Medina's acknowledgment that he was punishing conspirators and that without the conspiracy, he would have virtually disregarded their other acts. In this light, Judge Clark considered the conspiracy count pivotal, and finding none in the record, concluded, "A hearing therefore seems to me a prerequisite to punishment as a matter of law."[30] Judge Clark, in fact, found that "quite obviously this trial was not being . . . broken up, but did . . . proceed to an orderly conclusion; with what appears to be an improved attitude . . . if the drying up of untoward incidents is any test."[31]

Judge Hand wrote the lead opinion and, apparently, had little difficulty in sustaining the trial court's action in virtually every aspect, including the straight conspiracy charge. He brushed aside the petitioners' argument that they had been punished for engaging in a conspiracy—an act that the trial judge could not have witnessed. For Judge Hand, Medina's conspiracy merely "meant no more than that they were deliberate, and it was quite unimportant whether he believed that a prior conspiracy had been entered into."[32] In fact, Hand wrote, the acts Judge Medina "saw and heard" as the basis for his contempt charges were "enough to show willful obstruction of the trial."[33] Also, there was no need to impose punishment immediately, if doing so "would endanger the defense in a criminal case, or interfere with its conduct."[34] These decisions, Hand decided, were to be made by the trial judge and depended on the circumstances of each case.

Having rather facilely disposed of the conspiracy count that Judges Frank and Clark found more than troublesome, Hand reviewed the thirty-nine contempt specifications against each petitioner, one by one.[35] They, Hand concluded, more than justified the summary punishment Medina imposed.

Judge Frank concurred with Judge Hand, except for the conspiracy specification. On this issue, Frank agreed with Judge Clark that a hearing was required by Rule 42(b). Otherwise, his opinion was a devastating attack on the petitioners and their arguments. They were not courageous defenders of unpopular clients, he said, but were lawyers guilty of "outrageous conduct" and "crude antics" intended to "throw a wrench in the machinery of justice." These acts, Frank wrote, "can make no sensible man proud."[36]

During interviews in 1993 both Crockett and Goodman still expressed surprise and disappointment regarding Frank's opinion. Considering his liberal credentials and a well-deserved reputation for fairness, they expected a different result. Both believe that the "politics of the day," particularly fears of the "Red menace" and the lawyers who dared represent communists, tainted and influenced the appellate courts, just as they did virtually every other aspect of U.S. society in the 1950s.[37] Subsequent revelations gave much credence to their views.

While the internal workings of appellate courts, including negotiations, lobbying, and other forms of "deal making," are rarely made public, it appears that Frank originally sided with Clark for reversing the entire case but succumbed to pressures and changed his vote.

Frank's ambiguous opinion revealed a sharp division among the judges, but the split was actually much deeper than indicated in the published reports. Some months later, Clark confided to Supreme Court Justice Hugo Black that the contempt case was an "emotional strain." Older colleagues on the circuit bench, Clark reported, subjected him to enormous pressure. His doubts, furthermore, increased when "a younger colleague"—obviously Frank—who originally had sided with Clark changed his vote to create the tenuous majority. Clark confessed that his final decision to stand alone caused him great concern.[38]

This type of pressure is an extraordinary intrusion into the domain of judicial independence. Frank's vote "switch" was confirmed by one of his leading biographers, who concluded that his pivotal concurring opinion in "*Sacher* was not Frank's finest hour."[39] *Sacher*, along with Frank's upholding the death sentences of Julius and Ethel Rosenberg, stood in stark contrast to his reputation for a "scrupulous regard for fairness."[40]

There was no doubt that the defense lawyers would challenge the split
Second Circuit opinion, but they would have to persuade the United States
Supreme Court to grant certiorari and hear the case. Like every step in
their legal struggle, this would prove a difficult task. Meanwhile, the ten-
tacles of the Red Scare were spreading farther and deeper throughout the
country. On September 8, 1950, the Michigan State Legislature passed into
law the so-called Little Smith Act, a near replica of the national Smith Act.
Later, on November 7, 1950, with overwhelming voter approval, the state
constitution was amended to add a new Section 22 of Article II outlawing
subversion, which was defined as "consist[ing] of any act, or advocacy of any
act, intended to overthrow the form of government of the United States or
the form of government of this state by force or violence or by any unlawful
means."[41]

The State Bar Convention and the Uninvited Ghost

Unexpectedly, in the fall of 1950, Crockett once again had to face Judge
Medina. At the state bar's annual conference and banquet in Lansing,
the principal banquet speaker was none other than federal district court
judge Harold Medina. Goodman recounted the events:

> He was indeed a great drawing card. His name had been emblazoned
> in the press for almost a year....
>
> George and I discussed our strategy. Should we ignore the meet-
> ing and let Medina have the field to himself with George the unin-
> vited ghost? Or should George (and I) appear at the banquet where
> Medina would speak? We decided that the ghost of George would
> be unlikely to create much interest in his imminent disbarment by
> the State Bar....
>
> We thought that George's plight as the beleaguered lawyer
> would be highlighted rather than Medina's as the harassed judge....
> At any rate, George, by appearing, would dispel any notion that he
> felt he was ashamed of his conduct as a trial lawyer during the trial
> of probably the most important political case of this century.[42]

Crockett and Goodman decided they should attend the event.

We arrived on the evening of the banquet. The large banquet hall was crowded. As we walked in, we sensed an invisible barrier between us and the other guests. No handshakes or greetings. A coldness and aloofness. No one invited us to sit next to them or welcomed us after we selected our seats. During the dinner, we felt isolated and alone. We chatted together and pretended to be comfortable. At the early introductions, when Medina was introduced, all stood and applauded enthusiastically. We arose slowly and conspicuously and kept our hands to our sides.

The later introduction of the principal speaker was overlaid with the highest praise, extolling his judicial qualities and his enormous patience in the face of the most outrageous conduct by defendants seeking to discredit our system of justice (counsel for defendants was noticeably not mentioned). The speech itself was fairly routine and certainly not directed against George. At its conclusion, again the audience arose (including us—again hands by our sides) and heavily applauded. The banquet concluded and the guests quickly disbursed.

As we left the hall, we were met by a newspaper reporter I knew. He took us aside and asked us if we knew that during the proceedings the police were in the hall because of George's presence. That we found hard to believe. True, George had been sentenced to four months in prison. But it is doubtful whether many people, even lawyers, would consider contempt of court was a reason to believe that George would shoot or otherwise physically assault the judge who had found him in contempt at a banquet full of his peers. Yet the police had apparently been persuaded to deal with George as a potential threat to Medina. Perhaps they reasoned that the alleged conspiracy was still in effect. But if reason had governed such a weird decision, the police or the state bar, whoever instigated the action, would have noted that the theory of a conspiracy existed only in Medina's head. But in those days, as in similar periods of American history, prejudice and fear took the cloak of reason, and lawyers and judges succumbed to the transmutation as did most of the population. It was an interesting evening.[43]

The next day, a *Detroit News* story carried the headline, "Police Guard Judge Medina: Lawyer He Sentenced Spotted in Audience."[44] The *News* confirmed that, at the request of the state bar after Crockett's presence was known, three state troopers were dispatched to the banquet, and they kept him under surveillance the rest of the evening.

Also reported in the article was the state bar's adoption of a resolution that condemned communism and recommended that persons sympathetic to its principles be barred from government service and teaching. Only a single speaker opposed the resolution: Morton Eden, Crockett and Goodman's law associate, who called the resolution "another example of Red-baiting hysteria sweeping the country."[45] Eden stood alone. The dean of Crockett's law school alma mater, E. Blythe Stason, published an article in the *Michigan State Bar Journal* in 1951 advocating "disciplining subversive members of the bar."[46]

The hostile reception Crockett received from his brethren at the state bar convention, while not uncommon or unexpected, was not universal. Crockett recalled,

> It was sort of mixed. As I told you before, I had some friends who sort of shied away from me when I got back. I would see them walking down the street, and by the time we normally would get abreast of each other, they would've crossed the street or they would've turned their back to examine something that suddenly interested them in a store window, for example. So you had that experience. When I walked into court, I think, on balance, my standing was enhanced, sort of like a celebrity lawyer coming in.
>
> I remember one judge in particular, Judge Lederle, went out of his way to welcome me to his court and to be especially cordial with me when I was handling denaturalization cases before him.
>
> I got clients, but very few black clients. Most of my clients had to do with denaturalization and deportation proceedings. All of them were whites, who were identifiably associated with left-wing causes and wanted to demonstrate their support for me by coming to me with their legal matters. I'm sure Foley Square and the specter of communism closed me off from business from black leaders who traditionally ran scared from things like that.[47]

Ironically, Crockett, whom many people considered Red, knew little about communism before the *Dennis* case and never contemplated joining the party. Crockett was and would always remain a strong believer in the radical potential of the U.S. Constitution and the legal process. He was asked to join the party only once. His answer also suggests his sense of humor:

> During the trial, I walked out of the courtroom at recess. It was my practice to walk up and down the corridor. On this particular occasion, I was walking alone, really down in the dumps, and Ben Davis [the defendant] joined me. In some respects, Ben was very, very gruff. That day he was mad as hell, talking about "these god-damned capitalist bastards" and so forth and "what they're trying to do" and "the effect on black people" and so forth, and he ended up asking me why didn't I come on over and join the Communist Party. And I'll always remember looking at him and saying, "Ben, I catch enough hell being black. Why should I be Red, too? It doesn't make sense." [*Laughs.*] And that's the one and only time I've been invited to become a member of the Communist Party.[48]
>
> It was not assumed by those who knew me, but I'm sure it was assumed by the general public to the extent there was interest—the newspaper attacks and so forth. For example, the *Detroit Free Press* came out with a story in which they spoke about me as the "Communist lawyer." They forgot to put in the apostrophe and an *s*. I don't think they did it intentionally, and, as I recall, they later apologized.[49]

The Demise of the Sugar Firm and the Founding of the Goodman Partnership

The year 1950 was one of transitions. The factional infighting in the UAW that led to the ouster of Sugar, Goodman, and Crockett, among others, was devastating for the Sugar firm and for Sugar personally. Sugar receded from the active practice of law. "He had structured his firm as a makeshift confederation of associates, but it stayed tightly wound so long as Sugar was at its center."[50] The loss of Sugar and the ongoing UAW boycott of labor business for the firm were financially crippling. "The hoops were now coming off the barrel as the once-allied attorneys became competitors."[51] Some lawyers drifted away, while groups of others split off to form their own firms.

Four of the Sugar lawyers remaining were Ernie Goodman, George Crockett, Mort Eden, and the recent Wayne State University Law School graduate Dean Robb. They could not proceed as they had done in the past, but they could define a new vision and path forward, one that was more egalitarian. The new firm would have to be a real partnership: "A partnership that united its members in a defined structure of co-governance and shared liability would suit [Goodman's] more collaborative nature. Goodman would be the first among equals, but there would be no sidebar practice for the partnerships' members or competition for clients. All income would be pooled and shared according to the agreed-upon split."[52] There were other breaks with convention. Even though Mort Eden had more seniority than Crockett, Goodman insisted that Crockett's name would be listed second, underscoring the significance of the interracial nature of the partnership. With the signing of a simple two-page agreement consisting of only seven paragraphs and taking effect January 1, 1951, Goodman, Crockett, Eden & Robb became the first racially integrated law partnership in the country.[53]

That said, the firm was being founded in troubled times, and its economic viability was anything but certain. No matter how important civil rights work was, it did not pay the bills, even when such cases gained national attention. One illustration was the case of Willie McGee, a Black man wrongly convicted and sentenced to death for raping a white woman by an all-white Mississippi jury in 1945. Through the work of the Civil Rights Congress (CRC), his fate gained national and international attention as an emblem of southern injustice. After numerous legal maneuvers, an execution date was set for May 8, 1951. That spring, Goodman agreed to represent McGee without a fee but with the CRC covering expenses. Goodman helped mount a last-ditch federal civil suit seeking an injunction for Mississippi's violation of McGee's civil rights.[54] Unfortunately, the suit was unsuccessful, and McGee was tragically executed.

A postscript to the McGee case was a set of correspondence between the CRC and Crockett on behalf of the firm to collect payment for the firm's expenses—a total of $554.61. The case demonstrates how limited funds were at the time for civil rights work. Crockett wrote to William L. Patterson of the CRC asking, "Is there any reason that some of this cannot be paid at this time?" Patterson replied, "The answer is the only reason is there is no money."[55] Crockett replied in a friendly but honest manner: "We know 'your side'; you are doing the best you can. Our side is that none of us are able to draw a cent for the entire month of October."[56]

The Supreme Court Decides Dennis v. United States

The politics of the day always influence judicial decision-making. The perceived threat of the Red Scare was only growing in 1951. The anticommunist fervor in Michigan was deepening as well. The state's anticommunist constitutional amendment of the previous fall was followed by enabling legislation known as the Hittle Act. Among its many harsh provisions, the act imposed a life sentence in prison for "subversion" or its advocacy; made the mere knowing of "subversion" and failing to report it "as soon as may be" to a judge a felony; and required that any Michigan corporation knowingly contributing to or lending its name to a "subversion" would forfeit its charter and "be fined not more than the total amount of the corporation."[57]

As the government stepped up its prosecutions of communists throughout the country, the *Dennis* and *Sacher* appeals forced the Supreme Court to confront inflamed public opinion along with the troublesome legal consequences the convictions spawned. Within the Court, "deeply felt passions and vigorous politicking boiled beneath the seemingly placid surface."[58] The Court's long-awaited opinion in *Dennis* was announced on June 4, 1951, affirming the convictions of Crockett's clients and the other communist leaders.[59]

Chief Justice Vinson wrote for the majority of the Court. Still feeling the effects of Crockett's "nudge," Justice Clark had recused himself. Chief Justice Vinson characterized the case in terms of what powers Congress had to resist the violent overthrow of the government:

> The obvious purpose of the statute is to protect existing Government, not from change by peaceable, lawful and constitutional means, but from change by violence, revolution and terrorism. That it is within the power of the Congress to protect the Government

of the United States from armed rebellion is a proposition which requires little discussion. Whatever theoretical merit there may be to the argument that there is a "right" to rebellion against dictatorial governments is without force where the existing structure of the government provides for peaceful and orderly change. We reject any principle of governmental helplessness in the face of preparation for revolution, which principle, carried to its logical conclusion, must lead to anarchy. No one could conceive that it is not within the power of Congress to prohibit acts intended to overthrow the Government by force and violence. The question with which we are concerned here is not whether Congress has such *power*, but whether the *means* which it has employed conflict with the *First and Fifth Amendments to the Constitution*.[60]

In a somewhat tortured fashion, the Court reasoned that there was no First Amendment violation because the Smith Act was focused on "advocacy" and not "discussion":

The very language of the Smith Act negates the interpretation that petitioners would have us impose on that Act. It is directed at advocacy, not discussion. Thus the trial judge properly charged the jury that they could not convict if they found that petitioners did "no more than pursue peaceful studies and discussions or teaching and advocacy in the realm of ideas." He further charged that it was not unlawful "to conduct in an American college or university a course explaining the philosophical theories set forth in the books which have been placed in evidence." Such a charge is in strict accord with the statutory language and illustrates the meaning to be placed on those words. Congress did not intend to eradicate the free discussion of political theories, to destroy the traditional rights of Americans to discuss and evaluate ideas without fear of governmental sanction. Rather Congress was concerned with the very kind of activity in which the evidence showed these petitioners engaged.[61]

Holding that there was no constitutional violation, the Court upheld the conviction of the Foley Square defendants.

Writing in dissent, Justice Black countered the majority's characterization of the conduct at issue:

> At the outset I want to emphasize what the crime involved in this case is, and what it is not. These petitioners were not charged with an attempt to overthrow the Government. They were not charged with overt acts of any kind designed to overthrow the Government. They were not even charged with saying anything or writing anything designed to overthrow the Government. The charge was that they agreed to assemble and to talk and publish certain ideas at a later date: The indictment is that they conspired to organize the Communist Party and to use speech or newspapers and other publications in the future to teach and advocate the forcible overthrow of the Government. No matter how it is worded, this is a virulent form of prior censorship of speech and press, which I believe the First Amendment forbids. I would hold § 3 of the Smith Act authorizing this prior restraint unconstitutional on its face and as applied.[62]

Also in dissent, Justice Douglas warned of the devastating impact the Court's action would have for freedom of speech:

> The opinion of the Court does not outlaw these texts nor condemn them to the fire, as the communists do literature offensive to their creed. But if the books themselves are not outlawed, if they can lawfully remain on library shelves, by what reasoning does their use in a classroom become a crime? It would not be a crime under the Act to introduce these books to a class, though that would be teaching what the creed of violent overthrow of the Government is. The Act, as construed, requires the element of intent—that those who teach the creed believe in it. The crime then depends not on what is taught but on who the teacher is. That is to make freedom of speech turn not on what is said, but on the intent with which it is said. Once we start down that road we enter territory dangerous to the liberties of every citizen.[63]

These were unusual times, and the majority opinion stands as an aberration against U.S. constitutional traditions. Justice Black, with his characteristic candor, hoped for better days in the future: "Public opinion being what it now is, few will protest the conviction of these Communist petitioners. There is hope, however, that in calmer times, when present pressures, passions and fears subside, this or some later Court will restore the First Amendment liberties to the high preferred place where they belong in a free society."[64] As of that moment, however, a dark cloud was passing over the Constitution.

A few weeks earlier, on May 18, 1951, Crockett and the *Dennis* defense lawyers received yet another blow: their certiorari petition in *Sacher* had been denied by the Supreme Court in a 4–3 split.[65] After a motion for reconsideration was filed, intense lobbying began for the Supreme Court to take the case, primarily by Justice Frankfurter. Frankfurter, reportedly, had become deeply disturbed over the treatment being received by lawyers who represented communists. The bench and the bar, he believed, were fostering a climate of fear and "guilt by representation" that threatened the independent bar he regarded as vital in a democracy.[66] Members of the bar did not have to actually be taken to the woodshed to be collectively deterred. Frankfurter was particularly disturbed after a number of "reputable" lawyers refused to represent former U.S. vice president Henry Wallace during his appearance before a congressional committee.[67]

While Crockett's lawyers were fighting for a rehearing, he had an unexpected meeting with Justice Jackson:

> After certiorari was denied, we petitioned for a rehearing. Marty Popper was our lawyer, and he had requested a meeting with Mr. Justice Jackson, and he invited me and Isserman and Sacher to go with him. We went down to Washington, and Mr. Justice Jackson received us. This was my opportunity to actually see the chambers of a Supreme Court justice. Jackson was the presiding justice for the Second Circuit at the time. We were introduced but didn't say anything. Marty did all of the talking on why certiorari really should be granted in this case. But in a situation like that, you see, it's an independent judgment on the part of each justice. If you can get four justices to say that they want to hear a case, then you get cert. Marty did a good job convincing Mr. Justice Jackson. We picked up three other justices, and just by the skin of our teeth, we got into the Supreme Court.[68]

Notwithstanding the visit to chambers, it is more likely that Frank-furter, and not Popper, influenced Jackson's vote. That Frankfurter's efforts succeeded underscored both his influence and the case's importance. After Justices Jackson and Burton changed their votes, a majority of the Court had agreed to reconsider the appeal. The Court's review, however, was lim-ited to a single legal question: Did Judge Medina follow proper procedure under Rule 42 when he, the accusing judge, summarily adjudged and pun-ished his own contempt charges? The case was argued on January 9, 1952.

Crockett and the HUAC Hearings in Detroit

Although Crockett's fate was still hanging in the balance before the Supreme Court, he and Goodman were busy representing witnesses before the House Un-American Activities Committee (HUAC) in Detroit.[69] HUAC held its first set of hearings February 25–29, 1952, in room 740 of the Federal Building. During an earlier investigation in Massachusetts, the committee had been told by Herbert A. Philbrick, the notorious FBI infor-mant and surprise government witness at Foley Square, how the Commu-nist Party had infiltrated industry in the Massachusetts area.[70] As a result, HUAC came to Detroit to see if similar inroads had been made in the "Arsenal of Democracy" because there was "no area of greater importance to the Nation as a whole, both in time of peace and in time of war." HUAC wanted to determine "the nature, extent, character, and objects" of commu-nist activity "in this vital defense area."[71]

As the hearings opened, the chairman, Representative John S. Wood, announced that he expected the communists, their apologists, and fellow travelers to mount a smear campaign against the committee. The slander-ers, Woods said, would claim that the committee was motivated by a desire to damage the labor movement and to "raise racial issues."[72] Crockett's and Goodman's involvement in the hearings was substantial. Based on the hearing transcripts and news reports, they constantly angered and frus-trated the committee members.[73] Of those who were subpoenaed to testify, Goodman represented twenty, most of the leadership of Ford Local 600, and Crockett seven. Among Crockett's clients were several high-profile wit-nesses: Reverend Charles A. Hill, a prominent Black leader and pastor of the Hartford Avenue Baptist Church; State Senator Stanley Nowak; and

Detroit's future mayor Coleman A. Young. Reverend Hill, Young (who was dubbed a "defiant" witness),[74] and Crockett, the lawyer from Foley Square, received most of the press's attention, which was generally favorable in the Black press[75] and the opposite in white newspapers.

Crockett tried ably, but HUAC's rules were stacked against witnesses and severely constrained what their lawyers were capable of doing. Crockett sought unsuccessfully to make a statement for the record.

> **Mr. Crockett**: I would like to make a statement for the record.
>
> **Mr. Wood**: Statements by counsel are not permitted in this committee.
>
> **Mr. Crockett**: Counsel may not note anything on the record on behalf of his client ... ?
>
> **Mr. Wood**: Nothing at all.
>
> **Mr. Crockett**: May I inquire Mr. Chairman—
>
> **Mr. Wood**: Let us get this clear right now. You are at liberty to confer with your client ... and that is as far as counsel is permitted to go in this committee.
>
> **Mr. Crockett**: My advice to you—[*addressing his client Reverend Hill*]
>
> **Mr. Wood**: Counsel, give him your advice in private please.
>
> **Mr. Crockett**: He has no objection to my stating it out loud.
>
> **Mr. Wood**: We do.[76]

At one point, Chairman Wood threatened to expel Crockett from the proceeding: "One more address from you to this committee will result in your expulsion from the committee room. . . . This committee will not have its rules constantly violated in this flagrant manner, as you are undertaking to do."[77]

Crockett was not intimidated. When the first exhibit against Reverend Hill was being presented to the witness, tension emerged over the handling of the physical document. David Maraniss recounted the episode: The official transcript of the hearing later published by the U.S. Government Printing Office, noted in brackets, "[Whereupon, Mr. Crockett attempted to take the exhibit]." Reporter Fred Tew, covering the session for the *Free Press*, offered a more colorful description: "At one point in the testimony, a committee aide and Hill's attorney, George Crockett, nearly came to blows. Each held one corner of an exhibit that was being handed to Hill. They glared at each other as Chairman Wood rapped his gavel time and again for order."[78] Crockett may have been constrained by the rules, but he would be aggressive in defense of his client operating under them.

When it came time for Coleman Young to testify, Crockett was sitting by his side. Young's testimony was strident in tone and disarmingly aggressive. Newspapers reported long excerpts of his confrontations with the committee, and a phonograph record of his testimony became a "hit" in Detroit's Black community.[79] Crockett may have been silenced, but Young was not. Speaking in a manner that few others were able to emulate, Young made a strong stand:

Mr. Tavenner: But I desire to ask you the question which I
   have asked other witnesses: Are you now a member of the
   Communist Party?

Mr. Young: I refuse to answer that question, relying upon my rights
   under the Fifth Amendment, and, in light of the fact that an
   answer to such a question, before such a committee, would
   be, in my opinion, a violation of my rights under the First
   Amendment which provides for freedom of speech, sanctity
   and privacy of political beliefs and associates, and, further,
   since I have no purpose of being here as a stool pigeon, I am
   not prepared to give any information on any of my associates
   or political thoughts.

Mr. Tavenner: Have you been a member of the Communist Party?

Mr. Young: For the same reason, I refuse to answer that question.

Mr. Tavenner: You told us you were the executive secretary of the
   National Negro Congress—

Mr. Young: That word is "Negro," not "Niggra."

Mr. Tavenner: I said, "Negro." I think you are mistaken.

Mr. Young: I hope I am. Speak more clearly.

Mr. Wood: I will appreciate it if you will not argue with counsel.

Mr. Young: It isn't my purpose to argue. As a Negro, I resent the
   slurring of the name of my race.

Mr. Wood: You are here for the purpose of answering questions.

Mr. Young: In some sections of the country they slur— ...

Mr. Tavenner: I asked you no question regarding your individual views. I asked if you knew of any activities of the Communist Party in this community, which might be of some assistance to this committee in its investigation of un-American activities. I understood from your statement you would like to help us.

Mr. Young: You have me mixed up with a stool pigeon.

Mr. Potter: I have never heard of anybody stooling in the Boy Scouts.

Mr. Young: I was a member of the organization.

Mr. Potter: I don't think they are proud of it today.

Mr. Young: I will let the Scouts decide that....

Mr. Young: I am trying to answer the question, if you will let me.

Mr. Wood: No, you are not. You are trying to evade my question.

Mr. Young: You will have to wait for my answer in order to determine whether I am evading or not. I haven't finished.

Mr. Wood: You are assuming what you don't know.

Mr. Young: You are assuming what I am going to say.

Mr. Wood: I want you to answer in what way the preamble you read, of the National Negro Labor Council, differs, if any, in respect to the National Negro Congress.

Mr. Young: I would inform you, also, the word is Negro.

Mr. Wood: I am sorry. If I made a different pronouncement of it, it is due to my inability to use the language any better than I do. I am trying to use it properly.

Mr. Young: It may be due to your southern background.

Mr. Wood: I am not ashamed of southern background. For your information, out of the 112 Negro votes cast in the last election in the little village from which I come, I got 112 of them. That ought to be a complete answer of that. Now, will you answer the question?

Mr. Young: You are through with it now, is that it?

Mr. Wood: I don't know.

Mr. Young: I happen to know, in Georgia Negro people are prevented from voting by virtue of terror, intimidation, and lynchings. It is my contention you would not be in Congress today if it were not for the legal restrictions on voting on the part of my people. . . .

Mr. Young: I rely upon the Fifth Amendment of the Constitution of the United States, and refuse to answer that question.

Mr. Tavenner: The committee is informed that various petitions were prepared by the Civil Rights Congress, protesting the indictment of the 12 Communist leaders in New York City, and that you were one of the signers, a signer of one of the petitions. I am not interested, particularly, in whether you were or not. I am more interested in ascertaining the circumstances under which your signature, or that of any other person, was obtained. Will you tell us that?

Mr. Young: Sir, I have explained to you my refusal to answer such questions. I think it would be quite foolish on my part, in view of the hysteria stirred up by this committee; in view of the many bills having to do with people's political association, etc., to indicate to you on any question any information which amounts to testifying against myself. Therefore, under the Fifth Amendment, I refuse to answer.

Mr. Potter: If there is any hysteria in this country, it is generated by people like yourself, and not by this committee.

Mr. Young: Congressman, neither me or none of my friends were out at this plant the other day brandishing a rope in the face of John Cherveny. I can assure you I have had no part in the hanging or bombing of Negroes in the South. I have not been responsible for firing a person from his job for what I think are his beliefs, or what somebody thinks he believes in, and things of that sort. That is the hysteria that has been swept up by this committee.

Mr. Potter: Today, there are 104,000 casualties in Korea testifying to this fact of hysteria you so blandly mentioned, which is a cold-blooded conspiracy, which is killing American boys, and, you, as members of the Communist Party of the United States, are just as much a part of the international conspiracy as the Communists in North Korea who are killing men there.

Mr. Young: I see you have on a decoration, and, I will inform you,

I am also a veteran of the Armed Forces. I know you did your part. I want you to know I didn't have any part in sending anybody to Korea.

Mr. Jackson: Do you approve of the action of the United States in Korea?

Mr. Young: I refuse to allow this Committee to pry into my personal and private opinions. I got some opinion on it, however.

Mr. Jackson: So do I. Let us not lose individual freedom and human dignity by sacrificing it to an order of things which has filled concentration camps to overflowing. If you think of the lot of the Negro who have in eighty-some-odd years come forward to a much better position—

Mr. Young: Mr. Jackson, we are not going to wait 80 more years, I will tell you that.

Mr. Jackson: Neither are the Communists. They say they are going to overthrow the Government by force and violence and effect all the changes immediately.

Mr. Young: If you are telling me to wait 80 years, I will tell you I am not prepared to wait and neither are the Negroes.

Mr. Jackson: Neither is the Communist Party.

Mr. Young: I am speaking for the Negro people and for myself. Are you speaking for the Communist Party?

Mr. Jackson: I am speaking of the Communist Party.

Mr. Young: I thought you were speaking for the Communist Party.

Mr. Jackson: No. I think there are many in this room who are better qualified to speak for the Communist Party than I am. Mr. Chairman, I have no further questions.

Mr. Wood: Mr. Potter?

Mr. Potter: Mr. Young, I believe in your statement that you said that you were in the service fighting fascism during the last war.

Mr. Young: That is right.

Mr. Potter: Then it is proper to assume that you are opposed to totalitarianism in any form, as I am.

Mr. Young: I fought and I was in the last war, Congressman, that is correct, as a Negro officer in the Air Corps. I was arrested and placed under arrest and held in quarters for 3 days in your country because I sought to get a cup of coffee in a United States Officers Club that was restricted for white officers only. That is my experience in the United States Army.

Mr. Potter: Let me say this, I have the highest admiration, yes, the highest admiration for the service that was performed by Negro soldiers during the last war. They performed brilliantly.

Mr. Young: I am sure the Negro soldiers appreciate your admiration, Mr. Potter.[80]

Several other witnesses also defied the committee and, as the HUAC chairman had predicted, used the occasion to berate the committee, union busting, and racism in the United States. For example, James Watts, a Black official at the UAW-CIO Ford Local 600 and Crockett's client, testified:

Mr. Watts: I didn't come here with the intention of causing a scene. I know every member of the committee is anti-Negro. I know every member of the committee is opposed to President Truman's civil-rights program and the record so indicates.

Mr. Walter: The record doesn't so indicate. If you had done one-tenth for the cause of the Negro I have done, you wouldn't be ashamed to answer the question.

Mr. Watts: My heart bleeds for you—you love me.

Mr. Wood: One more outburst of that character and I will ask the officer to eject you from this hearing room.

Mr. Watts: I didn't come here on my own accord; you subpoenaed me.

Mr. Wood: If you are not going to be decorous, you are not going to stay. This is not a farce; this is serious business.

Mr. Tavenner: Did you testify in a proceeding or trial—

Mr. Watts: This is serious business. I have a picture here of a Negro being lynched in the State of Georgia. I think that is serious too.

Mr. Wood: Keep your mouth shut until you are asked questions.

Mr. Watts: One of the Negroes was being lynched in—

Mr. Tavenner: Have you got more pictures in your pocket that you want to show? Are you through?

Mr. Watts: I am through.[81]

Goodman, over four days, in a near miraculous effort, represented twenty witnesses before the committee. Virtually all were members or former members of the UAW-CIO Ford Local 600.[82]

The 1952 HUAC hearing in Detroit was a big deal for George and me. We represented most of the defendants, so called, before that committee, at least twenty to twenty-five—I forget how many. Most couldn't get lawyers to appear with them. I know, because I sent a number of them to the leading firms in Detroit who could handle their cases and could afford to do so. We were tired and needed help and rest. They all came back and said they were told to go to the Goodman firm. . . .

I especially remember one highly dramatic picture the press took of George. He was holding his hand over the microphone in front of his client, trying to communicate with him without the committee hearing his advice. That picture was used to take another blow at George. It became a graphic symbol, as if he had stopped his client from telling the truth, concealing the truth from the committee, and protecting the client from his just punishment, if he told the truth.

At any rate, it was a tough thing to take. You sat in the courtroom waiting for your client and had to sit in the corner they had reserved for the so-called hostile witnesses and their lawyers. It was very disheartening because you couldn't help people that way. You just had to protect them as best you could with the Constitution. This is what we had been doing from the very moment we formed our partnership—defending people with the Constitution. At that time, it was the communists, and those associated with them, who needed help.[83]

Later, HUAC released a long list of persons it had identified as communists following the Detroit hearings. While a witness like Coleman Young could turn the tables on the committee for an afternoon, real power resided with the government, which often used this power to destroy lives. The entire list of 319 persons was published in the Detroit newspapers.[84] Also published were the actions taken against the alleged communists since HUAC had left Detroit: six known communists were indicted under the federal Smith Act and were awaiting trial; others were fired from their jobs; the UAW-CIO had launched a "cleanup" of Ford Local 600, removing some officers and barring others from running for reelection; and several persons, including State Senator Stanley Nowak, were facing deportation proceedings for allegedly lying about communist affiliations when they became naturalized citizens.[85] These actions, of course, created even more legal work for Goodman, Crockett, and their firm.

The Supreme Court Decides Sacher v. United States

The Supreme Court decision in *Sacher v. United States* was announced on March 10, 1952, affirming Judge Medina's contempt convictions of Crockett and the other the *Dennis* lawyers.[86] The majority opinion, which was written by Justice Jackson, relied heavily on the circuit court. Rule 42, the Court held, gave a trial judge the discretion to punish contempt immediately and summarily or, depending on the circumstances, to delay until the trial's end.[87] On the conspiracy issue that divided the circuit court and that, as a result, was the petitioners' best hope, Jackson followed Judge Frank's "swing" position. The conspiracy specification, he wrote, was separate from and independent of the substantive offenses, and since the sentences were concurrent, the reversal of one did not require the reversal of the other.[88]

Justices Black and Frankfurter dissented. Justice Douglas agreed with both dissenters and in a terse opinion found ample blame on both sides of a "spectacle of the bench and the bar using the courtroom for an unseemly demonstration of garrulous discussion of ill will and hot tempers."[89] Black, whose strong dissent one critic described as "pithy,"[90] would have reversed the convictions because of Medina's manifest prejudice and the obvious hostility between the court and the defense lawyers.[91] He would have required that a second judge decide the contempt charges. In a nonsummary proceeding, Black reasoned, lawyers were entitled to proper notice, a hearing, and the opportunity to defend themselves with all the constitutional safeguards guaranteed criminal defendants, including a jury trial.[92]

Judge Frankfurter wrote at length and with the zeal he displayed during the reconsideration deliberations. Frankfurter, who disliked Medina personally, added forty-seven pages of the verbal exchanges between Medina and the defense lawyers to his opinion.[93] He, in essence, wrote Medina a lecture on improper judicial conduct and took him to task for his lack of judicial decorum.[94]

When informed of the decision by a reporter, Crockett stated that it was significant that the U.S. Supreme Court upheld his conviction at a time when he was "engaged in protecting the rights of the politically persecuted."[95] In an exclusive interview he gave to playwright Lorraine Hansberry for the Black journal *Freedom*, he warned of the decision's negative implications for civil rights. "A Negro lawyer will have to think twice before he presses any legal points for his client. In the back of his mind will always be this Supreme Court ruling which means he can be sentenced without a chance for defense or argument and sent to jail. The result of the ruling will be another source of intimidation for the Negro's fight for civil rights." He cautioned that the "all-out attack on the Communists is but a prelude to an all-out attack on Negroes. Therefore the fightback which must inevitably come must begin with the present fight for the civil rights of the Communists."[96] It was not lost on Crockett that the Supreme Court decision also meant that he would be going to prison for the crime of standing up for his principles and defending the rights of others, as a lawyer is trained to do.

March 12, 1952, was the last day of HUAC's second series of Detroit hearings. Despite the Supreme Court's decision in *Sacher*, Crockett was back at work. The fifth-to-last witness was Elliott Maraniss, father of the Pulitzer Prize–winning author David Maraniss. His lawyer was George Crockett. Elliott Maraniss, a journalist for the *Detroit Times*, was fired from his position on February 29, 1952, the same day he received a subpoena to testify before the HUAC hearings. While testifying, he invoked his rights against self-incrimination provided by the Fifth Amendment. The committee tried to leverage his assertion of rights into some implicit assertion of guilt. Crockett would not stand idly by:

Mr. Crockett: Mr. Chairman, do I understand that you are penalizing this man because he relies on the Fifth Amendment, and, because of that, you refuse to let him make a statement?

Mr. Wood: If he isn't a member of the Communist Party, I am
seeking to help him. If he is, I think the public is entitled
to know.

Mr. Crockett: The public isn't entitled to know anything that you
may properly claim a privilege from disclosing under the Fifth
Amendment.[97]

Elliott Maraniss, like Crockett himself, was yet another victim of the Red
Scare.

The exhaustion of appeals in *Sacher* also opened the door to Crockett's
potential disbarment. A "Request for Investigation of George W. Crockett Jr." was filed with the State Bar of Michigan Grievance Committee. On
March 13, 1952, Crockett responded with a lengthy letter requesting that
the state bar stay its actions until his application to the Supreme Court for
a rehearing had been decided or until he had been released from prison so
that he could properly defend himself.[98]

Crockett and Dr. Benjamin Mays

Later that same month, Crockett had an encounter with Dr. Benjamin Mays,
the revered and venerable president of Morehouse College. Mays was also
in the vanguard of the national Black leadership. After Crockett's family,
Morehouse College was his "second love." He stayed closely involved with
his alma mater and was an enormously proud "Morehouse Man." Dr. Mays's
approval would have meant almost as much to Crockett as the support he
received from his family during the trial. In the men's discussion, Mays,
however, expressed confusion and concern over Crockett's role in the Foley
Square trial. Crockett may have not cared what Judge Medina thought, or
even what the majority of members of the Supreme Court thought, but he
did care what Dr. Mays thought.

In response, Crockett crafted a careful rebuttal, one that he hoped
would help the fearful, if not skittish, Black leader understand why he
defended the communist defendants. Drafted with the knowledge that
he would probably go to prison for his beliefs, the letter provides deeper
insights into Crockett's thoughts and motivations:

March 24, 1952

Dr. Benjamin Mays
President Morehouse College
Atlanta, Georgia

Dear Dr. Mays:

I am grateful to you for the few minutes that we were able to con-
verse with each other on your recent visit.

I must confess that I was somewhat disturbed over the fact that
you did not know the real basis for my imminent imprisonment. I
recognize that if a person with your wide knowledge of current events
can be mistaken in this regard, then there remains a terrific job to
be done by way of educating the public generally concerning why the
defense lawyers in the Foley Square case were sentenced to jail.

With respect to the charges against me, I think you can understand them better if you read the enclosed report which was issued
some time ago by the Wolverine Bar Association of this city. You will
note that all of the charges stem from ordinary court room activity
engaged in every day by lawyers who defend vigorously the rights
of their clients. What happened to me is likely to happen in any
case where such a lawyer is confronted with a hostile judge and is
defending an unpopular client in a hostile community. It requires no
great deal of imagination to see how the precedent in my case might
live on to hound lawyers—especially in the South—who have courage enough to defend in court the rights of their Negro clients.

I think I told you that I am not too greatly disturbed about the
personal effect that my sentence will have upon me and my family.
What disturbs me most is the growin[g] patter[n] of repression as
evidenced by a long series of Supreme Court decisions interpret-
ing the Bill of Rights; the inability of the public generally to grasp
how the making of this new judge-made law provides the framework
for even greater repression of our civil rights; and the sad neglect on
the part of lawyers to speak out about these developments and to
bring such manifestations to the attention of the public generally.

It has been said before, and I am sure that in the coming years it will be repeated time and time again that this is precisely the pattern which made Nazism the ruling philosophy in Germany, and it was precisely the failing of the legal profession there that made it possible for Hitler to come into power and to enslave so many people.

I recall that during the Foley Square trial, or shortly thereafter, the student newspaper at Morehouse carried an article concerning Benjamin Davis, an alumnus of our school and one of the defendants in the Foley Square case. I can appreciate the courage manifested in the publication of that article. It is courage such as this that is so sadly lacking on the part of too many of us who are in position to direct the attention of our hearers to what is really the basic task of our day, namely, the prevention of Fascism and the preservation of our basic civil rights.

I think you will agree with me that any Negro who has lived for any extended period of time in the South knows more about Fascism and the evidences of Fascism than most people, for this was a part of the pattern of his life long before Hitler or Mussolini were heard of. It is for this reason that Negro leaders have a special function to perform in meeting what I have just described as the basic challenge of our times.

Your closing sermon here in Detroit was a step—a very excellent step—in this direction.

> With sincere personal regards to you and Mrs. Mays, I am
> Sincerely yours,
> Geo. W. Crockett, Jr.[99]

A few years later, with the tables slightly turned, Crockett would again write to Dr. Mays. This time, Mays was targeted in the press along with a group of prominent Black leaders. They allegedly had "past pro-Communists affiliations" and supported "pro-Communists enterprises in one form or another."[100] The group, which included six other Black college presidents, comprised the directors of the Southern Regional Conference. Knowing well the dangers and pains caused by such affiliation "smears," Crockett wrote the following letter:

December 6, 1955

Dr. Benjamin E. Mays
President Morehouse College
Atlanta, Georgia

Dear Dr. Mays:

I just came across a newspaper clipping indicating that the Hearst Press has taken the Fund for the Republic to task for aiding the Southern Regional Conference. The charge seems to be that the Conference is "Red" because its directors include Negro educators whom the Hearst Press regard as "pro-Red."

Included among the Negro educators mentioned are you, Dean Brazeal and several other leaders in the field of education and informed Negro opinion on social and economic issues.

My initial inclination upon reading the article was to let the matter pass without overt notice. But having been "smeared" so much and so often myself, I know that in such moments a cordial word from a friend—who knows that the smear is a lie, but whose friendship for you is unaffected whether the smear be true or false—can be most welcomed.

It must be apparent to all friends of Negro education, and most certainly to our fellow Morehouse men, that the progress our college has made under your leadership—and your militant advocacy of democracy for colored people everywhere—was bound, sooner or later, to incur the active displeasure of those who traditionally have been opposed to all that you have taught, preached and typified in your personal conduct so successfully for so many years.

Mrs. Crockett joins me in sending all good wishes to you and Mrs. Mays.

Sincerely yours,
Geo. W. Crockett, Jr.[101]

Dr. Mays responded with thanks:

December 8, 1955

Dr. George W. Crockett, Jr.
3220 Cadillac Tower
Detroit 26, Michigan

Dear Mr. Crockett:

I appreciate your letter of December 6, relative to the smear sheet of the New York Journal American. I think you are quite right in your interpretation of the situation. I think nobody takes the smear seriously because no one has even said anything to me about it—not even the members of my Board when we met in New York on November 17. I think the Hearst Press has little standing among people who think.

The Southern Regional Council is looking into the legal end of this thing to see if it is not possible to bring suit against the New York Journal American. Charles Johnson of Fisk University and I are awaiting counsel from the Southern Regional Council as to whether it will be a wise step.

Again let me thank you for your letter and kindly tender my regards to your wife and to your children. Tell the children I will be checking their grades when I come back to Detroit.

With kindest regards and best wishes, I am
Yours truly,
Benjamin E. Mays
President[102]

Crockett would cherish his connections to Morehouse for the rest of his life.

Crockett Goes to Prison, but the Firm's Work Continues

The HUAC hearings in Detroit fanned the existing, often rabid fears of communism. Michigan, similar to many other states, had already enacted laws to deal with the perceived Red menace. But because of the state's long and virulent history of political struggles within the UAW and other labor unions, Michigan, it seemed, had been particularly affected by the McCarthyite ideology. In 1950, Michigan enacted the Little Smith Act, which broadly defined "subversion" and outlawed it. In 1951, the state adopted the Hittle Act, which imposed a life sentence for "subversion" or its *advocacy*. To these was added additional legislation in spring of 1952, the Michigan Communist Control Act, introduced by Representative Kenneth O. Trucks and popularly known as the Trucks Act.

Goodman considered the Trucks Act one of the most dangerous laws ever enacted in the United States. Unlike Michigan's other anticommunist laws, which had been largely unenforced, the state placed its full police powers behind the new law. On the eve of its adoption, Michigan was poised to arrest citizens en masse,[103] firefighters, schoolteachers, and other public workers,[104] and deny the ballot to political candidates whom the law considered "subversives" and who failed to register as such.[105]

While prior laws required proof in court that an accused communist advocated the use of force and violence, the Trucks Act made one a criminal, and subject to prosecution, simply for being a communist or labeled a communist. Included among the many ways the Trucks Act defined "communist" were that the person "is a member of the communist party, *notwithstanding the fact he may not pay dues to or hold a card in said party*" and "*contributes funds or any character of property*" to the party.[106] Failure to register as a communist carried a maximum ten-year prison term and/or a $10,000 fine.

If, however, one was foolish enough to register, one's problems would be just beginning. The registration itself amounted to an admission or a "confession" to being a "subversive." The registrant, accordingly, was subject to immediate arrest and prosecution, without further proof, under Michigan's Little Smith Act and the Hittle Act. They were forced to be "stool pigeons" since they had to tell the state police the names of the organizations to which they belonged and provide a list of everyone they knew to be communists or members of "front" organizations. Also, they had to identify where they worked or their sources of income, apparently so they could be fired or fined the total assets of their businesses as required by the Hittle Act. Accordingly, the Trucks Act in combination with Michigan's other anti-communist laws created a sinister, "damned if you do, damned if you don't" legal dilemma for the communists, and they knew it.

Where could they seek legal help? The Michigan Communist Party, represented this time by Billy Allen, a communist and well-known journalist for the *Daily Worker* in Michigan, sought help where they always had: the Goodman firm. While Goodman believed that any challenge to the Trucks Act could eventually reach the U.S. Supreme Court, he did not think the firm could take it. With Crockett's departure to prison imminent, and Eden and Robb handling the "normal" work that kept the firm going, Goodman was reluctant. He sent Allen to five of Detroit's major law firms to seek representation: "I told Billy to go to these firms and tell them the party can pay a reasonable fee and that you've seen Goodman, and he can't take this case, as he's too busy working on other, similar matters. Tell them the constitutional issues are imperative and obvious and that they, as lawyers, have as much a duty as Goodman to represent the party on such an issue."[107] Within two days, Allen had returned. At each of the five firms, he had been politely received and had talked with a senior partner. They all agreed that the matter was urgent and compelling, but each, in turn, refused the case. Afraid to represent the Communist Party themselves, the five lawyers each gave Billy Allen what was virtually the same advice: "Go back to the Goodman firm. They know how to handle this kind of case."

Goodman was able to find an attorney to help in the cause: Joseph A. Brown. While Brown was not from one of the large, established law firms, he was a prominent lawyer and Michigan's first Black state senator.[108] "So I had no choice, and I had to figure out what to do. We were going to handle the case if no other lawyer was willing to; there was no doubt about it. We couldn't allow this law to go into effect without challenging it. Too many innocent people and organizations were at risk."[109]

Time was of the essence. "The Trucks Bill was damn unbelievable, a total disregard of basic federal First Amendment rights. Unlike normal legislation, which has a ninety-day waiting period, this law was given immediate effect. So you had a short time to register. . . . They knew if they didn't register, they would go to jail. They didn't intend to register, which would also get them arrested. So they wanted us to get an injunction to stop the law from going into immediate effect until the court could rule on its constitutionality."[110] Everything was happening at once. The Trucks Act was passed April 17, 1952. Four days later, another bombshell dropped. Crockett's day of reckoning finally came. On April 21, Crockett received a terse Western Union cable:

GEORGE W. CROCKETT JR=

3220 CADILLAC TOWER DET=

YOU ARE REQUIRED TO APPEAR UNITED STATES COURT HOUSE, FOLEY SQUARE, NEW YORK AT 10:30 A.M. APRIL 24, 1952. TO SURRENDER=

MYLES J LANE UNITED STATES ATTORNEY=[111]

Crockett recalled,

After I got the telegram, I had to prepare my family—the children. Ethelene, my wife, was incredibly supportive. We told the children that Daddy was going off to prison. They were very young, at the time. I think Elizabeth Ann, the oldest, was about twelve. But even they, by then, had become conditioned to the snide remarks made to them at school, the newspaper propaganda, me being called a "red," and all the fears that came from being associated with the trial.

For example, they understood why we had "black-out" drapes made for our windows to increase their security.

We told them we didn't know where Daddy was going to be, but that they could write. That was about it, there were no tears, no crying, just sadness.[112]

The pending challenge to the Trucks Act and Crockett's departure to prison were on a collision course, with the Goodman firm at ground zero. Goodman recalled,

On the day the governor was to sign the Trucks Bill, I had already prepared a complaint and a motion for an injunction. Joe and I were ready to go over to the federal district court. This was the same day George was to leave for prison. We went into George's office to say good-bye. He was standing at the window overlooking the Detroit River and Belle Isle, and I felt such a sadness, as if everything was going to hell. We seemed completely incapable of getting a handle on the massive problems that had been pushed down on us. We looked at each other. There were feelings we had that we couldn't express—that we didn't really try to express. The Constitution hadn't worked for George, and, by coincidence, we were on our way to federal court to seek the protection of the same Constitution. It seemed that something important was happening in our lives. In a way, we were going to court for George, trying to tell him that we weren't going to give up. We put on a good front, "smart-assed" a bit, and told George we would take care of things while he was gone. We said good-bye and left for court—George went off to prison. That was it.[113]

Goodman was off to court, while Crockett, one of the few lawyers in the country willing to provide such representation on the basis of his own core constitutional conviction, was heading off to prison for the crime of defending the rights of the politically unpopular. "We did well in court. The judge granted a temporary restraining order until a three-judge panel could hear the matter on its merits.[114] I believe George was proud of us that day. Later, however, a three-judge panel heard our arguments and read our briefs and found the law was constitutional on a two-to-one vote.[115] We drew two very conservative judges and one liberal, and that's the way they voted."[116]

While Goodman lost 2–1 before the three-judge panel, the lawsuit did accomplish something very important. While the case was being appealed to the U.S. Supreme Court, the Trucks Act was held in abeyance and would not yet be implemented.

5

"I Wasn't Alone"

From Prison to Fighting Disbarment

The night before "surrender day," friends, mostly from the Communist Party, gave George a going-away party. "There was this handicapped fellow; I think he had been a Ford employee. He sang a song that I had never heard. It was 'You'll Never Walk Alone.' I fell in love with it instantly. It became sort of a theme song for me. I thought of it many times during my troubles. The cause sustained me, but it wasn't enough. I had my family and many friends. I wasn't alone."[1]

Celebrity Convict #63624

Although Crockett had contemplated prison for two years, he was not fully prepared for the rituals that law enforcement sometimes reserves for its out-of-favor "celebrity" prisoners. It was clear Crockett and the other defense lawyers would not receive special treatment, and Crockett had resolved not to ask for any, with a single exception. He did not want to be sent to a southern segregated prison. Crockett requested incarceration in the Milan, Michigan, federal prison or some other northern facility. At Milan, which was about forty miles from Detroit, first and foremost, he would avoid segregated confinement, and, second, his family and others could visit conveniently. The government, however, had other plans. Not only did the Foley Square lawyers not receive any preferential treatment, but their surrender was staged for very special and humiliating media attention.

On April 24, 1952, Crockett and the other lawyers appeared together one last time in federal court. The presiding judge, who was not Medina, did not utter a word. The clerk called their names. After each had responded "Here," the judge, in a perfunctory gesture, simply waved his hand to the federal marshals as a signal to take them away. The lawyers were escorted to the court's basement, where they waited for three hours. Eventually, the federal marshal, whom Crockett described as "the big guy, not a deputy," came out. He engaged the lawyers briefly in casual conversation before saying it was time to go. They were then handcuffed over the protests of Sacher, who argued that, as lawyers, it was not necessary that they be cuffed for the short ride from the court to the West Street detention facility. Shackled, one to the other, the lawyers were taken outside onto a loading dock, where they were put on display for an assembly of newspaper reporters and press photographers who had been waiting patiently.[2]

> The prosecution, which included the judge, the district attorney, the marshal, and so forth, were very conscious of the fact that they were playing in an international drama. They wanted as much publicity as they could possibly get. So they wanted it to be seen walking with these lawyers in handcuffs. That's the picture that the *New York Times* and the rest of them came out with and publicized.
> [They] made no pretense of trying to prevent the glare of publicity. You'd think they had invited the cameras and reporters to be down there at the loading dock. They actually had us stand still, while they took pictures in handcuffs, so they could be plastered in newspapers all over the world.[3]

The parade was intentionally designed to be humiliating: "The deputy marshal marched us out. When he stopped, the whole line stopped. That probably accounts for the scowls on our faces in the pictures. The little black wagon was waiting. The television cameras were projected into that black wagon to see how we lawyers were taking it."[4] Crockett remained externally stoic, but internally angry: "But there certainly wasn't any pleading. As a matter of fact, I don't recall saying one thing, no. I think the best way I can describe my feeling: I was just downright mad, that's all, that this could be happening to lawyers for simply doing what they had been trained to do—to fight, to fight vigorously on behalf of their clients, not to take anything lying down, to challenge everything."[5]

After the lawyers arrived at the West Street detention facility, which was an old warehouse, they were searched thoroughly, issued prison garb, and instructed about the facility's routines. Shortly thereafter, they discovered they had one very good friend at West Street.

We were fortunate because we had an ambassador of goodwill [t]here. Gus Hall [one of the Foley Square defendants] was brought back to stand trial for a contempt citation. He is a big jovial fellow, and there isn't anyone who didn't know and respect Gus Hall. He told them some important people are coming in here today. They are my lawyers. He said, "First, I want to make arrangements; I want to make sure they are all in the same 'tank' with me. Secondly, I don't want any discrimination against George Crockett. He must be in the same tank with all the other lawyers." That was carried out.[6]

Later that evening, Crockett, now number 63624, wrote his first letter to his strongest and most ardent supporter, Ethelene. His tone was upbeat, obviously intended to calm his family's concerns:

From George W. Crockett, Jr.

April 24, 1952

To Dr. Ethelene J. Crockett
7263 American, Detroit, Mich.

Darling: For once I have difficulty beginning a letter; not because there are not many things to speak of, but because one is somewhat limited.

The court appearance was routine and uneventful. After waiting there for about 2 hours we were taken out—in the fashion I had anticipated—to the tune of a battery of photo flashes and

TV cameras and brought here. Most of the remainder of the day was taken up with checking in, examinations, etc. All of us are well, relaxed and right now in the process of penning our first letters.

Of course, I don't know how long any of us will be here or where we shall go from here. I'd rather not stay here and yet certainly have no desire to go anywhere South of here. This is not the most quiet place, but everyone is congenial and helpful.

I've listed you, the Carrolls, Mom, Mother & Dad and George as my correspondents. I can write three letters a week and receive seven. As I review the list of my correspondents I'm inclined to think the rule should be the other way around—I have the "least writingest" family possible.

It is interesting to see how a human can adapt itself. We were not far off when we jocularly referred to this period as a much needed, if enforced, vacation. Since I know you and the kids are O.K., I really have nothing to worry about.

Tell George III that I shall try to write to him at least once a week but sometimes I may have to substitute someone else. My letters to him will be for all of the children.

I shall be able to write to my partner, Goodman, about office matters and cases and he can write to me. That is an exception—for business letters....

All my love sweetheart. Please don't work too hard and remember there is nothing to worry about. Your George

George W. Crockett, Jr.
63624[7]

Crockett's second letter to Ethelene described his adjustments, the prison, and the respect he and the other lawyers were receiving from their fellow inmates. Surprisingly, he wrote that he did not want any visitors. This desire for an insular life continued throughout his sentence and apparently helped him cope with confinement.[8] That does not mean that all of his friends would honor his request.

From George W. Crockett, Jr.

April 28, 1952

To Dr. Ethelene J. Crockett
7263 American, Detroit, Mich.

My darling: We just finished dinner—which wasn't bad. Our stomachs are becoming adjusted I suppose. Funny how everything around here revolves around meal time. You tell time by it and what work you do is geared to it. Not much in the way of work—a bit of sweeping and mopping and you are through for the day. The remainder of the time is spent in sleeping, reading and conversation. The latter is mainly with someone who feels that he got a bad break in court and wants you to make him feel better by saying "yes." I try to stay away from such discussions, but newspaper pictures which appeared in most N.Y. papers have identified us. There is a healthy respect among the other fellows for political prisoners. Much of our concern is to prevent them from setting us apart or getting the idea that they should look up to us. You can't afford to be isolated or to isolate yourself in a place like this—anymore than you can in a boarding school.

I have not had any visitors and still do not want any though I have Rev. and Mrs. Carroll on my list. Still don't know how long I will be here or where we will go from here. But I do hope we can remain together. It will make the adjustment much easier for each of us. One problem we have here is inability to exercise. We try to solve that by extensive walks up and down the corridors. I understand that it takes some time for letters to clear the censor, so it is quite possible that you and George have not received my last letters. Tell little George and Ethelene that when I am finally settled I'd love to hear from them.

It really is not bad here once you get over the idea of the confinement. All clothing is furnished to you and it is the same as the clothes I wear when working in my cabinet shop or repairing something around the house....

I'll take 20 laps around the corridors; then read some more of Dalton Trumbo's "Washington Letters" and "The Stilwel Papers"—then sleep a bit. Sorta typical Sunday routine—except that I've boycotted the Salvation Army Service. Tell all my friends that there is more democracy in this jail than I've ever found outside. Your husband,

George W. Crockett, Jr.

63624[9]

Before Crockett's transfer to a permanent prison, he renewed his request to be sent to Milan or the federal facility in Danbury, Connecticut. His fears over government-imposed segregation in the South, not unexpectedly, were ignored. Crockett and Sacher were assigned to the Federal Correctional Institution at Ashland, Kentucky. Isserman and McCabe, on the other hand, were sent to Danbury. Gladstein drew Texarkana, Texas.

On May 1, 1952, Crockett received his first letter from his son, George III. He responded immediately—a father giving advice and encouragement to his son:

From George W. Crockett, Jr.

May 1, 1952

To George W. Crockett III
7263 American, Detroit, Mich.

Dear Son:

Your letter was handed to me a few minutes ago. I thought I'd better answer immediately because I expect to leave here tomorrow for Ashland, Kentucky.

I don't know what it will be like there, but I expect to make the most of whatever it is. As I recall, Ashland is just across the river from West Virginia—your home State—and I think it is near Huntington. So the climate should not be too bad. Probably very hot in the day and cool in the evening. . . .

I intend to follow your suggestion and rotate my letters to the three of you. Last night I sent a joint letter to you and Ethelene, which you can send on to Elizabeth Ann when you finish. Or maybe you will want to keep my letters so we can go over them when I come home. I don't know now how many letters I will be able to write each week but I'll try and get one in especially for you. . . .

So everything at home is fine and you are having a good time swimming and playing ball. That's good. I know I could count on you to take care of everything during my absence. Keep on being a good fellow; choose your friends wisely and don't do anything that you would not want to tell me about. Help mother whenever you can and look out for your sisters—but don't try to boss them. Just be their big brother and good friend. I really don't need to tell you all of this because you are like that anyway and I admire you very much for it. So until my next letter, here is love and affection from your Dad.

George W. Crockett, Jr.

63624[10]

The trip south began on May 2, 1952, and lasted three days, with overnight stops at prisons in Lewisburg, Pennsylvania, and Chillicothe, Ohio. During the trip, Crockett was handcuffed, and for the first time, he experienced the degradation of leg irons. He was manacled by the ankles to Harry Sacher. "We lost some skin as a result. You get to the place where you are accustomed to it and you expect it. [The] degradation and all that goes with it. And it is important to realize that prison is essentially a matter of the mind."[11]

As they arrived in Ashland, Crockett's first sight of the prison was from the road. He was impressed with its non-prison-like appearance. Ashland, known as the "country club" of federal prisons, had no fences. It was more properly called a correctional institution and was noted for individual resident rooms, abundant outdoor athletic facilities, and green lawns with colorful picnic grounds where inmates could spend full days lunching with visitors. Crockett thought it looked like an educational institution.

The arrival of the two Foley Square lawyers was not unexpected:

When we got to Ashland, our coming was known. By the time we walked in the gate, the word was to the farthest compound that the Foley Square lawyers had arrived.

One day an inmate came to me and said, "I have the deepest admiration for you and the fight you made in New York." I think two days later, I discovered he was in prison because he was a conscientious objector and had refused to go to war in Korea.

Sacher and I were classified as minimum security. This means we could be trustees. Sacher felt very much that he would like to teach school ... but for reasons that you will understand, they knew Crockett or Sacher will not be allowed to teach school. Harry has a heart condition, and he was made clerk of the storeroom. He worked about one hour a day.[12]

Following a week in the prison's quarantine unit, where, Crockett recalled, "you first become accustomed to prison life when you hear those gates clanking on you at night as you are locked in your cell,"[13] he began settling into life as a minimum-security federal prisoner. The regular residential units were segregated—Blacks had one dormitory and whites another. The dining room was shared, but separate, alternating tables were assigned each race. The weekly movies were similarly segregated, whites on one side of the room, Blacks on the other. Work crews, however, were integrated.[14]

Crockett's request to work in the prison's cabinetmaking shop was denied, but his carpentry skills landed him with the interior decorating crew assigned to paint guards' homes. None of the work was difficult, but the pace was incredibly slow:

My particular task with the crew was to unfasten any windows that were stuck, make sure that the windows were not stuck as a result of painting, and do the cleaning of the floors. If the floors needed to be sanded, I ran the sanding machine. As a matter of fact, I gave them a new way of doing it. I don't know whether they're still doing it or not. I said, "It's foolish to waste all this time and money and effort sanding these floors. Why don't you let me ... take a bucket of hot water, put a can of lye in there, and wash the floors and wash all of the old stain and varnish out of it and then just lightly sand it over and then cover it again with clear varnish and see what it looks like?" The guy says, "All right with me. If you wanna do it, do it that way." I did one floor, and from that time on, he said, "That's the procedure we will use."

My other job with the interior decorating crew was really the one that took most of my time and that was just to sit and oper- ate the little portable radio, to keep them company and entertain them while they were doing the painting. In other words, I was a disc jockey.

Now, after we finished decorating a house, it was customary for the woman of the house to bake cookies for us. And we would sit out on the lawn, and she would bring the pies out and lemonade or something like that. We would sit and enjoy ourselves [*laughs*].[15]

One lesson Crockett did learn was not to work too fast. Saving time means nothing in prison. "Among ourselves you recognize the union price. So I didn't paint, and they didn't want me to. It was the first time I saw it take four fellows two days to paint one room, 12 x 12. We have a motto . . . and that is 'all we have is time' . . . and if we don't finish it, there will be oth- ers, and all they have is time."[16]

Crockett's relationship with the guards and other inmates was cordial, if not somewhat deferential. "There was one guard who felt . . . that it was an opportunity of a lifetime to be able to just sit and talk with one of the Foley Square lawyers. And he would talk and ask questions and talk and ask questions about the trial, what he'd read in the newspapers, and so forth, and we'd sit there and talk."[17] Other inmates gave the Foley Square lawyers the respect due political prisoners. "Most of the inmates had the attitude that they should be there—they had done something wrong, but there was this fellow, Crockett, who had done nothing and he shouldn't be here. As a result, they treated me very special. When I got hungry, all I had to do was say so, and some food would appear."[18] It is strange how some rituals emerge and how personally meaningful they become.

My true status among the prisoners was best represented by what I called the "ping-pong caper." While mostly symbolic, it was a major issue for the prisoners. There was one ping-pong table in each dormitory. And each week, one ping-pong ball would be issued to each dormitory. I take it, it was the same in the white dormitory. I'm not sure. But if some rowdy happened to puncture that ping-pong ball, nobody could play ping-pong for the rest of that week. There was one exception, however, and that exception was convict George Crockett.

Somebody in the dormitory would get me a ball, and I alone had a personal ping-pong ball, so that if I wanted to play ping-pong, I could play anytime. When the game was over, I'd take my ball and put it in my locker and lock it up. The fellow who made sure that I always had a ping-pong ball referred to me as his lawyer. Actually, all I did was sit and listen to him talk about the problems he had had growing up and the prisons that he had been in and so forth.

There were no serious offenders there. A lot of them were comparatively young. They had been picked up for driving stolen automobiles across state lines, that sort of thing, or violation of the Mann Act, taking women across state lines for purposes of prostitution. There were a few income tax violators, but not among the blacks. I found out about the income tax violators during the recess period when I would speak to some guy next to me. Usually the second question after "Where are you from?" is "What are you in here for?"[19]

Crockett retained his healthy sense of humor. In a May 12, 1952, letter to Goodman mostly addressing a range of business matters, he strongly objected to his law partner's description of his present living conditions as a "penitentiary."

First, this is not a *penitentiary*; it is a *Correctional Facility*. Check your U.S. Code and you'll see there is a difference—I could not be in the former without my consent! Secondly, we are awfully proud of this place—indeed it is called a "Country Cub"—with some justification. It has housed some important persons in our National Life—including Congressmen. There is no wall around it—only a fence to keep you outsiders from disturbing our relaxation. We

have individual rooms with wash basin and toilet, fluorescent reading lights, silent switches with solid brass plates; a reasonable fac-
simile of a Beauty Rest mattress; complete change of bed sheets
each week and clothes and towel twice per week. A few bars are
around to give us a sense of security and our doors are electroni-
cally closed and opened for us each night and morning. Food is
excellent—not even touched while being served to you; everything
is spotlessly cleaned and polished wax floors; the halls are pas-
tel; our own library and theatre; music for our meals and broad
spacious green lawns and recreational facilities. Only the ungrate-
ful would quibble over being compelled to remain and partake of
these gratuitous pleasures.[20]

Friends and family appreciated his lighter side. His daughter Ethelene
recalled, "My father had a wonderful sense of humor. He was playful."[21]
Her mother, on the other hand, was the sterner parent. Even this became
a source of humor. Before George went to prison, the Crockett children
would wait at the bus stop for their father to return from work. "Usually the
first words out of his mouth were, 'How's the War Department?'" (referring
to his wife and their mother).[22] He would later refer to his time in prison as
"his government-paid vacation."[23]

Concerns over Disbarment Loom

While imprisoned, Crockett was concerned about the state bar's disbarment
proceedings, which had already begun. In March, Crockett had requested
that the state bar stay its actions until his application to the Supreme
Court for a rehearing had been decided or until he had been released from
prison.[24] The Crockett Defense Committee, which had been formed two
years earlier and which would be exceedingly helpful in the ensuing struggle, wrote every lawyer in Wayne County seeking support for Crockett's stay
petition. The letter claimed, in the words of Justice Black from the *Sacher*
decision, that the latest proceedings against Mr. Crockett constitute "an
overhanging menace to the security of every courtroom advocate in America" and that "the menace is most ominous for lawyers who are obscure,
unpopular, or defenders of unpopular persons or unorthodox causes."[25]

The requested delay was granted, but with disbarment looming, Crockett agonized over the expected ordeal and its probable consequences. In a letter to Ethelene on May 18, 1952, he raised the prospect of losing the fight and revealed that he was considering an entirely new career. In college at Morehouse, he had carefully weighed the pros and cons of becoming a lawyer or a dentist. If law was now somehow barred, maybe it was time to pursue dentistry. In addition, he had read all of the available newspapers and knew about General Douglas McArthur's visit to Detroit. Crockett had very little regard for the military hero, as the letter indicates. By this time, he had a new convict number—8995.

From George W. Crockett, Jr.

May 18, 1952

To Dr. Ethelene J. Crockett
7263 American, Detroit, Mich.

How is my darling? This is Sunday about 9:45 a.m., so the family should be just about ready to start the day. I suppose George and Ethelene are making breakfast and you are in for a cold cup of coffee. We have had breakfast (at 7) and have finished our chores for the day. The day is rainy so we will be inside all day and the fellows will be telling one lie after another and disputing all sorts of inconsequential points—I'll spend my time reading except when I am requested to "settle" some argument!

One of my "corridor mates" "comforted" me this morning with the comment that he is convinced that in my case and his case "it is nothing but persecution." (Smile) His is an income tax charge. In New York, the guy who was in for leading the ring of basketball fixers said that he and "we lawyers" were likewise "victims of filthy politics." So we have lots of friends; they are just in the wrong places!

... I've been giving some thought to my future. Of course the attempt to disbar me will be fought tooth and nail. But, against the possibility that it may be successful, I think it would be smart for me to begin thinking in terms of getting in some dental school in September of '53. That gives me about a year to brush up and take any pre-dental courses which I may lack. Will you check Wayne and U of M catalogues and let me know the requirements? But first let me know what you think of the general idea. It can be financed by refinancing our home. Think it over. Heard from Mother and Dad and William. I did not want any visits....

It's all the same to me that the kids did not see McArthur. I read of his Detroit appearance. I should prefer to really tell them who he is and what he represents before taking them to see him. The heroes of Bataan were the fellows who had to stay there while McArthur used valuable plane space to move out his furniture and other "mementoes!"

...I'll be glad to get the Detroit News too. Saw the May 2nd issue of the Guardian and several of the N.Y. papers, pictures and stories about our incarceration. I'm really fortunate to have a wife like you sweetheart. Otherwise this would be a tough burden to shoulder. You manage to make all of your letters cheerful and so encouraging. I know how busy you are and it takes time to write. Why not make them shorter? The real joy comes in just getting a note which in itself says you and the kids are O.K. It is enough for me. I can sit for hours with my pipe and just dream of home and you, the kids, friends, etc., and I am not alone and neither am I imprisoned. I'm just temporarily detained from doing many of the things I like to do or should be doing. But, fortunately, we are still young and still have time and this experience is likely to be the making of both of us. All my love, sweetheart. Your George.

Geo. W. Crockett, Jr. 8995[26]

On the occasion of having served half of his sentence, George wrote to Ethelene. He assured her that prison had not changed him or his convictions. The letter began, however, with his disapproval of their daughter's summer work in what he called a "Negro job."

From George W. Crockett, Jr.

June 20, 1952

To Dr. Ethelene J. Crockett
7263 American, Detroit, Mich.

My Sweetheart: Your letter came this afternoon so I'm answering
in the hope you get this by Monday. Ethelene's comments do not
surprise me because it was my reaction also. There are fellows here
who actually do not want to leave. They have at last found security
in a life which heretofore offered them nothing. They don't have
to think or plan for tomorrow. Awfully glad Mother and Dad are
there. George told me in his letter and Elizabeth told me about
her job. This letter leaves me with mixed feelings. Had I been at
home, I think I would have opposed it; but there may be considerations that I do not know about. I don't especially care for the way
the job was obtained; absent the personal, friendly element—for
example assisting someone like Norman—I can't get away from
the fact that it is a "Negro job"—if you know what I mean. Our
task—especially those like us who can afford to take it or leave it
in such circumstances—is to break away from "Negro" jobs and
seek employment at our highest skill. I'd much rather see [Eliz-
abeth Anne] and her girlfriends in the neighborhood spending
the entire summer if need be picketing the five and ten stores on
Warren Avenue. Or spend the entire summer doing those scrap-
books for me in the manner I indicated. These are going to play
a vital part in my defense because I'm going to have to show (by
comparing the newspaper accounts with the actual record) just
the defense was misrepresented in the press. But, as I say, this is
a question for [you] and [Elizabeth Anne] to decide so I accept
the decision.
    . . . This week has passed very rapidly and Sunday will be the
end of two of my four months. If imprisonment (of the body) is
intended to make the individual penitent, remorseful, sorry for
his alleged offense, etc., then Medina can take small comfort from

my incarceration. I've never had a conscious moment when felt imprisoned—even when they put handcuffs and leg irons on me and locked me in the prison van. I was "demobilized"—and still am—but my mind and my conscience was free. . . . So, in a way, sweetheart, you do me a slight (very, very slight) injustice by even expecting to find me change or my "quiet smile" missing. I'll be quietly smiling, I'm afraid, when the Medinas and the forces who produce their ilks are seething in a hell created by their own misdeeds. My incarceration and that of the many [who] are bound to follow just added straws on the camel's back—eventually the break will come. . . .

See, I'm still your George—just a bit more mellow.

Geo. W. Crockett, Jr. 8995[27]

On August 16, 1952, an obviously buoyed husband wrote his wife for the last time from the Ashland Prison:

From George W. Crockett, Jr.

August 16, 1952

To Dr. Ethelene J. Crockett
7263 American, Detroit, Mich.

Sweetheart:

Your letter reached me yesterday together with a note from the front office letting me know they are holding my ticket for me. So everything is all set and I'm glad of it. . . .

Glad to hear Maurice wants to know when I'll be up. I'm not so sure now that I'll have the time. I'd like to get that disbarment proceeding over and done with before November if possible; which means I should get to work on it as soon as possible. Moreover the fellows at the office have been swell carrying on [in] my absence and I should give them some relief. Yet, I would like to see Maurice and Jane in their habitat. Maybe I can get away for Labor Day weekend.

Seems strange to realize that the kids are getting ready for school again. I really have been away for a while. This time next week, though, I'll be well on the way home to you. Thanks for everything, darling. Your George.

P.S. That birthday card was a Scream.

Geo. W. Crockett, Jr. 8995[28]

Crockett Goes Home: The Bar Acts, and the Smith Act Returns

A week later, Crockett, having served his full sentence, was freed from custody.[29] He headed home with thoughts of the joyous reunions to come. "The Civil Rights Congress and the Michigan Committee for the Protection of the Foreign Born hosted a welcome home party for him at the Jewish Culture Center in Detroit. He was greeted by more than three hundred friends and admirers who gave him a standing ovation."[30] However, he was still under close surveillance: "The FBI continued watching his every move, taking note even when Hellen Winter, the wife of his Foley Square client, Carl Winter, 'kissed George Crockett' at the homecoming banquet."[31]

Potential disbarment was an even larger threat than the FBI. Crockett was plagued by a growing preoccupation with the State Bar of Michigan—his next formidable and seemingly intractable nemesis. As the other Foley Square lawyers completed their sentences and returned home, they, too, were already under the scrutiny of their state bar associations. Officially, the disciplinary actions were professional misconduct investigations allegedly triggered by their contempt convictions. In reality, they were motivated as much, if not more, by the hatred that mainstream lawyers had for communism and by the campaign, led by the American Bar Association, to drive communists and their advocates out of the legal profession. These extralegal proceedings provided few, if any, constitutional protections and were primed for high-toned harassment by the bar's elite. The profession's "legal woodshed" was also costly and time-consuming, and because it threatened the attorneys' very livelihoods, it caused enormous frustration and constant emotional distress. McCabe, who had received the group's mildest contempt sentence, was charged in Pennsylvania, but the investigatory proceedings against him were dismissed.[32] For the other lawyers who endured the disbarment ordeals, the results were troubling but mixed.[33]

In January 1952, a federal judge in New York permanently disbarred Sacher and suspended Isserman from federal practice for two years.[34] New Jersey disbarred Isserman. The punishments imposed on Sacher and Isserman made them the first American lawyers disbarred for forensic misconduct.[35] After Isserman's state disbarment, he was disbarred by the U.S. Supreme Court.[36] His disciplinary experiences were the group's most severe, even though he was far from the worst offender, according to Judge Medina's contempt sanctions. New Jersey began its disciplinary action against Isserman two weeks after the Foley Square trial ended, and it was pursued with a vengeance until the New Jersey Supreme Court ordered his disbarment in 1952.[37] He was eventually reinstated to practice in the federal district courts and the U.S. Supreme Court,[38] but the New Jersey Supreme Court doggedly refused to lift his disbarment until 1961.[39] Isserman never returned to the practice of law.

Sacher appealed his disbarment. In 1954, after an affirmance by a divided Second Circuit Court of Appeals,[40] the U.S. Supreme Court overturned the disbarment order in a terse decision that concluded that Sacher's punishment had been "unnecessarily severe."[41] Sacher resumed his law practice and lived in "relative obscurity and with a diminished practice" until his death in 1963.[42] Gladstein, who was a highly respected San Francisco labor lawyer, avoided disbarment in California but only after contesting disciplinary charges for seven years. He, similarly, had to fight a *sua sponte* suspension order that had been initiated and pursued by a territorial judge in Hawaii after he appeared there as the lead defense attorney in a Smith Act trial.[43]

After Crockett returned home, he also faced disbarment proceedings, and the "pain, costs, and turmoil . . . [were] every bit as torturous" as those suffered by his Foley Square colleagues.[44] His outcome, however, would be decidedly different from those that befell Sacher and Isserman.

On October 16, 1949, the *Detroit Times* announced, "Detroit Lawyer Faces Discipline." The accompanying story reported that "George W. Crockett Jr., 40, a Negro," was to face a state bar disciplinary action, but charges were being delayed until his appeal had ended. On March 13, 1952, only three days after the Supreme Court affirmed Crockett's conviction, the State Bar of Michigan received a "Request for Investigation" from its secretary of grievances. Crockett, the preliminary complaint charged, had "committed various acts constituting professional misconduct in the presence of the court," for which Judge Harold Medina had sentenced him to imprisonment.[45]

Even before the contempt citations were issued, Crockett and his allies commenced a counterattack. First, they sought to delay the disciplinary actions until his sentence was over or until a planned request for reconsideration had been decided by the Supreme Court. This effort succeeded. Second, Crockett's supporters launched an elaborate campaign attacking the merits of the complaint, whose predicate, of necessity, was Judge Medina's findings. Crockett, the lawyer, became the centerpiece of the campaign. The professional esteem that Crockett enjoyed after eighteen unblemished years in practice made him an unlikely candidate for disbarment. His seminal work at high levels in the federal government and the UAW had earned him an impeccable reputation in Detroit and nationally. Lastly, the publicity techniques that Goodman, Sugar, and other leftist Detroit lawyers had perfected in gaining popular support for their causes became mainstays of Crockett's defense.

The publications that the Crockett Defense Committee had sent to virtually every member of the Michigan bar and bench as early as 1950 and again in 1952 had already begun to neutralize the opposition.[46] In addition to the Detroit Chapter of the National Lawyers Guild and the predominantly Black Wolverine Bar Association, Crockett was supported by local labor leaders and other prominent citizens. A petition to the state bar on his behalf was signed by nearly two hundred lawyers, Black and white, including several sitting judges.[47]

In August 1952, a resolution to support Crockett, "Statement of the National Bar Association in Opposition to the Disbarment Proceedings against George W. Crockett Jr., of the Michigan Bar," was placed before the National Bar Association (NBA) at its annual meeting, which, coincidently, was held in Detroit. Since 1911, Black lawyers had been denied membership in the American Bar Association. As a consequence, the NBA, which was formed in 1925, had become the Black lawyers' preeminent professional organization and their only national voice.[48] The NBA's backing would add an important and prestigious cornerstone to the Crockett campaign. The five-page resolution was carefully and succinctly worded. It devoted as much space to Crockett, focusing on his merits as a nationally prominent attorney, legal scholar, bar leader, friend, and defender of unpopular clients, as well as the severity of the punishment he had already endured, as it did to Judge Medina's contempt citations. As the Wolverine Bar Association presented the resolution for adoption, it encountered a powerful opponent: Thurgood Marshall. This was the second time that Marshall had opposed Crockett publicly on a Foley Square matter.

What Thurgood did I didn't think was very principled, and for that reason, as well as his similar opposition when we sought the help of the NAACP during the trial, we've not been bosom buddies, although we respected each other. Thurgood got up and made a speech in connection with the resolution. The substance was, "Look, George Crockett might be a good lawyer, a hell of a lawyer, good friend to all of us, but as an organization, we cannot take a position on something like this with no knowledge of what there is in the record showing what, if anything, he actually did." So Thurgood's position was that unless they were prepared to read the entire trial record and form an independent judgment as a result, he didn't see how they could pass the resolution.

Now, Thurgood knew it was literally impossible to find someone who was going to sit down and read over twenty volumes of transcript. Plus, we had a summary of the transcript prepared and available. It was all gratuitous. He didn't have to get up and say anything. He could just have kept quiet. . . . The resolution passed anyway.[49]

It was not only the prospect of disbarment that followed Crockett home from prison. In the wake of the success against national leadership of the Communist Party at Foley Square, the United States Department of Justice extended its prosecutions nationwide against the leadership of state parties. On September 17, 1952, the FBI arrested the top six members of the Michigan Communist Party under Smith Act indictments for conspiring to advocate the violent overthrow of the government. The group, which included Saul Laurence Wellman, Nathan Kaplan (aka Nat Ganley), Thomas Dewitt Dennis Jr., Philip Schatz, Helen Mary Winter (wife of Carl Winter, convicted in the New York trial), and William Allan, would come to be known as the "Michigan Six," and they sought legal representation from the Goodman firm. Less than a month after returning from prison for bravely representing the defendants in *United States v. Dennis*, Crockett was being asked to walk down that same road in potentially representing the Michigan Six. This raised difficult strategic questions about how Crockett should fight disbarment at the same time the Goodman firm took on the representation of the latest round of Smith Act defendants.

Earlier that year, Crockett had explained in a letter to his son his reasons for *not* taking a similar case representing Smith Act defendants back in New York. As always, the letter reflects a careful consideration of all the facts. Crockett was convinced that it would be impossible for him to participate in the trial without once again being found in contempt of court. He further doubted his own ability to be fully focused on the trial with the Michigan disbarment proceedings hanging over his head, recalling that saying something as innocuous as "seemingly unintentional" to Judge Medina was the basis of one of his contempt charges. More importantly, the charged political environment and hysteria associated with these trials would almost certainly produce a range of contempt citations. Finally, Crockett understood that he would be a particular target: "I would be a magnet drawing the fire of both the prosecution and the judge. The other defense lawyers would naturally come to my defense, a move which would serve only to implicate them. So that I must necessarily either be so inhibited in the defense of my clients as to impair my usefulness to them or else run the risk of incurring the displeasure of the judge not alone for myself but for other defense counsel as well. This could only have disastrous effect upon my client's case."[50] Every consideration pointed in the same direction: Crockett should not take the case. That was the rational decision, but it still tore him up inside.

> So that I am compelled to weigh on the one hand the value of any contribution I could make in winning the case as against the detriment that is likely before me, my co-counsel and the clients from

my participation. I have reached the conclusion that the detriment far outweighs the advantage. I've decided not to participate in the trial of the case.

I despise the situation which makes this decision necessary. This is one of the few times in my life when I am compelled to reach a decision induced by fear. I say this because no matter how you dress it, the fact comes through that I am not taking this case because I'm afraid of the consequences. It may well be that in the long run these consequences really do not matter. But, unfortunately, there are times when a decision must be made based upon a present evaluation of a current situation. When courts and judges are afraid to do justice or when they are willing to ignore the dictates of justice in order to bask in the light of publicity and enjoy the prospects of promotion—when these times are upon us, then lawyers are in danger and their whole futures are in danger.[51]

Crockett's first priority, understandably, had to be fighting disbarment. Following the extensions he had received, Crockett's answer to the "Request for Investigation" was filed in October 1952. Initially, Crockett's lawyers were his friend and state senator Joseph A. Brown (Goodman's cocounsel in the Trucks Act litigation) and Harold A. Cranfield, who, at the time, was general counsel for the UAW. Cranfield's involvement carried the imprimatur of the UAW and was a major coup for Crockett's defense. Cranfield, however, had agreed "without any clearance."[52] Later, because of high-level national politics, Cranfield, as Crockett wrote to Maurice Sugar, "had to withdraw as my counsel. The union [e.g., Walter Reuther] thought he was 'right on principle' in wanting to serve but that the newspapers would play it up to the detriment of the union's effort to support [Adlai] Stevenson."[53] After Cranfield's withdrawal, Brown was joined by Willis M. Graves,[54] and, thereafter, the two prominent Black lawyers represented Crockett.

The Crockett Defense Committee, which had met as early as January 1950, remained active throughout the disciplinary proceedings. Among its stalwarts were Crockett's law partners, Goodman and Robb. The most influential member, however, was Crockett's longtime mentor and his "father in the law," Maurice Sugar. Sugar himself had been disbarred in the federal courts and knew firsthand what the profession's ultimate sanction meant.

From his retirement home at Black Lake in Onaway, Michigan, he was regularly informed of developments and kept himself deeply involved.[55] Sugar's participation and his influence with Crockett would become critical.

Defending the Michigan Six and the Continuing Struggle against the Trucks Act

By December 1952, both Goodman's and Crockett's attention was back on the Michigan Six. In one sense, this gave Crockett a second bite at the apple. Crockett was brought into the Foley Square case late, after key strategic decisions had been made. In retrospect, he was very critical of many of the defense tactics. Crockett believed that lawyers, and not their clients, should be in charge of legal strategy and courtroom conduct. Crockett also deeply believed that the common law tradition in England and the United States was ill suited for "political trials" and that defendants who undertook such a strategy seriously undermined their own efforts. Finally, Crockett believed that the best defense rested within established constitutional norms of the First Amendment, not in esoteric defenses of Marxist-Leninist ideology. These beliefs would define the core of the Goodman firm's proposed legal strategy for the Michigan Six. How that strategy could be implemented in such a charged political environment was a more complicated question.

There is a series of extraordinary memos, all dated from December 1952, outlining the Goodman-Crockett defense strategy. None of the memos identify their authors, but several that draw extensively on first-hand knowledge of the Foley Square defense are clearly written by Crockett. Regardless of individual authorship, the memos reflect the considered opinions of both Goodman and Crockett. One of the most telling is dated December 11, 1952, titled "Memorandum to Smith Act Defendants Subject: Staff." It states, "Trial Staff encompasses both lawyers who will be actively engaged in the court room as well as lawyers who will be primarily concerned with out-of-court preparation."[56] Crockett was envisioning a key role for himself but one that would be behind the scenes. "In addition to the trial team, there must be at least one seasoned attorney outside of the court; preferably someone who is familiar with the legal issues which a Smith Act trial presents and who is in a position to direct the preparation of motions, briefs and legal memoranda."[57]

There were good reasons for all involved that Crockett play an essentially invisible role. This strategy resolved the dilemmas that Crockett outlined in the letter to his son. In fighting against disbarment, charges based on his actions representing the Foley Square defendants, it would not be wise to reprise that same role in Detroit, with the adverse publicity and public reaction that might result. Moreover, he and Goodman were trying to employ a strategy that marked a sharp break with the tactics used at Foley Square. Crockett's presence inside the courtroom would make this more difficult, to the detriment of their own clients.

While Crockett would not be in the courtroom, it is significant that the staffing memo still strongly called for an integrated defense team.

Now with respect to trial counsel: It is our view that there should be at least two trial attorneys, one Negro and one white. This, we think, is required not only because of the presence of both races among the defendants and because it is consistent with the defendants' policy of always giving visual manifestation of their opposition to racial discrimination; but also because of the volume of work and the difficult questions of trial tactics which will have to be evaluated and decided on the spur of the moment. The job is too big to rely entirely upon one lawyer's appraisal and decision.[58]

The memo also addressed the thorny issues of defendant self-representation, or what the memo somewhat awkwardly termed "self defense," and recommended strongly against the tactic. "This technique has been employed in most, if not all, of the previous Smith Act trials. Our appraisal of the results leads us to the conclusion that the technique should not be employed in the Detroit trial."[59] The analysis reflects both Crockett's lessons and his frustrations concerning the legal tactics employed at Foley Square. "We believe the idea of using this technique to get some defendants before the jury in a favorable light other than as a witness is an illusion. It is safe to say that while the speeches made to the jury by self defendants in prior Smith Act cases may be excellent for public consumption, they have not contributed one iota towards influencing a favorable verdict. On the contrary ... they have harmed the defense."[60]

The memo further warned against the past practice of centering the legal strategy on the defendants' political ideology. "The idea of using the opening and closing as an opportunity for a self-defendant to present his political ideology is also illusory and, in any event, is of insufficient importance to risk the consequences." One danger is that the "jury is likely to conclude that they are, in effect, being asked to approve the defendants' political ideology." Additionally, the very mechanics of the rules of evidence would incur "frequent interruptions by the prosecution or warning or expressions of displeasure by the Judge all of which make an orderly presentation of the defendant's ideology impossible." The memo pleaded to let the lawyers control the legal process: "If we are to win this case, our strategy must be based on legal principles; the gimmicks and the usual will not do." The document concluded with the strong recommendation that none of the defendants seek to represent themselves in court: "Accordingly, it is our recommendation that there be no self defendants and that all court room activity be strictly in the hands of trial counsel—acting with the advice and consent of his clients."[61]

If this was not enough of a break from past Smith Act trials, Crockett and Goodman were advocating one more. In the same file as the December memos is an undated document titled "On U.S. History."[62] It does not designate an author but illustrates how Crockett and Goodman believed that the defense of the Michigan Six should be framed for the jury in positive terms, based on the constitutional protections of the First Amendment. This positive frame would be combined with a theory of social change focused on the peaceful advocacy of beliefs.

The memo is significant on many levels. At one level, it illustrates the development of a legal strategy for the case that stands in sharp contrast with previous Smith Act trials. At a deeper level, it sheds light on the question of how Crockett and Goodman could zealously protect the rights of communists (and others) and not be communists themselves. This reasoning centers the two lawyers' life work on a sophisticated understanding of the radical potential of established legal structures. It reveals how lawyers could be revolutionary in their aims yet still dedicated to constitutional means to accomplish those ends. The memo defined the central challenge: "If progressive social change was inevitable, and in fact desirable, a legal system was necessary to facilitate that change in a peaceful and non-violent manner."[63]

According to this analysis, no one understood this challenge better than our founding fathers. The founders were conscious that their historic moment of revolutionary change *was not* unique. Change would always take place. As such, their legal vision for the new country had to incorporate this reality.

> Thus the fathers of our country believed in social change and when they looked back in history they saw that society had developed from one stage to another, but always as a result of struggle, conflict and bloodshed. They did not assume that the economic, political and social basis of their own society would always continue. They knew that changes, probably fundamental changes, would eventually take place. What they were concerned with was not that such changes be prevented, but rather to develop a system of government within which such changes could take place without the bloodshed and violence which had heretofore accompanied such changes in history.[64]

To answer to this challenge, these American revolutionaries established clear protections for freedom of speech and political expression.

> [The founders] sought to lay the bases within this country for fundamental changes to take place through peaceful and non-violent means. Their idea that such changes could take place was predicated upon this belief: That if everyone could hold and advocate his ideas, beliefs and opinions as to change in society, be free to express these ideas and to organize others in support of them, it would then be possible for the people of this country to accept and adopt those ideas which appear most feasible to them and to reject those ideas which appear to them to be erroneous.[65]

To be effective, however, these rights must reside in a robust legal framework. One can find these institutions within the founding documents of our country:

> According to this view, America's legal system was born of revolution and embodies a framework that could facilitate future social change.

The Declaration of Independence (July 4, 1776), the Constitution of the US (1787) and the Bill of Rights (1791) were adopted as a framework upon which our country was established [and] were based on one overriding principle. This principle was that change in societies occurred in the past and would continue in the future.

The Declaration thus proclaims the equality of men in certain unalienable rights such as life, liberty and the pursuit of happiness; it proclaims the revolutionary right to alter or abolish old forms of government and to institute new government; it proclaims the peaceful efforts of the colonies to achieve this revolutionary change in government....

The first declared right in the constitution was to "form a more perfect union" which was implemented by Article 5[,] the right to amend the Constitution. On this basis, under the mass pressure of the American people . . . and through peaceful Constitutional means, the Bill of Rights, the first 10 amendments, were written into the Constitution providing for freedom of speech, press, and assembly, religious freedom, trial by jury and other rights of the people.[66]

Within this framework is an important irony: it is not the expression of ideas (whatever they may be) that leads to violence but rather the official suppression of ideas that leads to bloodshed:

[The founders] knew that if any idea or group of ideas were suppressed, or the persons who held or advocated them persecuted, and if these ideas should prove to be consistent with the needs and desires of the people, the change, if it came, could only come through force and violence. It was their considered view, looking back upon history, that it was suppression and persecution which, in the end, bred force and violence, and not beliefs and advocacy. By adopting the First Amendment, which guaranteed full freedom of expression, they hoped to create in our society the legal basis upon which all ideas could be advocated and change within our society be accomplished peacefully.[67]

As historical illustrations of these principles, the document pointed to how the violent suppression of antislavery views in the South before the Civil War necessitated and accentuated the violence of that conflict; how the relatively less violent suppression of the women's suffrage movement facilitated significant and important social change without comparable force and violence; and, finally, how the level and nature of violence in the labor movement were often calibrated to the degree to which the voices of labor advocates were being suppressed.[68]

Certainly, this historical analysis makes a number of heroic assumptions, whether it is approached as a trial strategy or a life philosophy for progressive lawyers. One can see its wisdom as a trial tactic. It gives jurors a framework to uphold the defendants' unpopular beliefs, with which the jury might disagree. As a progressive lawyer's philosophy, it maps well onto the lives of both Crockett and Goodman. This view of history, law, and the Constitution fit comfortably with the struggle for labor rights and defending communists during the Red Scare, as well as the impending struggle for civil rights and ultimately standing up for the rights of Black Power advocates.

The group that had the most difficulty embracing this view of history, however, was the Michigan Six. A "Memo on the Memos," dated December 1952, whose authorship Babson, Riddle, and Elsila attribute to lead defendant Saul Wellman,[69] expresses skepticism about the view of history being put forth by Goodman and Crockett, if not necessarily the legal strategy. "Of course Counsel views and our views on the subject are not and need not be the same. Hence even with my amendments, Goodman theses still remain a bourg[eois] liberal rather than a communist concept of Amer[ican] history."[70]

As 1952 was coming to a close and the legal strategy to defend the Michigan Six was falling into place, another tragedy of the Red Scare was unfolding that would generate an additional significant legal case for the Goodman firm. On Christmas Eve, while the former state senator Stanley Nowak was at home decorating the tree with his family, he was served with a set of legal papers. Crockett had represented Nowak in the HUAC hearings. "The papers notified Nowak that the federal government had filed suit in federal court to cancel his naturalization as a U.S. citizen. Nowak was to be stripped of his rights and deported to Poland, the land he had left forty years before as a ten-year-old child. According to the government, he had lied in his 1938 application for U.S. citizenship when he told the examiner that he was not a member of the Communist Party."[71] The work-load of the Goodman firm and its lawyers continued to mount. The firm faced the tremendous burden that so long as the threat of disbarment loomed, Crockett would have to remain a silent partner in the firm's most controversial cases.

February 2, 1953, would, once again, find Goodman on the steps of the United States Supreme Court. Goodman was appealing the adverse decision denying the requested injunction against the Michigan Trucks Act. This time, however, he was not alone. The ACLU had filed a support-ing amicus brief in the case. Underlying the clear constitutional threats embedded in the Trucks Act, however, was the more technical legal issue of abstention, whether the federal courts should defer first to the state court to interpret and apply state law before assessing its constitutionality.

The stresses on Goodman were great. He recalled,

I had to write the brief and prepare to argue the case before the U.S. Supreme Court during a difficult time for me, personally, and I argued the case on a day I was ill with the flu and had a high fever.

The case was a difficult one; it had many constitutional com-plexities. When I got to Washington and stood in front of the Court, it was [one of] the most unhappy legal experiences I've had. It was made worse because there was a clear division among the justices as to what to do with the case. Some of the justices, par-ticularly Douglas, wanted to hear it on its merits. On the other hand, there was Frankfurter, who wanted to send the case back to have the state courts first decide the constitutional issues.

Justices Douglas and Frankfurter began to argue this issue bit-terly, but they were doing it through me. I was just a foil. They would ask questions about it and expected me to answer in a cer-tain way. Frankfurter was as nasty as he could be, and he could be damned nasty. All the time I was trying to make the constitu-tional argument—about the merits of this kind of law—but they kept pulling me back to this other issue. Finally, I was so tired and harassed that when Frankfurter asked another question along the same line, I told him in effect, "Justice Frankfurter, all I can tell you is there are cases that go both ways. You can decide it on the merits if you wish, or you can send it back. You're going to have to decide it one way or the other; don't ask me to do it for you." I just wanted to quit the argument and go to the hotel and go to bed, and that's what I did for a couple of days until I recovered.

Well, the Court followed Frankfurter's view. Douglas wrote a dissent, supported by Justice Black. The case was sent back to Michigan for the state courts to decide it.[72]

In the moment, while feeling ill, Goodman might have negatively characterized the argument and the Supreme Court decision to send the case back to the Michigan courts, but the result was a positive outcome. The federal case was stayed while the state proceedings continued. As such, the Trucks Act continued to be held in abeyance. If Goodman started the suit seeking an injunction to prevent the implementation of the Trucks Act, he was accomplishing that end. The only question was, "How long would it last?"

Crockett's Disbarment: A Stalemate over an Apology

Sugar, Goodman, and Crockett had perfected the techniques of multipronged mobilizing in support of liberal legal causes. All of those efforts were brought to bear to support Crockett in his fight against the state bar. This elaborate and determined support network kept enormous pressure on the state bar. Before the bar filed a formal complaint, a decision was made to try and settle the case, thereby avoiding what were expected to be lengthy and strongly contested hearings. A Grievance Committee member, Hobart Taylor, a well-connected Black lawyer who would later become associate counsel to Vice President Lyndon B. Johnson and a board member of the U.S. Export-Import Bank,[73] approached Crockett with the offer of a "deal." Taylor proposed that Crockett agree to a "private reprimand." "Private" meant a written record would be made, but the reprimand itself would be done in a judge's chambers, not in open court. Also, Crockett would have to apologize to Judge Medina.

In 1953, legal practice in Detroit was highly segregated, and the community of Black lawyers was small and close-knit. Virtually every Black lawyer belonged to the Wolverine Bar Association, which represented their interests, particularly in matters of race. When the state bar filed its formal charges against Crockett, it gave what seemed was unmistakable evidence of a desire for rapprochement. Appointed to represent the bar as its prosecutors were two Black attorneys, Assistant County Prosecutor Elvin L. Davenport[74] and former assistant prosecutor and criminal court judge Charles W. Jones.[75] Both were Wolverine Bar members and friends of Crockett. In fact, Davenport had sponsored Crockett's admission to the bar. The matter appeared to be at an end. Crockett, however, could be stubborn and balked. "I didn't think I was guilty of anything, and I wasn't willing to accept a reprimand, particularly if it required I apologize to Medina. Sugar, however, talked with me, and he wanted me to do it. I didn't agree."[76] The matter had reached a stalemate over the issue of an apology.

During the time the "deal" languished, Harry Sacher wrote Crockett on May 4, 1953. He reported on the status of his and Isserman's appeals and then got to "the business at hand":

Dear George:

I have thought of you a good deal these last few days. April 24th marked the first anniversary of the commencement of our sentences. And today, May 4th, marks the anniversary of our arrival at Ashland, where we forged our lasting friendship, not without some travail to be sure; but then again, things excellent are as difficult as they are rare.

Now, to the business at hand, namely, the question of an apology to Medina. However distasteful such a thing must be to you, as it would be to me, I think you ought to do it—whether in the less painful manner of a letter, or the more painful one of a personal appearance. The important—the critically important—thing is that you remain at the bar. The enemy must not be permitted to disbar any of us if there is any way in which it can be avoided. Besides, if an apology is not tendered after they have said that they would take it, the responsibility for disbarment will rest on you, not them. This would take them off the hook—a hook of which the 4 dissenters in Abe's case were quite conscious. So, my dear friend, my thought is that you do it. A long and distinguished career lies ahead of you, and it will in the shortest order wipe out the unpleasantness that an apology will temporarily leave in your mouth. . . .

Sincerely,

Harry[77]

Despite the urging from Sacher, Sugar, and others, Crockett refused any compromise that required him to appear before Judge Medina and apologize.

The Trial of the Michigan Six

Not everything goes according to plan. The previous December, Crockett had helped outline a careful, unified defense strategy for the Michigan Six, calculated not to repeat the mistakes of Foley Square. The key to that strategy was to have the lawyers in charge of courtroom activities, representing all clients. This unified front started to fall apart on the eve of trial. Despite the defendants' earlier agreements, they came back to Goodman and Crockett wanting to present a political defense, similar to all previous Smith Act cases.[78] "Feeling, no doubt, betrayed, Goodman flatly refused to accept their late-hour demand. Crockett seconded his decision. The defendants would have to find another lawyer if they insisted on this change of course. They agreed to talk it over and return the next day with their decision."[79] The defendants returned and proposed a compromise. Three of the defendants would represent themselves, and the Goodman firm would continue to represent the rest according to the original plan.

After seeing how far off the legal rails a trial can go when the lawyers lose control of their clients, Crockett, like most lawyers, knew that having three clients represent themselves is little different than having all clients represent themselves. All of the difficulties he outlined in his December memos would probably face the Michigan Six under their proposed strategy. Nevertheless, with more than a year invested in the defense and knowing full well that no other lawyers would be willing to step up and take the case, Goodman and Crockett agreed to the change in representation. On October 19, 1953, the paperwork was filed with the court.[80]

The trial began on November 3. There was no integrated defense team *inside* the courtroom. Goodman worked the entire trial by himself. Despite having lost a unified defense strategy under the lawyers' control and having three of the six defendants represent themselves, there were significant ways in which the trial of the Michigan Six was different from the trial at Foley Square. Goodman insisted that there be no pickets outside the courtroom.[81] This helped depoliticize the contest and changed the experience for the jurors and the media. Neither the press nor the jury had to pass bands of police and protesters to get to the building and could better focus on the events in the courtroom. There were fewer fireworks there as well. Goodman maintained a good rapport with the presiding judge, Frank A. Picard, who treated even the self-representing defendants with more respect and deference than had Judge Medina.

In other ways, the two cases were similar. Though Judge Picard had a more pleasant demeanor, his substantive rulings were just as pro-prosecution as had been Judge Medina's.[82] Judge Picard ruthlessly held the unrepresented defendants to the strictures of established rules of evidence,[83] making many of their efforts to integrate their political beliefs ineffective and counterproductive, as Crockett had predicted. The inevitable pressure that defendants who took the witness stand faced to implicate others was also the same, as were the severe legal consequences for their silence.

When Wellman and Schatz went to the witness stand and refused to name fellow party members, the judge immediately cited them for contempt and sent both men to jail. Thereafter, they appeared in court every morning in handcuffs; in the meantime, the government's paid informants were happy to lie on the stand, admit it under cross-examination—and then walk out of the courthouse free men.[84]

The trial lasted four months. The jury deliberated over two half-day periods. On February 17, 1954, they returned with guilty verdicts for all defendants.[85]

Disbarment Revisited and Resolved

During the impasse over Crockett's apology, negotiations were held periodically between his lawyers and the bar's lawyers. Crockett proposed that if he had to apologize, a letter from him to Medina should be enough. His offer was refused. With the apology issue unresolved, on February 17, 1954, the same day as the conclusion of the Michigan Six trial, the state bar set the date for the commencement of disciplinary hearings on Crockett's disbarment: March 22, 1954.

Sugar, fearing the worst and realizing that if formal proceedings were conducted, they "just can't know what will happen—and it may be serious"[86]—continued to press for the compromise. Finally, just two weeks before the hearing was to take place, Crockett reluctantly agreed to apologize to Medina in person.

Crockett immediately wrote a terse letter to Judge Medina requesting an audience.[87] The same day, Sugar, without Crockett's knowledge, also wrote a letter. Sugar's was to a friend, the NLG member and prominent New York lawyer Osmond K. Frankel. After explaining why the apology had to be made and its urgency, Sugar wrote,

And here, Osmond, is where I am asking your aid: Judge Medina can handle this matter in one of two ways: he can receive the apology in open court and create a situation making for the utmost of humiliation for George, or he can handle the matter in chambers and dispose of it in a quiet, dignified manner without publicity.

Are you willing to see him and endeavor to persuade him, if necessary, to pursue the latter course? You may of course advise him that you are aware that George proposes to come to New York to tender the apology....

... One thing more: This request is coming to you from me, not George. I am sure that he would not make it. Indeed, I feel so certain that he would disapprove of my making it that I have not informed him that I am doing it.

You will appreciate how important this is not only to George but to his host of friends and admirers. Will you do it?

I hope so.

Sincerely
Maurice[88]

On March 19, 1954, Crockett, accompanied by Joseph A. Brown and Elvin L. Davenport, appeared before Judge Medina in his chambers. The session was brief, less than five minutes. Crockett made a short and respectful apology. Medina's only response on the record was, "I accept your apology, Mr. Crockett."[89] After short statements by Brown and Davenport, the ordeal that Crockett later described as "galling" ended.[90] He left New York with only the Detroit hearing remaining to complete the "deal."

The Goodman firm was engaged in one more important trial defending individual rights against the government's anticommunist campaign. State Senator Stanley Nowak was served his papers on Christmas Eve 1952. Eighteen months later, on July 13, 1954, Goodman was defending Nowak's right to citizenship in a bench trial, once again in front of Judge Picard. Two days later, Judge Picard rejected Goodman's defense and stripped Nowak of his citizenship. Nowak had become one more victim of the Red Scare and joined the Michigan Six and the anti–Trucks Act litigation in a trilogy of prominent civil rights cases defended by the Goodman firm.

Crockett did not contest the findings of the State Bar of Michigan Grievance Committee. He was found guilty of professional misconduct, and the committee recommended that he be reprimanded *publicly*.[91] Once again, Crockett felt cheated since a private reprimand had been promised. He, however, did not contest the recommendation, which meant that no greater punishment than a reprimand could be imposed. In fact, his reprimand was almost private. When he finally appeared before a three-judge Wayne County Circuit Court panel on October 11, 1954, the courtroom was nearly empty.[92]

Crockett, far from contrite, addressed the court at some length. He explained that his defense of communists and the First Amendment against a flawed Smith Act caused his problems with Judge Medina and that Supreme Court decisions after *Dennis* and *Sacher* demonstrated that the punishments he had already endured were unjustified. He concluded by informing the court that the lawyers who dare defend unpopular clients were being intimidated and "smeared," contrary to the Canon of Legal Ethics. "I am literally swamped with clients who are defendants in these Communist political cases. [T]hey can get no other lawyer to represent them. . . . I am not and never have been a member of that [Communist] Party. But I do reserve the right to carry out my sworn obligation; and that is, that I have not and will not refuse any man's case because of considerations personal to myself."[93]

The court's opinion, delivered by presiding judge Herman Dehnke, implied that if the judges had any latitude, they would have imposed a more severe penalty. Crockett's statements, the panel wrote, showed "substantial doubt" about his "sincerity in acknowledging . . . [his] misconduct" and "his obligations as a lawyer." Crockett, nevertheless, was asked to rise, and the order carrying out recommended punishment was entered, "similar to the responsibility which rests upon a father with respect to his children." The court, in a not too veiled reference to Crockett's race and the barriers it created for Black lawyers, said that it recognized "the obstacles which have impeded [his] progress, which do not impede the progress of many others," but advised him to "re-check" his attitudes and "disabuse" his mind of "mistaken and erroneous notions."[94]

In the court's final comment, in a less patronizing way, it addressed Crockett, directly and personally. The judges were unexpectedly laudatory and unknowingly prophetic: "Because of your more than average ability, we feel that you are still young enough to reach distinguished heights in the profession which you have chosen, and, so far as we are personally concerned, we genuinely and heartily wish you well. Court stands adjourned."[95]

As Crockett and Goodman left the courthouse, relieved that their Foley Square travails finally were over, they shared a rare laugh about the case. Goodman turned to Crockett and said, "I'll be damned if I could tell if they were reprimanding or complimenting you."[96]

Legal Vindication

The legal vindication that Crockett predicted on the day he was held in contempt of court slowly started to unfold. The *Sacher* opinion, as precedent, was short-lived. The case, which Crockett had described as "extremely dangerous for all lawyers," began to legally erode less than two years later, in 1954. In *Offutt v. United States*, the Court broke with its "fresh" *Sacher* ruling and required that when a contempt case against a lawyer involves personal attacks on the judge or "is entangled with the judge's personal feeling against the lawyer," the charges should be heard by another judge.[97] Later, in what Justice Rehnquist called "a total repudiation of the principle laid down in *Sacher*" in "the course of only 20-odd years,"[98] *Sacher* was effectively overruled by *Taylor v. Hayes*.[99] After *Taylor*, the due process rights denied

Crockett in 1950 became firmly established in law. Adding the guarantee of a jury trial when a jail term greater than six months was involved,[100] *Taylor* required that lawyers confronted with posttrial contempt charges receive notice of the specific charges and the opportunity to be heard. Also, when the alleged contemptuous conduct, even if short of personal attacks, provokes the trial judge and "so embroil him in controversy," the contempt charge should be decided by another judge.[101]

The year 1955 was full of appeals for the Goodman firm. With the threat of disbarment gone, Crockett was now playing a more public role in the fight. Goodman and Joseph Brown continued the Trucks litigation through the Michigan state courts. Crockett was the principal author on the firm's brief to the federal Sixth Circuit Court of Appeals in the Michigan Six case and joined Goodman on the brief in the Nowak appeals.[102] Both efforts before the Sixth Circuit were unsuccessful. On November 18, 1955, the appellate court affirmed Judge Picard's Smith Act convictions of each of the six defendants.[103] The following year, the Sixth Circuit affirmed Judge Picard's removal of Nowak's citizenship.[104]

From the standpoint of an individual defendant, legal change seems to take an eternity. Change occurred too slowly to save the defendants and their lawyers in the Foley Square case. By the law's own slow standards, however, changes started to take place very quickly as the Supreme Court started to reexamine its initial Cold War doctrines. The cases following *Dennis* and *Sacher* confirmed that Crockett and his colleagues were sacrifices to the "politics of the day" that had temporarily encrusted and perverted First Amendment law. *Dennis*, as the later cases demonstrated, was an out-and-out political trial, one calculated to silence those who dared teach Marxism as the Cold War raged, with a majority of the then-constituted Supreme Court, led by Chief Justice Fred Vinson, willing helpers.[105]

Justice Black's prophecy that in "calmer times" the Court would restore First Amendment liberties unfolded a mere six years after *Dennis* was decided. Although anticommunism remained strong in the late 1950s, the draconian excesses of McCarthyism and the witch hunts it spawned had been exposed and condemned. In 1954, Senator McCarthy was censored by the U.S. Senate for unethical conduct and for impairing the dignity of the Senate. After *Sacher*, the second domino to fall involved state legislation similar to the Michigan Trucks Act. In 1956, the U.S. Supreme Court heard a challenge to comparable legislation in *Pennsylvania v. Nelson.*[106] Reasoning that the Constitution gives the federal government sole responsibility for the conduct of foreign policy, the Court held that states could not enact laws against foreign subversion. Shortly thereafter, the Michigan Supreme Court held that the Trucks Act was unconstitutional.[107] While not the vindication of the rights embodied in the First Amendment that Goodman and Crockett might have wanted, the Goodman firm, with the help of Joseph Brown, had prevented the Trucks Act from ever being implemented.

The biggest target was still *Dennis v. United States.* By 1957, appeals from the convictions of "second string" communist leaders like the Michigan Six in a comparable case from California, *Yates v. United States,* reached the Supreme Court.[108] Senator McCarthy had died, and his namesake, McCarthyism, was in decline. Furthermore, the composition of the Court that heard *Yates* was decidedly different from the one that decided *Dennis.*[109] Without expressly overruling *Dennis,* the Court in *Yates* drew a sharp line between the advocacy of action and the advocacy of ideas. The mere doctrinal teaching, even of forcible overthrow, that was condemned in *Dennis* the *Yates* Court deemed "too remote from concrete action" to be considered a "clear and present" danger.[110] *Yates,* in essence, was a return to the Court's original standards. It also signaled to the government that its wholesale prosecutions of "second string" communists that followed *Dennis* had become constitutionally suspect.

Later, in *Noto v. United States,* the Court held that the Communist Party's teachings fell within the realm of "abstract doctrine" rather than "advocacy of action."[111] After *Yates* and *Noto,* the government, realizing that communist teachings had been removed from the scope of the "clear and present danger" doctrine, stopped its Smith Act prosecutions. The damage had been done, however. The declines in membership and resources were dramatic, and for all practical purposes, the Smith Act trials had decimated the U.S. Communist Party.[112]

While these changes came too late for the Foley Square defendants, they did help the Michigan Six. In light of the Supreme Court's decision in *Yates,* the Court vacated the Sixth Circuit decision and remanded the case for reconsideration in light of the Court's new precedent.[113] Not surprisingly, Justice Clark dissented. In March, the Sixth Circuit ruled that the convictions had to be thrown out and the case retried. The Department of

Justice determined that it had insufficient evidence to support a new prosecution, and all charges against the Michigan Six were dropped.[114]

Vindication next came for Senator Nowak. In a 6–3 decision authored by Justice Harlan, the Court reversed the conviction and restored Nowak's citizenship. The Court was critical of the weak nature of the government's evidentiary case and of the circuit court's failure to give appropriate legal weight to the basic right of citizenship.[115]

The trilogy of Nowak, the Michigan Six, and the Trucks Act litigation was an extraordinary series of accomplishments for one relatively small firm in Detroit, Michigan. Goodman reflects, "Looking back, I'm somewhat amazed that we could handle these major cases with our small firm and limited resources. But this was why George, Mort, Dean, and I started the firm in the first place. This is why George went to prison." The Trucks litigation and Crockett's incarceration were particularly connected in Goodman's mind. "Somehow, when I think of Trucks, I think of George and the day he went to prison. It's almost as if we dedicated the case to him. Trucks was a great ultimate victory, not only for our firm and Joe Brown but for the Constitution."[116]

Crockett's Reflections

After the "Battle of Foley Square" and Crockett's imprisonment, he had many occasions to reflect on his involvement. In a speech he gave shortly after his release from Ashland, he showed a strong resolve to fight on. The occasion may also have been the first time he spoke publicly about a future in politics.

> One conclusion is that if the choice is between sacrificing your convictions and going to prison then actually going to prison is not nearly as bad....
>
> You have the fear of how the family is getting along. Well, I didn't have that fear because ... I knew my family would be safe. You ask yourself whether you should ... hold fast to your convictions and go to prison. Whether it would be more difficult going to prison or your son saying "my father turned out to be a coward."
>
> Now a lot of people have asked me since I returned why [I] don't have any bitterness.... I have a sense of bitterness but it is

classified as a better understanding of the class nature of our society. My bitterness is not against the puny officials at Ashland. My bitterness is against those who are higher up. As a result of the rest I have enjoyed down there, I am a better fighter in carrying out the program . . . to eliminate such places as Ashland and Milan, [and make] prisons no longer necessary. . . .

If, therefore, I have any contribution to make as far as my city and nation are concerned in the next few months and years, it is to carry on the fight for peace, security and prosperity for all. . . .

We have seen the continued movement of this country in the direction of fascism. Yet, so long as they go more and more to the right, I must necessarily be progressing farther and farther to the left.

I am only concerned about the fact that none of the labels shall deter me from what I believe needs to be done around Detroit—and that is to continue this fight in every avenue that is available today whether in the courts or in the field of politics.[117]

In truth, the ordeal for Crockett never really ended. Despite the resolve reflected in his words, the wounds of the Red Scare were deep and would take substantial time to heal. During the years that followed, as he worked toward the "heights" that Judge Dehnke predicted, the *Dennis* case "hounded" him. That said, nothing could ever shake Crockett's internal resolve. Over forty years later, after his life had been changed in ways that few lawyers can know, he spoke about Foley Square and its aftermath with the convictions and the passion he had in 1950. In one respect, he said going to prison was good for him:

I haven't been bothered with fear since then. I don't fear going to jail like you or some others who've never done it. Now, I weigh my choices one way or the other, impartially, and decide—well, if this means going to jail, then I go to jail. I'm still going to do it, if I think it is the right thing to do. Later in my life, having been in prison helped me greatly as a lawyer, a judge, and a man. When I joined the bench, I knew, as a few judges can, what it means to send a man to prison.[118]

Crockett's grandfather, Moses Jenkins (1861– 1934), a farmer and lay preacher.

Crockett's parents, Minnie and George Crockett Sr., circa 1928.

Crockett family: George Jr., mother Minnie, brother John, and sister Alzeda, circa 1913.

Crockett in Hartford, Connecticut, after one year at Morehouse College, 1928.

Morehouse College Yearbook staff, Crockett seated front left, circa 1930–31.

Crockett graduates from the University of Michigan Law School, June 18, 1934.

Crockett's wife, Dr. Ethelene Crockett, with their children, George III, Ethelene, and Elizabeth Ann, 1941.

Crockett and Ethelene, 1956.

Crockett at UAW-CIO office, 1944.

Crockett's "father-in-the-law" Maurice Sugar. (Photo by Isadore Berger)

UAW President R. J. Thomas (seated, center) introduces Crockett as director of the Fair Practices Department. Crockett is standing to Thomas's right, 1944. (Courtesy Walter P. Reuther Library, Archives of Labor and Urban Affairs, Wayne State University)

Sensationalized mug shots of defendants Eugene Dennis, William F. Foster, and Jack Stachel in Look Magazine *article by Attorney General Tom Clark, August 30, 1949.*

Ebony Magazine *features Crockett and Ethelene in their Detroit Lafayette Park home, 1969.*

Crockett in the basement workshop of his Lafayette Park home.

Ebony Magazine *showing Crockett relaxing on his couch at home, 1969.*

Foley Square trial defense lawyers. From left to right: Abraham Isserman, Crockett, Richard Gladstein, Louis McCabe, and Harry Sacher.

Foley Square defense lawyers strategizing over challenging jury selection process.

Life Magazine *courtroom sketch of Judge Medina reading charges to the jury,* October 24, 1949. Life *claimed sketches were the most comprehensive pictorial record of trial.*

Seven of the eleven defendants depicted in Life *sketch: Eugene Dennis, Carl Winter, Robert Thompson, John Gates, Henry Winston, John B. Williamson, and Benjamin J. Davis, October 24, 1949.*

Life *sketch depicts alleged "contemptuous behavior" of defense lawyers: Crockett, Louis F. McCabe, Eugene Dennis (self-represented), Harry Sacher, Richard Gladstein, Abraham J. Isserman, and "Attorney Counsel, Maurice Sugar," October 24, 1949.*

Life *sketch depicts jury forewoman, Mrs. Thelma Dial, announcing a guilty verdict for all defendants, October 24, 1949.*

FREEDOM
IS
Everybody's Job!

The Crime of the Government
Against the Negro People

Summation in the Trial of
the 11 Communist leaders

BY

× GEORGE
W.
CROCKETT, Jr.

(1949)

10¢

Crockett's closing statement in Dennis *published as pamphlet: "Freedom Is Everybody's Job!"*

First formal interracial law partnership in the United States. From left to right:
Mort Eden, Ernie Goodman, Crockett, and Dean Robb, effective January 1951.

Crockett
representing
George L. Ellery
before House
Un-American
Activities
Committee, 1952.
(Courtesy Walter P.
Reuther Library,
Archives of Labor
and Urban Affairs,
Wayne State
University)

Crockett representing
Coleman A. Young
before House
Un-American Activities
Committee, 1952.
(Courtesy Walter P.
Reuther Library,
Archives of Labor and
Urban Affairs, Wayne
State University)

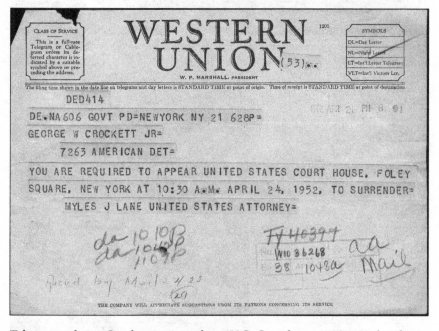

Telegram ordering Crockett to surrender at U.S. Courthouse in New York to begin
prison sentence.

Handcuffed and ready for "perp walk" before the media, the Foley Square lawyers on their way to prison: Abraham Isserman, Crockett, Richard Gladstein, Louis McCabe, and Harry Sacher. (New York Times)

Lorraine Hansberry interviews Crockett about adverse implications of contempt charges on lawyers in civil rights struggle, Freedom 1952.

Goodman firm. Back row, from left: Crockett, Ernie Goodman, Dean Robb, and Mort Eden; front row, front left: Harry Philo, Claudia Morcom, Ty Mackie, and Richard Goodman.

Rev. Martin Luther King Jr. and Dean Robb at Guild-sponsored "Seminar for Lawyers on Civil Rights and Negligence Law," Atlanta, December 1962.

Ernie Goodman and Crockett in the "Confederate Room" of the New Orleans Hilton for a Guild-sponsored law conference, the first integrated law conference in the city's history, October 1962.

Attorney Sam Sporn at Guild's Jackson, Mississippi, office, Summer 1964.

6

Early 1960s

Crockett, the Guild, and Civil Rights in the South

The Aftermath of the "Red Scare"

While the most intense passions of McCarthyism started to fade even before the death of the disgraced senator, the hysteria of the Red Scare remained a defining characteristic of U.S. politics, leaving tremendous damage in its wake. Among its many victims were the National Lawyers Guild (NLG), George W. Crockett Jr., and the Goodman firm itself. As late as 1961, the House Un-American Activities Committee's *Guide to Subversive Organizations and Publications* continued to list the NLG as a "Communist front organization."[1] The NLG was pushed to a point where its continued viability was in question: "From its formative years in the late 1930s, when the NLG boasted 5,000 members and thirty-five chapters nationwide, dues paying membership had fallen by 1957 to just 489 attorneys willing to brave the gale-force winds of the Red Scare."[2] Victor Rabinowitz, former NLG president, reports, "A low point was reached at the 1960 guild convention, where serious consideration was given to dissolving the organization.... This suggestion was quickly put down, but it was a disturbing moment."[3] Only New York, Detroit, and San Francisco continued to have functioning chapters. "Respectable" liberal organizations like the ACLU, the NAACP, and the latter's Legal Defense Fund (LDF) kept their distance.

Thurgood Marshall resigned from the NLG in the early years of the Cold War. His successor at LDF, Jack Greenberg, tells a story that would

169

have been particularly hurtful to Crockett. Marshall resigned because the NLG "passed a resolution condemning Judge Harold Medina for his conduct of the Smith Act trial, in which eleven Communist party leaders were found guilty essentially of being members of the party."[4] Even though the resolution called for an investigation of Medina's conduct, Marshall stated, as he had concerning a similar National Bar Association resolution, that the investigation should be completed *before* the resolution was adopted. According to Greenberg, this explanation was largely pretextual. "Thurgood's reasoning may sound technical, but that was in reality a non-confrontational way to leave the group, of which he disapproved politically."[5]

Not every prominent Black lawyer acted in the same manner. Crockett's friend Bill Hastie, who as a young law school graduate had edged him out of a potential teaching position at Howard Law School, stayed with the NLG. Greenberg explained, "People were Guild members for various reasons. Some, like Bill Hastie, joined in part because, at that time, it was a nonracist alternative to the ABA. Being the man he was, nobody was going to push Hastie into quitting when the Guild came under fire."[6]

For Crockett, the aftermath of the "Battle of Foley Square" endured. It would hound him in different ways for the balance of his career.[7] Like W. E. B. Du Bois (who describes his own life as consisting of four different stages: "the Age of Miracles, The Days of Disillusionment, The Discipline of Work and Play and the Second Age of Miracles),"[8] Crockett experienced ups and downs in his career. He began with an Age of Miracles—Morehouse College, University of Michigan Law School, U.S. Department of Labor, Fair Employment Practices Commission, and the UAW. After Foley Square, he was in the Days of Disillusionment, with no guarantee about what would follow. "It affected my law practice, too, because people wouldn't come to me. . . . You'd have to be a very brave soul to do so."[9] Ultimately, he decided that the stigma of prison was so overwhelming that he would give up the practice of law: "Frankly, I thought it would be too difficult to get re-established and to build up confidence."[10] Crockett had a lifelong love for carpentry and went to see a friend about a job as a cabinetmaker. His friend listened to his reasons for wanting to stop practicing law and then wisely advised, "We need you more as a lawyer than we do as a cabinetmaker. So I'm not going to encourage you to leave the law by offering you a job as a cabinetmaker."[11]

In later years, Crockett claimed that his *Dennis* involvement set his career back a decade: "I had to spend about ten years rehabilitating myself and convincing people that I was a good lawyer that they could come to and trust."[12] Goodman concurs: "Although George returned and practiced law . . . he seemed to lose an interest in the law that he never regained."[13] Goodman recalled that "he more and more came in and went into his office and closed the door and didn't keep it open as the office did": "We had a feeling that he wanted to be left alone—even with his partners."[14] The problem became so serious that Goodman, on behalf of the firm, took Crockett out for a long lunch and told him that "he was creating an atmosphere which was not healthy for him or healthy for the firm." The proposed resolution was for Crockett to "to get involved in local organizations and politics."[15] What this meant in practice was not clear.

The Goodman firm was another victim of the Red Scare. Reuther's purge of Maurice Sugar and others at the UAW and the UAW's subsequent boycott of the Sugar firm were devastating to Sugar personally and led to the destruction of his loose confederation of practicing lawyers. The firm of Goodman, Crockett, Eden & Robb was spawned in crisis. It responded in a reactive manner, largely as a matter of survival. Serendipitously, however, it cobbled together an innovative portfolio of work including workers' compensation and negligence cases, led by Eden and Robb, that enabled the firm to cross-subsidize the civil rights work led by Goodman and Crockett. As the 1950s came to a close, however, the Goodman firm had to ask serious questions about its own future and its reasons for existence.

The tensions inside the firm were reflected in an interesting exchange of letters between Ernie Goodman and his son Dick. In 1959, Dick Goodman, now a lawyer himself, critically assessed what he thought the firm's problems were in a series of letters with his father: "The position of the firm after the collapse of the labor law work had not been clear." Dick worried that "the firm and some of its partners had fallen into a rut. . . . [George Crockett] seemed 'immobilized' by the politics of the Red Scare and needed to 'pull himself out of his tremendous intellectual rut and start thinking again.'" Dick further challenged his father to "rethink the firm's future course." Ernie responded in an equally frank and honest manner. "There is a place for you here if you want it," Goodman told his son. "If I have given the impression that I feel too old to embark on new projects or entertain new ideas—perish the thought. I am thinking, examining, and seeking."[16] As these letters were exchanged, a new day was already dawning.

From the Red Scare to the Civil Rights Movement

Crockett, the NLG, and the Goodman firm would all ultimately find renewed energy, motivation, and purpose from the same source: the emerging fight for civil rights in the South. The struggle for racial justice had been Crockett's main passion since his youth. His oratory on the Civil War amendments helped finance his Morehouse education and chart his course to law school. He founded a new NAACP chapter in West Virginia and employed litigation as a tactic to integrate public facilities. While some people might classify him as a labor lawyer in light of his time at the Department of Labor, the Federal Fair Employment Practices Commission, and the UAW, his work was primarily at the intersection of labor law and racial discrimination. As the only Black lawyer on the Foley Square team, he constantly highlighted issues of civil rights and racial justice as central themes in his opening and closing statements. With the NAACP's 1954 victory in *Brown v. Board of Education* and the 1955–56 Montgomery bus boycott, the nation's attention started to focus on civil rights. Crockett was well aware of these developments. His lifetime participation in the National Bar Association gave him an excellent platform to remain informed and engaged.

The student-led sit-in efforts to desegregate lunch counters in 1960, followed by the Freedom Riders' trips south to integrate interstate bus transportation the next year, sent a jolt through the nation, as well as the "establishment" in the civil rights community. For years, the NAACP had followed a methodical, well-calculated, and tremendously successful litigation strategy to integrate schools and other public facilities. In tandem, individuals like Dr. Martin Luther King Jr. and his organization, the Southern Christian Leadership Conference (SCLC), plotted carefully organized campaigns to advance civil rights objectives. The sit-ins and the emergence of groups like the Student Nonviolent Coordinating Committee (SNCC) and the Congress of Racial Equity (CORE), with its Freedom Rides, however, indicated that new forces, energies, and tactics were afoot.

While much has been written about the impact that youth activism had on civil rights organizations and the civil rights movement, less attention has been paid to the implications these developments had for the nation's lawyers. As the civil rights movement took a more proactive stance, expanding the scope and intensity of its work, the need for lawyers on the front lines, particularly lawyers who could be as nimble as the activists in the face of crises, increased as well. Tellingly, this was not the traditional role played by civil rights lawyers, and few attorneys were ready to meet the call.

The American Bar Association (ABA), the nation's largest organization of lawyers, was virtually no help. Indeed, the ABA had a history that was downright hostile to the cause of civil rights: "The ABA's relationship with Black lawyers was openly racist—Blacks could not be members."[17] The official ABA policy of exclusion did not change until 1943, but it was not until 1950 that it knowingly admitted its first Black lawyer as a member. No meaningful integration occurred until the mid- to late 1960s.[18] In contrast, the NLG was an interracial bar association since its inception. The NBA was formed in 1925 to support Black lawyers in reaction to discrimination at the ABA. The NBA was committed to civil rights from its very beginning.[19]

As the 1960s dawned, the need for civil rights lawyers in the South was great. George Crockett documented the state of affairs in a letter he sent to the *New York Times* in 1965:

The immensity of the need is disclosed by following figures:

States	Pop. (1960)	All lawyers	Negro pop. (1960)	Negro lawyers
Alabama	3,267,000	2,712	980,271	17
Georgia	3,943,000	4,806	1,122,596	30
Mississippi	2,178,000	2,190	915,743	4
S. Carolina	2,382,000	1,884	829,291	22

The almost 4,000,000 Negros in these four of the most highly segregated states, where the need is greatest, can look (except for the less than a handful of white lawyers) to only 73 lawyers for legal representation in their courageous struggle against concentrated opposition of state and local power.

Even these figures don't plumb the depth of the problem. Not all of these 73 lawyers are in a position to handle civil rights cases. And others can handle only a few and still carry on their law practices. A lawyer who really fights for his client's right not only risks a great deal in becoming (in the eyes of the white community) a party to conspiracy to destroy its way of life; but, in most cases, he must appeal from one court to the next for a chance of ultimate success.

Until the Southern bar takes up its professional responsibilities there can be no possibility of equal justice for millions of Negros in that section of our country.[20]

There were many reasons for the dearth of Black civil rights lawyers in the South. Serious institutional constraints restricted Blacks from access to basic education at the elementary and secondary levels, let alone meaningful access to universities and professional schools. Equally significant is the fact that Blacks who did become lawyers had a very hard time making a living.[21] Crockett faced these obstacles, typified best perhaps by his law school professor's recommendation that he take courses in family law because that would be his most likely area of stable employment. Crockett struggled to make a living in private practice in West Virginia and again in Detroit after being forced out of the UAW. His government salary at the Department of Justice and the FEPC provided him financial stability, but these types of jobs were the rare exception for Black lawyers, not the rule.

Black civil rights lawyers, on the other hand, could often barely pay the bills. One need only recall that in 1951 Goodman and Crockett struggled mightily to get paid $554.61 for actual expenses paid from the Civil Rights Congress for their pro bono representation in the Willie McGee capital case in Mississippi. Crockett's wry quip could have been made by nearly every Black civil rights lawyer in the country: "If we hope to stay around to render legal services at greatly reduced rates, we gotta eat and pay rent!"[22]

Conditions were even worse in the South. Black civil rights lawyers risked their livelihoods (as well as their lives) doing civil rights work. They were targets of judges, prosecutors, and opposing counsel in ways that could damage their interests and the interests of future clients. Most Black clients with money would seek white lawyers. Herein lay the dilemma for the civil rights movement. A long-term solution to the dearth of Black civil rights lawyers in the South lay in seeing that these lawyers could make a decent living. With so few white southern lawyers willing to do civil rights work and the obstructionist role of the ABA and southern state bar associations, the short-term solution would have to lay elsewhere: in encouraging lawyers from the North to take up the southern cause.

The Guild's Committee for Assisting Southern Lawyers (1962)

The National Lawyers Guild had always been concerned about social justice, including civil rights, but civil rights had never been its core mandate. The NLG's focus would soon change, in no small part due to the efforts of the Detroit chapter and the leadership of Crockett and Goodman. In 1959, the Detroit chapter of the NLG brought Robert Williams, the leader of the NAACP chapter in Union County, North Carolina, who had been suspended from his duties for advocating that Blacks had a right to self-defense, to speak to the organization.[23] Williams would go on to author the influential book *Negroes with Guns*.[24] In 1961, the Detroit chapter invited the North Carolina lawyer James Walker to speak; the title of his address was "The Role of the Negro Lawyer in the South."[25]

Landmark changes began at the February 1962 NLG national convention, held in Detroit. The NLG is a bar association, not a civil rights organization; but the civil rights movement needed lawyers, and no other bar association in the country was addressing this pressing concern. It was also true that the NLG needed to find a cause that could give it renewed energy and purpose as it entered a new decade. In a bold move, the convention voted to make providing lawyers to the South the major focus of its activities and to devote a substantial portion of its limited resources to that cause.

A memo coauthored by Crockett and Goodman summarized the details:

A Committee to Assist Southern Lawyers was established by the Convention of the National Lawyers Guild at Detroit in February 1962. It has received an original appropriation of over $6,000 by subscription among the delegates.

The purpose of the Committee was to attempt to fill the gap left by the failure of the Bar in the Southern States to provide adequate and effective legal representation necessitated by the massive resistance of the Southern States to the growing desegregation movement.

*   *   *

Having in mind the limited resources of the Guild and the immensity of the problem, the Committee was directed to channel its efforts in the direction of providing legal assistance to Southern lawyers, rather than to attempt to provide direct legal aid.[26]

The committee's interracial leadership team consisted of Crockett and Goodman as cochairs and Len Holt and Ben Smith as cosecretaries. Holt was a Black lawyer from Virginia and a veteran of the civil rights struggle. Indeed, Holt gave a stirring speech at the guild's February convention that brought the members to their feet, building momentum for the new direction of the organization.[27] Goodman recalled that "Holt dramatized the concept of the developing historical struggle by the Blacks in the South to which the Guild should be committed, and he wanted the Guild to come in."[28] Ben Smith was a white lawyer from New Orleans who was deeply involved in the civil rights struggle.

The NLG's new initiative was publicly announced on March 28, 1962, at the First Baptist Church in Petersburg, Virginia, during a rally at which Dr. Martin Luther King Jr. was the principal speaker. Ernie Goodman addressed the crowd:

Those who are seeking to deny Constitutional equality to Negroes are those who possess all the power. And they use this power, without hesitation and with little restraint. Those who possess the constitutional rights but no power and little money, must resist—must defend themselves—must fight back as best they can.

Because the Negro people and their leaders, have chosen the road of non-violent resistance to freedom (by sit-ins, freedom rides, prayer meetings, peaceful marches and lawful boycotts) they are brought (some say "hauled") into courts. They sometimes try to use the legal machinery of our courts—particularly the federal courts—to seek justice.

To defend themselves and to fight back, they need lawyers. Under our law, under the law of practically every nation on earth, even South Africa, they are entitled to lawyers.

But we sometimes deny in practice what we give in theory. Only a few lawyers will take these cases. Some will take them but are not prepared to really fight for the constitutional rights involved— for this would require them to fight against the institution of seg- regation itself.

And the few lawyers who have the courage—the guts—to take these cases have suffered the consequences.[29]

The NLG was charting new territory, and Crockett was taking new lead- ership responsibilities. While the Committee to Assist Southern Lawyers (CASL) was certainly a team effort, with the presence of many talented law- yers and some very large personalities, Crockett was central to the emerging enterprise. There were times when he took a direct role. There were other times when he exhibited quiet leadership, sometimes from a distance, like in the trial of the Michigan Six, overseeing the design, strategy, and tactics of the operation. CASL would be yet another significant episode in Crock- ett's life, as well as a critical but seldom-told chapter in the civil rights movement.

CASL's early activities focused on building the knowledge base and per- sonal relationships that would be essential to its future work. CASL lawyers attended civil rights conferences sponsored by the SNCC in Atlanta and Birmingham. NLG attorneys explained the legal dimensions of the civil rights struggle, conducted basic "know your rights" training, and answered the questions of front-line SNCC soldiers in the struggle. CASL put together a "Handbook for Laymen" that provided easily understandable descrip- tions of legal rights, remedies, and procedures in desegregation cases. In addition, the NLG prepared a "Manual for Lawyers" to guide lawyers in the North and South on how to undertake cases relating to desegregation. NLG lawyers were helping to build the basic legal infrastructure needed to sup- port the movement. While national in scope, this work was being directed by Crockett and Goodman out of their Detroit offices.

CASL's main contribution remained recruiting lawyers to assist on civil rights cases in the South. Many of the cases stemmed from peaceful efforts to integrate businesses. *Abercrombie v. Option* was one such example. The case arose out of an effort by Black and white citizens in Durham, North Carolina, to break down segregation at a local movie theater. The theater owner sought an injunction to restrain picketing and other peaceful efforts to protest segregation. The case demonstrated the benefits of connecting veteran lawyers of the labor movement with those of the civil rights movement. NLG lawyers advocated using the equitable doctrine of "unclean hands" as a defense to the injunction. "This doctrine may permit the attorney in a typical case in the South, where an injunction is sought to prevent peaceful protest of segregation, to prove the illegal character of segregation in the particular circumstances, and thus allow the basic constitutional and moral issues to be openly raised and decided in the injunction proceeding."[30]

Other cases involved defending Black civil rights lawyers themselves who were attacked for taking civil rights cases. Sam Mitchell was a lawyer in Durham, North Carolina, and one of the few attorneys in the state willing to do civil rights work. As a result, he also had a very hard time making a living. He was indicted for failing to file income tax returns. "His failure to file and pay his modest taxes for these years was undoubtedly related to his non-lucrative, harassing work on desegregation cases. Having no defense, he pled guilty, hoping to be able to pay the taxes and penalties out of his current income. The judge, in addition to paying taxes and penalties, imposed a fine of $7,000, more than his tax and penalties combined."[31]

Unable to pay the fine, Mitchell was going to have to serve a year in prison. The NLG lawyer Morton Lesson from Flint, Michigan, was assigned to assist. The trips south were often eye-opening experience for the northern lawyers. "I went to North Carolina thinking that I was going to represent a foolish lawyer who couldn't understand the simple language of the Internal Revenue Code that requires a person to file a tax return on time. I found instead that Sam Mitchell is truly a lawyer's lawyer, whose biggest fault is that he can't refuse to handle cases where the clients can't afford to pay a fee. The result is that his yearly income ranges from $2,200.00 to $4,300.00."[32] Lesson was able to get Mitchell a seven-month extension to pay the fine.

Other NLG lawyers reported equally moving tales. Irving Rosenfeld of Los Angeles traveled to the SNCC civil rights conferences in Birmingham and Atlanta to conduct "know your rights" trainings. With a little flair for the dramatic, he recounted his arrival to the meeting at the St. Paul Methodist Church in Birmingham: "We were greeted at the steps of the church by photographers from the Birmingham Police Department and by many parked police cars, each containing a large fierce-looking police dog. I felt like a 150 Pound of Dr. Ross dog food at that point. The church was surrounded by many police officers." The meeting was closed with a prayer asking the Lord to keep everyone safe as they walked home through the streets of Birmingham. "I could not help but be impressed that for these people, citizens of the United States though they were, a simple walk through the streets of their own home town could be fraught with danger and the fear of harm or death." At the same time, the room was filled with powerful leaders. "Before leaving the church, I had the great pleasure of meeting Rev. Fred L. Shuttlesworth, Jr. (a cofounder of SCLC). He smiled when he shook my hand and said that he was always happy to have lawyers in attendance. In fact, the more lawyers that he had around him, the happier and safer he felt."[33]

CASL was also charged with encouraging other bar associations to join the fight. This was an easy request of the National Bar Association, which had been involved in the civil rights fight long before the NLG. However, it was nearly impossible for the bar associations in southern states and for the nation's largest organization of lawyers, the American Bar Association, to come to the assistance of CASL. On May 26, 1962, at the Mayflower Hotel in Washington, DC, Crockett and Smith met with the ABA Committee on Civil Rights to urge the organization to strongly encourage southern bar associations to take on civil rights cases and defend civil rights workers engaging in lawful protest.[34] The ABA committee members acknowledged the importance of and difficulties associated with persuading their southern affiliates to become more involved. The ABA's only substantive recommendation fell flat, particularly for Crockett: "The Chairman of the Committee stated that at its Boston Convention in 1953 the American Bar Association had adopted a broad resolution calling for the members of the Bar to provide legal assistance for defendants in so-called 'unpopular cases.' While the immediate purpose of the resolution related to pending Smith Act prosecutions, the Committee was of the view that the resolution was sufficiently broad to encompass the present day situation in the South. This was the closest to any approximation the Committee was likely to do."[35]

Crockett knew better than anyone how meaningless the ABA resolution was during the Red Scare and how meaningless the resolution would prove in getting southern lawyers to support civil rights cases.

One of the most significant CASL events in 1962 was its November 30–December 1 interracial legal conference held in Atlanta: "A Workshop Seminar for Lawyers on Civil Rights and Negligence Law." The title of the conference should give lawyers pause, then and now. What is the relationship between civil rights law and negligence law? The answer reflects the innovative thinking of Goodman, Crockett, Eden, and Robb. The perennial question was, "Why are there so few Black lawyers in general and even fewer Black lawyers doing civil rights work in particular?" The difficulty lay in making a living. The Goodman firm had merged civil rights work and negligence law out of necessity at the firm's founding. They were now extending this model to the South as part of a more sustainable framework for lawyers to engage in civil rights work. A key purpose was to "make it possible for more lawyers to accept civil rights cases by making their practice in other areas more lucrative. We believe that if the attorney's proficiency in this area is improved, his income will be improved and he will be more willing to accept civil rights cases." With Dean Robb participating, the conference featured seminars titled "Building a Negligence Practice," "Investigation and Discovery Techniques," "Medical Management," "Evaluation and Settlement," and "The Trial and the Factor of Race."[36]

The overriding purpose of the gathering, however, was civil rights. "The Civil Rights Seminar is not designed as a mere review of previous decisions in civil rights cases. Instead, we expect to emphasize new approaches and techniques for the defense of constitutional rights and liberties and to suggest additional ways in which the judicial process may be used to advance the struggle for integration in American life." This was a gathering for lawyers doing the work, by lawyers doing the work: "The emphasis will be on practice, rather than theory; it is a How-Do-You-Do-It-Conference."[37]

In addition to the NLG, the NBA and the SCLC sponsored the event. It was important for all parties to establish the credibility of their joint efforts. Dr. King was a featured speaker, as well as the Honorable Wade H. McCree Jr., of the U.S. District Court for the Eastern District of Michigan, the first Black judge to hold that position. His presence was another strong endorsement for the movement, as well as an indication of how well respected the NLG, Goodman, and Crockett were in Detroit's Black community.

NLG Lawyers on the Front Lines (1963)

The front line of the civil rights movement was constantly shifting, as was the need for lawyers. In early 1963, one of the front lines was in Birmingham, where Dr. King and SCLC were focusing their efforts. The NAACP's LDF had a long-standing relationship with SCLC, going back to the 1955–56 Montgomery bus boycott. LDF brought expertise and legitimacy to its work, but it also brought a certain top-down way of doing business. The LDF perspective was longer term and at a higher strategic elevation than that of a single lawyer's advocacy centered on the needs of a single client. From the LDF perspective, one waits for the right case, not the first legal case. This inevitably means that many injustices go unaddressed, leading to a type of legal triage that other lawyers find unacceptable.

As 1963 dawned, LDF wanted to exercise greater control over the legal dimensions of the civil rights movement. LDF chair Jack Greenberg explained, "We needed control—where possible—over how demonstration law developed. We didn't want conflicting theories and unattractive facts before the courts."[38] One aspect of this control was an attempt to lock down SCLC as an exclusive client. Top officials of LDF and SCLC met in Washington early in the year. Not surprisingly, SCLC feared external efforts to control its organizing strategies. LDF feared the effects of legal competition. "We promised that we would never tell them what to do, only inform them of the likely legal consequences. . . . From then on SCLC was represented almost exclusively by LDF."[39] Consequently, as civil rights issues erupted in Birmingham and Sheriff "Bull" Connor unleashed his dogs, LDF marshaled the legal work.[40]

Another front in the 1963 civil rights struggle arose in Danville, Virginia. The Virginia-based NLG lawyer and CALS cosecretary Len Holt was at the center of the controversy. Danville was an example of bottom-up movement lawyering. The primary objective was not to use the law to effectuate some broader legal change but to use the law in conjunction with the emerging social movement to radically transform the political and social milieu governing the lives of Danville's Black residents. Socially, Danville was in the heart of the heart of the Deep South. Its white citizens were prepared to defend every aspect of its oppressive racialized hierarchy. For example, when students led a sit-in movement to desegregate the public library, the city closed the library to all patrons. When a federal court ordered the library opened to all, the city removed the chairs and tables from the facility to prevent Black and white citizens from actually sitting together in a public facility.[41]

The Black citizens of Danville were committed to change and used assertive tactics to effect such change. In the summer of 1962, with NLG support, Holt and other local lawyers filed an innovative "omnibus" desegregation suit, challenging the segregation of all local public facilities in a single legal proceeding. The aggressive lawsuit fed the local movement, and the local movement, in turn, fed the legal proceedings. Against this rising tide, local officials ramped up their efforts of oppression, always attempting to give their actions a thin veneer of legality. During the course of the struggle, this became known as the "Danville Formula." First, the judge at the local municipal court issued a temporary injunction forbidding any further demonstrations. Second, the local prosecutor started issuing indictments under a pre–Civil War law known as the "John Brown statute," punishing "any person conspiring to incite the colored population to insurrection against the white population."[42] Finally, the City Council adopted a stringent antipicketing ordinance.[43]

The city's suppression efforts ratcheted up in tandem with the movement's level of resistance until, as Len Holt described it, "all hell broke loose" on June 10, 1963.[44] In defiance of a court injunction against further demonstrations, student-led protests began in the morning with some sixty high school students marching toward city hall, only to be met with firehoses and waves of police. Over fifty students were arrested. The police went so far as to arrest the parents of the student leaders for "contributing to the delinquency of a minor."[45] In response, a mass meeting was held that evening at the Bibleway Holiness Church. Some fifty people, mostly women, marched while singing hymns from the church to the jail, where their children were held. The women knelt in prayer beside the jail. The kneeling women were met with firehoses and beaten by a mob of police and white vigilante men armed with clubs and truncheons. By the end of the day, over two hundred people were arrested and awaiting imminent trial.[46]

The Danville movement was facing a legal crisis. How would the lawyers respond? The struggle, in part, reflected the tensions between the top-down and bottom-up styles of civil rights lawyers. An important meeting was held the following day, June 11, which included representatives of the Danville Movement, Black Danville lawyers, and representatives of the state NAACP, as well as the LDF and NLG lawyer Len Holt.[47] It was intimated that the LDF was willing to do the legal work and cover the expenses, but the funds would not come without strings. Consistent with its more top-down approach, LDF wanted to influence the scope and nature of the Danville Movement's future demonstration tactics. It also wanted to exercise control over who would do the legal work. When asked specifically about the role of Len Holt, the NAACP and LDF responded, "NAACP money can go only to NAACP lawyers, and Holt is not an NAACP lawyer."[48] This was a deal breaker for the local leaders. "'Ol' Snaky'—the Snake Doctor was a nickname affectionately bestowed upon Len Holt by movement people—'is the movement lawyer. If you want to put some people here to work with him, good. Otherwise. We're sorry.'"[49]

The Danville Movement stayed with Holt, and the LDF withdrew support at a critical juncture. The Danville activists may have been acting out of principle in rejecting the LDF offer, but the decision left them in the lurch. Where would they find the legal help they needed? Holt moved to activate his own networks of support. He made two calls. One was to his CASL allies Crockett and Goodman in Detroit; the other was to the progressive New York lawyers William Kunstler and Arthur Kinoy (Kinoy also had strong NLG connections). Immediately, Detroit NLG lawyers Dean Robb and Nathan "Nate" Conyers were dispatched to Danville. They were joined by Kinoy and Kunstler.[50]

A legal strategy meeting was held Saturday, June 15, just two days before the first trial of the arrested protesters was to begin. What could be done to keep the Danville Movement alive in the face of such suppression? This group of lawyers was in no mood for a cautious, defensive strategy working through racist Virginia state courts with only distant hopes of U.S. Supreme Court review. That would take years. By then, the Danville

Movement would be long dead. The lawyers decided on an aggressive two-pronged approach. On one track, they would challenge the constitutionality of the Danville formula—injunctions, the antipicketing ordinance, and John Brown statute prosecutions. On the other track, they would seek removal of all the pending prosecutions of those who were arrested from state court to federal court, under a rarely used Reconstruction-era statute: the 1866 Civil Rights Act.[51] These were bold moves reflecting the necessity of the moment. The lawyers knew they were taking chances, but they also knew they had few other alternatives. Kinoy recalled the moment: "No one asked. 'Can we technically do this? Will it hold up in court?' We just did it. The objective was to fight back, and we as lawyers had to find ways to assist that objective."[52] Moreover, the legal rules that applied in the rest of the country did not apply to Black litigants in the South. The courts and the police did whatever they wanted. As Nate Conyers observed, "This was not the law I was taught at Wayne State."[53]

The Danville lawyers' two-pronged approach began a series of pitched legal battles in tandem with street-level demonstrations. There are a number of excellent accounts of the Danville struggle from June through August 1963.[54] From start to finish, CASL cochairs Crockett and Goodman were deeply involved in the Danville summer. They sent rotating sets of NLG attorneys in and out of the city. "Ernie Goodman and George Crockett were coordinating the efforts from Detroit, including the work of local Guild members who were drafting briefs and petitions for use in Danville. CASL's formal meetings and continued bull sessions in the Cadillac Tower developed strategy and offered advice to the volunteers on the ground, ringing up a substantial phone tab in long-distance calls to Virginia."[55] Nate Conyers recalled that "Crockett called every day and talked with Holt and others.... He was the lifeline."[56]

In 1963, the distance between the needs of the street and the sensibilities of the people in political power was immense. On June 21, 1963, President Kennedy summoned 244 lawyers to the East Room of the White House to examine the response of the nation's lawyers to the emerging civil rights crisis. The conference was held while the city of Danville was still in the midst of crisis. Detroit NLG lawyers George Crockett and John Conyers were in attendance. Presidential recognition of the problem was a significant victory, but the outcome was disappointing to the Detroit attendees.[57]

Establishment powers would be just as happy if the mass protests simply stopped, whether or not underlying injustices were addressed. Moreover, the trajectory of the response of the traditional legal community was nothing like the front-line lawyering the NLG was engaged in at that very moment in Danville. Rather, the crowning achievement of the White House meeting was the formation of the Lawyers Committee for Civil Rights under Law, also known as the President's Committee.

In early October, Crockett and Goodman were convening the second CASL interracial legal conference modeled after the successful program a year earlier in Atlanta. This year the event would be in New Orleans, marking the first integrated meeting of lawyers ever held in the city.[58] In addition to the NLG, sponsors included the state chapter of the ACLU and the Luis A. Martinet Society, an organization of Black lawyers in New Orleans. The conference had a now familiar theme—a dual focus on negligence law and civil rights. One goal was to create an economically stable model in which Black lawyers could engage in civil rights work and still make a living. The conference's primary objective, however, was to further buttress the legal infrastructure required to support the expanding civil rights movement.

As events unfolded, it was difficult to stay focused on the conference agenda. The civil rights movement was increasingly a target of the white power structure in the South, at the local, state, and federal levels. Many of these officials blindly conflated northern support for the southern civil rights cause with alleged communist infiltration of the movement. Crockett, Goodman, and the NLG were already on the list of usual suspects. What unfolded in New Orleans, however, was not just an attack on the NLG and its key Louisiana supporters but a targeted attack on whites generally supporting the cause of civil rights.

In the direct line of fire was New Orleans lawyer Ben Smith, cosecretary of CASL, and his legal partner, Bruce Waltzer, also an active NLG member. On the afternoon of the first day of the conference, Smith got a phone call; he hurriedly spoke with his partner, and both left the room.[59] "More than a hundred state and local police cordoned off the streets in front of the homes and law offices of local Guild activists Ben Smith and Bruce Waltzer. With guns drawn, they began a three-hour search of the two lawyers' files, bookshelves, and personal belongings."[60] Both Smith and Waltzer were arrested. The charges: subversion and failure to register as a subversive organization. These were the exact same Cold War McCarthy tactics of the 1950s. That same day and in a similar manner, the police raided the offices of the Southern Conference Educational Fund (SCEF) and arrested its director, Dr. James Dombrowski. Dombrowski was one of the few white civil rights leaders in the South.[61]

The timing of the raid was no accident. The NLG and SCEF were being targeted in a high-profile manner, as were, by extension, all potential white supporters of the civil rights movement. Kinoy writes, "If the power structure could illegalize SCEF and the Lawyers Guild, they could use the same technique throughout the South. And if being a lawyer for the movement was a 'subversive crime,' no one who lifted a finger to help Black people was safe."[62] The NLG was in the crosshairs, and the stakes were high.[63]

In response, the NLG lawyers employed the same type of aggressive legal tactics they had honed in Danville. With Arthur Kinoy taking the lead, the lawyers filed a complaint to stop the state proceedings using another Reconstruction-era statute that provided federal protection against conspiracies under color of state law to deprive citizens of their rights guaranteed under the Constitution. The complaint charged a conspiracy by state officials "to harass and intimidate [SCEF] members into abandoning their constitutional rights to fight for equality and against segregation in Louisiana."[64] In a hopeful sign that the legal struggles of the 1960s might fare better than those of the 1950s, the legal challenge ultimately succeeded. In *Dombrowski v. Pfister*,[65] the Supreme Court held that the federal courts did have the power to enjoin the state criminal proceedings under the subversion statute as a threat to the parties' First Amendment rights.

While the events in New Orleans were a serious strike against the movement, there was a brighter moment in fall 1963 when it looked like a broader coalition of legal groups might coalesce, including the NLG, to coordinate work in the South. On November 10, 1963, a group of civil rights lawyers met in the Manhattan offices of the ACLU to map out possible collective strategies for the following summer. The meeting included Ernie Goodman and Ben Smith, along with Kunstler and Kinoy, Mel Wulf, legal director of the ACLU, and lawyers having affiliations with SNCC, CORE, and NAACP.[66] There was a respectful desire not to interfere with the work of LDF but also a strong feeling that the field was wide enough for new coalitions and tactics. Participants were interested in the volunteer-based model the NLG had developed and the legal tactics recently deployed in Danville.[67] The group discussed the feasibility of the plan, as well as potential funding. Before moving forward, however, the ACLU lawyers stressed the need to consult with LDF and the newly formed President's Committee about the advisability of the proposed undertaking.

With the response of establishment legal actors still tentative, the NLG moved forward on a still bolder path. The NLG Executive Board met in New York in November 1963. In many respects, the future direction of the organization was at stake. A united Detroit contingent was pushing to make civil rights work in the South the primary focus of the organization and to devote the organization's financial and personnel resources toward that end. A larger but less united New York contingent wanted the NLG to continue to pursue a range of issues. Rabinowitz explained that New York "had developed a full program ranging from social security legislation to concern about nuclear war and the growing East-West tensions on the international front": "No one wanted to drop civil rights issues, but we were not prepared to give up everything else."[68] By a close margin, the proposal to make the civil rights struggle the primary emphasis of the organization passed. The site of the February 1964 NLG national convention was shifted from New York to Detroit. The national convention would help deepen and refine the NLG's new civil rights focus.[69]

The NLG National Convention (1964)

The NLG national convention in February 1964 marked an important inflection point in NLG history. The theme of the convention was "The Legal Revolution: Challenge to the Legal Profession." In preparation, Crockett and Goodman drafted a report on CASL's work over the previous two years and provided a set of recommendations for moving forward. Without a doubt, serious needs in the South remained: "While CASL has served a useful function and has been of practical assistance to a number of lawyers and individuals, it has only scratched the surface of the problem. As of today, it would be a fair conclusion to say that due process and equal justice does not exist in most sections of most southern states."[70] A significant cause of the racial injustice was the ongoing failure of national and state bar associations in the South to ensure the enforcement of constitutional rights. The ABA was largely to blame, not only because of its inaction but for its failure to acknowledge the nature of the underlying injustices.

> The position of the American Bar Association is set forth in its Statement adopted by its House of Delegates on August 13, 1963. It equates the "demonstrations" undertaken by the integration movement with the "action or inaction of public officials who refuse to carry out the mandate of the courts," and places primary emphasis upon "law and order" and the use of the judicial process to attain constitutional rights.
>
> This position of the ABA misinterprets or fails to understand the nature of the problem in the South, and therefore fails to deal with its own responsibility as a bar association. The report fails to recognize that it is impossible to obtain justice in most Southern courts, and the only means presently available to the Negro people is by organized protest and the use of economic and other pressures. Until enough white lawyers in the South are willing to adequately serve the legal needs of the Negro people and to challenge every aspect of segregation; and until the judges are committed to a policy of enforcing federal constitutional rights in their courts and in their decisions, it is hypocritical to urge the Negros to curtail their demonstrations and to rely on judicial proceeding to secure their rights.
>
> The primary duty of CASL, as it should be every bar association, is to take the practical steps necessary to transform the system of justice in the South from one which supports an illegal, unconstitutional system of segregation to one which supports the federal constitution. Only then can the bar think of lecturing Negroes about law and order and the duty of citizens to follow judicial process.
>
> Such transformation of a judicial system is difficult, of course. And we have no illusions that it can take place except in a general climate of social and political change. However, there are things which we, as lawyers, can do NOW, which will give practical assistance and which will carry the seeds of ultimate change.[71]

This was not a time for business as usual. Crockett and Goodman, based on their experience in Danville, advocated more aggressive tactics:

The case-by-case legal attack on discrimination is inappropriate to meet the problem in the South. There is insufficient personnel, insufficient funds and insufficient time for this approach.

Moreover, there is becoming more and more evident a studied pattern on the part of many federal district court judges in the South to engage in unreasonable delays and innumerable dilatory moves before acting upon requests for emergency relief in civil rights cases—relief which frequently involves no more than a local declaration of rights already established in previous Supreme Court decisions.

A more expeditious method must be found to cut through the morass of legalities and lay bare the cancer of state-instituted segregation and discrimination in the South.

Accordingly, it is recommended that CASL undertake responsibility for devising the strategy and doing the necessary research incident to the prosecution of selected all-encompassing judicial attacks on specific, yet far-reaching, aspects of discrimination and segregation.[72]

The report outlined a number of innovative strategies. Building on the experience of Danville, one tactic was to take the "omnibus suit" and direct it at the state level: "A suit challenging the legality of the entire political power structure in a given Southern state which can be shown to systematically exclude its Negro citizens from the full and equal participation in critical aspects of the state or state supported activity."[73] It is impossible to imagine this type of idea being actively discussed at the President's Committee or even the LDF. The NLG was pursuing bold new ideas.

In addition to exploring more aggressive legal tactics, the report recommended that CASL stand vigilant in the defense of lawyers who were facing criminal or disciplinary charges for taking civil rights cases, including the NLG's own cosecretaries, Len Holt, arrested in Danville, and Ben Smith, arrested in New Orleans.[74] Programmatically, the report recommended establishing a southern field representative to work on behalf of CASL and that the "Guild should orient its dues and fund raising toward CASL."[75] In essence, the report advocated that civil rights work become the NLG's primary focus.

R. Hunter Morey, legal coordinator for the Council of Federated Organizations (COFO), was a featured speaker at the convention. COFO was a loose coalition of civil rights groups. Morey outlined COFO's plans for what was being termed the "Mississippi Summer Project," where more than a thousand people would go to the state as volunteers. He expressed an "urgent need" for lawyers to represent COFO workers, in light of the almost certain violent retaliation that was expected. "As Guild lawyers pondered his request, the question arose: what happens when the system of justice breaks down in one part of the country; what is the obligation of lawyers who practice elsewhere?"[76] NLG lawyers were ready to accept the challenge.

The convention enthusiastically supported the CASL recommendations. "Delegates at the Guild's National Convention, held in Detroit February 21–23, voted overwhelmingly to devote the full resources of the organization to aid Negroes in their struggle for equal rights with other Americans."[77] The new course for the organization was clear. "Recognizing the imperative need for legal aid to participants of the 'Negro Revolution' and the general failure of the organized bar to respond to the challenge, the Convention directed the national officers of the Guild to devote their full energies to the development of a three-part program designed to bring about full equality for Negroes in the South, integration within northern communities, and integration within the legal profession itself."[78]

The convention made a number of other important decisions. Ernie Goodman was elected the new president of the organization. The national headquarters of the NLG would move from New York to Detroit to facilitate coordination of the civil rights work. The NLG would open up a regional office in the South to coordinate its civil rights work.[79] Ben Smith was named the new cochair of CALS, joining Crockett. Finally, CALS was renamed the Committee for Legal Assistance in the South (CLAS).

While the NLG was mapping out an aggressive new path, establishment legal groups were moving in a very different direction. For a brief moment in the fall of 1963, it looked like a broad national coalition, including the NLG, would be formed and move forward together. Given the divisions between LDF and NLG and the tensions between top-down and bottom-up forms of movement lawyering, what actually transpired was not surprising.[80] Ultimately, a broad coalition of establishment legal groups came together without the NLG. The Lawyers Constitutional Defense Committee (LCDC) was created, consisting of LDF, ACLU, CORE, the American Jewish Conference, and the American Jewish Committee. Ironically, however, the new organization would employ a model of rotating volunteers in the South almost identical to that pioneered by the NLG in 1962 and 1963.[81]

The NLG and the Mississippi Project (Summer 1964)

Among the Deep South states, Mississippi was by far the worst at protecting its Black residents' civil rights, particularly the right to vote. In 1960, over one million Blacks lived in Mississippi. Although they were 43 percent of the total population, only 5 percent of voting-age Blacks were registered voters. Whites, often through the Ku Klux Klan, White Citizens Councils, and corrupt police and politicians, prevented Blacks from registering to vote by threats, intimidation, and acts of violence, including beatings, murders, and lynchings. In Mississippi, it was generally understood that it was not a crime that anyone would prosecute to kill a civil rights worker or a Black person. Here, civil rights were the exclusive domain of the white man. At the polls, registrars used post-Reconstruction innovations such as poll taxes, so-called intelligence tests, and good-character evaluations to deny Blacks the franchise. Mississippi had only three Black attorneys who would accept civil rights cases, while white court-appointed attorneys would not raise relevant constitutional issues.

With all of these endemic challenges, Mississippi became ground zero for the civil rights struggle in the summer of 1964. COFO would take on voter registration as one of its top priorities. Based on past experience, it anticipated an extremely hostile response. Its workers had been shot, beaten, and arrested by the hundreds on a variety of trumped-up charges ranging from armed robbery to traffic violations. Accordingly, it regarded legal protection for its workers as crucial for the program's success. It was also essential that lawyers be based locally so that the legal responses could be immediate. With the NLG structure realigned so as to be entirely committed to civil rights, CLAS was prepared for its most ambitious undertaking, helping to support COFO's Mississippi Summer Project.

The Mississippi Summer Project was the undertaking of COFO, with SNCC and CORE taking the lead, joined nationally by SCLC and the NAACP, along with numerous state and local organizations in Mississippi. COFO's primary focus was on electoral reform and a massive voter-registration project, but it recognized the need to address a number of other pressing social concerns at the same time. Its "educational and social" programs included most famously the Freedom Schools, "to implant habits of free thinking and ideas of how a free society works."[82] COFO planned for one thousand volunteers, who included college students, teachers, nurses, artists, and legal advisors.

Much of the unity suggested by the name Council of Federated Organizations, however, was more aspirational than anything else. In reality, relationships between the partnering organizations were highly divisive. CORE wanted to make sure that it had a coherent geographic area in which it could work (and raise funds). As a result, CORE was assigned the Fourth Mississippi Congressional District, with counties including the cities of Canton, Meridian, and Philadelphia. "Into this area, CORE placed 20 field secretaries; it paid their salaries but, otherwise, made only minor contributions to the over-all budget of COFO."[83] Support from other national organizations was similarly lacking. "The NAACP contributes neither staff nor money to COFO programs."[84] Roy Wilkins, executive director of the NAACP, "privately distrusted the militant leaders of Freedom Summer and quietly withheld staff and funds from the campaign."[85] SCLC's presence was similarly light. In the end, COFO was really a SNCC project. As Len Holt reported, "Civil Rights in Mississippi is COFO. SNCC for all practical purposes, is COFO. And SNCC is people."[86] SNCC staffed all four remaining congressional districts.

The divisions within COFO mapped onto divisions within the legal community supporting the Mississippi Summer Project. SNCC was the primary motivating force and the principal decision-maker on the ground. While LDF had a near exclusive relationship with SCLC to do its legal work, it had no comparable relationship with SNCC, although it desired one. SNCC, however, quickly made it clear, as a matter of principle, that it was willing to accept legal help from anyone willing to provide it—including the NLG. One of the first activities of the NLG's newly formed CLAS in 1962 was to dispatch three NLG lawyers—Len Holt, Irving Rosenfeld, and Vic Rabinowitz—to SNCC conferences in Atlanta and Birmingham. There were multiple sessions of intense interaction between the SNCC student leaders and the NLG lawyers. "Over meals, into the night, the questions and answers flowed as the SNCC staff gulped in the presence of the three Guild Lawyers, who were responsive, unaloof and 'regular' and seemed to know *where it is at*."[87] This was in sharp contrast with other movement lawyers SNCC had worked with. "Why aren't the NAACP lawyers like you guys?"[88]

SNCC's relations with LDF were tenser. SNCC's executive secretary, James Forman, recalled that SNCC leaders believed that LDF was too defensive and too willing to mirror the positions of the Department of Justice.

> So we were in a box, with almost no one then either willing or able to do the kind of aggressive legal work that we needed done— except members of the Lawyers Guild. During the spring of 1964, the COFO staff—including CORE workers—agreed to use the services of any lawyers we needed and could get. [Bob] Moses [SNCC's leader] then wrote a letter to Jack Greenberg saying that this would be COFO's position. Greenberg sent a strong reply stating that the decision was Bob's, but that the Legal Defense and Education Fund would then pull out of Mississippi.[89]

Greenberg somewhat derisively wrote elsewhere that "SNCC went to any lawyer who would help it."[90] But SNCC recognized that another dynamic was also at play. Not only was the bottom-up movement lawyering of the NLG more in tune with its own tactics, but the very presence of the NLG worked to increase, not decrease, the commitment of legal organizations, like LDF. After LDF threatened to withdraw support, Greenberg reversed his decision.[91] LDF was not about to cede Mississippi to the NLG.

The NLG's Mississippi Summer Program was announced to NLG members on April 15, 1964, and to the public on April 17, 1964.[92] Despite its new focus on civil rights, the NLG was still and would continue to be a bar association. "The Guild is *not* a civil rights organization. It is a national bar association of attorneys, professionally and personally committed for the past twenty-seven years to the defense of the civil rights and liberties of all people."[93] This distinction would govern how it approached its work: "The distinction is important because it explains why the Guild itself cannot become an integral part of a lay defense organization or association of such organizations. Our concern in the Mississippi Project is to attempt to redress the lack of available lawyers in Mississippi ready, willing and able to handle civil rights cases. And we would hope that our example might bring an increasing awareness to their professional obligations to members of the Mississippi bar, which would permit us to reduce and eventually withdraw our commitment."[94]

In relatively short order, CLAS recruited 125 attorneys to volunteer for forty hours of work, some traveling to Mississippi and others to prepare briefs and motions from their home offices.[95] Orientation for the sixty lawyers going to Mississippi was held at Wayne State University in Detroit on June 5–6 with workshops on the Mississippi constitution and statutes, criminal practice and procedure, and habeas corpus and removal problems. The last scheduled "workshop" of the orientation was a cocktail party at the home of George Crockett.[96]

Substantial work was needed to get the NLG's Mississippi Project up and running in time for summer. Most of the responsibility rested with George Crockett, who was also selected to head the NLG regional office in Jackson, Mississippi. There were many pressing logistical challenges. First and foremost, the project needed an office. Space was located at 507½ North Farish Street in Jackson, Mississippi, four rooms over a store. "After a week's work building office cubicles and repainting the premises (supervised by master carpenter Crockett), the office opened for business on 9 June, less than two weeks before the arrival of the first student [COFO] volunteers from the North."[97] An NLG publication concedes, "Let us say it is unpretentious. That is certainly the most charitable way to describe the Guild's new field office."[98] What it lacked in amenities it made up for in personnel. "The office will be under the immediate supervision of Guild vice president George Crockett of Detroit. He will be assisted by attorney Lawrence Warren of the Michigan Bar, Michael Starr, a student at Georgetown University Law School and Miss. Cornelia McDougald, a student at Harvard University Law School."[99] Larry Warren was law clerk to Michigan's first Black Supreme Court justice, Otis Smith, who was loaning him to the Mississippi Project for the entire summer.[100]

Everyone understood the seriousness of the undertaking. The NLG volunteer lawyers and the thousand COFO student volunteers were walking into hostile territory, and the white power structure was prepared. "The Jackson *Daily News* and other news media had characterized the coming summer volunteers as an invasion. The City of Jackson, Mississippi, took this literally: the police force was expanded from 200 to 390; Mayor Allen Thompson bought 250 shotguns, and the mounts for them were installed in squad cars and motorcycles."[101] As Goodman announced the CLAS project to NLG members, he also warned them of the dangers: "Mississippi officials are prepared for all-out resistance. According to *Newsweek* (2/24/64), the mayor of the capitol city of Jackson boasts of a 'riot-trained police force' which is 'twice as big as any city our size'; the acquisition of two 'detention compounds' for 'demonstration POWs'; and a specially built '13,000 pound armored battle-wagon.'"[102]

Demonstrators were often not safe on the streets, but they could be under even greater threat if they were arrested and placed in jail. COFO volunteer Eli Hochstedler signed a chilling affidavit on April 21, 1964: "On Thursday April 6, Marian Gillon, Negro, and I, Eli Hochstedler, white, were attempting to integrate the Jackson Municipal auditorium to attend the Holiday Ice Show. We were charged with Breach of Peace."[103] Both Gillon and Hochstedler were sentenced to six months in prison. In Hochstedler's first night in jail, the jailer made sure that the other white prisoners understood why he was in prison. He detailed a horrendous beating in the prison cell by the other white inmates. "I was told that they were going to show me and any other people from the North thinking about coming down to stir up trouble, what would happen to them if they came."[104]

Against this backdrop, it was Crockett's job to orient and supervise lawyers coming into a hostile state. In one respect, his instructions were dispassionate and matter-of-fact, but in another sense, given the obvious tensions, they were chilling:

All attorneys coming to Mississippi on the Guild's project will come first to the Jackson office and receive their assignments from that office. As nearly as practicable, they will be transported by automobile to the community where their services are needed and they will be accompanied at all times by either another lawyer or a law student.

It should be realized that living accommodations for civil rights attorneys in Mississippi are not likely to be ideal. None of the white hotels will be available to an attorney who is known to be sympathetic to the civil rights struggle: and Negro hotels are practically nonexistent. Moreover, local mores outside of Jackson tend to frown on white persons living in the homes of Negroes. To some extent the experience of the "Freedom Riders" have tended to alter this picture and in the City of Jackson, it is accepted that white people interested in the civil rights struggle will be furnished living accommodations with Negro families. Also, Negroes and whites in Mississippi do not frequent the same restaurants. As of this writing, two (2) Jackson restaurants are "open" to interracial groups.

Wherever it is necessary, therefore, that living accommodations be provided in communities other than Jackson, such arrangements will be made by the Council of Federated Organizations District Leadership; otherwise the attorney will return to Jackson where such accommodations will be available at all times.[105]

Crockett also admonished that the lawyers were going as lawyers and were to conduct themselves accordingly: "We must at all times demean ourselves in a matter befitting our status as lawyers. Attorneys should not become active participants in demonstrations, picketing and other lay activities in which it is reasonable to expect that they later may be called upon to represent professionally persons charged with law violations as a result of such activities."[106] There was a specific geographic footprint in which the work would be staged: "CLAS lawyers operated primarily from three bases in the field—Greenwood, Hattiesburg and Meridian—serving as a sort of 'House Counsel' to the COFO workers and to the local Negros involved in the Freedom Movement."[107]

No orientation program, no matter how good, could completely prepare a volunteer for what was waiting in Mississippi. How does one, including Crockett himself, prepare for the fear that waited? "'I would be lying if I said I wasn't afraid when I first went down there,' Crockett admitted years later. Called upon almost immediately to secure the release of a local civil rights worker arrested in Hattiesburg, Crockett asked himself ('trembling like I don't know what') how the arrival of a black attorney from

Detroit would be received in the Piney Woods of Mississippi?"[108] When abstract fear confronts the reality of oppression, radical transformation is possible. "It was his client's dire condition after only one night in jail that snapped Crockett out of his nervous state. '[He] took off his shirt to show me the welts across his back, how he'd been beaten.'" Crockett filed a petition for habeas corpus. "'After that,' Crockett remembered, 'I wasn't afraid, just angry.'"[109]

On June 14, the first NLG lawyers, Don Loria from Detroit and Charles Markels from Chicago, arrived at the newly opened Jackson office.[110] The next day, they were on assignment to Meridian, Mississippi, eighty miles to the east. Some thirty-five protesters had been arrested for obstructing the sidewalk while picketing three national five-and-dime stores.[111] Meridian was in the CORE-staffed congressional district. Before going to court, Loria and Markels met with and were briefed by the CORE local organizer Michael Schwerner. The husband-and-wife team of CORE organizers Michael and Rita Schwerner had been working in the city since January. "Michael and Rita Schwerner were staunch CORE people. They had a passion to change things: to change things *now*."[112] The Schwerners were teamed up with James Chaney, a twenty-one-year-old Black man and native of Meridian. "'Chaney was one of our best men,' CORE's James Farmer said. 'He was a native of Mississippi. He was a child of the soil. He knew his way around. He was invaluable.'"[113]

In court, the NLG lawyers challenged the clearly segregated nature of the proceeding, the "blocking the sidewalk" statute itself for being "void for vagueness," and the fact that the prosecution was in violation of the defendants' First Amendment rights. They also challenged the factual predicates of the proceeding. "They argued that the young demonstrators, walking in single file with small cardboard signs, were no more blocking the sidewalk than the portly police officer who arrested them."[114] As was becoming the norm in such civil rights cases, just like in Danville, Virginia, the case was ultimately removed from state to federal court.

While Loria and Markel were defending the demonstrators, Michael Schwerner and James Chaney were preparing to go to the Western College for Women (now Miami University) in Oxford, Ohio (more than seven hundred miles away from Meridian), to participate in the orientation of the first wave of CORE student volunteers. The Oxford training was for the hundreds of volunteers, mostly college students, who were headed south to participate in Freedom Summer. One of the volunteers in the audience was twenty-one-year-old Andrew Goodman, a native New Yorker and student at Queens College. Goodman would be assigned to the CORE town of Meridian and teamed up with veterans Schwerner and Chaney.

As later reported by Louis E. Lomax in *Ramparts* magazine, the orientation leaders did not mince words about the potential dangers that lay ahead. R. Jess Brown, one of the few Black lawyers in Mississippi willing to do civil rights cases, was frank with his warning: "Now get this in your heads and remember what I am going to say. They—the white folk, the police, the county sheriff, the state police—they are all waiting for you. They are looking for you. They are ready; they are armed. They know your names and your description even now, and before you get to Mississippi."[115] Representatives of the federal government made it clear that there was little if anything they could do to ensure the safety of the volunteers. Civil rights lawyer William Kunstler was at the orientation and recalled, "When confronted with the unmistakable evidence of both official and unofficial violence, Attorney General Robert F. Kennedy consistently maintained that the Justice Department did not have the power to do any more in Mississippi than it was doing—which was very little. During my trip to Oxford I heard John Doar, the second in command at the Department's Civil Rights Division, reiterate the refrain at one of the orientation sessions in Peabody Hall. 'We simply do not have the necessary tools,' he explained to his frankly incredulous audience, 'to cope with the problem.'"[116] The students were heading into a hostile land, and there would be very little, if any, external help.

The events in Philadelphia, Mississippi, at the Mount Zion Methodist Church on June 16 illustrated the violence and danger that were unfolding. A number of church elders and their children were meeting in the church that evening. "It was the same church in which the Schwerners had held a civil rights meeting on May 31 to rally support for a Freedom School COFO planned to open in the area." These church members were assaulted and beaten as they left their meeting. Hours later, the church was in flames, burned to the ground by an arsonist.[117]

After the orientation, Goodman joined Schwerner and Chaney for the long drive back to Mississippi, arriving in Meridian the afternoon of

June 20. The trio was immediately met with the news of the Philadelphia church burning. Seeking advice, Schwerner made a hurried call to one of the few sources of legal counsel available—George Crockett, who recalled, "He wanted to know was there any legal recourse for that type of situation. And I explained to him that it might be possible to get some sort of federal proceeding going but we'd have to have more information, and we'd have to have witnesses when we go into court. He said, 'Well, we will go to Philadelphia tomorrow morning, Sunday, and see some of the people who've been at the Freedom School and who attended these churches.' I said, 'All right, you do that and we will come over to Meridian and talk with you on Monday morning.'"[118]

Andrew Goodman was not the only northern volunteer who went to Mississippi that weekend. Crockett was joined by the Detroit lawyers Anna Diggs, the wife of Michigan congressman Charles Diggs, and Claudia (Shropshire) Morcom in the Jackson NLG office. Morcom, a 1956 graduate of Wayne State University Law School, joined Goodman, Crockett, Eden & Robb in 1960 as its first Black female associate.[119] With the first large wave of volunteers arriving, Freedom Summer was now a reality.

While some violence was anticipated during the Mississippi Summer Project, no one anticipated the horrendous events that were about to unfold. On June 21, Schwerner, Chaney, and Goodman left the Meridian COFO office to examine the just-burned Black church in Philadelphia, Mississippi. They wanted to boost the spirits of the residents and maintain momentum for the Freedom School. As Crockett had suggested, they also wanted to gather information that might facilitate an FBI investigation or other federal action.[120] By noon that Sunday, they were at the burned-out church. Sometime after 3:00 p.m., on their way back to Meridian, they were arrested by a Neshoba County deputy sheriff and placed in jail. Sometime after 10:00 p.m., they were released from jail and shortly thereafter fell into the hands of a murderous mob.[121] They were never seen alive again. Their disappearance touched off a statewide search by both federal and state organizations.

Two days later, on June 23, three CLAS lawyers, George W. Crockett Jr., Anna Diggs, and David Finkel, along with two law students, went to Philadelphia to interview Sheriff Lawrence Rainey and inquire into the church-burning incident. Rainey was later implicated and charged with conspiracy in the three slayings. According to Diggs, "We felt that as attorneys we could accomplish such a routine task without the difficulties encountered by the COFO students, to whom the sheriff had given conflicting stories."[122] Before the CLAS contingent could enter the courthouse, however, a crowd of a hundred people closed in on them. They were asked their identity and reason for being there. When Crockett led the contingent into the sheriff's office, the hallways were so filled with townspeople that, Diggs recalled, "we were effectively intimidated by their number and threatening attitude before a word was exchanged with the sheriff."[123] After Crockett introduced each member of the group to the sheriff and stated the reason for their appearance, the sheriff said that there had been no injuries at the church and that the state was investigating. The sheriff then gave them directions to the burned-out church, but according to Finkel, "he gave them so loud, he obviously was telling everyone in the courthouse we were going there."[124] Crockett made an appropriate change of plans. "When we came out of the Sheriff's office, there was unanimous consent. . . . We ain't going to look for any church. We are going to get the hell out of here and get back to Meridian."[125]

Later that night, after returning to the Jackson office, Diggs wrote to President Lyndon Johnson for help. In her telegram, she related the incident in Philadelphia earlier that day, the connection with the missing civil rights workers, and how desperately direct federal protection was needed:

Dear Mr. President:

I would like to report my experience as an attorney, a negro, and as the wife of a United States Congressman, in Philadelphia, Mississippi on June 23, 1964. I went there, a volunteer legal counsel from Detroit. . . .

On arrival in Jackson, I was assigned to the investigation of the burning on June 16th of the Mt. Zion Church and the reported pistol-whipping of its member in Philadelphia. . . .

Our group had sent the three civil rights workers who disappeared in Philadelphia on June 21st to locate possible witnesses for interview by our attorneys.

Attorney George W. Crockett Jr., of Detroit, Attorney David B. Finkel of Los Angeles, Mr. George Johnson, a Yale Law Student and my brother, Lowell Johnston, a Harvard Law Student, accompanied me to Philadelphia on June 23rd to interview its sheriff and inquire into the church burning. . . .

On arrival at the Philadelphia court house, we were instantly made to realize that no civil rights lawyer was welcome in town. Mr. Crockett was temporarily blocked from the Sheriff's office by an assembled crowd outside its door. By the time we were able to enter the Sheriff's office townspeople had crowded in and filled the hallways so that before a word was exchanged with the Sheriff we were effectively intimidated by their number and threatening attitude. . . .

Nevertheless, Mr. Crockett introduced each of us to the Sheriff, stating our business. The Sheriff advised that there had been no injuries at the church and that the state was still investigating. He would not escort us to the church but gave directions to its site. Because the crowd inside and out of the courthouse had grown so large and hostile, we left at once to avoid incident. . . .

Were it not for the fact that another civil rights lawyer had been detained the previous day by local townspeople at Mathiston, Mississippi, I would prefer to evaluate our experience as peculiar to the drama of the three missing COFO workers in Philadelphia, but it is apparent that what we experienced is a problem faced by all civil rights workers in their efforts to aid Mississippi Negroes. If lawyers have no safe access to the Neshoba County Courthouse at Philadelphia, it is apparent that the students who are arriving in this state will not be safe without federal protection. Indeed, the fact that we saw not a single Negro on the streets of Philadelphia suggests that local Negroes are in equal peril. . . .

Hence, the purpose of my report to you, Mr. President, is to plead for immediate federal assistance toward halting a blood bath before it grows to mass scale, not by suggesting the ending of the civil rights movement, because it will not be stopped, but by providing federal protection to the citizens of these United States who seek to exercise their rights in Mississippi.

Respectfully yours,
Anna Johnston Diggs[126]

The impact of Diggs's letter is not known. The NLG issued a press release reproducing key portions of the telegram to amplify its effects and its call to action.[127] The day after Diggs sent her letter, the burned-out shell of the station wagon driven by Schwerner, Chaney, and Goodman was found near a swamp.

The killing of the civil rights trio unfolded in the first days of Freedom Summer. As traumatic as these events were, there was still important work to be done. The NLG project continued. Volunteer lawyers would typically fly into Jackson on Sunday and begin their orientation in the car, while Crockett drove them to the office. "'Most of the trip was spent trying to quiet their fears,' said Crockett, 'without at the same time making them complacent.'" It was important they always kept in mind their role as a lawyer in the struggle. "We constantly had to remind them that their job was to get people out of jail and not land there themselves."[128] Crockett was a critical anchor for the Guild program during a turbulent summer. "George was the perfect man for the job. He walked into a tense situation in Jackson and kept his cool throughout," reports Victor Rabinowitz. "Everytime I saw George, he was impeccably dressed in a white suit; he was probably the only man in Jackson who wore his white Panama hat every day, whatever the temperature."[129] He was a calm and steady presence.

There was much work to be done. The NLG lawyers "were on hand to put out fires—get people out of jail, arrange bail or present removal papers before the appropriate Federal Judge in time to head off a trial in the first instance."[130] What happened in Greenwood, Mississippi, is illustrative. "Crockett would receive a call from COFO legal department: 'Ninety-eight arrested at a Freedom Day in Greenwood,' and the Guild office would begin to hum."[131] The Jackson office would contact the two lawyers already stationed in Greenwood and relay the facts. "Legal forms had to be run off on the mimeograph machine. . . . One of the law clerks had to research the statute that the 98 were accused of violating; another had to gas up the Guild station wagon for a drive to Greenwood with the bail money."[132] While defenses in state court were planned, removal of the proceeding was simultaneously being sought in federal court. Ironically, speed with bail money was particularly important for white protesters. Crockett explained that the white worker would "usually share a cell along with other white inmates, who, having been alerted by the guards that he is a COFO worker, are likely to beat him."[133] That said, the mere presence of northern attorneys seemed to temper some of the more serious abusive practices.

Not surprisingly, the large influx of northern lawyers triggered resistance from local attorneys. Mississippi did not lack lawyers; the state lacked lawyers willing to do civil rights work. Even when white lawyers would represent Black clients in criminal matters, they would seldom, if ever, raise basic constitutional questions that challenged the institutional racism embedded in southern legal systems. The white lawyers in Mississippi did find one law they desired to enforce. An obscure provision of state law, section 8666 of the Mississippi Code, permitted any two members of the Mississippi bar to challenge the qualifications of an out-of-state lawyer. If this happened, the out-of-state lawyer must withdraw from the case.

Section 8666 was invoked against two NLG attorneys representing seven Blacks arrested for distributing handbills in Columbus, Mississippi, in violation of a recently enacted city ordinance banning distribution of literature without a city permit. The handbill consisted of explanations of provisions of the newly enacted federal Civil Rights Act. Crockett wrote a letter to the bar association of Lowndes County, where Columbus is located. After reciting well-known facts about the absence of effective legal representation for Blacks in Mississippi and the justification for the NLG program, he outlined the qualifications of the challenged lawyers: "Mr. McGee was for several years an Assistant State Attorney for Cook County (Chicago), Illinois, and Mr. Shapiro of New York City has extensive experience in the litigation of cases presenting constitutional issues."[134] He chided the lawyers making the challenge for failing to raise the clear manner in which the new local statute violated the First Amendment rights of the defendants. Finally, he called on the lawyers to refrain from future challenges until members of the local bar were willing to provide effective representation.

> However, there will undoubtedly be many more arrests and criminal prosecutions of civil rights workers in the coming months, both in your county and in other areas of Mississippi. If local counsel continues to file petitions under Section 8666, those defendants will be effectively deprived of counsel. We therefore urge that unless and until competent local counsel are prepared to volunteer to defend those prosecuted without fee and to raise and

diligently press the constitutional and federal issues involved, they be requested by your Association to refrain from filling petitions under Section 8666 where it is obvious that the out-of-state attorney is evidently qualified to handle the matter and is volunteering his services.[135]

Obviously, one could not wait on the good graces of the Lowndes County Bar Association. The NLG lawyers removed the case to federal court, where the federal constitutional claims could be pursued and the rights of the individuals to choose their own lawyers could be respected.

The larger problem of these challenges remained. Section 8666 was a threat to the NLG's work and to all other programs sponsoring northern lawyers. A collective challenge to the practice in federal court would be the most effective legal tactic. Such common sense, however, ran headlong into the unfortunate politics dividing the legal community. In a letter to Samuel Koenigsberg, Crockett assessed the situation:

A great deal of interest has been garnered down here in favor of filing the suit which you proposed to challenge the constitutionality of Section 8666 of the Mississippi Code. We had proposed to Mel Wolf [of the ACLU] and lawyers [of the President's Committee] that we work on the suit as a cooperative venture since it concerns both of our programs. I feel confident that Mel was in favor; but I am equally confident that he has met opposition among some of the "top brass" in his outfit. Accordingly, I have had several unofficial comments to the effect that they intend to file their own suit.[136]

As a result, the NLG filed its own suit to challenge the provision.

Throughout Freedom Summer, there were numerous calls for greater federal protection for civil rights workers. In the wake of Anna Diggs's letter to the president, NLG president Ernie Goodman wrote an open letter to President Johnson on July 14. The letter refuted the government's claim that it lacked appropriate legal authority to intervene in Mississippi and appended an NLG legal memorandum justifying the guild's legal analysis: "We respectfully submit that the Memorandum establishes that the Federal

Government does have explicit and adequate powers by which it can protect the voting rights of the Negro citizens of Mississippi, or any other
State, through the use of whatever Federal agencies it deems necessary to
overcome systematic resistance to the execution of Federal law or the exercise of Federally protected rights." The letter called for federal "powers to
be used with all possible speed in order to bring to an end the intimidation
of voters in Mississippi and those who would assist them in voting."[137]

Sadly, very little federal protection was forthcoming. On August 4,
1964, the dreadful moment everyone feared but knew was inevitable finally
arrived. The bodies of Michael Schwerner, James Chaney, and Andrew
Goodman were found buried in a newly constructed dam. It was clear
from the start that the abduction and killing of the trio was a lynching,
orchestrated and executed by an age-old conspiracy between the Ku Klux
Klan and southern law enforcement. The timing of the attack, at the very
start of the appearance of northern COFO volunteers, was also no accident.
William Kunstler noted, "From the moment of their disappearance, I was
convinced that the three civil rights workers had been killed in order to
stop the thousand COFO volunteers who were to follow them."[138] Fortunately, it was equally true that the Klan conspiracy had failed and that fear
and intimidation did not stop Freedom Summer. "But, to the everlasting
credit of the volunteers and their families, there were no defections. Two
days after Mickey [Michael], Andy and James had disappeared, hundreds of
frightened but resolute college students were proceeding to their assigned
projects throughout Mississippi."[139] Equally true is the fact that the bravery
and dedication of the volunteers was more than matched by that of the
COFO workers and the Black citizens of Mississippi.

Working in tandem with COFO, the NLG's Mississippi Summer Project was a tremendous success. Under Crockett's leadership, from its inception to its end on August 30, 1964, the NLG office handled forty-five cases
involving 315 defendants. Sixty-six lawyers participated, as did four law
students, with lawyers like Carl Maxey coming from as far away as Spokane,
Washington. The bulk of the lawyers, twenty-three, were from Michigan, and
fifty-four were NLG members; twelve were women, and fourteen were Black.
Each typically served for a week. Among the eleven lawyers from Detroit
were four future judges: George W. Crockett Jr., Warfield Moore, Claudia
Morcom, and Anna Diggs. Morcom and Diggs received some celebrity

attention when they were featured on the cover of *Jet* magazine with the headline, "Women Lawyers to Aid Mississippi's 'Freedom Corps.'"[140]

The lawyers were often too busy to be scared, but the dangers were real. While Morcom was fully aware of what she was facing, as a Black woman, she believed that it was even more dangerous for Crockett to be in Mississippi in 1964: "If you're a black male, it doesn't matter if you're a professional or a lawyer or anything else, you still are in jeopardy." She considered Mississippi a virtual police state: "Our phones were tapped. We were constantly watched, and the local police, along with the FBI, refused to respond to the obvious lawlessness." In reflecting on the important contribution they made, Morcom said, "I don't think we even understood how much impact that we had on Mississippi as lawyers at that time because we were too busy. We were running all over the state representing people, trying to get them out of jail, trying to get bail for them. And it wasn't until later when we could look at what had been accomplished, that we understood George Crockett had created history with what he did and what he was able to build in Mississippi."[141]

The accomplishments were many. The mere presence of the lawyers functioned as a partial deterrent. "'There have not been nearly so many arrests this summer,' said Crockett, 'and certainly not as much police brutality and harassment as did exist here last summer.'"[142] Moreover, the joint efforts of the lawyers and the civil rights workers helped create a sense that legal rights have meaning. "The 'lift' given to Negroes and sympathetic Southerners was invaluable. Not a small part of the profound impact of the summer project is the undeniable *preventative* effect of the project: no longer can legal rights be violated with impunity and courtroom behavior be so lax. If no other achievements are credited to the project, this new respect, this new appreciation of the inviolability of the rights of even the lowest and the poorest has changed for all times the legal climate pervading the courts of Mississippi."[143] All participants realized, however, that much work remained to be done. "The project, a giant act of love, has already cracked for all time the walls of exclusion and hate in Mississippi. Much, much more will be required before they crumble."[144]

The work was also exhausting. With the CLAS office closed on August 30, a bone-weary, frustrated Crockett returned to Detroit from what he called a "hell-hole."[145]

The NLG in Mississippi after Freedom Summer

Plans for the CLAS's next chapter were being made even before the Jackson office had closed its doors. In an August 12, 1964, letter to Goodman, Crockett mapped out the strategy. Noting that there were twenty-five cases pending with as many as two hundred clients, he observed, "Obviously, our 'Mississippi Program' must continue until these cases are completed."[146] The letter sought to balance a number of competing tensions in the work. Clearly, the civil rights needs in the South were substantial and would probably only increase. "There also is a growing feeling, commonly shared, that greatly increased repressive actions on the part of State officials and the various anti-segregation organizations can be expected after the conclusion of the Summer Program. . . . Hence, the Guild's Southern program also must contemplate some setup which will permit us to assist in this connection whenever and wherever needed in Mississippi."[147] Additional tensions lay in the ongoing, contested relationship between the NLG and other national legal groups. This relationship was complicated and contradictory. Ironically, the NLG's presence actually helped ensure the ongoing commitment of establishment legal groups. "The feeling at COFO is that the presence of the Guild has been primarily responsible for the large number of lawyers brought or sent into the state by other lawyer groups; and they would like some sort of arrangement whereby the Guild was still available to help and thus furnish pressure on LCDC and the Legal Defense Fund to make a maximum effort here."[148] LDF's animosity toward the NLG remained strong. "The antipathy the leadership of the Legal Defense Fund has for the Guild is such that, I am told, any increase in lawyer personnel in Mississippi will be made and financed by that Fund if this insures the absence of the Guild. On the other hand, however, the Legal Defense Fund is adamant in its refusal to follow through on any of the cases handled thus far by the Guild."[149] These tensions would not be resolved.

The NLG office in Jackson reopened in October 1964. Claudia Morcom returned to Mississippi to head the project and continue, in heroic fashion, the mission that Crockett had begun. "I told Crockett that I had family in Mississippi, that as a woman I felt reasonably safe, and since someone had to do it, I'd be a good choice."[150] Much of the work continued to be the front-line legal defense of protesters. In a memo Morcom typed herself "on an old beat up machine that someone left from the challenge," she outlined the cases that were in the office.[151] One individual had been arrested in Indianola, Mississippi, for distributing fliers without a license. Sixteen individuals had been arrested in Meridian for picketing a segregated hotel. These cases were removed to federal court, where the judge remanded them back to the state. The NLG lawyers appealed that decision to the Fifth Circuit U.S. Court of Appeals. Eighty-six people had been arrested in Indianola for picketing a second-rate segregated public library that had been created only when integration was threatened at the all-white public library. People were charged with disturbing the peace and failure to obey a police officer. Seven people had been arrested in Vicksburg for picketing a supermarket that decided to close its lunch counter rather than integrate it. They were charged with obstructing the sidewalk. These cases "represent arrests arising out of peaceful demonstrations and picketing in protest to segregation and discrimination which still exists everywhere in Mississippi. It is noteworthy that all of these arrests are since the Civil Rights Bill and evidence that there is still going to be a long struggle in Mississippi."[152] The memo also detailed Morcom's first brush with the law: "The law finally caught up with me. I got my first ticket during the challenge when I had the white court reporter from New York with me and one of the white COFO workers. The motorcycle officer who finally stopped the car had been right on our bumper for over twenty blocks.... My big trial is this coming Thursday. Raise the bail money, I may need it."[153] The incident is reported with a sense of humor, but the threats to her security and that of the people she worked with were very real. (Schwerner, Chaney, and Goodman had originally been detained for an alleged traffic violation.)

Part of the Jackson office's new assignment was to help support the ongoing struggle of the Mississippi Freedom Democratic Party (MFDP). The MFDP was an outgrowth of the resistance COFO had encountered in registering voters and trying to work within the traditional party system. As a bypass, the MFDP operated as a separate political party and ran its own registration and voting processes. The intention was to challenge establishment structures and to document the eagerness with which Black citizens wanted to engage the political process. The MFDP gained national attention in late August in Atlantic City at the 1964 Democratic National Convention, when it sought to be seated instead of the Mississippi Democratic delegation. Television broadcasts of the Credentials Committee hearings were riveting. In the end, the MFDP rejected a weak proposed compromise in which the Mississippi delegation would remain seated while the MFDP would be given two at-large seats. MFDP delegate Fannie Lou Hamer made it clear for the world to hear: "We have compromised with compromises too long. We will not compromise now."[154]

The MFDP tried to register its candidates for the fall election and was rejected. Instead, it held its own parallel elections from October 30 to November 2, yielding a slate of MFDP representatives for Mississippi's federal congressional districts.[155] The stage was now set for the MFDP's next challenge to Mississippi's racist political structure: trying to unseat Mississippi's congressional delegation. A team of lawyers consisting of Kinoy, Kunstler, and Ben Smith mapped out the legal strategy. An obscure provision of Title 2 of the United States Code permitted citizens of a state to challenge the seating of a member of the House of Representatives by filing a complaint with the clerk of the House and serving it on the House member in question.[156] The MFDP challenge was filed in December. The next step was to have a member of the House object to the seating of the Mississippi delegation when the chamber reconvened in January. On January 4, 1965, Representative William Fitts Ryan of New York rose to his feet: "'Mr. Speaker,' he began, 'on my responsibility as a member-elect of the Eighty-Ninth Congress, I object to the oath being administered to the gentlemen from Mississippi.'"[157] Although the body voted 276–149 to seat the delegation anyway, the law provided a hearing process to consider the challenge.

The third step was gathering evidence. The law gave the challenger forty days from January 4 to gather evidence and documentation on the systematic exclusion and intimidation of Black voters in Mississippi. Significantly, the challenger wielded federal subpoena power to aid their cause. Documenting evidence requires lawyers. The NLG now shifted into high gear. In what became known as the "deposition caravan," evidence was gathered throughout Mississippi and the country. "The response was magnificent. By the time the first depositions were scheduled, more than 130 lawyers and a sufficient number of court reporters had signed up for Mississippi service."[158] In that short forty-day window, more than six hundred depositions were taken documenting the violence, intimidation, and oppression involved in excluding Blacks from the electoral process.[159]

The NLG's work, however, extended beyond the struggles of the MFDP. The NLG began to plan the Mississippi Summer Project for 1965, which would be significantly different from its 1964 Summer Project. While the Jackson office focused primarily on defensive, front-line representation, the 1965 project outlined a bold new agenda. The NLG recognized that establishment legal organizations were filling the breach first entered by the guild and that its front-line legal efforts might soon be eclipsed in this regard, hence the need for a new plan for the summer. Ernie Goodman wrote, "Our pioneering effort in this area has inspired other lawyers associated with civil rights or liberties organizations to carry out programs similar to that of the Guild."[160] The NLG wanted to continue its leadership role and shift from defensive to offensive legal action.

> It is time for the Guild to move on again and pioneer with a new concept for combatting the continuing inequalities in the South. It is time, too, for the Guild to act, not merely in defense of civil rights, but affirmatively on behalf of those rights. Accordingly, it is proposed that the Guild concentrate its efforts in the South this summer on a program to provide legal assistance to the Negro people in their efforts to enforce Title III of the Civil Rights Act of 1964 which provides for the desegregation of Public Facilities, such as courthouses, libraries, hospitals, public parks, golf courses, etc.[161]

This time, the NLG would partner with the MFDP instead of COFO as its main ally in the litigation. In the midst of the MFDP's challenge to unseat the Mississippi delegation to the House of Representatives, the MFDP also committed to being the boots on the ground to help gather data and make the personal connections needed to support the NLG's desegregation litigation.

The scope of the work was ambitious. "The project consists of bringing together approximately 20 Teams composed of attorneys and research workers. Each Team will assume responsibility for desegregating the public facilities in a given county in Mississippi, Louisiana, Alabama or other selected southern states, including the institution of omnibus law suits pursuant to Title III of the 1964 Civil Rights Act."[162] To outsiders, particularly from the North, the palpably entrenched segregation in the South and the strong powers inherent in the new federal law led the NLG lawyers to expect that these would be easy cases to litigate and win. "Such techniques as interrogatories and requests for admissions will greatly reduce the necessity of oral testimony and might well serve as the predicate for a motion by the plaintiffs for Summary Judgment. Moreover, in many instances it will be found that the kind of discrimination practiced in public facilities is required by state statute and the presumption is that the state statute has been used and observed. Thus, it is anticipated that in most cases the actual 'trial' will be the argument on the motion for summary judgment."[163]

In a prediction that indicated a tremendous level of confidence, tinged perhaps with a bit of optimistic naiveté, Goodman anticipated that these goals could be accomplished within a few months. "It is believed that in most instances the amount of time required for such litigation will not exceed three months and hence, we are hopeful that several counties can be desegregated by the end of the summer."[164] The MFDP issued a press release announcing the joint effort, with Crockett making similarly ambitious predictions. "We hope that the work of these lawyers will be completed by the time the 1965 summer is over."[165]

To be sure, some NLG lawyers raised more cautionary notes while the project was being formed. Charles Markels, one of the first lawyers to arrive for the 1964 Summer Project, thought that the scale of the project was too large; he favored a "pilot" program using the skills of the NLG's most experienced lawyers.[166] Others questioned whether this was the right moment to pivot from voting rights to desegregation in light of where the broader movement was heading.[167] The prominent California NLG lawyer Hugh Manes worried whether they were stepping on the toes of the NAACP and whether there was sufficient support for the project inside Mississippi.[168]

Goodman's best rejoinder to those who were expressing a more cautionary note was to channel the lessons of history: "The promises inherent in the 1964 Civil Rights Act have yet to be fulfilled. That law, adopted last fall as a result of nationwide protest, has no self-enforcement provisions. It can become a dead letter, much as the 13th, 14th, and 15th Amendments did for 100 years, unless the rights guaranteed the Negro people in this law are exercised by them."[169] Despite the caution expressed by some people, there was broad, enthusiastic support among the membership for the NLG's 1965 Summer Project. Everyone knew that aggressive lawyering would be necessary to give meaning to the new Civil Rights Act. Goodman proclaimed, "The lack of lawyers in the South who are willing to institute such affirmative litigation, designed to desegregate their own states, will vitiate the Act unless other lawyers supply the need. I think the Guild can meet that need!"[170]

Just as had happened the year before, an orientation seminar was planned for the NLG's 1965 Mississippi Summer Project, chaired by George W. Crockett Jr.[171] The program was held on June 12 at the Bismarck Hotel in Chicago. Lawrence Guyot, chairman of the Mississippi Freedom Democratic Party, conducted a session titled "Survey of Public Facilities in Mississippi and the Practice and Effect of Segregation and Discriminatory Practices."[172] Other sessions covered the background of Title III, how to obtain voluntary compliance, and framing the lawsuits. Finally, Claudia Morcom and her colleague Leonard Rosenthal gave an overview of the administration of the program, including the role of the Jackson office, the relationship between lawyers and the civil rights movement, and the participation of local counsel.[173]

Tellingly, conflicts and the threats of violence were never very far away. Within days of presenting at the Chicago orientation seminar, Morcom was back in Jackson writing Goodman a letter reporting on the most recent crisis. Nearly a thousand MFDP supporters had been arrested as they marched to the state capitol to protest newly proposed state voting laws. Lacking room, some were being held in the livestock barn at the state fairgrounds.[174] "The cops were herding the demonstrators into garbage trucks and caged-in vans, and of course, the 'white ladies' had the plush accommodations of the City Jail, while most everyone else was taken to the Fairgrounds."[175] One of those arrested was Morcom's nephew. Despite clear evidence of police brutality, she wrote, "the stupid News-casts yesterday, in mentioning the arrests, said 'There was no violence—several people were treated at the Hospital for head injuries.' Unquote! All in the same breath."[176]

The commotion was distracting from the "work." "With all of the excitement going on down here on Farish Street it's a little difficult to concentrate on the business at hand."[177] Part of the "business at hand" was gathering the data necessary to support the 1965 Mississippi Summer Project. "I will do follow ups on the other counties as soon as my F.D.P. people get out of jail. Right now, most of them plan to sit in jail, including [Lawrence] Guyot, for a while."[178] Ironically, responding to these mass arrests was one of the few incidents that galvanized the lawyers on Farish Street, leading to united action on the part of the NLG, LCDC, and the LDF.[179]

Unfortunately, the NLG's 1965 Summer Project did not produce the results the lawyers had hoped for. Ongoing chaos on the ground was certainly a factor, but the problems ran much deeper than that. The initial vision was audacious and probably exceeded what the resource-strapped organization could accomplish. Goodman later acknowledged, "It was a rather ambitious program which, as it turned out, had only limited impact. We were never able to find the money and resources to institute more than a couple of lawsuits."[180] The NLG's local partner, the MFDP, was more concerned about its national efforts to unseat the Mississippi delegation in the U.S. House of Representatives than about the desegregation suits. Crockett was frustrated by the lack of results: "It seems to me that the MFDP is not interested in and lacks the broad local leadership essential to working up the factual basis and arousing local support for the desegregation suits."[181] The final results were not impressive. "Although nine (9) teams of lawyers participated in the Guild Summer Program to desegregate public facilities on a county-wide basis for the Freedom Democratic Party, only three (3) suits have actually been filed since mid-July."[182] Morcom questioned the viability of the volunteer model: "This summer's experience has proved that it is not feasible to have out of state attorneys who are present in the state for a short period, handle long range litigation."[183]

The MFDP faced its own setbacks as well. In September, the leadership of both the Democratic and Republican Parties joined in favor of seating the Mississippi representatives. By a vote of 228–143, the MFDP's challenge was formally rejected, and the all-white Mississippi delegation was seated.[184]

With a mix of successes and setbacks, Morcom assessed the future of the NLG's work, making a number of insightful recommendations. She recognized that a focus on what was traditionally called civil rights was not enough. Hundreds of years of racism not only produced segregation and discrimination but generated systems of endemic poverty. Lawyers, she said, had a role to play here too: "What is still needed is adequate representation for local Negroes, who still get inadequate jury verdicts, lose their property through legal maneuvers, get no share of the profits of the crops they harvest and invariably end up owing plantation owners at the end of each and every year."[185] She advocated that the NLG set up neighborhood legal services programs. "It is unquestioned today, that one of the critical areas where legal assistance is most needed is in poverty stricken areas and services to the poor. This is particularly true in the South and equally true in the North. It is recommended that the Guild investigate setting up neighborhood law offices in these needy areas."[186] These recommendations foreshadowed the direction of Morcom's own career. In 1966, she left the Goodman firm to focus her energies on neighborhood legal services for poor Blacks.

The NLG's near-exclusive focus on the civil rights movement in the South was also coming to an end. There would be no 1966 Mississippi Summer Project. The Jackson office was closed, ending an important chapter of the guild's civil rights campaign.

The Implications of the NLG's Civil Rights Work in the South

The 1950s and the Red Scare had left many scars on the NLG, the Goodman firm, and George W. Crockett Jr. The NLG's active engagement in the civil rights movement not only made a significant external impact but also positively energized all who had participated. For the Goodman firm, it was a period of transition and changing personnel. New lawyers like Dick Goodman, Claudia Morcom, and Robert Millender joined the firm, with old soldiers like Eden and Robb remaining. The firm now openly embraced its diverse portfolio of negligence, workers' compensation, and public interest litigation, not as a lack of focus but as a model that could inspire others as a sustainable formula to support civil rights work. The firm regained its footing and direction and was prepared to meet the new challenges of changing times.

Similarly, the NLG's commitment to civil rights through CLAS provided renewed energy and purpose to the venerable organization. Goodman reflected that "as important as the Guild was to the Civil Rights Movement, the Movement was as important to the Guild." More colorfully, he noted, "Our participation in the Civil Rights Movement turned out to be a shot in the arm, or a kick in the ass, whichever way you prefer to describe it."[187] By the mid-1960s, the NLG was on a new and positive trajectory that would serve it well in future years. CLAS gave the Guild "a direction, gave it a purpose, shook off the fear of being labeled a 'communist' and pushed it ahead toward constructive activity in many new directions: the campus upheavals, segregation in the North, urban problems, the Vietnam War, women's equality, gay rights and international issues."[188]

The impact on Crockett was just as profound, both personally and professionally. Crockett had been deeply wounded by the Battle of Foley Square and its aftermath. He was withdrawn, even with his partners, and had lost interest in the practice of law. Years earlier, in the late 1950s, Goodman had taken him for a long lunch, encouraging him "to get involved in local organizations and politics" as a possible remedy. Crockett's work on civil rights in the South broke him out of his rut. He was finding a new sense of self and a new focus for his career. In many ways, the North, particularly a city like Detroit, was just as rife with economic inequality, racial injustice, and civil rights violations as the South was. Crockett may have left Mississippi, but he brought the fight for civil rights back to Detroit. He was ready to get involved in local politics. With his partner Bob Millender serving as campaign manager, Crockett ran for Common Council in the fall of 1965, Detroit's equivalent of the City Council at the time. He lost the election, but the race would forever change his professional trajectory. In 1966, he prepared for his next election campaign, this time to be a judge on Detroit's Recorder's Court, the court hearing all of the city's major criminal matters.

7

Election to Detroit Recorder's Court, the 1967 Rebellion, and the L. K. Tyler Case

Civil rights abuses and police brutality were not just southern problems. George W. Crockett Jr. had been deeply committed to constitutional principles since his youth. Few issues angered him throughout his life more than police misconduct. The 1948 tragedy of Leon Mosely was a case in point. The Mosely incident highlights the profound dangers of bigotry on the part of judges, as well as the police. Judicial complicity coexists with and helps enable police brutality.

"Officer, Please Don't Shoot That Boy": In the Matter of Leon Mosely

From the inception of the Detroit Police Department in the late nineteenth century, it had maintained an openly hostile relationship with Detroit's Black community.[1] Detroit was among the worst urban police departments with regard to chronic, unaddressed complaints by Blacks of police brutality, harassment, warrantless house searches, and the unjustified use of deadly force. In 1943, the year before George Crockett moved from Washington, DC, to Detroit to accept a position at the UAW, Detroit experienced one of the most devastating race riots in U.S. history. The police were severely criticized for their blatant attacks on Blacks, with seventeen of twenty-five Blacks killed during the riot slain by the police.[2]

In 1948, Detroit police practices remained openly brutal. Protests against police abuse and recommendations by civil rights groups went unheeded. Discipline within the department for abuse of Blacks was nonexistent. Even more difficult, if not impossible, was the prospect of having an officer criminally charged for killing a Black citizen.

On June 4, 1948, the police shot and killed an unarmed, fifteen-year-old Black high school student named Leon Mosely. His death from a bullet in the back was the fourth such incident within a year. Three thousand people attended his funeral on June 11, 1948, and then marched to downtown Detroit in protest.[3] Mosely came to the attention of the police by allegedly driving erratically. The police claimed they shot Mosely as he was fleeing arrest. Many witnesses, however, testified that Mosely had been beaten by the police and was shot in the back when he tried to stumble away from the police.[4] In addition to the bullet wound, Mosely's autopsy revealed a fractured skull, bruises, and other injuries not related to being shot. Notwithstanding the forensic and witness evidence, the case was destined to become just another "justified" killing by police officers, who at the time could lawfully use deadly force to apprehend a "fleeing felon." The Civil Rights Congress of Michigan (CRC) asked Goodman and Crockett to conduct an independent investigation of the shooting, hoping to force the prosecutor to bring criminal charges against the officers.[5] These efforts failed, but in a creative maneuver, Goodman and Crockett were successful in forcing the prosecutor to request a coroner's jury to determine the cause of Mosely's death. The coroner's inquest opened on June 21, 1948, before a jury composed of six citizens, three white and three Black.

Representing the Prosecutor's Office was Assistant Prosecutor Robert C. McClear, who apparently had replaced Willis F. Ward, a Black assistant prosecutor and former University of Michigan football star who was originally assigned to the inquest.[6] Goodman and Crockett were joined by the Black lawyers Elvin L. Davenport and Elvin A. Wanzo, representing the Mosely family. Attorneys for the Detroit Police Officers Association, Henry S. Sweeny and Frank G. Schemanske, represented the accused officers.[7] The two sides clashed frequently during the proceedings: for example, one confrontation occurred when Goodman tried, unsuccessfully, to have photographs of Mosely's body introduced to show he had been beaten. Crockett, however, successfully obtained autopsy and police investigative reports that had been denied them but were given to the police officers' attorneys.[8]

Evidence presented by the police was calculated to show that Mosely had been shot while escaping from the police. On the other hand, numerous eyewitnesses called by Goodman and Crockett testified that Mosely had been captured, beaten by the police, and then shot without warning as he staggered away from the beating.[9]

The graphic testimony of one witness whom the press dubbed the "hanging witness" was reported in the *Detroit Free Press*:

> "I saw the police slugging that boy," he said. "I ran out of the house. My wife came out behind me screaming, 'Please don't do that, Officer, please don't do that.'
>
> The boy staggered up the street like a drunken man after they quit.
>
> My back was to the police. My wife screamed, 'They're going to kill him.' I turned around and said, 'I'll get him for you, officer. Don't shoot him.'
>
> The boy staggered against a car. That officer wasn't more than 15 feet away from him when he shot him.
>
> The officers dragged him back and dropped him on the ground, face down. One of them pulled that boy's shirt up and pushed around the wound and blood gushed out."[10]

After six days of testimony, from fifty witnesses, the jury began deliberations. Eight hours later, the jury returned a verdict that the Mosely shooting was "unnecessary, unwise and unjustifiable."[11] Following the coroner's jury verdict, Officer Luis Melasi, the police officer who shot Mosely, was charged with involuntary manslaughter and slated for trial in Detroit's Recorder's Court. The Recorder's Court was a state court with jurisdiction for all criminal felony cases committed in Detroit. Its judges were elected by the citizens of Detroit. Melasi waived his right to a jury and was tried in a bench trial before Judge Arthur E. Gordon. Not unexpectedly, he was acquitted.[12] Melasi returned to work immediately. He was given $2,021 in back pay and told by the police commissioner, "[Be] as fearless an officer as you were before this happened."[13]

In historical context, Judge Gordon's verdict, notwithstanding the coroner's jury verdict and the spate of eyewitnesses to the contrary, was not surprising to Goodman or Crockett. The judge's written opinion, however, was highly provocative and particularly unjudicial. He displayed blatant prejudice toward Black people and a passionate political dislike, if not hatred, of Sugar (who was not even directly involved in the case) and Goodman. That such venomous remarks would appear in a judicial opinion underscored a pervasive judicial bigotry, serving as a reminder that police brutality cannot exist without judicial complicity. Following Judge Gordon's statement of case facts, he wrote his opinions about the witnesses and the lawyers:

> From this point, the testimony differs. One group [Black witnesses], which had been herded into the office of Ernest Goodman, the brains of Maurice Sugar's law office in the Barlum Tower [later the "Cadillac Building"], by some of the pink members of the NAACP, insisted dramatically that from two to seven police officers beat the driver with pistols and fists, until he escaped from them and that the defendant, a police officer, shot him in the back while he was running or staggering away....
>
> Another group testified, quietly and soberly, that they heard shots in the alley, heard and saw the chase of the cars on Waterloo Street, heard the crash of the dark car against the tree, saw the officers try to grasp the driver of the dark car as he tried to escape through the right hand door of the stolen car, heard cries of "halt" or "stop," saw the driver run west [on] Waterloo Street, saw the defendant shoot once at the fugitive; saw the fugitive fall onto the brick pavement of Waterloo Street; saw the police officers pick up the fugitive and carry him to a place of safety between the curb and the sidewalk....
>
> It is worthy of notice that those witnesses who made the wildest accusations of beating with fists and pistols by three, four and even seven policemen, were of the group produced by the NAACP and sent to the Barlum Tower to be interviewed by the pink devotees of agitation. And their testimony was contradicted by others of the same racial group, of equal or superior intelligence, and with the same opportunities for observation.[14]

Judge Gordon concluded, "The defendant is Not Guilty of the charge here presented. He should be commended as an alert police officer. If the handful of communist agitators, who are trying to ruin the creditable work of the NAACP, cared to do a good deed for once in their pink lives, they would raise money to replace the automobile stolen by Mosely."[15] The outcome was a shattering exhibition of judicial bigotry, but this was the reality of Recorder's Court.

After the opinion was released, Goodman wrote to Judge Gordon objecting that the judge's opinion "dramatizes the prevalent discrimination against the Negro people."[16] Bigotry on the bench can be even more dangerous than police bigotry; it is a toxin that corrodes the very foundation of the rule of law. Goodman wrote, "I believe, however, that if left unchallenged, your intemperate opinion may dissuade other lawyers from vigorously representing the victims of discrimination as is their right and duty. And your opinion may well have the effect of creating wide distrust of our judicial system as an instrument for dispensing equal justice."[17] Maurice Sugar also put pen to paper: "For myself, having reflected upon Judge Gordon's observations, which of course had no place in the performance of his judicial duties, I wonder whether his reference to the 'herd,' obviously intended as an insult, does not flow naturally from a deep and dangerous prejudice against Negroes—and others who strive to eradicate racial discrimination and justice."[18]

Goodman, Crockett, and Sugar ensured that Judge Gordon's opinion gained wide circulation in Michigan and throughout the United States. Police brutality in Detroit's streets did not end. Incidents similar to the killing of Leon Mosely continued unchecked in Detroit into the 1960s and beyond.

Justice in Detroit would not change until the racial composition of Recorder's Court changed. After Crockett's unsuccessful run for Detroit Common Council, his eyes were now fixed on Detroit's Recorder's Court. After fighting for civil rights in Mississippi, he was now ready to take the fight to Detroit.

Crockett's 1966 Campaign for Recorder's Court

On Friday, March 25, 1966, surrounded by 150 supporters at the Rondora Hotel, George W. Crockett Jr. announced his candidacy for Recorder's Court judge.[19] Learning lessons from his campaign the previous year, Crockett entered this race with maximum preparation. He was the first to announce

formally his candidacy in what he knew was going to be a crowded field
for an unprecedented ten open judicial seats. Crockett was introduced by
the chair of the Thirteenth Congressional District Democratic Organization as the district's "favorite son." A telegram was read from Congressman
John Conyers, then in his first term, representing the First Congressional
District: "I'm pledging you my full and unqualified support."[20] The chair of
the First Congressional District Democratic Organization also spoke and
pledged his personal support.

Crockett's campaign issues mirrored his principles. In April, he was in
the news again, speaking on behalf of a blue-ribbon panel composed of
both citizen and police representatives, urging the Michigan Civil Rights
Commission to address more seriously the problem of police misconduct.[21] In the report, Crockett said that quick and vigorous action on citizen complaints was necessary for equal enforcement of the law. He noted,
however, that police departments "unfortunately leave much to be desired"
in how they handle complaints. Problems included "protracted delays in
investigations, frequent and almost automatic exoneration of the accused
officer, and the tap-on-the-wrist punishment, even when there is substan-
tiation of the claimed misconduct."[22] This was more than just politics for
Crockett; it was a deeply held passion and a critical reason for his campaign.

Crockett's campaign materials stressed his experience, temperament,
and integrity, particularly highlighting his work in labor and civil rights.
One of his campaign fliers read as follows:

CROCKETT: "BEST QUALIFIED"

That's what you hear in Labor circles, Legal circles, Civil Rights
circles and throughout the community whenever there is a discussion of CROCKETT for RECORDER'S COURT JUDGE.

WHY?

BECAUSE CROCKETT IS EXPERIENCED: Many appearances and oral
arguments before the United States Supreme Court are only a part
of the thirty years of George Crockett's solid legal experience. . . .

BECAUSE CROCKETT HAS JUDICIAL TEMPERAMENT: He exhibits courtesy, dignity, patience, tact, humor; and above all, he has the ability
to listen and to keep an open mind.

BECAUSE CROCKETT HAS INTEGRITY: In 1963, together with other nationally known attorneys, Crockett met at the White House with President Kennedy and Vice President Johnson to discuss civil rights. His demonstrable moral courage in this area includes defending freedom of speech and advocacy for all groups; volunteering three months of legal services in Mississippi to defend civil rights workers; and participating in the Selma, Alabama March with Rev. Martin Luther King.[23]

Two photos accompanied the flier. One was captioned, "George Crockett in Mississippi directing National Lawyers Guild Committee for Legal Assistance to the South." The other photo was of Crockett with his grandson: "George Crockett, an expert cabinet maker, teaches his grandson his hobby."[24]

Into early summer, news coverage of Crockett was largely factual, accurate, and positive. In a June 9, 1966, article, the *Detroit News* reported, "Crockett, 56, of 1327 Nicolet, is a graduate of Morehouse College and the University of Michigan Law School. He was a senior attorney for the U.S. Department of Labor, and head of the international UAW's fair employment practices commission program."[25]

One of the first indications of potential trouble was the failure of the AFL-CIO Committee on Political Education (COPE) to endorse Crockett's candidacy. Without a doubt, Crockett was one of the most qualified candidates in the race, particularly with regard to labor credentials. When COPE announced its endorsements for the August 2, 1966, primary, however, Crockett's name was absent.[26] After purging him from the ranks of the UAW nearly two decades earlier, Reuther's labor establishment was trying to undermine his judicial candidacy. Sugar, Goodman, and Crockett had learned years earlier that a good defense requires decisive action. Crockett's supporters responded in an advertisement in the *Michigan Chronicle*. Under a banner reading, "George W. Crockett: The kind of man Recorder's Court needs," the advertisement declared, "AUTO WORKERS WILL REMEMBER!" There was a large photo of Crockett being appointed in 1944 as the first director of the UAW Fair Practices Program, surrounded by Black labor luminaries such as Horace Sheffield, William Bowman, Oscar Noble, William Latimer, and John Conyers Sr. "This picture shows how

George Crockett gave leadership to the formation and growth of the UAW's Fair Practices Program." The text listed Crockett's many accomplishments in service of nondiscrimination and the labor movement and concluded, "Auto workers will remember his loyalty and ability on behalf of working people, both as Union member and official and as a civil rights attorney!"[27]

Crockett received the fourth largest number of votes in the crowded August primary. As the general election approached, opponents on the left and the right increased their attacks. The focus of the attack on Crockett was yet another reprise of his involvement in the Battle of Foley Square. On October 17, 1966, with the November election looming, the *Detroit News* published a lengthy story under the headline, "Hectic '49 Trial Haunts Crockett's Bid for Bench." The opening lines of the article read, "Is George W. Crockett—who went to jail 14 years ago for insulting a federal judge in his courtroom—now ready to dispense justice as a Recorder's Court judge of Detroit? This is the election issue dividing the city's legal and liberal communities as they debate the related question of whether Crockett is simply an able lawyer and civil rights crusader, or whether he is a handyman for the radical left."[28] What followed was a lengthy rehash of Crockett's role in the Foley Square trial, Judge Medina holding Crockett and the other defense lawyers in contempt, and the protracted legal proceedings before the U.S. Supreme Court.

Crockett was given space in the article to defend himself:

I don't believe the Smith Act is constitutional, I think that it is important that Congress be kept within the free speech guarantees of the First Amendment.

Congress should not be allowed to restrict a person's right to teach and advocate anything, including the violent overthrow of the government.

That does not mean that I believe in the violent overthrow of the government. I oppose it completely, but the difference between speaking and doing is tremendous, and that is a difference clearly recognized in the Constitution.

I also believe that every defendant should have the benefit of every defense.

Just because you might think a man is guilty, or you know people might think badly of you for defending a member of an unpopular minority, or you think you might lose other clients, doesn't
allow you to disregard your duty as a lawyer to give every man the
defense he deserves under the legal system.[29]

Crockett vowed to ensure proper decorum in his courtroom if elected.
He made clear, however, that he would enforce stronger due process standards than had Judge Medina in exercising the contempt power. "But
only in those cases where it was perfectly obvious and where it was necessary to continue the trial, would I invoke summary contempt power.
Any other, I would refer to a prosecutor for trial before another judge
and jury."[30]

The political divides were sharp, and Walter Reuther's knives were long.
The AFL-CIO political arm, COPE, refused to endorse Crockett in the primary or the general election. The growing controversy led the First Democratic Congressional Committee to withdraw its earlier endorsement after
bitter internal disagreements. Ironically, the candidate selection committee
of the Detroit Bar Association stood by Crockett, conferring on him its
"outstanding" rating.[31]

Attacks against Crockett by mainstream labor on the left were matched
by attacks from far-right activists, orchestrated, remarkably, by the FBI: "In
1966, a memo from Hoover's office instructed agents to derail the electoral efforts of George Crockett Jr."[32] These instructions were implemented.
"Agents wrote a letter under a false name assailing Crockett and mailed it
to a right-leaning organization. Unaware of the true source of the letter,
the group disseminated fliers emblazoned with a hammer and sickle, calling Crockett an 'enemy collaborator.'"[33] The flier was quite remarkable. It
showed Crockett's photo, surrounded on each side by a hammer and sickle,
labeled "Enemy Sympathizer" and "Enemy Collaborator." The banner read,
"Why We Must NOT Elect George Crockett to Recorders' [*sic*] Court."[34] Chief
among the allegations were Crockett's involvement with the National Lawyers Guild, a purportedly communist-front organization, his opposition to
the war in Vietnam, and a trip he had made to the Soviet Union to study
its legal system. The flier ends with a crescendo: "The election of GEORGE
CROCKETT to a Judgeship on Recorders' [*sic*] Court would be a MOCKERY OF

JUSTICE, a NOD OF APPROVAL TO TREASON, a SOURCE OF ENCOURAGEMENT TO THE ENEMY and a BETRAYAL OF OUR AMERICAN FIGHTING MEN!!!"[35] FBI agents then made sure the flier was widely distributed to groups like the state bar association, unions, and newspapers.[36] Fortunately, even in 1966, the sting of these Red Scare tactics had begun to wear off.

The controversy over Crockett also signaled growing tensions between white establishment labor, aligned with white establishment Democratic Party leaders, and the increasingly vocal Black community. Crockett had substantial support in Black Detroit, a community that was increasingly frustrated and resistant to being told how they should behave. Crockett supporters circulated their own flier that was a reproduction of a political advertisement in the *Michigan Chronicle*, titled "Solidarity House Must Not Control the Negro Community." A subheading of the flier declared, "The Issue Is the Political Independence of Detroit's Negro Community." Strong language pervaded the document. "No longer can patronizing, paternalistic political guidance be accepted by Negroes in Detroit." In what was tantamount to its own Declaration of Independence against the UAW Solidarity House, the flier stated,

> Detroit's Negro Community has been handed a challenge by the International UAW-CIO. Through their strong-armed attempts to "dump Crockett" the political henchmen from Solidarity House are ignoring a choice overwhelmingly made by the Negro people and their friends in the primary election.
>
> Atty. George W. Crockett, rated "Outstanding" by the Detroit Bar Association, was nominated second among the non-incumbent candidates for election to the Recorder's Court bench. Now he is the target of an unprecedented attempt by the UAW Solidarity House power group to prevent his election and thus defeat the acknowledged choice of Detroit's Negro-liberal white community.
>
> If we allow them to get away with this, we will demonstrate a shameful form of political immaturity that will be difficult, if not impossible to outlive.
>
> If we allow them to get away with it, it will be another step backward, reminiscent of Reconstruction days when the rights

won by blood were taken away by backroom swaps, by paternalistic
deals and by self-centered apathy.

If we allow them to get away with this, the independent action
of a united Negro-liberal white political thrust will be dissipated.
THIS MUST NOT HAPPEN![37]

Members of the Black community knew George Crockett better than anyone else. The authors of the flier understood the significance of the political moment and the increasing need to support Black leaders who would
stand up to traditional power structures. Other passages expressly called
out Crockett's strength and independence: "To Solidarity House Crockett
has one fault: He is a civil rights leader that cannot be dictated to!" Many
of these statements would prove to be prophetic: "Only through the support of a man of Attorney Crockett's proven integrity, wisdom and courage
can we prove that Negroes and their friends are ready to stand behind
those who are willing to give us responsible, independent leadership." They
knew that if Crockett were elected, he would be no ordinary judge: "He
is and will continue to be uncontrolled."[38] He would answer to his own
principles.

Some of the newspaper endorsements, to their credit, saw through
the smoke of the Foley Square reprise. The *Detroit Free Press* editorialized,
"Crockett has an undeserved reputation for leftist leanings because of his
defense of 10 Communists 15 years ago. . . . When he was asked to help
the defense against a law whose constitutionality is still in question, he
felt he could not refuse."[39] On the eve of the general election, the *Detroit
Free Press* spoke out again. Since Crockett "finished fourth in the primary,
the UAW and AFL-CIO have pulled out all the stops to defeat him. In the
process they've rekindled old charges of union domination of Detroit's
Democratic Party, alienating the Negro community and placed themselves
in the same camp with Breakthrough [an extremist right-wing organiza-
tion]. Crockett is one of Michigan's finest constitutional lawyers, has judicial temperament and he has lengthy experience in Recorder's Court. He
merits your vote."[40]

On Election Day, Detroit citizens voted for Crockett. Recorder's Court
now had a judge who would not be controlled by traditional political forces
or notions of "business as usual."

Judge Crockett Assumes the Bench

On January 1, 1967, the firm of Goodman, Crockett, Eden, Robb & Millender sent a public notice, announcing with pleasure that "George W. Crockett, Jr. will begin his elected responsibilities as a Judge of the Recorder's Court for the City of Detroit and will resign as a member of the firm. The firm will continue in the practice of law."[41] Crockett was leaving the professional home he had enjoyed since the Sugar team's collective ouster from the UAW.

All his life, Crockett had been guided by deep personal convictions about what was right and wrong, an unshakable commitment to racial and economic justice, and strong beliefs in constitutional principles. While he had principles, he did not have the power needed to implement and enforce what he believed was right, often suffering the consequences as a result. Power lay with racist forces in the U.S. Department of Labor that imposed a promotional glass ceiling for Black lawyers. Power lay with the reactionary political forces of the Red Scare that ostracized him for his legal defense at Foley Square and sent him to prison for contempt of court. Power lay with racist sheriffs and judges, against principle, in the civil rights struggle in the South.

In assuming the role as a Recorder's Court judge, Crockett joined his principles with meaningful state power, and he knew it. He later wrote, "The battleground today is the trial courts—and especially the lower trial courts. It is in these tribunals that legally approved racism-classism flourishes in its most virulent form. If the battleground against racism has shifted to the trial courts the chief artillery, if that battle is to be won, has to be the trial judge himself. He is the one in absolute command; and he is the sole repository of that tremendous force for good or evil which we call 'judicial discretion.'"[42] Crocket understood how race and class interacted within oppressive systems and the critical role law played in enforcing and protecting those systems. He also knew how progressive lawyers and judges could work to disrupt these systems. In many respects, he had spent his whole life preparing for this role.

Crockett became a Recorder's Court judge amid a revolution in the U.S. Supreme Court's understanding of criminal law and criminal procedure. In 1961, the Court decided *Mapp v. Ohio*,[43] ruling that evidence obtained in violation of a defendant's Fourth Amendment rights should be excluded in the trial proceedings. *Miranda v. Arizona*[44] was decided the year Crockett was running for Recorder's Court judge; individuals now had to be informed of their rights before being subject to questioning. These decisions triggered substantial backlash from police, prosecutors, and judges. Crockett was soon mired in these controversies.

Judge Crockett made clear that he disagreed with what were then the prevailing views of other Recorder's Court judges as to the scope of *Mapp v. Ohio* and its relationship to certain Michigan state constitutional provisions. "Not too long after I got on the bench, a reporter asked me about my views." Crockett told the reporter that the state constitutional provision was "in conflict with the Federal constitution" and that he "did not intend to follow it": "Immediately there was a story on the front page of the paper attacking my statement." But Crockett stood his ground: "I became the only judge on my bench who was dismissing cases of illegal search and seizure and I incurred considerable displeasure from the police." In the end, Crockett was proven right. The Michigan Court of Appeals and then the Michigan Supreme Court adopted positions similar to his. "Now the point is that, all too frequently, if you get one judge who is willing to stick his neck out and say I'm not going to be moved, eventually he draws other judges to him."[45] Such legal victories, however, do not come without their costs with regard to relations with police and prosecutors.

After *Mapp*, Crockett's next legal battle involved the question of whether the police had properly complied with *Miranda*. A woman had stabbed her husband after overhearing a telephone conversation he was having with a female friend. The man died on the way to the hospital. The woman later confessed in police custody. Judge Crockett ruled that the confession could not be admitted because, under the circumstances, she had not knowingly and voluntarily waived her *Miranda* rights. He dismissed the charges.[46]

In a favorable editorial, the *Detroit Free Press* noted, "Of all the judges on Detroit's Recorder's Court, none is more of a constitutional expert than George Crockett. None is more of a stickler for it either." The Wayne County prosecutor, William Cahalan, had a different perspective; he "called Judge Crockett's decision 'an abuse of discretion.'" The *Free Press*, however, disagreed and editorialized in support of better police practices: "Police and prosecutors must be as aware of the rights of the defendant as is the judge, and must be just as determined to see that those rights are enforced."[47] The police seemed to have taken away a different message. Rather than a call for greater adherence to the rule of law, the police increasingly viewed Judge Crockett as the enemy.

It is likely that the FBI had a file on every member of the Detroit NLG chapter as a result of their actions in the 1930s, 1940s, and 1950s. This was certainly true of Crockett and Goodman. It was substantially less common for local police to open secret files on a Recorder's Court judge before whom they routinely appeared, but that is just what the police did. The May 28, 1967, edition of the *Detroit Free Press* published an article with the headline, "Police Keep Secret File on Judge Crockett." The article read, "Detroit police officers, dissatisfied with the performance of Recorder's Court George W. Crockett, are keeping at least two secret files on the judge's decisions."[48] Less than six months into his tenure on the bench, the message was clear: relations between Judge Crockett and the Detroit police would not be business as usual.

Crockett had his defenders, but divisions often fell along racial lines. One supporter was the Wolverine Bar Association: "In specific response to a recent newspaper article attacking Judge George W. Crockett's performance of his duties and, by implication, his integrity and character, the officers and members of the Wolverine Bar Association on May 23 passed a resolution. 'We hereby reaffirm our complete confidence in Judge Crockett's ability and his personal and professional integrity and loyalty.'"[49] The Black attorney and activist Milton F. Henry also penned a letter to the *Free Press* expressing his support for Crockett: "I simply cannot contain myself any longer in the face of the continuing program of unjustified abuse being heaped on Recorder's Court Judge George Crockett." Henry continued, "What right have police officers to keep a dossier on any judge? None; and to do so is a gross intimidation of that Judge. Further, what right has any prosecutor to dissent from a court's ruling in a newspaper? Again, absolutely none, and to do so is to commit a contempt of that court. A prosecutor's remedy from a claimed abuse of discretion is an appeal to a higher court."[50]

If the road was rocky in June, it would get infinitely more so in July with the outbreak of the 1967 Detroit Rebellion. Although Crockett was a relatively new and inexperienced judge, he had spent his whole life fighting institutionalized forms of racial violence. By any measure, he was ready for the looming challenge.

The 1967 Rebellion

The Rebellion began in the early morning hours of July 23, 1967, near the corner of Twelfth and Clairmount Streets in the midst of a mass arrest after police raided an afterhours drinking establishment (a "blind pig"). The violence on the streets and the subsequent response of police and prosecutors resulted in an onslaught on the judicial system with major racial and class overtones. Crockett recalled, "In the Detroit riots of 1967 a total of 7,200 persons were arrested. Virtually all of these defendants were lower income or indigents. Virtually all were black."[51] The *Law Review* at the University of Michigan Law School conducted a comprehensive study of judicial practices during the Rebellion. The pressures on the court system were tremendous, challenging the very notion of constitutional due process:

> Apparently, it was commonplace during the disorder for a group of suspects to be "rounded up" and arrested at the same place (often a store which had already been broken into or burned), charged with the same offense (typically, entering without breaking but with intent to commit larceny), brought to a police station for booking, and taken to the court to be arraigned—still as a group—before one judge. Moreover, most of the judges continued the pattern of group treatment by addressing the defendants collectively, rather than as individuals, and by setting identical bails for all. Obviously, the adoption of these procedures precluded any consideration of individual circumstances or of the probability that any particular defendant would return for trial on the appointed day. Bail was set for offenses, not for people.[52]

Would the Recorder's Court judges defend constitutional principles and adhere to legal notions of individualized process, or would they fall in line with the call of police, prosecutors, and politicians to impose a very racialized sense of order?

The first test came in judicial determinations of the bail to be imposed on the thousands of individuals arrested. Wayne County Prosecutor William Cahalan called for bonds at $10,000 or higher to prevent anyone arrested from being able to return to the streets, without regard to what actual risk the individual might present.[53] The Recorder's Court judges almost immediately fell into line, following the prosecutor's recommendation for extremely high bail. There was, however, one exception: "The dissenting judge was George W. Crockett, Jr. who, on Wednesday, July 26, wrote a letter to his fellow judges on the Recorder's Court informing them of his 'disagreement with [the] suggested high bond policy' and of his view that 'each of us has the sole responsibility of fixing bonds in cases assigned to us. I intend to exercise that responsibility as well as accept the responsibility for my action.... In my judgment [$10,000 and $25,000] bonds are not only excessive, they are prohibitive.'"[54] Crockett later wrote that in "the court's rush to 'keep those people off the streets,' these bail amounts were imposed in assembly-line fashion, with no individual inquiry to determine whether such bail was reasonable and justified in the particular case."[55]

In addition to unconstitutionally high bail, the courts imposed additional and unsanctioned burdens on those who were actually granted bail. Judge Vincent J. Brennan, executive judge of the Recorder's Court, ordered sheriff officers to report back to his office with additional types of information before a prisoner who had met bond would actually be released. These requirements "met with considerable resistance from some Recorder's Court judges, notably Judges Crockett and Schemanske. Judge Crockett in fact told Sheriff Buback that if the bonds he had set were not honored, he would cite the sheriff for contempt of court."[56] The practice soon ended.

How should courts respond to a crisis of social unrest? Crockett began with the premise that while thousands of people might be arrested and detained, each detainee was, in fact, an individual and should be treated as such. "People with long residence records, regular jobs, and with no previous police records found themselves separated from families and jobs, incarcerated in maximum security prisons, out of contact with their world—all without benefit of counsel, without an examination, and without the semblance of a trial."[57] Crockett responded to the logistical challenges with creativity and ingenuity. Taking advantage of his preexisting network of relations, he fashioned new processes to meet the needs of the moment. His former colleague Claudia Morcom had moved from the Goodman firm to Neighborhood Legal Services (NLS) and offered to help by gathering the information necessary to set appropriate levels of bail. Defendants were interviewed privately by NLS staff, "the information was presented to the judge, the advice of the interviewer was requested, and bond was then set. And, a stern and clear warning was given on the consequences of lying to the court."[58] This system proved workable.

> Judge Crockett's experience indicates that in fact it took very little extra time to arraign defendants his way, and that in the long run it actually saved his court a great deal of time by eliminating the necessity of reviewing every bond at a later date. Moreover, he felt there was very little misrepresentation by defendants, and that questionable bail risks and dangerous persons could be weeded out by the volunteers or the court. In addition to the warning to the defendant about lying, telephones were available to the volunteers to aid in verifying information when that was possible and necessary.[59]

Crockett maintained that if the will existed, problems could be solved in a manner that respected the Constitution and individual rights.

He was willing to take other independent action to correct perceived injustices, particularly those inflicted by the police. Given the extreme circumstances and the dearth of defense attorneys involved in the process, there was almost no use of habeas petitions to protect those who were wrongfully imprisoned. Again, there was one exception: "Judge Crockett handled only one habeas corpus petition during the entire period of the arraignments, and that one he himself suggested for a prisoner in the court bullpen who had been seriously beaten, allegedly by a policeman, and for whom insufficient information was available for arraignment. Judge Crockett appointed an attorney, told him to petition for a writ, granted the writ, and released the man on personal bond."[60] When principles and power are combined, justice can be done, even during a crisis.

When the results of the *Michigan Law Review* study were published, Judge Crockett received some well-deserved good press. The *Detroit Free Press* editorialized, "Judge Crockett proved that even under trying circumstances it is possible for the courts to be what they ought to be. Consideration of the suspects' rights at the beginning of the court process actually turned out to save time and prevented the necessity of back-tracking."[61]

In 1968, Crockett wrote a law review article for the *Journal of Urban Law* titled "Recorder's Court and the 1967 Civil Disturbance." In it, he

focused on the role of race, noting that 83 percent of the seventy-two hundred people arrested in the Rebellion were Black: "I suggest that this fact
accounts in large measure for the unconstitutional procedures uniformly
followed by the authorities after their arrest."[62] An indication of the degree
of police overreach was the number of actual felony convictions as compared with the number of felony arrests: "Of these 3,230 Detroit riot felony
defendants, the most recent court data shows that only 9 were found guilty
of charges serious enough to warrant prison sentences in the state prison."[63]

Crockett credited forceful lobbying by the Black community of the
Recorder's Court judges for breaking the logjam of unconstitutional practices: "By Friday afternoon, a sizable delegation representing Detroit's
black community demanded and received a hearing with our bench and
they lodged a vigorous protest against the flagrant denials of their civil
rights and liberties, the killing of some thirty-three Negroes by police and
guardsmen, and the indiscriminate kicking in of doors and the searching black people's homes. It was not until these encounters occurred that
we judges returned to our judicial senses. Within a matter of a few hours
orders were entered releasing the overwhelming bulk of these defendants
on personal bond. But the damage had been done."[64] Tension between the
police and the Black community, including high levels of police brutality, was a leading cause of the 1943 Detroit race riots. At the time of the
1967 Rebellion, the Detroit police were frequently described as an army of
occupation. What transpired during and after the Rebellion, including the
behavior of the Recorder's Court, only deepened these divides. "It is not
surprising that police-Negro tension in our City today [1968] is almost as
high as it was immediately after last summer's events. The simple truth is
that Detroit's black community has no confidence in the administration
of justice in their city; they believe that the temple of criminal justice is
sagging, is tottering. They feel the beams resting upon their necks. What
is particularly disturbing is the refusal of the establishment to open its eyes
to the fact and take corrective measures before it is too late."[65]

History often trades in irony. In March 1968, Judge Crockett was called
on to preside over the trial of Michael Lewis, the man allegedly charged with
"starting" the Rebellion. "Lewis, at the time a factory worker, was arrested
August 13, when three officers cruising the 12th street area said they recognized him as the man who had harangued the crowd gathered at the scene

of a raided after-hours drinking spot in the early morning hours of July 23, and incited them into attacking the raiding officers."[66] Prosecutors charged Lewis with six felony counts of "inciting a riot and rioting" under old English common law, claiming that Michigan statutes contained no provisions for punishing such offenses. Each felony carried a possible five-year term, raising the prospect of potentially thirty years in prison. As a matter of law, Judge Crockett disagreed, holding that statutory provisions provided that acts not otherwise covered by statute should be treated as a misdemeanor, punishable by a potential of ninety days in jail and a $100 fine.[67]

The Lewis case also provided Crockett a chance to express his views as to the real causes of the Rebellion and on police conduct on the morning of July 23, 1967: "Crockett questioned the prosecution charge that Lewis 'started' the riot, commenting that 'most competent observers agree that causes for the riot existed long before July, 1967.'" Crockett spared no criticism of the police: "He said testimony concerning the raid and the situation existing outside immediately following it 'suggest that any incitement to riot is attributable as much to the ineptitude of the raiding officers as to the profane insults allegedly hurled at those officers by the defendant.'" Finally, Crockett expressed his view that it was inappropriate for the police to make the mass arrests that triggered the Rebellion in the first place: "Crockett suggested that in raids, as with traffic and other ordinance violations, patrons should be given a summons to appear in court. If they fail to appear on the court date, he said, then a warrant for his arrest should be issued."[68] These incidents should not be the predicate of mass arrests.

Crockett's convictions could not be shaken, even by the forces of the 1967 Rebellion. Crockett believed that rigorous enforcement of constitutional principles was the key to addressing historical inequities. While others in Detroit and the nation were moving to more radical positions of Black Power, Crockett stood his ground. Just as he and Goodman had articulated their defense of the communist Michigan Six, they believed that aggressive resort to democratic processes was the best way to effect essential social change, not fanciful notions of revolution. While Crockett was advocating democratic change, others in Detroit were mapping out a more radical agenda. In March 1968, at the same time Crockett was trying the man who allegedly started the Rebellion, the attorney Milton Henry and his brother, Richard, were busy hosting a national meeting of Black

Power advocates. Out of the Henry brothers' meeting emerged the Republic of New Africa (RNA). "The RNA called for nothing less than the establishment of an independent black nation comprising the states of Mississippi, Louisiana, Alabama, Georgia and South Carolina."[69] This was a radically different agenda from that advocated by Crockett: "The best way for the Negro to get justice and the better conditions he seeks is to do it at the ballot box. The answer is not riots or the idea of setting up another state for Negros some place."[70]

Crockett's and Henry's paths would cross again in July 1968 at the NLG national conference in Santa Monica, California. The NLG may have been the first integrated national bar association and it may have done pioneering civil rights work in the South, but it still had a difficult time attracting significant numbers of Black lawyers. Crockett was not shy about criticizing his white NLG colleagues. One implication of the lack of substantial Black membership, Crockett believed, was that NLG members often failed "to really understand black America's point of view. So the [NLG] Convention concludes that every black man who speaks long enough and loud enough must speak 'for the Negro.'"[71]

Crockett was responding to a speech Milton Henry made at the convention on behalf of the RNA. "A majority of the Guild delegates found this convincing enough to elect Henry a vice president of the organization and to call for the drafting of 'a memorandum of law setting forth the legal authority for the establishment of the aforesaid separate black nation.'"[72] Crockett was offended by the spectacle and advocated a very different view, in which every state in the United States would belong equally to Black and white. Crockett wrote that he would "'fight like hell' until white America recognized 'that every state in this Union is as much ours as it is theirs, and that we don't intend to voluntarily surrender our right to mutual sovereignty over a single acre.'"[73] Crockett and Henry were reacting to racial injustice in very different ways and staking out very different paths.

Lloyd K. Tyler: The Tempest before the New Bethel Storm

Detroit roiled in 1967 and 1968; 1969 was no different. Judge Crockett remained in the crosshairs of the police, prosecutors, and the press. The case of Lloyd K. Tyler highlighted these tensions as they played out in the early months of 1969, on the eve of the so-called New Bethel Church Incident.

Lloyd K. Tyler, a twenty-five-year-old Black male, was attempting to rob a jewelry store on Detroit's east side with two associates when they were surprised by the police. According to the press, Tyler ran out the front door, while his two associates escaped through the back door. Tyler got into a running police car and drove off, abandoning the car some five blocks away, and proceeded by foot. When he was spotted by a police patrol, "he then took the pistol from the waistband of his trousers and threw it to the ground and surrendered himself."[74]

The contrast is striking between how Judge Crockett tells the story and how it was reported in the newspapers:

> [A] young man, Mr. Tyler, charged with armed robbery came before me. The defendant was pleading guilty to the charge of assault with intent to rob. According to the probation report, he was a narcotics addict. Before sentencing I inquired if he had anything he wanted to say. He said, "I am no good at talking your honor. I have written out what I want to say and I would like to hand it up to you and have you read it." The statement told me about his addiction and that he was in the throes of withdrawal when two of his associates came by and offered him a chance to go along to get some money. Since he was unable to work he went along on this serious crime. He told me of the beating he allegedly received from the police. His parish priest stepped forward and said he could verify the beating. The priest had seen him the day after he had been arrested. The priest said his head felt like a bunch of grapes. His mother then spoke up and said when she saw her son his eyes were closed, his nose was broken and blood was all over his clothing.[75]

Police brutality was one of Crockett's strongest triggers. It was behavior he found absolutely intolerable. "I said, in substance, 'that when it appears to me and I am satisfied a defendant, while in police custody, has been brutalized, I will not add to his punishment by sending him to jail. The state has an obligation to protect people in its custody. When the state, acting through its officers, punishes suspects without trial, it usurps the judicial function. When a man has been punished, I will not send him to prison or punish him again.'"[76]

We will return to the issue of the police's treatment of Tyler, but the first part of the story focuses on the issue of sentencing and addiction. Portions of Tyler's letter to Crockett read as follows:

> I would beg you to see the importance of narcotics in this crime and how sick I was from the lack of it. My body was aching and sore, my mind was not my own. I wish the court to consider this, to see that I did not intend to commit this, and to see that I am begging for help on my addiction problem. I would never have done what I did if I could have helped myself. I had no will. I was nervous, afraid, and full of pain. They said I shot at the policemen, which I did not do. I stole the police car in an insane attempt to get away or get killed. Even after being handcuffed, I couldn't feel the savage blows of enraged police who screamed out dirty names. Two times I was knocked unconscious, but never long enough to numb the great and increasing pain of (drug) withdrawal.[77]

Crockett had long viewed alcoholism as a public health problem, not a criminal matter.[78] "Drunkenness is a disease, just as drug addiction is a disease. The common drunk should get treatment, not incarceration." He was also sensitive to the class dimensions of the issue. "He pointed out that members of Detroit's swank clubs get drunk every night of the week, but never go to jail: 'If wealthy drunks don't go to jail, then poor drunks shouldn't either.'"[79]

Crockett viewed Tyler in a similar light. "'The issue is whether or not I should do anything about your narcotic addiction.' I told him I would put him on probation on condition he went to Lexington, Kentucky to get treatment for his addiction."[80] Crockett made the necessary arrangements and sentenced Tyler to treatment.

For the already agitated police, prosecutors, and press, the Tyler case was just more red meat. "After I recommended that Tyler go to Lexington the newspapers came out with screaming headlines about dope addicts loose on probation and what does this Judge Crockett think he is doing, etc."[81] The *Detroit Free Press* columnist Judd Arnett observed, "A few days ago Judge George Crockett paroled a four-time loser to a Federal institution which treats drug addicts, and since then the air has been blue with the invective of aroused citizens. The old Gray Lady Down The Street [the *Detroit News*] ran 14 hell-raising letters on its editorial page shortly after the incident occurred and has consistently beaten the judge over the head and shoulders with the heaviest weapons in its arsenal."[82] In almost all the coverage, the name of "Lloyd K. Tyler" disappeared completely as a human being and was replaced only with the repeated label of "addict" and "four-time loser."

With all of the venom spewing forth, some stories rehashed old attacks on Crockett, while others anticipated future ones. The *Detroit News* published numerous letters from readers attacking Crockett: "Readers Rap Judge for Felon's Release." One letter stated, "I say 'hooray' for police power and down with criminal power and judges like Crockett." Another read, "Why should policemen with families risk their lives to catch criminals, if our judges are going to make justice a joke?"[83] The *Harper Woods Herald* ran an article with the headline "George W. Crockett Jr.: A Communist Agent in Judge's Robes."[84] A political cartoon in the *Detroit News* showed a disheveled man labeled an addict with a criminal record receiving a bus ticket to the rehabilitation center from a judge dressed in black robes with the admonition, "Try not to get any irresistible impulses en route."[85] The columnist Al Blanchard wrote that Crockett's ruling was just another legitimate justification for further white flight: "But it is safe to assume that these unfortunates, . . . the appeal process being what it is, . . . will now use the Crockett-Tyler ruling to seek their freedom, which will mean that we can probably empty the prisons and return these men to Detroit. This will all be good because they will certainly be needed to fill the population gap left by those citizens who will be fleeing because of Judge Crockett's decision."[86] The racism was blatant.

Some rebukes came from more establishment sources. The chief justice of the Michigan Supreme Court made public statements critical of Crockett's decision: "The 'mild sentences' handed down by Recorder's Judge George W. Crockett Jr. in two recent cases are 'a bad policy to follow,' according to Thomas E. Brennan, chief justice of the State Supreme Court."[87] Perhaps most troubling, echoing Crockett's previous fights over threatened disbarment, the *Detroit News* columnist Will Muller advocated that Crockett be brought before the newly created Judicial Tenure Commission and removed from office. "One of the first tasks of the state's new Judicial Tenure Commission, once it is constituted, might well be to review the tempestuous course of Recorder's Court Judge George W. Crockett Jr. It's rare that a criminal court judge doesn't collide with the police and the prosecutor's office over leniency with lawbreakers some time in his career. That it should be a persistent pattern running counter to the judicial policy of his colleagues, as in Crockett's case, is of significant public concern."[88]

Crockett did have his supporters. Letters to the *Detroit Free Press* were different from those sent to the *Detroit News*. When asked, "Did Judge Crockett make right decision?" the *Free Press* readers largely answered "yes." "Most people agree that our present legal and penal system needs a very critical overhauling. Instead of giving in to the cries for oppressive 'law and order,' Judge Crockett takes a courageous stand. He believes in rehabilitative treatment which respects the dignity of the person no matter who he is. Whether his decisions will prove successful remains to be seen."[89] Not surprisingly, his colleagues at the National Lawyers Guild expressed their support.[90] The Democratic Committee for the Thirteenth Congressional District sent a telegram expressing its continued backing of Crockett: "Please be advised that the official 13th District of the Democratic Party went on record unanimously continuing its endorsement of Judge George W. Crockett and censoring the news media for its bias and incomplete reporting of the facts of the case."[91]

Tyler was not a one-day story; it was a spectacle. Reporters went to Lexington, Kentucky, to follow Tyler to the rehabilitation facility and monitor his progress. On the positive side, the reporters learned that there were few facilities available to treat drug addiction and that the recovery process was difficult. The *Detroit News* published a story with a byline from Lexington, "Entry, Cure Hard to Get at Dope Hospital."[92] Sadly, after twenty days of evaluation, Tyler was released from the facility as not being an appropriate candidate for treatment. He returned to Detroit to appear before Judge Crockett for sentencing.[93]

With treatment for addiction no longer at issue, Judge Crockett turned his attention to the alleged police brutality. Crockett later stated, "I told him my sending him to prison depended on whether or not I was convinced he had been a victim of police brutality. I informed him that I would appoint counsel to investigate his charges. . . . I fixed a date for the hearing."[94] The press made a big deal of the fact that Judge Crockett did not report the alleged abuse to the police commissioner.[95] Crockett remarked in one interview, "The police are the last people in the world I would report this matter to," noting that he had done that before with no result.[96] Judge Crockett did, however, put the police commissioner and the prosecuting attorney on notice, "so they could give any evidence they wanted to offer" at Tyler's sentencing hearing.[97] Crockett later recounted,

On the appointed date the prosecutor appeared and announced his office would prefer not to have anything to do with the hearing. I told him he was welcome to stay and observe; so he sat down. No one appeared for the police commissioner. The young lawyer, representing the defendant, had done a good job. He had gone to the community and found two young witnesses, kids about 17 or 18 years of age. They had been on their front porch, witnessed the arrest, and saw the police beat the defendant. They saw another man come up and whisper to the police who then stopped beating him. The police put the defendant in the car and punched him as the car was leaving the scene. The probation department representative had gone to the police department and examined their files which included mug shots. There was a mug shot of the man taken right after he was arrested showing his broken nose, eyes puffed up and blood splattered over his shirt. The police offered no evidence in contradiction. For the record, I again heard the priest's testimony. I concluded that the defendant had been the victim of police brutality and that he should not be sentenced to prison. He was placed on probation for three years under the joint supervision of the probation department and his parish priest. I told him, from the bench, that if he had any difficulty, the doors to my chambers were always open and he could come to my chambers and I would discuss his problems.[98]

The silence of the police and prosecutor spoke volumes.

Sadly, the Tyler story did not have a happy ending. Crockett recalled, "He strayed from the beaten path on one occasion, but our probation department straightened him out. He did not commit a crime that time. [In 1971] he was [involved] in a shoot-out and was killed." There was a silver lining: "The opinion of the man in the street was that dope addicts should be locked up in jail. I think the Tyler case persuaded more people to think seriously about the problem and consider the necessity for providing medical assistance for narcotics addicts."[99]

Carl Parsell, president of the Detroit Police Officers Association (DPOA), continued the charge against Crockett. The headline of the *Detroit News* on Friday, March 28, 1969, continued to sound the growing drumbeat: "Crockett Is Blasted by Parsell." Parsell accused Judge Crockett of "letting his prejudice against the police show," referring to "allegedly lenient sentences he has imposed on confessed criminals." Among other things, the article rehashed details of the Tyler case. While these criticisms had become routine, the spectacle of the white DPOA president publicly chastising a Black judge cannot be lost. Parsell was quick to reassure people, however, that this had nothing to do with race: "'Before someone accuses me of being prejudiced,' Parsell said in reference to his opinions of the Negro judge, 'I am glad to say that we have several good black judges.'"[100]

If the Tyler case set the pot boiling, the New Bethel Baptist Church Incident would cause it to explode, the very next day.

8

The New Bethel Baptist Church Incident

The Incident

On Saturday, March 29, 1969, the Republic of New Africa (RNA) held its second annual convention, renting New Bethel Baptist Church to host the event; the pastor at New Bethel was Reverend C. L. Franklin, father of the famed singer Aretha Franklin.[1] The church was at the corner of Linwood and Philadelphia in the Tenth Police Precinct, not far from the intersection of Twelfth and Clairmount, the epicenter of Detroit's 1967 Rebellion.

In the wake of the Rebellion, police relations with the Black community had become even tenser: "Sometimes the contact is violent, sometimes abrasive, sometimes only chilling in the manifestation of white indifference."[2] Police patrols in the Tenth Precinct were often spoken of in military terms: "Many officers now approach their tours of duty almost like combat patrols. Loaded carbines are commonly carried in the front seat of scout cars, sometimes leaning conspicuously against the dashboards. Some officers have them in hand when answering 'hot runs.'"[3]

The RNA had a packed agenda: RNA Supreme Court justices were elected, resolutions debated and voted on, and updates provided.[4] An important question from the beginning was whether and to what extent the police had the meeting under surveillance. "Police officials from headquarters and the Tenth Precinct either denied or refused to comment on the possibility that extra surveillance was already underway in the area before the shooting."[5] It is difficult to imagine a significant Black Power meeting in Detroit, or anywhere else in the country in 1969, that was not subject to some level of police surveillance. In an interview years later, Crockett flatly stated, "The police had had the building and the situation under surveillance because of the nature of the organization having the convention."[6] The subsequent release of law enforcement documents confirms Crockett's assessment. The RNA and its convention were under surveillance by the FBI's COINTELPRO campaign, Michigan State Police, and the Detroit Police Department's Intelligence Bureau.[7] There were numerous undercover informants from various agencies at the meeting.

RNA work went late into the evening. At end of the meeting, the Black Legion, an honor guard, wearing military fatigues and leopard-skin epaulets, escorted Vice President Milton Henry to his car, and he drove away. Uncertainty still shrouds exactly what happened next. According to police reports, at about 11:42 p.m., around the same time Henry drove away, Tenth Precinct scout car 10–5 with patrolmen Michael Czapski and Richard Worobec aboard was driving north on Linwood. The officers reported "seeing 10–12 Negroes some armed with rifles, entering cars" outside the church.[8]

What took place in the eighteen minutes that followed is still a blur. According to early press reports, the "policemen leave the car to approach the men. Czapski was shot seven times, fatally. Worobec, hit three times, crawls back in the car under fire." At 11:43 p.m., Worobec was able to radio back to the station: "They're shooting at us, they're shooting at us. We need help." According to the *Free Press* timeline, at 11:44 p.m., "police cars from four precincts begin to arrive." At 11:50 p.m., some fifty policemen entered the church, guns firing. In the flurry of gunfire, four people inside the church were shot, and one person suffered a broken leg. By midnight, the building had been secured.[9]

Not surprisingly, widely divergent stories of the incident emerged almost immediately. According to the police, the persons responsible for shooting officers Czapski and Worobec fled back into the church, and people inside the church actively shot at the police officers as they arrived on the scene.[10] Police "smashed their way through front and side entrances guns blazing. They were met, they said, by a line of Negroes kneeling inside the church in firing position."[11]

RNA members tell a very different story. It was nearly midnight, and the meeting was coming to a close. "[The] Minister of Culture had just finished giving a benediction which asked 'the help of our direct ancestors who have helped in the struggle and died.' Police entered the church, some of them shooting as they came in."[12] RNA members denied the accusation that they shot at the police as they arrived or during the raid on the church.

Given how quickly police secured the building, it is doubtful that they met very much active resistance. The police, however, did meet 142 members of the RNA, many women and children, and arrested them all. "Those inside the church were lined up against both walls of the building. Another group was confined in the basement. Squad cars and police buses began carrying prisoners away."[13]

Subsequent investigations solicited complaints of ill treatment from those who were detained:

> Rep. [Nelis] Saunders, having interviewed some of the persons arrested that night charged that police used unnecessarily rough tactics in effecting arrests of people who offered no resistance. "Women told us how their dresses were pulled up over their heads and how they were patted down—an illegal act—by police officers," Rep. Saunders said. "The women also told us how the police kicked them and their children and how they hit men who were innocent of any wrong. Men and women told us how they were dragged from the floor and how they were hit over their heads and about their bodies with guns."[14]

Other sources reported similar abuses: "A Republic of New Africa member from Cleveland said officers were 'walking down the line hitting us in the back with rifle butts.'"[15] By the time the police attack was over, there was substantial damage: "church walls and pews were spattered with blood."[16] Over eighty-four bullet holes were found in the altar, doors, walls, and pews.

While the building had been secured quickly, the episode was by no means over. City officials were concerned about the potentially dangerous implications of yet another mass arrest. "Fearful of further incidents, police were ordered on tactical alert immediately after the battle. A cordon of shotgun-armed officers was formed around Police Headquarters."[17]

Milton Henry had departed just before the violence. He said that "he heard gunfire as he drove away, but did not turn back because he has feared

assassination ever since the shooting of Malcolm X."[18] In another indication that the police had the entire RNA convention under surveillance,
Henry, a short time after his departure, was pulled over by the police at
Webb and the John C. Lodge Service Drive. This was only two miles away
from the church and less than a five-minute drive. "They shook me down
for weapons and when they didn't find any, they let me go."[19] Soon thereafter, Henry called the Black state representative James Del Rio. Del Rio
called Reverend Franklin.[20]

Del Rio arrived at police headquarters at 12:40 a.m. All those who
were arrested were being detained in the police headquarters' underground
garage, which had no sanitation facilities. By 4:35 a.m., "Del Rio, angry,
leaves to get Recorder's Court Judge George Crockett, claiming suspects'
civil rights were violated."[21] It just happened that, as presiding judge of
Recorder's Court that week, Crockett was the right person to contact.
Moreover, his house in Detroit's Lafayette Park was close, less than a three-
minute drive away.

The Habeas Corpus Proceeding

This is how what later came to be known as the New Bethel Incident literally came to Crockett's doorstep. Reverend Franklin had joined Del Rio at
Crockett's home. Crockett recalled that Franklin let Del Rio do most of the
talking. They explained the situation. Crockett reported later, "The first
thing that went through my mind was whether or not we were on the verge
of another riot in Detroit."[22] As a judge, he began to process the facts of the
mass arrest through the lens of a writ of habeas corpus, a legal mechanism
to determine whether persons are being unlawfully detained.

The scope of habeas writs under Michigan law was expansive. Rule 712 of
the General Court Rules of 1963 authorized a judge to "issue the writ without
any formal or written application therefore 'and upon his own motion' whenever he learns that any person within his jurisdiction is illegally restrained
of his liberty."[23] The judge was further authorized to designate the time and
place where the prisoner was to be produced, as well as where the hearing was
to be held, and to command the presence of the prosecutor. The court rule
further provided, "The Court shall proceed promptly in a summary manner
to hear the matter and render judgment accordingly."[24]

Crockett, Franklin, and Del Rio arrived at police headquarters around 5:00 a.m., just as the tactical alert was being called off.[25] Crockett asked the sergeant at the front desk to see a list of all people who had been arrested, but no list existed. Crockett asked to see Police Commissioner Spreen but was told he was unavailable. Crockett, Franklin, and Del Rio huddled in a small room in the station, as Crockett filled in the relevant facts in the habeas form.

The habeas form read, "In the name of the People of the state of Michigan to the person or his superior having custody of _____." Crockett filled in the form, writing by hand, "any person arrested and detained in connection with the shooting incident which allegedly occurred at the New Bethel Church, Linwood and Philadelphia Streets, Detroit, at or about midnight on March Twenty-Ninth-Thirtieth, 1969." The writ listed Reverend Franklin and Representative Del Rio as the applicants. With regard to the timing of the habeas hearing, the writ simply stated, "forthwith." As to the location for the hearing, the writ specified the "First Police Precinct Station, Detroit," which was located in the police headquarters building. Finally, the order was signed: "George W. Crockett, Jr."[26]

Crockett did everything by the book. The police commissioner was the most appropriate person to receive the writ, and Crockett knew where the commissioner's office was located. With the writ in hand, along with Franklin and Del Rio, Crockett took the elevator up to Commissioner Spreen's office. "We informed the Commissioner of the complaint made by Reverend Franklin and Representative Del Rio and of our intention to proceed with a habeas corpus hearing with respect to the arrested persons. We requested that the Commissioner notify the Prosecutor and that we be furnished with a list of all of the arrestees in order that their names could be inserted in the Writ. We also requested that a room be made available for the hearing."[27]

The commissioner provided a room in the police station, and the habeas proceedings started at 6:40 a.m. The hearing was open to the public, and even at that early morning hour, the press was in attendance. The Prosecutor's Office was represented by Assistant Prosecutor Jay Nolan. He informed the judge that twenty-five women had already been released fro custody. Judge Crockett ordered the remaining arrestees be brought do in groups of ten, beginning with the women. Every person brought for was questioned individually by Crockett in the presence of the prosecutor. Fifteen Detroit residents were released on their own recognizance with a $100 personal bond and ordered to return at noon that same day to Crockett's Recorder's Court courtroom. With the consent of the prosecutor, another Detroit resident, the janitor at the church, was discharged. A resident of Springfield, Ohio, was ordered released with a $100 personal bond but was also ordered to appear in court at noon. Twenty-two other out-of-town residents were remanded back into custody.[28]

The hearing was running smoothly, with a total of thirty-nine individuals processed, until Wayne County Prosecutor Cahalan arrived. In the presence of the court, he ordered the rearrest of James Wheeler, one of the Detroit residents released on his own recognizance. Notwithstanding the court's warnings that Cahalan would be held in contempt, he actively prevented the police from bringing any more arrestees before the court. In the face of such defiance, Judge Crockett terminated the habeas proceedings. Crockett ordered the hearing to reconvene at noon in his courtroom, where Prosecutor Cahalan was directed to appear and show cause why he should not be held in contempt of court.[29] When the hearing reconvened, Cahalan was not present.

Assistant Prosecutor Nolan gave the court a significant update on the number and status of detained individuals: "We have released upwards of a hundred people since we had our earlier session of Court this morning.... We proceeded with our investigation and determined that we had no basis to hold them." A total of ninety-nine individuals were released by the prosecutors "as a matter of routine as soon as [they] got the necessary information."[30] According to Nolan, only ten individuals remained—two of whom prosecutors were seeking warrants to arrest and eight others ᵗ whom prosecutors were seeking an extension of time to continue investigation.[31] Prosecutors sought to adjourn the habeas hearing for ᵗ of twenty-four hours. Some of the eight had allegedly tested posiᵗaffin test for nitrate. Others were simply from out of town and ᵗht risks.

ᵗes of the men were called, they were brought before the ᵗ informed them of their right to an attorney and asked ᵗrepresented by a lawyer. Each indicated yes. Judge ᵗ there any lawyers present who will volunteer their services just for this proceeding?"[32] As an indication of how quickly the Black legal community had been called into action, present in the courtroom were some of Detroit's best attorneys. Among those willing to provide representation were Alan Chalfin, Kenneth Cockrel, O. Lee Moulette, Lucius Patrick, Cornelius Pitts, Myzell Sowell, Myron Wahls, and, ironically, Milton Henry, the RNA vice president. Each arrestee was assigned a lawyer and given space and opportunity for consultation.

In the meantime, the court called the names of the Detroit residents who had been released on their own personal recognizance earlier that morning, including James Wheeler, the man Cahalan had ordered rearrested. Despite Cahalan's earlier antics, Nolan recommended that they *all* be discharged. Judge Crockett granted Nolan's requests and dismissed the prisoners.[33]

The court then called the cases of David Brown Jr. and Kirkwood Hall, the two men for whom the prosecutor was seeking arrest warrants.[34] After Brown and Hall were advised of their rights, Brown was assigned attorney Robert Mitchell, and Hall was assigned attorney Marshall Hill. Both lawyers were Black senior members of a loosely organized group of attorneys practicing in Recorder's Court known as the "Clinton Street Bar Association."

Crockett next turned his attention back to the contempt charges against Cahalan. Aloysius Suchy, chief of the Civil Division, asked to address the court. Suchy made a number of unsuccessful efforts to diffuse the contempt issue and to explain away the continued absence of Cahalan. He suggested that no formal order to show cause had been issued and that in the "early morning hours" Cahalan did not "fully understand what the Court's order was."[35] Judge Crockett showed little patience. He reminded Suchy that the contempt had taken place in the court's presence, that the order to show cause had been clear and direct, and that it was not necessary to issue a written order under these circumstances. Nor, having himself arrived at the police station at 5:00 a.m., was Crockett sympathetic to the alleged "early morning" nature of the episode.

Crockett made it clear that he believed that Cahalan's conduct constituted contempt. Nevertheless, having learned from his own experience before Judge Medina in the *Dennis* case, he believed that basic norms of due process should be followed:

It is my considered opinion that the Wayne County Prosecutor is in contempt.... However, and notwithstanding the Court is authorized to punish that contempt because it was committed in my presence, I have always been of the view that where the contemptuous conduct amounts to a personal affront to the Judge—notwithstanding that Judge is authorized to hear and punish—he should, as a matter of discretion, refrain from doing so and refer the matter to another Judge. I not only think this is a personal affront but I am persuaded that it had racial overtones—and that is an additional reason why I think I should disqualify myself from sitting in judgment of the Prosecutor.

Instead, I shall prepare the usual affidavit that is required by law for contempts not committed in the presence of the Judge and I will present those charges to the Presiding Judge of this Court with notice that I have disqualified myself and with a request that another Judge be appointed to hear this matter.[36]

The court returned to deliberations for the eight arrestees whom the prosecution wanted held for further investigation. The most contentious cases involved those who allegedly tested positive for nitrate following a paraffin test. The first involved Mr. Valrie Jackson, who was represented by Milton Henry. Nitrate tests were controversial. Henry said, "I think Mr. Nolan would have to admit that nitrate can come from anything. It could come from dealing in junk. It could come from a number of things other than gun powder." Henry was further concerned about constitutional protections: "Now for them to come here and say there was nitrate on this n's hands when they illegally arrested him to begin with ... and now for to take the fruits of the poisonous tree" was a problematic issue.[37]

kett had a number of concerns of his own. "These people are being municado, as my certificate indicated, without an opportunity or to get in touch with relatives or consult with anyone. helpless position and you take advantage of them to get he evidence to convict, not to identify them. This is ing or making mugshots." Crockett was concerned been taken despite his orders to the contrary: ng that you requested that I allow time for a nitrate test to be made. I said that I would not and I said that I wanted those people brought directly before me without any nitrate test. It would appear that notwithstanding that order, the police decided to go on and make the nitrate test anyway. That is a factor I will take into consideration in exercising my discretion that the statute gives me with respect to the release of this man on bond."[38]

The court proceeded to release all eight arrestees whom the prosecutor had sought to detain. Release at this stage did not prevent further lawful police investigations. "You still have the right to get a warrant if you have sufficient evidence to show probable cause and you have the right to come back to this Court and I am sure that any Judge of this Court will give you a warrant under those conditions. For the present, you fail to show probable cause and the police have violated the constitutional right of this defendant."[39]

The court turned to the prosecutor's requests for warrants to arrest two of the detained men. First was David Brown Jr., charged with assault with intent to murder. Not many details are provided in the transcript, but according to the news coverage, "Patrolman Chester Harkiewicz said that as he moved through the church he heard a noise from above, followed by several shots fired in his direction from an opening in the ceiling. Harkiewicz said he returned the fire. A youth later identified as David Brown Jr., 19, of Compton, Calif., tumbled through the opening, dropping an Italian automatic carrying six live cartridges, Harkiewicz said. Brown was not wounded in the gunfight."[40] Brown pled not guilty.[41] Judge Crockett ordered Brown held without bond pending further court proceedings.

Kirkwood Hall was considered next. Prosecutors were seeking a warrant to charge him with "Possession of a Gas Ejecting Device."[42] According to the news accounts, Hall was arrested in the church basement carrying a can of chemical mace.[43] During the hearing, it was revealed that Hall was a graduate of Virginia Union University and was working in New York as a social worker. He claimed that the device was legally purchased in New York and used for his personal protection.[44] Similar to Brown, Judge Crockett ordered Hall held without bond pending further court proceedings.

The confusion flowing from the mass arrests was evident through the habeas proceedings. Accurate lists of those arrested, those released, those still being held were difficult to obtain. At one point, Judge Cro was made aware that "a substantial number of persons are apparently still being held in custody by the police." The court was finally given a list of twenty-two persons still detained in the basement of the First Precinct. These individuals were finally released, and the court had all of their names entered into the record. The prosecutor later informed the court that an additional ten persons were still somehow being detained. Still later, another seven individuals were identified as still in custody.[45] The names of all were read into the record. The habeas proceeding adjourned at 2:30 p.m.[46]

While an intense drama played out in Judge Crockett's courtroom that Sunday, much of life in Detroit proceeded largely as usual. Amazingly, services at the New Bethel Baptist Church went on as scheduled. "The church was almost full ... with almost 1000 persons to hear Rev. Franklin preach his Palm Sunday sermon at 11 a.m."[47] The real storm would begin on Monday, March 31, 1969, with the arrival of the morning newspapers.

The Backlash of the White Establishment

Monday, March 31. The New Bethel Incident would come to mean different things to different people, but some facts were clear. In a confrontation between the RNA, a Black nationalist group, and the Detroit police, one white officer was killed and another lay wounded in the hospital. In any other city and at any other time, this would be the main focus of the story. On Sunday morning, however, something even more frightening and unimaginable occurred. A Black judge stood up to enforce the law and protect the constitutional rights of those who were subject to a mass arrest. ʼas Judge Crockett's actions and not those of the RNA that became the ʼtory. As the *New York Times* observed, "Judge Crockett had done it ꜜ the prosecutor's office, the police, the newspapers and the makꜜne telephone calls would soon be after him—again."[48] *Time* ꜜ a similar observation: "In racially tense Detroit, the inciꜜared into a riot. Instead—at least so far—it has turned ꜜver the conduct of Negro Judge George W. Crockett, ꜜr's Court."[49]

ꜜ coverage was so charged was because the press prosecutors as their almost-exclusive sources. One headline read, "Police Group President Assails Judge Crockett."[50] Police spokespersons, particularly Detroit Police Officers Association (DPOA) president Parsell, continually made outrageous and irresponsible comments. Parsell accused Crockett of giving "people a free license to shoot policemen . . . without fear of punishment."[51] Parsell continued to stoke resentment among police and in the community: "Feeling is running extremely high with the men (policemen), and it will run high in the community when citizens view the weekend justice we have just witnessed."[52]

Tuesday, April 1. The police were not the only members of the establishment stoking the flames of resentment. Twenty-one state senators cosponsored Senate Resolution no. 44, "A resolution to invoke action by the Judicial Tenure Commission of Michigan":

> Whereas, Public allegations of misconduct in office concerning Recorder's Court Judge George W. Crockett have been made, most recently in the March 29–30, 1969 affair in Detroit, and in a Sunday session which Judge Crockett consequently opened, allegedly ten key suspects were discharged and released, despite official protest by Detroit law enforcement officers who produced evidence indicating warrantable suspicion.
>
> *　　*　　*
>
> Whereas, Such allegations and statements, if true, would clearly cast doubt upon the fitness to hold judicial office of the said Recorder's Court Judge George W. Crockett and would interfere with the orderly process of justice.[53]

The senate resolved that "the Judicial Tenure Commission be urged and is hereby requested to investigate promptly any and all charges of misconduct as are alleged to have been committed."[54] The resolution passed on a 25–5 vote.

One of those who voted "no" was State Senator Coleman A. Young. Young criticized his colleagues for their rush to judgment: "I'm one of the few who went to the scene to get the facts—and they're not clear. If we don't have the time to get the facts, let's keep our noses out of the judicial branch." For Young and the four other senators opposing the resolution, a clear double standard was at play: "You didn't hear this kind of request for an investigation of the courts during the Detroit riots—where people were held on $100,000 bonds. You didn't hear this kind of request when the accused murderer in the Algiers Motel Case was released on $5,000 bond." Crockett was being targeted because of his race: "'Let's stop kidding ourselves,' said Young. 'This is the Crockett lynching session.'" Young predicted that the white backlash against Crockett would not bode well for race relations: "'We seem powerless to change our direction.' At the end of the day, Young said, 'This action to lynch the black judge will be understood for what it is in the black community.'"[55]

That same day, Reverend Ralph Abernathy, who assumed the leadership of the Southern Christian Leadership Conference after the assassination of Dr. Martin Luther King Jr. less than a year before, arrived in Detroit. He was there "to help cool down the black community and investigate the conduct of police after the shooting of the two officers." Abernathy was critical of the conduct of the police: "He contended that police fired into the church without provocation and said that the forty officers who responded could have used a bullhorn or tear gas 'before resorting to frontal tactics of [risking] taking lives and injuring people.'"[56]

Some 150 white policemen picketed the Tenth Precinct Station, protesting Crockett's actions.[57] When the spokesperson for the officers was asked why no Black police officers were part of the picket, he stated that "most black officers worked the afternoon shift and were at work during the hours of the demonstration." That assertion was contradicted by his superior: "Lt. Richard Szymoniak, of the [Tenth Precinct] Station, said however that black officers were assigned to all shifts like white officers. Black officers at the [Tenth Precinct] Station were reluctant to discuss why no black officers were marching with the white officers."[58]

Wednesday, April 2. Governor William Milliken waded into the fray and joined the state senate in calling for the Judicial Tenure Commission to investigate Crockett. "I am extremely concerned about the allegations made with regard to Judge Crockett's handling of this matter. . . . And I want to strongly encourage the tenure commission to investigate the case thoroughly. This is a logical and proper approach." Milliken was joined by Detroit mayor Jerome Cavanagh in calling for a Judicial Tenure Commission probe of Crockett: "I think Judge Crockett acted with haste in exercising what obviously were his judicial prerogatives."[59]

The divide between Black and white leadership over Crockett and the New Bethel Incident continued to grow. William T. Patrick, Detroit's first Black councilman and president of New Detroit, Inc., a civic organization formed in the wake of the 1967 Rebellion, called Crockett "an authentic hero of these trying times."[60] Unprecedented support for Crockett was forming throughout the Black community, leading to the creation of the Black United Front (BUF), headed by Dan Aldridge, an employee of the Detroit Commission on Children and Youth.[61] The growing coalition included representatives from across the wide spectrum of Black political representation. The Black United Front included "the highly controversial Negro militant Black Panthers, the Wayne State University Association of Black Students, the Guardians (a Negro police officers group), the Eastside Voice of Independent Detroit (ESVID), two Negro churches and representatives of Democratic Congressmen Charles Diggs and John Conyers and State Rep. James Del Rio, D-Detroit."[62]

Police protests against Crockett continued. "Much of the action was spearheaded by angry policemen and their wives. About 500 of them picketed Recorder's Court, completely ringing the building on St. Antoine between Macomb and Clinton." The protesting policemen carried signs reading, "Crockett justice? Release Killers, Prosecute Prosecutors, Give License To Kill Policemen." A group of a dozen police wives presented a petition to Robert Grace, the U.S. Attorney, charging that Crockett had "conspired with known revolutionaries, people that advocated the overthrow of our government," and demanding that the U.S. Department of Justice conduct an investigation.[63]

Some of the police officers' statements appeared contradictory. The group's spokesman, patrolman Joseph Whall, said that "although in a technical sense Crockett was probably right in releasing the prisoners, his actions is like a guy who gives a speeding ticket for traveling one mile over the speed limit." What everyone seemed to agree on was that this was all somehow about race. Whall added, "Frankly, I don't understand the man. He must be a racist himself. Or else I just don't understand him."[64]

Thursday, April 3. The momentum of anti-Crockett sentiment generated by the media, the DPOA, and leading politicians from the governor to the mayor was amplifying racial tensions throughout the city. Morrie Gleicher, a civil rights activist and public relations expert who often provided services to progressive politicians, observed that "the tension grew so fast ... that in two days, this whole city was on the verge of another riot on the basis of Crockett's activities as a judge releasing these so-called suspects." Gleicher held the media directly responsible, recalling that all the news coverage was "condemnatory of Crockett." Speaking of the coverage by the *Detroit News* and *Free Press*, he stated, "They weren't news reports. They were editorials about Crockett putting criminals back on the streets, being easy on crime, being a racist because these were all blacks."[65]

Gleicher reached out to Crockett, his longtime friend, and told him that he had to take affirmative steps to address the growing crisis. "But he was calm and said, 'Look, I did the right thing.' And I said, 'George, the people don't understand that you did the right thing—it has to be explained.'"[66] The two agreed that Crockett should hold a press conference to counter the media firestorm. Gleicher and Crockett got together around midnight on the evening of Tuesday, April 1, and worked through most of the night drafting a prepared statement. A press conference was scheduled for Thursday, April 3, and Crockett decided that it should be held in his courtroom.[67]

Gleicher recalled, "That Wednesday, the momentum, the tempo was accelerating even more, as far as the tension in the community, about the so-called outrage that had been perpetrated by Judge Crockett."[68] Gleicher was with Crockett in his chambers that Thursday morning with the press conference scheduled for 11:00 a.m. "I said, look, let's go, get ready to go and he said, 'Well, let's take another look at this statement'—very calm, very relaxed."[69] Crockett's personal copy of the statement shows a number of handwritten revisions to the text.[70] While Crockett was calm, Gleicher was not. "I was kind of tense because outside I could hear the shouting and screaming of people who were still picketing [the courthouse] and we could hear it through the window of the courtroom." When he entered Crockett's courtroom and saw the media, cameras, radio reporters, and assorted onlookers, Gleicher recalled, "you couldn't get another soul in that courtroom."[71]

The stage was set for what Gleicher calls "one of the most dramatic statements in the history of the city's political life."[72] As reported by the *Miami Herald*, the atmosphere was charged. "Chants of 'Judge Crockett must go, Judge Crockett must go!' could be heard through the windows in Crockett's second-floor courtroom, where he explained to newsmen and a throng of applauding supporters the actions that sparked the growing controversy. Earlier, uniformed police had kept order between about 500 off-duty policemen protesting Crockett's actions and a crowd of about 1000, mostly Negro, supporting the Judge, also a Negro."[73] *Jet* magazine ran a photo of the protest outside the courthouse showing a Black policeman carrying a sign saying, "Black Cops Support Equal Justice."[74]

Judge Crockett began by reading his prepared statement.

The distortions of fact and the confusion over this Court's actions in the recent events of the New Bethel Church compel me to make certain facts clear. I am personally deeply affronted by reports and stories which have clearly and deliberately twisted the truth and the law in this matter.

More serious than any harm to me personally is the profound damage being done to the Court and to our entire community by those who would use this tragic affair to intensify community hostilities which were already so deep and divisive.

The actions taken by me in my capacity as presiding judge, following the New Bethel Church shootings and the mass arrests, were legal, proper and moral. Indeed, it is precisely because I followed the law, equally and without partiality, that questions and accusations are being raised. If I were to have reacted otherwise, if I were to have ignored my judicial and constitutional responsibilities and followed the often accepted practices of condoning long police detentions, of ignoring prisoners' rights to counsel and of delaying the hearings of writs of habeas corpus, possibly the adverse publicity about Judge Crockett may have been averted. But in doing so, justice would have been denied.

I deplore the senseless shooting of the policemen. I also deplore the armed assault on a church, particularly a church occupied by men, women and children, whom we must presume to be innocent until and unless evidence to the contrary is presented. I deplore, too, that so many innocent people were rounded up by the police, incarcerated for many hours in violation of their rights as citizens, and that some officials who are sworn to enforce equal justice have complained because I have done so.[75]

Crockett proceeded to outline the clear legal basis for his actions, just as he had done in the transcript of the habeas proceedings. He stated that he had acted completely in accordance with the law: "Justice last Sunday demanded prompt judicial examination and processing of the persons arrested. If there was any sound legal basis for their detention, they were detained; otherwise they were entitled to be released and they were released upon reasonable bond."[76]

Judge Crockett stressed a point virtually absent from the media coverage. The prosecutor "himself released or requested the release of some 130 arrestees. It is essential to emphasize that the vast majority of those released, approximately 130 persons, were released with the prosecutor's concurrence. Despite this fact, the press has several times referred to my actions in terms of 'unwarranted leniency.' There was no unwarranted leniency."[77] Because this had been a mass arrest, there was absolutely no basis for the police to hold the vast majority of those who were imprisoned, and the prosecutors knew that.

Next, Crockett made clear the legal basis for his actions. He held over two arrestees, David Brown Jr. and Kirkwood Hall, because the police and prosecutors presented sufficient evidence to get a warrant for their arrest. These individuals were being held without bond. With regard to the individuals whose hands allegedly tested positive for the nitrate tests, Crockett was clear as to his reasoning: "I hold that such tests are unconstitutional when taken without the presence of counsel or at least upon advice to the prisoner that he is entitled to counsel at this critical step of the interrogation. For me to have held those nine men, without objective evidence and under those circumstances would have been improper."[78]

It was the police and the prosecutors who shouldered the responsibility of the investigation: "The police had many hours to identify those nine men. They should know who they are and present enough legal grounds for their arrest and detention. They still can do so if their investigation warrants it." Crockett defended his actions as principled and legal: "I am most anxious that criminals be apprehended, tried and brought to justice. But I will not lend my office to practices which subvert legal processes and deny justice to some because they are poor and black."[79]

With regard to the political backlash and growing tensions in the community, he held the prosecutor and the media responsible: "I understand, of course, why the hue and cry arose. An angry prosecutor, lacking police evidence or testimony which might produce a probable suspect, and resentful that ordinary and undemocratic police practices were challenged, chose to divert public attention to Judge Crockett. And some of the media, particularly the *Detroit News*, picked up that lead and began their campaign to help the police and the Prosecutor's office continue their efforts to dominate and control the courts and legal processes. The judiciary cannot allow its independence to be threatened in this fashion."[80]

Crockett ended by placing the controversy directly within the frame of race, racism, and discrimination:

Finally, and regrettably, let me repeat that this whole case does have racial overtones.

Can any of you imagine the Detroit Police invading an all-white church and rounding up everyone in sight to be bussed to a wholesale lockup in a police garage? Can any of you imagine a church group from, let us say, Rosedale Park, being held incommunicado for seven hours, without being allowed to telephone relatives and without their constitutional rights to counsel? Can any of you justify the jailing of 32 women all night long when there was admittedly not the slightest evidence of their involvement in any crime? Can anyone explain in other than racist terms the shooting by police inside a closed and surrounded church?

If the killing had occurred in a white neighborhood, I believe the sequence of events would have been far different. Because a terrible crime was committed, it does not follow that other wrongs be permitted or condoned. Indeed, constitutional safeguards are needed even more urgently in times of tension than in ordinary times.[81]

Crockett then placed the episode in an even broader social context. Only the rigorous protection of constitutional rights can prevent violence and ease racial tensions:

The best guarantee to avert the kind of social disaster that occurred in Detroit in 1967 is prompt judicial action with strict observance of constitutional rights.

I intend to continue to maintain law and order in my court by dispensing justice equally and fairly, by protecting each individual's rights, and most importantly, by upholding the independence of the judiciary and the dignity of this court.

If the real dangers to our community are to be uprooted, let the news media and all other forces of truth and justice concentrate in the underlying causes of crime and social disorder as described by the Kerner Commission and as identified by virtually every responsible commentator in America. The causes are steeped in racism ... racism in our courts, in our jails, in our streets and in our hearts.[82]

When Crockett finished the statement, he took questions. In response to the first question, he stated, "My whole purpose in making the statement is an effort to acquaint the public in Detroit with what happened to dispel the garbled accounts that members of the press have spread and let the truth itself quiet any tensions." He made clear what avenues of review were open for those who disagreed with what he had done: "I had jurisdiction to act on Sunday morning. Whether I acted properly or improperly, is a matter to be determined by a superior court, not by the prosecutor standing before me."[83] The press conference had the definite air of theater and performance. The Black community demonstrated strong political support for Crockett. "As the conference ended, Crockett was applauded, as he had several times during the conference, by an audience which included Congressman John Conyers, State Representative James Del Rio, NAACP President Tom Turner, American Civil Liberties Union chief Ernest Mazey, Rev. Albert Cleage and county supervisor Fred Burton."[84]

The media following Crockett's press conference was impactful. Gleicher recalled, "It was on the 12:00 news, the first item on the news—and all day long and all night long his speech was at the top of the news."[85] The headlines were favorable; one article with the title "Crockett Defends Action as 'Legal, Proper, Moral'" reported, "Recorder's Court Judge George W. Crockett came to his own defense Thursday and called 'legal, proper and moral' his release of several persons arrested following a shooting of a policeman. To do otherwise, the Negro jurist said, would 'have ignored my judicial and constitutional responsibilities.'"[86]

In what appears to have been a coordinated media strategy, Crockett's press conference was not the only media event that day related to the New Bethel Incident. Only an hour before the Crockett event, "New Detroit Chairman Max M. Fisher spoke out in Judge Crockett's defense, praising his 'very good judgment' in freeing persons in the [New Bethel] incident."[87] New Detroit, Inc. had been formed in the wake of the 1967 Rebellion as a coalition between the corporate and civil rights communities to improve race relations. Fisher was no radical. He was a conservative, Republican business leader. Judge Crockett and New Detroit were not the only entities holding press conferences. "At another press conference attended by about 200 persons, Crockett was defended by the Interfaith Action Council, a liberal group working for improved race relations."[88]

Crockett's press conference was a pivotal turning point. While the impact was not as immediate as Gleicher would later recall, things would start to be significantly different after April 3 than they had been before. "It was as if . . . there was a steaming boiling kettle and all of the sudden it was dropped into a vat of cold water. It stopped and rationality began to take over."[89] Rationality may not yet have taken over, but the kettle was not boiling quite as intensely.

Friday, April 4. Black support for Crockett was never in question, as symbolized by the Black United Front. Additional support for Crockett, however, appeared from a somewhat surprising source: the legal establishment. "The President of the American Bar Association and the heads of three Michigan lawyer groups urged public restraint Friday in the furor surrounding Recorder's Court Judge George W. Crockett Jr. Pending any official review of his actions, the four bar association presidents said in a statement, Judge Crockett 'is presumed to have acted in good faith and in accordance with the law and his obligations as a judge, and his decision is entitled to be respected.'"[90] In addition to the American Bar Association, the state groups included the State Bar of Michigan, the Wolverine Bar Association (a predominantly Black bar association), and the Detroit Bar Association. The unifying message was one of respect for the judicial system and the rule of law.

Crockett got additional legal support the following Monday from Chief Justice Thomas E. Brennan of the Michigan Supreme Court. The *Free Press* reported, "In an unusual public statement at a Meeting of the State

Bar of Michigan, [Chief Justice] Brennan said, in effect, that Crockett had acted within his judicial discretion in releasing all but two of those arrested because Cahalan had not issued or recommended warrants charging the detained persons with a criminal offense."[91] Particularly in the wake of the 1967 Rebellion, new procedures needed to be adopted to handle mass arrests. "[Brennan] said that if this had been done at the church, the furor over Recorder's Court Judge George W. Crockett Jr. might have been avoided."[92]

Black Political Unity

While the white legal establishment was slowly solidifying its support of Judge Crockett, the controversy was unifying support in the Black community at unprecedented levels. The police attack at New Bethel and the mass arrests that followed were deep affronts to Detroit's Black citizens, triggering decades of racial divisions. The quick actions of Judge Crockett and the use of constitutional authority finally to protect the rights of Black citizens sparked tremendous pride and a sense of vindication. Reverend Albert B. Cleage Jr. of the Church of the Black Madonna expressed this sentiment: "At long last 'Law and Order' had come to Recorder's Court and to Detroit. Tension was high in the Black community. The desecration of a Black church by the police and the mass arrests of women and children would have been enough to have sparked a citywide rebellion. Only the actions of Judge Crockett prevented this outbreak. Only the feeling in the community that at least the black man could find justice in at least one court kept the people calm."[93]

To see Judge Crockett vilified by virtually every corner of the white power structure triggered an even deeper sense of outrage and indignation. Reverend Cleage continued, "The communication media misread the temper of the black community and they turned a good judge into a black hero. Their denunciations did for Judge Crockett just what Bull Connor's brutality did for Dr. Martin Luther King." The New Bethel Incident was becoming a defining moment in Detroit racial politics: "The white police, prosecutor and mass communication media have done what no black leadership had been able to accomplish. They have united 95 percent of the black community which is necessary to elect a black mayor in 1969. If the election were tomorrow, certainly Judge Crockett could win hands down."[94]

Deep anger was a central theme uniting the whole community. The *Michigan Chronicle*, the city's leading Black newspaper, reported, "Crockett's backing cut across community, racial, and social lines, with prominent public and private leaders joining 'the man on the street' in indignation over calls for his censure and/or removal from office." The actions of white politicians had produced anger and resentment: "Dr. John P. Eagan [the first Black orthodontist in Michigan and a civil rights activist] in an angry response on Crockett's behalf, called Milliken's move 'a slap in the face of the black community' and accused him of echoing the 'bigotry' of the Detroit police and the white news media."[95]

The intensity of Black feelings is found in the archetypal symbols and imagery used to express these strong views. Not surprisingly, given that these events were playing out during Holy Week 1969, Amos A. Wilder, executive vice president and general manager of Motown Records and part-time columnist for the *Michigan Chronicle*, used the imagery of crucifixion: "The New Bethel Baptist church incident of this past week only moved forward the date of crucifixion for Judge Crockett, by the news media, the prosecutor's office, the police hierarchy and others." Crockett was widely respected in the Black community: "Judge George W. Crockett Jr., today stands high as a symbol of hope, in the law, for black people everywhere." The disrespect exhibited toward Judge Crockett by the white establishment was palpable: "The issue is whether the decisions of a black judge, obviously qualified, are respected and recognized by citizens, news media, the police department, the prosecutor's office, and by his fellow jurists. Note, we did not say agreed with, but respected and recognized." A clear double standard applied when the New Bethel Incident was contrasted with the Algiers Motel Incident in 1967, in which white police officers essentially assassinated three Black teenagers during the Rebellion: "Public indignation over the processes of justice in the courts was never so vociferously expressed in the 'Algiers Motel' case, where legal gymnastics have prevented the trial of the alleged murderers of three black youth." All of these emotions became a clarion call for action: "The black community in Detroit, must unite behind this man and provide him the kind of assurances that he will not become the sacrificial victim of the arrogance of power, now being misused in the hands of a few."[96]

The *Michigan Chronicle* columnist C. C. Douglas evoked the archetype of "lynching" as his primary symbolic frame, just as Senator Young had done earlier. Lynching has always been used as a tool of white supremacy to violently control Black men who asserted too much power and authority. This was the case with Judge Crockett. "The issues at hand in the power structure's race to lynch Judge Crockett are clearly racial. The daily press and others are calling for Crockett's job because he used *their* legal system to give *justice* to black people." White condemnation of Crockett was combined with paternalistic critiques of so-called responsible Black leadership: "Each of the papers ran an editorial which, in effect, called upon 'responsible Negros' and 'responsible Negro leadership' to step forward and denounce Crockett and embrace 'law and order.'"[97]

What the white establishment failed to recognize, however, was that times had changed. Their hypocrisy and double standards were understood at a visceral level in the Black community. "The local establishment, including the daily papers, Jerry Cavanagh, William Milliken and a host of others, certainly did not know what they were getting into when they formed a lynching bee to go after Recorder's Court Judge George Crockett. The overt and blatant racism of the anti-Crockett position in the issue is apparently not clear to such as Cavanagh and Milliken, but it is very clear to thousands of black Detroiters." This time, white racism was met with political action and resistance; a new generation of Black leadership was asserting itself: "While the newspapers were weeping and wailing about the loss of 'responsible Negro leadership,' the truly responsible black leadership was meeting to form the Black United Front to support Judge Crockett and denounce police actions during the [New Bethel] incident."[98]

Detroit Police Officers Association Mounts Its Attack

Political unity and support of the Black community was important because Judge Crockett remained under strong attack, particularly from the DPOA. On Tuesday, April 15, the DPOA paid for a full-page advertisement in the *Detroit News* captioned, "Detroit Police Officers Association. GOD BLESS YOU GEORGE [CZAPSKI]! The Complete Story of the Assassination of Patrolman Czapski." The ad reprised the account of the New Bethel Incident from the DPOA perspective and, yet again, assailed Judge Crockett: "Judge

Crockett maintains that he is objective and wants to see justice done. This is hard for us to swallow in view of his previous actions." The ad ended with a call to action: "Anyone wishing to assist in petitioning for the removal of Judge Crockett or in the demanding for changes in the present law or court procedure—or interpretation of the law: contact DPOA."[99] President Parsell defended the DPOA actions, stating that it took out the "full-page newspaper ad attacking Recorder's Court Judge George W. Crockett Jr. only after waiting in vain for 'so-called community leaders' to act." In the same article, Parsell attacked the leaders of New Detroit: "He said that New Detroit, Inc., president William T. Patrick and chairman Max Fisher had 'abdicated their position of responsibility when without benefit of the facts, they took it upon themselves to elevate Judge Crockett to sainthood.'"[100] Judge Crockett, for his part and consistent with his deep constitutional principles, defended the DPOA's right to free speech.[101]

Unlike the way the press acted in the wake of the initial incident, it no longer simply echoed DPOA statements. In an editorial, the *Free Press* called out the DPOA tactics as highly racialized and ultimately self-defeating: "Detroit Cannot Afford to Follow DPOA Lead." The editorial warned that the "DPOA will not end, with this move, the danger of racial polarization. It will not end the feeling among many of the black community that the police are racists and that this is a racist society. The police cannot win, in this way, the broad support of the whole community which police demand and have the right to expect."[102]

The DPOA mounted a sustained campaign to get Judge Crockett removed from office. It circulated fliers asking people to call the police station directly to register their complaints against Crockett. "The Leaflet said: 'Attention!! Anyone interested in having their name added to the formal protest list against the actions of Judge Crockett should call the Beaubien police station, 224-4425, and give your name address and phone number. This list is being compiled by the Detroit Police Department for submission to the Honorable John H. Gillis in Lansing.'"[103] Judge Gillis was the chairman of the Judicial Tenure Commission. The police were using official time and resources in their battle against a Recorder's Court judge.

The DPOA orchestrated a statewide effort against Crockett, circulating petitions to the new state Judicial Tenure Commission, asking that it remove Judge Crockett from office for improper conduct. Channel 10, WILX

TV, editorialized against the campaign: "At this point the removal campaign seems ill-advised and may cause great harm without proving anything."[104]

Crockett's Supporters Fight Back

Dual political and legal battles were emerging over the New Bethel Incident, with the Judicial Tenure Commission taking center stage. On the legal side, Judge Crockett was racking up more victories. The Michigan Trial Lawyers Association (MTLA) expressed its support; its board "issued a statement commending Crockett as 'an able conscientious judge' whose actions in the New Bethel incident were consistent with the highest ideals of the American judiciary."[105] On April 22, the U.S. Supreme Court issued an opinion extending Fourth Amendment protection to overturn a conviction because fingerprint evidence had been obtained during an illegal arrest. Crockett believed that the opinion supported his actions invalidating the even more intrusive paraffin tests for nitrate.[106]

Even though no formal complaint had been brought against Crockett, the Judicial Tenure Commission held a preliminary investigation on April 23.[107] The DPOA did not file a formal complaint until April 30.[108] The DPOA complaints against Crockett now extended far beyond just the New Bethel Incident. "The attack had been broadened, the sources say, to list what Crockett critics consider to be a number of unjustified decisions that the judge has made during more than two years in Recorder's Court."[109] Crockett testified for nearly two hours before the commission.[110] The commission deferred its decision on whether to investigate.[111] "Meanwhile, four of Michigan's criminal law instructors at a press conference at Wayne State University said the Judicial Tenure Commission had no right to investigate Crockett. The professors said that all of Crockett's disputed actions in the New Bethel Incident were based soundly on Michigan law."[112]

Within days of the Judicial Tenure Commission's informal, confidential hearing, the Law Committee of New Detroit issued "The New Bethel Report: 'The Law on Trial.'" As the *Free Press* reported, "A well documented 26-page legal brief endorsing all actions by Recorder's Court Judge George W. Crockett Jr. in the [New Bethel] incident has been drafted by the Law Committee of New Detroit, Inc. . . . The report, commissioned and then endorsed by the Law Committee, will be presented to the entire

30-person board of trustees of New Detroit, Inc."[113] The wake of the New Bethel Incident was characterized by press-fueled panic and hysteria. The New Detroit legal analysis was a sober second look. Significantly, the report stressed that no evidence existed to connect anyone arrested with the actual shooting of the police officers. "During Crockett's two court sessions on March 30, the prosecution introduced no evidence that the shooting of the two police officers occurred from inside New Bethel Church, or any evidence to connect guns or ammunition seized inside the church with any of the 142 arrested persons."[114]

The New Detroit report had legal and political significance. With regard to the legal analysis, it largely vindicated Judge Crockett's actions: "There is little question that Michigan law placed upon this judge as the presiding judge of Recorder's Court, the responsibility of being available for making the judicial inquiry into the challenges of illegal detention." The report sought to reset the frame of analysis: "Contrary to the reporting at the time, it is now clear that virtually all (132) of these persons were released by or at the request of the Assistant Prosecutor."[115] The report carefully examined and supported Judge Crockett's actions in convening the habeas hearing at the police station, the issuance of the writ of habeas corpus, and, most controversially, his release of suspects over the prosecution's objection with allegedly positive nitrate results from a paraffin test. The report concluded, "First, that the nitrate tests were not sufficiently reliable evidence to require a finding of probable cause to hold the suspects. This conclusion is supported by the apparent lack of confidence in such tests shown by the Prosecutor's office. Although they had positive test results they neither sought a warrant nor brought a charge. Second, that even if the tests were *prima facie* probable cause, the tests were taken in such a questionable time and manner that their exclusion by the Judge was justified."[116] More significantly, the report placed the New Bethel Incident in the context of a long and troubling pattern in Detroit of unlawful arrests for the purpose of police investigations. It was standard practice to arrest to investigate. "The Detroit Bar Association has been concerned with the problem for years and as early as 1960 the Special Civil Rights Subcommittee sought to end the practice in Detroit."[117]

The illegal tactic of "arrest to investigate" had become business as usual for Detroit police, prosecutors, and judges at Recorder's Court. "The practice of holding suspects for the purpose of investigating them has been effectively sanctioned by the Detroit Courts and the Prosecutor's Office."[118] This was true even in the face of a valid writ of habeas corpus. The normal routine would proceed this way: "If a Writ of Habeas Corpus was brought by or on the behalf of a person held in investigatory custody, it was the practice of the Prosecutor to request and the Court to grant an adjournment for up to seventy-two hours so that the police could complete their investigation." What was most surprising to police and prosecutors that Sunday morning of March 30 was that Judge Crockett actually enforced the law: "This history makes it clear that when Judge Crockett refused to allow continued detention solely to permit investigation, he was not breaking new ground in stating that the practice was illegal." The only shock was that national legal standards were being applied in Recorder's Court: "In view of the long history of unhampered power of the police to arrest suspects for investigation, it is understandable that both the Prosecutor and the police were disturbed and surprised by Judge Crockett's refusal to permit this illegal method of investigation."[119] Whether it pleased the police and prosecutor or not, Crockett was simply enforcing the law and protecting individual rights.

The New Detroit analysis has withstood the test of time. The historian Say Burgin characterizes the "Jim Crow Judiciary" in the North as consisting of "taking the police at their word, presuming that the role of the judge is to support the police, and assuming bias, if not blatant deceit, on the part of African Americans."[120] In New Bethel, Judge Crockett put an end to this oppressive business as usual.[121]

The political significance of the New Detroit report was even more important. "New Detroit is disturbed that much of the criticism surrounding Judge Crockett's ruling after the New Bethel shooting has been provoked by inaccurate reporting of facts and inadequate understanding of law. We hope that this memorandum will be helpful in dispelling widespread misapprehensions of fact and law, explaining the judicial role in our legal system and restoring calm and perspective to our society."[122] In the wake of the crisis, the entire white power structure, from the mayor to the governor, came out against Crockett. In subsequent weeks, a growing number of leaders in the legal establishment started to speak in his favor. New Detroit was created in the wake of Detroit's 1967 Rebellion expressly to improve race relationships; now it was doing just that. Under the leadership of William Patrick and Max Fisher, the organization was in a unique position to help calm the waters.

As the newspapers knew, New Detroit could wield real power. "Endorsement by New Detroit would give [Judge Crockett] support from the city's top white leaders."[123] Still, the New Detroit Law Committee was overly optimistic in suggesting that it hoped that the report would "be the end of the matter."[124] Backlash by the DPOA was almost immediate, but its statements were now starting to sound just a little more shrill and desperate: "The Detroit Police Officers Association (DPOA) Friday characterized as 'fools or cowards' New Detroit Inc. committee members who endorsed Judge George W. Crockett Jr.'s actions on the New Bethel Baptist Church case."[125] The organization vowed to fight on. According to the DPOA statement, "The Detroit Police Officers Association may be alone in this fight at the present time, because those public officials who know the truth are afraid to speak out. However, we promise the citizens of this city that we will demonstrate Judge Crockett's actions in the New Bethel incident are merely one example of his hatred and contempt for any man who wears a badge."[126]

Crockett had many friends, but none more loyal than Ernie Goodman. Goodman joined attorneys Robert Millender and Edward Bell to defend Crockett before the Judicial Tenure Commission. Goodman also penned a letter to the editor of the *Michigan Chronicle* placing Crockett's actions in the New Bethel Incident in the context of a lifetime commitment to constitutional principles: "It might be well to mention that Judge Crockett's actions do not arise out of impulse or hasty judgment—they are predicated upon a philosophy based on thoughtful study of the Constitution and the historical forces which have brought about its adoption and from careful and critical analysis of the interpretive decisions of the U.S. Supreme Court." Goodman made clear his friend's deep commitment to equality: "I view the reaction to Judge Crockett's judicial philosophy as a reflection of our community's and our nation's unreadiness, after 200 years, to accept the simple, but hard principle: that all men and women, at the bottom of the well as at the top of the economic and social scale, are really entitled to the full and equal protection of the Constitution." In what was a refrain throughout both men's careers, Goodman stressed that the equal application of constitutional rights was the remedy for and not the cause of racial unrest: "Those who talk so piously about the desirability of peaceful racial integration but are unwilling to accept the minimum step which Judge Crockett insists upon—equality of Constitutional rights—should be prepared to accept the alternatives of violence and racial separation."[127]

Strategic action was needed to fend off the coming storm before the Judicial Tenure Commission. Money was also necessary. Crockett supporters organized a fundraiser for Saturday, April 26, 1969, at the Howard Johnson's New Center Motor Lodge on West Grand Boulevard and Third Avenue. For a donation of ten dollars, guests would be treated to dinner and a lecture by Judge George W. Crockett Jr. He was slated to give a speech titled "Crime and Punishment in the Black Ghetto."[128]

This was the first of an important series of events. The Committee to Honor Judge Crockett in Support of Law and Justice organized a two-dollar-per-person brunch of pancakes and sausages where some two thousand interracial supporters attended. The judge stated, "As long as we have this inter-mingling, this sense of unity, we don't need to worry about the future of Detroit." According to the *Free Press*, "At one time a double line extended a block down the sidewalk outside." Crockett remarked, "I wish my colleagues in the Michigan Supreme Court and the Michigan Judicial Tenure Commission could see this." Supporters purchased buttons and bumper stickers saying "I support Judge Crockett." The organizers of the event were honoring him for everything his critics decried: "his courageous actions making habeas corpus and other constitutional rights a reality for the black and poor; [h]is relentless exposure of systematic brutality against black people by segments of the Detroit Police Department; his prudent efforts to encourage rehabilitation of narcotics users; and his steadfast courage in the face of bitter ... attacks."[129]

On Tuesday, May 13, a formal tribute dinner for Judge Crockett was held at the Latin Quarter. More than one hundred people helped arrange the tribute to the judge.[130] The prayer opening the occasion was inspiring: "So, right now, dear God, we thank Thee for a great-hearted and clearminded, courageous Judge Crockett—one who can keep his head when all about him are losing theirs and blaming it on him; one who can trust himself when all men doubt him, but make allowances for their doubting, one who can wait and not be tired by waiting, or being lied about, won't deal in lies; or being hated won't give way to hating."[131] Remarks for the dinner were delivered by Congressman Charles C. Diggs: "There have been few times in local history when the honorable actions of one man have done so much to unify the forces of liberation in Detroit. This is the real cause and purpose of our presence tonight ... to send forth to the reluctant dragons who would resist the forces of changing values and rising aspirations a message they cannot help but hear loud and clearly."[132] Significantly for Crockett, his family was in attendance. Photos of the event show his parents, Reverend and Mrs. George W. Crockett Sr., his son, George W. Crockett III, and his brother-in-law, Reverend Leroy Hacker of Pittsburgh.[133]

Crockett was riding a wave of increasing local and national attention. He was invited to be the law school graduation speaker for the University of California at Berkeley. The *California Law Review* was also publishing his book review of *Crisis in the Courts*. The invitation to speak at Berkeley followed Judge Crockett's speaking engagements at the law schools of the University of Michigan and University of Illinois, the Urban Studies Institute at Morgan State College in Baltimore, and the annual meeting of the American Society for Public Administration at Miami Beach.[134]

Important support was solidifying locally through the ongoing work of New Detroit. The organization's report had been approved by the New Detroit Law Committee in April. In late May, it was presented to and approved by the New Detroit Board of Directors. This was a significant endorsement. The *Free Press* reported, "The board of trustees of New Detroit Inc. (NDI) said Friday justice was done on the morning of the New Bethel incident and adopted a committee report endorsing the actions of Recorder's Court Judge George W. Crockett Jr. Thirty of the board's 39 members, including the cream of Detroit's business community, met at a closed-door meeting and approved the 26-page report." The New Detroit statement included high praise for Crockett: "Justice was afforded promptly and effectively in this instance. It should provide a basis for renewed confidence that we are a government of laws and not men."[135] Given Detroit's historical racial dynamics, the actions of New Detroit were monumental: "It would have been far easier to have made no comment about this event. But New Detroit saw a need to thwart what appeared to be developing: an almost-solid white attitude that Judge Crockett, a black, was wrong. New Detroit also saw this as one of those significant occasions in which the law was made to work for the black just as effectively as it works for the white who is used to justice as a matter of course."[136]

In a separate process, the Detroit Commission on Community Relations (CCR) was conducting its own investigation. A draft of the CCR staff report leaked in late March but received only limited public attention.[137] With the actions of the New Detroit board, renewed attention was given to the CCR report, which was not only supportive of Judge Crockett but also highly critical of police conduct. A key part of the police story was that officers were met with gunfire coming from inside the church. The CCR found little support for this claim: "Citing police reports that police were met with a hail of fire when they neared the church, the report said: 'A painstaking examination of the church interior, exterior and immediate surroundings, however, does not reveal any physical evidence to support this claim. Command officials admit that few shell casings were found inside or outside.'" The CCR also confirmed earlier allegations of abusive police conduct targeting those who were arrested: "The report says that the CCR staff members were provided with 'detailed accounts of expressions of verbal epithets and commission of physical brutality in considerable amounts by the police. The verbal epithets were predominantly racial. The physical brutality allegedly included two unprovoked shootings of unarmed persons and menacing of individuals with ends of rifles and pistol barrels against their heads.'" These reports match those made by Black state legislators: "After arrests were made, the report says that testimony from persons in custody suggests an 'appreciable lack of concern for minimum attention to certain basic human needs. To begin with, a considerable amount of testimony indicates that there was an open and unrestrained searching of females by male police officers at the church.'"[138]

Finally, the CCR was critical of the media coverage of the incident, particularly that of the *Detroit News*. In an editorial, the *Detroit News* struck back. With more than a little irony and sarcasm, the paper blamed the CCR for stirring public discontent over the issue: "The patient can't get any rest because someone keeps waking him up to give him a sleeping pill. Every time public passions regarding the New Bethel Baptist Church affair begin to cool, some self-appointed investigative body issues an inflammatory 'report' telling the community to remain calm. The latest such report comes from the Detroit Commission on Community Relations, which charges the news media—and particularly this newspaper—with misstating the facts and polarizing the community. It's as reckless and distorted a document we have ever seen." Not surprisingly, the *Detroit News* doubled down rather than apologize: "The *News* is not about to apologize for using words which are not in themselves offensive and which we think accurately describe existing conditions. Judge Crockett's conduct in this affair was, we think, questionable; he did feed fuel to the flames of racism by acting according to the belief that it is his job to advocate the interests of a race rather than to act as an objective jurist." The *News* was very clear: the issue was not that the newspaper did not like Black judges; it just, distinctly, did not like Judge Crockett: "CCR apparently feels that because Crockett is black, he should be immune from criticism. We disagree. And let's put to rest right here the charge that *The News*'s criticism of Judge Crockett arises from race prejudice. This newspaper has supported the judicial candidacy of every Negro on the major courts with the exception of Judge Crockett."[139] The *Detroit News* was not going to change its mind.

The CCR report triggered a backlash from Mayor Cavanagh. The report had been prepared by the CCR staff and its director, Richard V. Marks. Unlike New Detroit, it had not yet been presented and approved by the CCR board. "Cavanagh said that the CCR—not the CCR's staff and director—runs the agency and the report was not official CCR policy but only the finding and opinions of the staff." In a dispute between the CCR and the police department, the mayor sided with the police: "The mayor said he has read all police reports of the incident and thinks they are accurate. He said the CCR report contains inaccuracies." Politics were clearly involved. Marks had "aroused Cavanagh's ire last April 17 when he charged a 'leadership vacuum' existed within the city following the New Bethel Baptist Church incident." Undaunted, Marks stood by the report: "The report was prepared in good faith. If there are facts which contradict the assertions in that report I would like to see them."[140]

The Judicial Tenure Proceedings Begin

At the end of the day, it would be the Judicial Tenure Commission and not the Detroit Commission on Community Relations or New Detroit that would decide Judge Crockett's fate. The DPOA was mounting an increasingly shrill political battle. In announcing its intent to file a brief in support of its motion, President Parsell repeated his charge that Crockett had "hatred and contempt for any man who wears a badge."[141] The DPOA was not alone. It had spearheaded a statewide attack with the support of the Police Officers Association of Michigan (POAM). POAM filed in the governor's office petitions bearing two hundred thousand names calling for Crockett's impeachment.[142]

The previous year, Michigan voters had approved a referendum adopting a new constitutional provision creating the Judicial Tenure Commission, a nine-member body to hear complaints of judicial misconduct and to make recommendations to the Michigan Supreme Court for disciplinary actions. While Crockett surely felt frustrated having to defend his conduct before the commission, in all likelihood, the creation of the official body gave him the best opportunity to save his judicial career. If his fate was left to the hyperracialized politics of the moment, when the governor, state senate, and mayor had all condemned his actions, it is likely that he would have been impeached within weeks, if not days, of the incident. Instead, with the creation of the Judicial Tenure Commission, his future would be decided through a less partisan process. Passions would be cooled, and the process would largely be outside the spotlights of politics and the media.

The very confidentiality of the process, however, created challenges in telling the whole story. After the highly publicized "informal" hearings in April and the filing of the DPOA complaint, there was very little press coverage. Later, reporters reconstructed events: "The *Free Press* has learned . . . that Crockett was accused of 71 acts of improper conduct on the bench. More than 50 of the charges were contained in affidavits filed by individual policemen. The DPOA, in a formal complaint against Crockett, charged the judge with 'intemperance towards the police department and conduct which is clearly prejudicial to the administration of justice.'" The scope of police complaints went far beyond the New Bethel Incident and constituted a laundry list of objections to virtually everything Judge Crockett had done since taking the bench: "The DPOA accused Crockett of 'refusing to listen to the testimony of police officers, refusing to believe uncontradicted testimony of police officers, outright refusal to convict persons charged with public drunkenness and/or vagrancy' and other alleged improprieties." Crockett and his attorneys were deeply critical of the entire undertaking.

Crockett's attorneys said that "'similar condemnation has never before been visited upon any white judge in the same or similar circumstances.' The DPOA, they said wanted to 'punish or remove' Crockett because of his color."[143]

Crockett Continues to Speak Out

Most people facing an official investigation that could lead to their removal from office would keep a low profile and avoid further attention until the process concluded. Crockett, however, was not like most people. He maintained a high public profile, traveling nationally and giving speeches challenging the racism and classism embedded in the legal system. On August 1, 1969, speaking before the National Bar Association, where he received an award for outstanding judicial service, Judge Crockett declared, "The causes of crime are steeped in racism—racism in our courts, in our jails, in our streets and in our hearts." If racism and poverty were the root causes of crime, then jail was not the solution: "A man or youth who has been denied human dignity his whole life, and who is daily faced with starvation, nakedness, homelessness and unemployment in his ghetto existence, is not afraid of prison. . . . He has been in prison his whole life."[144]

Later, while answering questions following an address in Cleveland, Crockett made clear how his analysis was different from that of the advocates of Black Power. "He called black power a myth and said the only three kinds of power are money, moral suasion and political power. Money is what black people lack, moral suasion is too slow, so the tactic is for blacks to strive for state political power."[145] The key to political power was to transcend the historical racial wedge dividing poor Blacks and whites and to unite both around common class interests. "We had better address ourselves to a program of reclaiming all of our alienated poor, black as well as white before it is too late." He called for "the alienated poor white and the alienated poor black" to "forget about their race and color differences and come to understand that class and economic distinctions—not racial and color cleavages—dominate American life today."[146]

In this political process, Crockett firmly believed that there was a special role for Black judges: they must "be especially mindful of class justice and rule against it." "Black judges have a responsibility to the people . . . and the people have a responsibility to make sure more black judges are elected to the bench."[147] In these speeches and remarks, he fused and combined his lifelong commitment to racial and economic justice in a manner that spoke directly to the needs of the political moment.

In September 1969, back in Detroit, Crockett made a speech in the Community Arts Auditorium at Wayne State University assessing contemporary issues facing the city. The headline of the article reporting on the speech focused on Crockett's public endorsement for Richard Austin for Detroit mayor: "Crockett Endorses Austin."[148] Austin, a Black candidate, would go on to lose a close and divisive campaign for mayor by a 51 to 49 percent vote.

The primary focus of Crockett's address, however, was, once again, race, law, and politics. He was highly critical of the ongoing waves of white flight, stating that "the exodus is criminal" and warning that "integration of the inner city is essential to relaxing racial tensions." He argued that whites in Detroit must be willing to vote for Black candidates, just as Blacks had been historically willing to support white candidates. He warned that the failure to breach this racial divide could be extremely dangerous: "If Detroit does not elect a black mayor, it would be 'anybody's guess' what actions the blacks of Detroit would take. Increased black representation is 'the best guarantee of the continuance of the present cooling off period.'" Crockett also called for greater integration of the police department as essential for healthy community relations. Reflecting his core political convictions, he advocated aggressive action within existing legal and political institutions as the path forward: "'Let's cool it' and 'give the democratic process a chance to work.'"[149]

Tellingly, Crockett also warned against efforts to undermine Detroit's Recorder's Court. "The blacks of Detroit see this as an effort to get rid of black judges and dissolve the only truly integrated bench in the nation." He reasoned "that black votes are not a strong force in county-wide elections and noted that half of the present Wayne County Circuit Court judges live outside Detroit."[150]

The Attacks on Recorder's Court

Crockett's warning about the need to protect the Recorder's Court was prophetic. As summer turned to fall and fall began to transition into winter, there was still no word from the Judicial Tenure Commission. However, forces in the state judiciary were taking aim at both Judge Crockett and the entire Recorder's Court. On November 20, 1969, the *Free Press* headline read, "Big Court Shakeup Asked to End 4,000-Case Backlog." According to the article, a "major shakeup of the Wayne County and Detroit court systems—with at least 20 judges changing jobs—was proposed Wednesday to the State Supreme Court." The changes would have the dramatic effect of eliminating the Recorder's Court and merging it with Wayne County. But this was not all. The proposal specifically targeted Judge Crockett. Without providing any reason or justification for the action, the plan provided that "Recorder's Court judge George W. Crockett would be moved from criminal to civil cases."[151]

Pushback against the proposal was immediate. The *Free Press* reported, "Several judges strongly oppose the proposal, which would have to be approved by the State Supreme Court." Crockett publicly called the plan out as a racially targeted attack on the court: "Recorder's Court Judge George W. Crockett Jr., one of those most affected by the plan, suggested it was an attempt to prevent a possible majority of Black Recorder's Court judges in the next few years. 'If the present political set up continues, within three or four years Recorder's Court would be predominantly black,' Crockett said. 'They don't want that to happen.'"[152]

The *Michigan Chronicle* echoed Crockett's view: "We see in the proposed plan to reorganize the courts of Detroit and Wayne County, another scheme to thwart the efforts of the black community to achieve equal representation in all areas. This is a glaring fact to anyone who has any knowledge of the political arena, and it is not too difficult for the novice to understand." The *Michigan Chronicle* was equally vocal in calling out the direct attack on Judge Crockett: "The black community knows very well that there are forces that are eager to the point of desperation to remove George Crockett from criminal cases. And the proposed plan would help them kill two birds with one stone, by removing George Crockett now, and getting the rest of the black judges later."[153] There appeared to be no other justification for the proposal. The plan was ostensibly intended to eliminate a backlog of cases, but all it did was shift personnel around without adding any additional resources or judges to increase the capacity of the court.

Given the strong pushback, the reorganization plan was short-lived. "After hearing an earful from protesting Wayne County Judges involved in a proposed massive shift of jurisdictions," Michigan Supreme Court Chief Justice Brennan declared that the plan "will not be adopted."[154] Instead, a committee was appointed to study the backlog problem and come up with alternative recommendations.

The Judicial Tenure Commission's Secret Decision Is Made Public

The quick sidelining of the plan to eliminate Recorder's Court only begged the question of why the proposal specifically targeted Judge Crockett for removal from the criminal docket. The Michigan Supreme Court, in essence, was proposing a disciplinary action against Crockett undertaken with no transparency and no due process, outside of the formal process of the Judicial Tenure Commission. But what was the status of that proceeding? There was no public answer to this question. The commission operated under a complicated set of confidentiality rules. Its report would be public only if it found cause to recommend discipline. If it found that there was no actionable case, then no one would learn anything. In most cases, given reputational interests of those who were accused, this is entirely proper. Given that everyone was (improperly) aware that Judge Crockett was being investigated, the process created its own complications.

Slowly, details of the commission's findings started to leak, largely as a by-product of the implosion of the Michigan Supreme Court's proposed reorganization plan for the Recorder's Court. The same day that the newspapers announced the reorganization plan's demise, they reported the results of the Judicial Tenure Commission investigation. The commission had ruled in favor of Crockett, and the investigation ended with no disciplinary action. "A sharply split State Judicial Tenure Commission, operating in secrecy, has cleared controversial judge George W. Crockett Jr. of charges of improper conduct on the bench." Details about the process were scarce, but the decision was not unanimous: "A spokesman said the decision to clear Crockett was hotly debated and opposed by at least one-third of the commission members."[155]

Not all standard commission rules were followed, however. The decision not to proceed should have ended the matter. It did not. The decision, along with dissenting options, was forwarded to the Michigan Supreme Court.[156] There was a backstory to this action as well. On September 25, 1969, Judge John H. Gillis, chairman of the Judicial Tenure Commission, wrote a letter to Chief Justice Brennan. The letter was captioned, "Confidential: Complaint No. 3, George W. Crockett, Jr.": "The Michigan Judicial Tenure Commission wishes to advise the Supreme Court that by majority vote the Commission has terminated their investigation pertaining to the above matter for the reason that the Commission has not been able to establish grounds upon which the Commission can properly act under Rule 932. Furthermore, I have been directed by majority vote of the Commission to forward our complete file pertaining to the investigation to the Supreme Court with the request that your court review the problem and determine for yourselves whether the Supreme Court can properly act via your power of superintending control."[157] Amazingly, given the prevailing rules, neither Crockett nor his attorneys were informed of the decision in his favor.[158]

Even though Crockett had prevailed before the Judicial Tenure Commission, his ordeal was not over. A *Free Press* editorial bemoaned the particular lack of vindication that a judge like Crockett received when no action was taken by the commission in a high-profile investigation: "The *Free Press* learned, and reported, that the commission decided on a 5–4 vote that it had no cause of action against Judge Crockett. Yet even this fact cannot be publicly acknowledged because the Supreme Court has required the commission to proceed in secret unless a decision is made to take formal action against a judge." The editorial called for action: "Someone, some agency, should say forthrightly that there is no official cloud over Judge Crockett's work as a judge."[159]

Rather than official vindication, it was later revealed how Crockett became the extrajudicial target of the Supreme Court's reorganization plan. No one was following the rules or respecting the law in this case. "A court reorganization plan that would shift Recorder's Court Judge George W. Crockett Jr. away from criminal trials was apparently the result of the State Judicial Tenure Commission." In accordance with no legitimate rule, reason, or process, the "recommendation apparently accompanied a report on the commission investigation of Crockett that was presented to Brennan three months ago."[160]

Official oddities did not end there. The *Free Press* editorial triggered a highly unusual letter from Michigan Supreme Court Justice Eugene F. Black addressed to both the *Free Press* and the *Detroit News*. In a taunting manner, he suggested that Crockett could petition the Supreme Court for the release of the entire file: "I will promptly move our Court to open the entire record to public gaze; confident that there are at least three Justices who will support such a motion." He suggested that the Supreme Court was split between "five Crockettphiles and four Crockettphobes" and indicated his willingness to "provide the press the Roman Holiday it wants." Justice Black ended his letter stating that the "showdown should be perfect."[161]

The Battles against Crockett Continue

As the dust began to settle around the New Bethel Incident, Crockett's enemies searched for new reasons to attack him. On Saturday, December 6, 1969, in another writ of habeas corpus proceeding, Judge Crockett released two robbery suspects because police produced no evidence to justify holding them. Learning from the past, he had a transcript of the proceeding typed that night and released it to the press the next day—Sunday.[162] At least the *Free Press* gave sympathetic coverage: "It is, indeed, a shame that men charged with so serious a crime as armed robbery were released. But the error is not that the judge released the two suspects. It is that the prosecutor's office and the police—in a case involving only 2 arrests not a massive dragnet—did not produce enough testimony to hold the suspects."[163]

Crockett's foes in the state legislature leapt at the opportunity. In a reprise of motions passed in the wake of the New Bethel Incident, the Michigan Senate introduced "A Resolution to invoke action by the Judicial Tenure Commission of Michigan" directed at George W. Crockett Jr. The resolution noted the alleged "precipitous release on Saturday December 6, 1969 of two men suspected of participating in an armed robbery."[164] "Sen. Stanley F. Rozycki, D-Detroit, assailed Crockett as a coddler of suspected criminals and an 'enemy of the society he is elected to serve and sworn to protect.'" Crockett still had his defenders among the small group of Black legislators: "Sen. Basil W. Brown, D-Highland Park, denounced the move as 'another witch hunt,' and defended Crockett as 'the most worthy trial court judge in the state.'" State Senator Coleman A. Young accused his fellow senators of having "'lynch-the-black-judge' motives and wishing to 'suspend the constitution for blacks.'"[165] Despite these protests, the state senate again adopted a resolution that "the Judicial Tenure Commission be urged and is requested to investigate promptly charges of misconduct as are alleged to have been committed by Recorder's Court Judge George W. Crockett on December 6, 1969."[166]

Less than a week earlier, Senators Brown and Young had introduced Senate Resolution No. 163: "A Resolution commending the State Judicial Tenure Commission and expressing public acknowledgement of the propriety of the action and fitness for office of Judge George W. Crockett."[167] The rules permitting a vote were not suspended, and the resolution was referred to the Committee on Senate Business. No further action was taken.

For Crockett, the official ending of the Judicial Tenure Commission investigation came quietly and only after much public fanfare. On December 16, his good friend Ernie Goodman received a very brief letter from the chief justice. It read, "Dear Mr. Goodman: I enclose copy of letter which I received from the Tenure Committee on September 25, 1969. The Court has made no reply. It is forwarded to you without comment."[168]

As usual, Crockett had the final, correct diagnosis. The real solution to challenges to his judicial conduct and his continued tenure on the bench should not lie with the Judicial Tenure Commission or the state senate but rather with the democratic process and the citizens of the city of Detroit. "This is the way our democratic process works and must continue to work if we are to maintain the principle of separation of powers and uphold the independence of the judiciary."[169] Democracy would also be the greatest source of Crockett's protection on the bench, with the increasing strength of Detroit's unified Black community.

Jet Magazine *featuring attorneys Claudia Morcom and Anna Diggs: "Women Lawyers to Aid Mississippi's 'Freedom Corps,'" July 1964.*

Claudia Morcom working in Guild office in Jackson, Mississippi, Summer 1964.

Crockett filing for unsuccessful run for Detroit Common Council, 1965.

Crockett campaigning for judge of Recorder's Court, 1966. (Detroit News)

WHY WE MUST **NOT** ELECT
GEORGE CROCKETT

ENEMY

SYMPATHIZER

ENEMY

COLLABORATOR

TO RECORDERS' COURT

(Following are facts about GEORGE CROCKETT'S background which you are not likely to read either in his campaign literature or the daily newspapers.)

FBI-backed anti-Crockett election flyer, 1966.

*Crockett,
victorious, in
his Recorder's
Court courtroom.
(Courtesy Walter
P. Reuther
Library, Archives
of Labor and
Urban Affairs,
Wayne State
University)*

*Celebration of Crockett's victory in his judicial chambers. From left to right:
Dean Robb, Robert Millender, Maurice Sugar, Crockett, Ernie Goodman, and
George Bedrosian, 1966.*

Judges of Recorder's Court. Back row, from left: Crockett, Samuel Olsen, Joseph Maher, Thomas Poindexter, Robert Colombo, and Joseph Gillis; front row, from left: Donald Leonard, Geraldine Bledsoe Ford, Gerald Groat, Vincent Brennan, Frank Schemanske, Elvin Davenport, and Robert DeMascio, December 1967.

Detroit News *political cartoon attacking Crockett's decision in the L. K. Tyler addiction case: "Try not to get any irresistible impulses en route," February 20, 1969.*

Full-page ad by Crockett supporters backing his decision in the L. K. Tyler addiction case, March 1969.

New Bethel Baptist Church, Detroit, Michigan.

Crockett, State Representative James Del Rio, and Reverend C. L. Franklin confront desk officers at the First Precinct Police Station early Sunday morning following the New Bethel Incident mass arrests.

Time Magazine *documents police protest against Crockett outside Tenth Precinct. Protesters carry signs reading: "Crockett Justice? Release Killers, Prosecute Prosecutors, Give License to Kill Policemen," April 1969.*

Crockett supporters stage mass protest in front of Recorder's Court, April 1969. (Courtesy The South End, photo by Gerald Simmons)

Crockett gives press conference in his courtroom to counter attacks by media and politicians (note portrait of Frederick Douglass on wall), April 3, 1969. (Courtesy The South End)

Crockett provided police escort from home to courthouse in the wake of death threats, April 1969. (Courtesy Ebony Magazine)

Detroit News *political cartoon shows armed militants emerging under a judge's bench as he calls "next case," April 9, 1969.*

Baltimore Afro-American *political cartoon contrasts the views of* Detroit News: *"You can't break the law, officers," April 19, 1969.*

Like father like son. George Crockett III, with his father, after being sworn in as a Recorder's Court judge, 1976.

Unexpected Reunion. Judicial Council meets with retired Supreme Court justice Tom Clark (center). Crockett seated right, 1974.

Judge George W. **CROCKETT**, Jr.

for U.S. Congress
13th District
Democrat

- *Experience*
- *Integrity*
- *Leadership*

A remarkable record
of historic achievement

VOTE TWICE!
AUGUST 5

☒325
☒341

Crockett's campaign brochure for his first run for Congress, 1980.

Crockett on election night, waiting for results, November 4, 1980. (Courtesy Detroit News)

Crockett celebrating congressional election victory with his second wife, Dr. Harriet Clark Harris, November 4, 1980. (Courtesy Detroit News)

Crockett with Speaker of the House Thomas "Tip" O'Neill, his mother, Minnie Jenkins Crockett, and his son, George W. Crockett III, on the day he is sworn in to fill Congressman Charles Diggs's term, November 12, 1980. (Courtesy Dr. Ethelene Crockett Jones)

Crockett with Archbishop Desmond Tutu. (Courtesy Dr. Ethelene Crockett Jones)

Crockett with Nelson Mandela during his visit to the United States, June 1990. (Courtesy Dr. Ethelene Crockett Jones)

Black power: Mayor Coleman A. Young, Mayor Harold Washington, Congressman John Conyers, and Congressman George W. Crockett Jr. (Courtesy of Dr. Ethelene Crockett Jones)

Reflective moment. Crockett and Mayor Coleman A. Young.

9

The Struggles in Recorder's Court, 1970–78

Judge Crockett survived the New Bethel Incident and emerged even stronger, becoming a nationally prominent advocate for racial justice and the special role that Black judges play in the fight for civil rights. No part of this struggle would be easy, especially given the difficult and changing politics of Detroit at the dawn of a new decade.

The Trials of the New Bethel Defendants and Their Aftermath

The New Bethel Incident would define Crockett for the balance of his life. With the beginning of 1970 and the end of the Judicial Tenure Commission proceedings, his official involvement with the controversy ended. However, the pending trials of the accused shooters guaranteed that the fallout from the New Bethel Incident continued to dominate the headlines.

Prosecutors decided to try four individuals for the shootings of Officers Michael Czapski and Richard Worobec: Alfred Hibbitt (also known as Alfred 2X), Kirkwood Hall, Raphael Viera, and Clarence Fuller. Hall was one of two persons (along with David Brown Jr.) whom Crockett had held over with a warrant, denying their habeas petitions in the mass arrests. Hall was found in the church basement, allegedly carrying a can of mace. Hibbitt and Hall were tried first, in what came to be known as "New Bethel One," while Viera and Fuller were tried second, in "New Bethel Two." These trials cemented the legacy of the New Bethel Incident as fundamentally transforming understandings of race and law in Detroit.

The Pulitzer Prize–winning historian Heather Ann Thompson writes that "battles on city streets" in Detroit were quickly transformed into "clashes in the courtroom."[1] The New Bethel Incident typified this transition. These trials also spotlighted a new generation of radical Detroit lawyers; first among them was Kenneth (Ken) Cockrel.

Although Crockett and Cockrel were united by a common commitment to racial justice, the contrast between them was striking. For all of the controversy that surrounded Crockett, he believed that law and democracy, properly applied, provided the most effective path forward to vindicate Black civil rights. Cockrel, on the other hand, was an unapologetic Marxist and member of the executive board of the League of Revolutionary Black Workers.[2] In one interview, Cockrel called Crockett a "Brahmin" and contrasted Crockett's national image with his reputation in Detroit. "You mention George Crockett on the East Coast or the West Coast in certain circles and they think you're talking about a fire-breathing radical. . . . He is not seen as the vanguard flaming leftist in Detroit or by anyone who's close to him."[3] Speaking specifically about the New Bethel Incident, Cockrel commented that "everyone is going around saluting Judge Crockett for having followed the law which is not a revolutionary act, but had revolutionary consequences in a state that is not accustomed to the law being followed."[4]

Cockrel brought his passion and radical views to the courtroom. Al Hibbitt was a thirty-eight-year-old Detroit factory worker. His bond hearing in New Bethel One was highly contested. Recorder's Court Judge Joseph E. Maher set bail at the almost unattainable level of $50,000. Cockrel stormed out of the courtroom, muttering under his breath, but within earshot of the press, that Judge Maher was "a racist monkey, a honkie dog, a racist pirate and a bandit."[5] Judge Maher held Cockrel in contempt of court when he learned of the statements. In what was becoming best legal practice two decades after Judge Medina sentenced Crockett to jail for contempt in the *Dennis* case, Judge Maher sent the matter to be heard by an independent Recorder's Court judge. A generation later, Cockrel was afforded due process protection that Crockett had been denied, on the basis of laws that Crockett helped change.

Cockrel was undaunted. His strategy was to defend the truth of his statement and use the contempt proceeding to prove beyond a reasonable doubt that Judge Maher was in fact "a racist monkey, a honkie dog, a racist pirate and a bandit." Cockrel recruited a small army of supporters including linguists, etymologists, and civil liberties experts. He put the judge himself on trial. The courtroom was packed, with additional crowds of supporters protesting outside. True to his word, Cockrel presented expert witness after expert witness documenting the truth of his statement. After two days of hearings and mounting public and media pressure, the prosecutor quietly suggested the voluntary dismissal of the charges, and the judge, accordingly, dismissed the contempt proceeding.[6]

This was just the beginning of New Bethel One. Cockrel aggressively used the jury-selection process to probe deeply the racial beliefs of prospective jurors. He deftly used his permitted challenges and surprisingly produced a representative jury of six Black and six white members. Such racial balance was virtually unheard of in Detroit at the time. Historical prejudices in the Recorder's Court's jury-selection process virtually guaranteed majority-white juries, despite Detroit's dramatically changing demography.

From the beginning of the jury selection and throughout the trial, Cockrel focused on the deep racism that, in effect, defined the Detroit Police Department. As Thompson reports, "He had decided early on that the best way to defend each of those accused of the New Bethel murders was to remind members of the jury that these were black men being charged with attacking white police officers—officers, he maintained, who had a well-known reputation as being violent, untrustworthy, and racist every time they stepped foot into the black community."[7] Cockrel's aggressive lawyering was aided by the prosecutor's relatively weak case. This combination yielded an outcome that virtually no one expected. The jury voted to acquit both defendants. "In doing so, they sent shock waves through the radical and conservative communities of the Motor City alike."[8]

From the standpoint of public opinion and probably jury sympathies, the trial in New Bethel Two would be substantially more challenging for the defense attorneys. The acquitted defendant Hall in New Bethel One was a social worker holding a can of mace, and Hibbitt was a local factory worker. The defendants in New Bethel Two, Clarence Fuller and Raphael Viera, in contrast, were vocal members of the Republic of New Africa (RNA) and unapologetic in their commitment to Black nationalism.[9]

In New Bethel Two, Cockrel was joined by the defense lawyer Milton Henry, vice president of the RNA and the individual who had been escorted from the church by the RNA's Black Legion honor guard just prior to the police shooting. The defense was hampered in the jury-selection process and was unable, this time, to get significant Black representation. They faced the further challenge of the prosecutor's new star witness, David Brown Jr., a nineteen-year-old resident of Compton, California, who testified that he had seen both Fuller and Viera shoot at the police officers.

Like Kirkwood Hall, David Brown was one of the individuals whom prosecutors had sought arrest warrants for in the initial New Bethel habeas proceeding before Judge Crockett. Brown was charged with assault with intent to murder. According to the police, he was firing at them from an opening in the church ceiling before tumbling to the floor after police returned fire. Judge Crockett had ordered Brown held without bond pending further court proceedings. Now, surprisingly, he was testifying on behalf of the prosecution. It is very possible that Brown was an undercover FBI informant.[10] The nineteen-year-old Brown flew from Los Angles to Detroit for the RNA convention. If he was an informant, then it is also likely that the elaborate story of his shooting at officers and tumbling to the floor with a weapon of Italian make and six live cartridges was a fabrication to increase his credibility with RNA members. There was no credible evidence of RNA members firing on police as they stormed the church.

Cockrel attacked the credibility of Brown as a witness by establishing that prosecutors had paid Brown's father a fee for persuading his son to testify for the state. Cockrel further used his cross-examination to have Brown testify to "the police-induced chaos and violence of the New Bethel incident."[11] In essence, Cockrel used Brown to give the jury a front-row seat, through the prosecution's own chief witness, to the police violently storming the church and engaging in mass arrests. Brown further testified to the abuse he suffered at the hands of the police, including numerous kicks to the head that required medical attention.

While these were effective trial tactics, they were unlikely to overcome the prejudices that white jurors brought to the trial. As a result, the defense returned to the issue of jury selection. In a move that took a page right out of the playbook of Crockett and his fellow defense lawyers in the *Dennis* case, in which the attorneys put the jury-selection process of the federal Southern District of New York on trial, Cockrel and his team started to investigate the Recorder's Court jury-selection process. "What they found chilled them and would change the course of legal history in the Motor City."[12]

Cockrel and his partner Justin Ravitz documented systematic biases and prejudices in the jury-selection process that explained why, in a city that was split almost evenly between Blacks and whites, so few Blacks ever served on Recorder's Court juries. The work culminated in a "Joint Motion to Quash Jury Panel and for Other Relief and Affidavit Thereon." After additional hearings, the court granted the motion. Rather than seeking a mistrial, however, the defense sought the unusual remedy of merging wrongly excluded jurors in the case with some number of already-empaneled jurors. The result, according to Ravitz, was the first ever majority-Black jury panel in Recorder's Court history.[13] Furthermore, the controversy triggered systemic changes in the jury-selection process for the entire Recorder's Court.

The trial resumed with a jury of twelve Black and two white members. On June 16, 1970, after deliberating some twenty-eight hours, the jury acquitted both defendants. After more than a year, the New Bethel Incident, which began with the RNA convention and involved police shootings, mass arrests, a firestorm over Judge Crockett's habeas corpus proceedings, investigation by the Judicial Tenure Commission, and two high-profile criminal trials, was finally over. As Thompson concludes, "The New Bethel trials were not about criminals winning out over cops; rather, they were glowing examples of how any violation of black civil rights—even by members of law enforcement—would effectively be censured by the judicial process."[14] Because of Judge Crockett's principled courage in the early morning hours of March 30, justice in Detroit would never be the same.

The legal changes from the New Bethel Incident trials had many ripple effects. The attorney Justin Ravitz and his partner Neil Fink filed a motion for a new trial before Judge Crockett in a separate matter on behalf of their client, Robert Mason. They alleged the same improprieties in jury selection uncovered in the New Bethel Two trial. Mason had been convicted for arson and was serving a prison sentence in the Jackson State Penitentiary. Crockett ordered Mason's release on a $1,000 bond pending a hearing.[15] All in all, it was determined that 200–250 other prisoners would have comparable claims. Wayne County Prosecutor Cahalan sought and received an emergency stay of Judge Crockett's order from none other than Michigan Supreme Court Justice Thomas Brennan.[16] The Michigan Supreme Court later overruled Crockett's release of Mason as an abuse of discretion.[17] Crockett stood alone on principle in trying to extend the New Bethel Two precedent to other cases.

Crockett was not shy about making controversial rulings or about commenting on other important legal controversies of the day. One example involved William Kunstler, his friend and fellow civil rights lawyer during the Mississippi Summer of 1964. Kunstler was representing the "Chicago Seven," who were charged, among other offenses, with efforts to incite a riot by leading protests during the 1968 Democratic National Convention. Reminiscent of what had happened to Crockett and other defense lawyers at the end of the *Dennis* trial, Kunstler was summarily charged and convicted of contempt and sentenced to more than four years in prison by Judge Julius Hoffman—the same judge who, like Judge Medina, had conducted the underlying trial. Crockett made his position clear: "In a political trial, it is necessary for the defense counsel to identify with his clients to some extent, but this means he runs the risk of offending the judge, who often feels a part of the establishment which is under attack.... The greater duty for maintaining an orderly trial lies with the judge, and engaging in continuous bickering with the defense attorney influences the jury and denies the case of a fair hearing."[18] Following new judicial best practices, Crockett said that Judge Hoffman should have disqualified himself from hearing the contempt charges and referred the case to the presiding judge. On appeal, Kunstler's conviction was overturned.

Crockett's national enemies had not disappeared. During closed-door testimony to the House Appropriations Committee, FBI director J. Edgar Hoover specifically criticized Crockett. The *Detroit News* reported, "Although he did not mention him by name, one of those upbraided by Hoover is Detroit Recorder's Court Judge George W. Crockett Jr."[19] According to Chip Gibbon, he "refused to call Crockett by his name, as internal documents show he and the Bureau felt Crockett was too 'despicable' to dignify in such a way. Besides, after internal deliberations, the FBI felt Crockett's rulings were so 'reprehensible' that people would recognize them without Hoover having to demean himself by uttering a name so odious."[20] Hoover detailed how Crockett had sent Lloyd Tyler for treatment, rather than to prison, to address his addiction. Hoover also testified that the "same judge outraged society by immediately releasing on bond a gang of trigger-happy radical militants, who were arrested after two officers were shot, one fatally, at a Detroit church building." According to Hoover, "concerned citizens of Detroit have been completely astounded by the judicial machinations of one judge who has demonstrated latent contempt for investigative and prosecutive officials, and had reportedly proclaimed that he will deliver light sentences to anyone claiming mistreatment by police."[21]

Hoover had always been Crockett's nemesis on the right. The year marked the passing of one of Crockett's long-term nemeses on the "left:" Walter Reuther. Reuther and his wife, May, died in a plane crash in the spring of 1970. Despite the fact that Crockett never spoke with Reuther after he ran Crockett, Maurice Sugar, and Ernie Goodman out of the UAW, Crockett somehow received a telegram invitation to the Reuthers' memorial service: "You have shared with May and Walter Reuther their hopes and aspirations to build a world of peace and brotherhood. On behalf of the members of their family we would be honored if you would join us in the Memorial service."[22] It is not known how Crockett responded to the invitation. Obviously, much had changed in the intervening years.

The National Bar Association's Judicial Council and the Role of Black Judges

The year 1971 marked Crockett's fifth year on the Recorder's Court. In no small part due to the attention generated by the New Bethel Incident, Crockett had gained a national reputation. On January 9, 1971, the Executive Board of the NBA, of which Crockett was a lifetime member and supporter, adopted a resolution creating the Judicial Council, an independent section of the NBA with its own officers, bylaws, and treasury. The newly formed Judicial Council replaced the NBA's Judges' Section, acknowledging the growing role of Black judges in combating racism in law enforcement. The Judicial Council held its founding convention in Atlanta in August, with U.S. Circuit Court of Appeals Judge William H. Hastie as keynote speaker. Elected as its first chairman was Judge George W. Crockett Jr.[23]

The Judicial Council had a clear mandate. Its first priority was a drive for more Black federal judgeships. It sought meetings with both President Richard Nixon and Attorney General John Mitchell.[24] The need for more Black lawyers and judges was a long-standing concern for Crockett. Black

judges represented an extreme minority of those on the bench. The dispari-
ties were particularly acute in the South. "'The population in Mississippi,
for example, is 50 percent black,' Crockett said. 'Yet they have lily white
courts.'"[25]

Crockett's inaugural address to the Judicial Council highlighted his
views on the role of racism in U.S. law and the special role that Black
judges must play in the national struggle for equity. In what can be read as
a judicial manifesto, he fused the twin motivations of racial and economic
justice that had motivated him since his youth and grounded the power
of Black judges in the knowledge they posses in understanding how racism and political oppression function in their own daily lives. He called
on them to use this knowledge and access to state power to undo racist
systems and find creative ways to use the law to new ends:

> Racism pervades every area and facet of American life. It is a
> characteristic of American life; and hence, it is a characteristic of
> American law.
>
> Racism is evident in our courts whenever and wherever a Black
> litigant is involved. It is indigenous to the law as applied to Blacks
> whether the proceeding be in Michigan or Mississippi, in a Federal
> or a State tribunal, or in a court of civil or criminal jurisdiction.
>
> None of this is startlingly new information and we did not
> have to come to Atlanta to learn the facts we were born with and
> live with every day. What is revealing, however, and what this con-
> vention underscores is Black America's growing understanding of
> the inner workings of our social order and the interaction of law
> and economics. There is apparent[ly] an increasing realization by
> Black judges that race discrimination and class discrimination are
> integral parts of our present day judicial system; that these twin
> evils affect profoundly every phase of our work as lawyers, law pro-
> fessors and judges and—most importantly—that we ourselves, will
> perpetuate and extend the cancerous effect of these evils unless we
> identify and fight them unceasingly.[26]

The exercise of power lies at the root of racism, but racialized capitalism
harms poor people of all colors: "Racism was born, nurtured and sustained

in the interests of a few against the many. The economics and the psychology of slave traders, plantation owners and corporate employers are essentially the same and undergone no basic change since the first slave ship sailed from Africa to the West Indies. Thus, what we judges and lawyers observe today in our courts is more than racism. The poor white derelict, the indigent, and the unemployed, the dispossessed, no matter what race or color are given like treatment."[27] Trial courts and trial court judges must play critical roles in the struggle for new liberation:

So the struggle continues. In recent years the battleground has largely shifted from the legislature and the repeal or enactment of statutes. The battleground today is the trial courts—and especially the lower trial courts. It is in these tribunals that legally approved racism-classism flourishes in its most virulent form.

If the battleground against racism has shifted to the trial courts the chief artillery, if that battle is to be won, has to be the trial judge himself. He is the one in absolute command; and he is the sole repository of that tremendous force for good or evil which we call "judicial discretion."

There are approximately 285 Black judges of courts of record out of 12,500 such judges in the nation. Many of us are convinced that this paucity of Black judges and the frantic effort which is constantly being made to block the election or appointment of more stems from the fear in some quarters that the awesome power of the state which inheres in the trial judge will be used by Black judges to correct many of the racist and discriminatory class practices of our judicial system.

Happily, these fears are not far-fetched. A Black New York judge has ruled that a Black mother is not an unfit custodian of her child merely because she elects to live in unconfirmed wedlock; a Black Detroit judge has held a high-ranking city official in contempt of court for his willful destruction of public records showing building code violations in ghetto housing; several Black Chicago judges have released non-white victims of police brutality; and a Black Baltimore judge has given leadership in defeating a referendum proposal that was calculated to seriously impair the further integration of Maryland's judiciary. These and many other non-conformist rulings and actions by Black judges confirm what Mr. Justice Cardozo wrote several years ago: that we judges are the products of our experiences and our environment. These actions also demonstrate that we Black judges have not forgotten from whence we came to our present exalted positions, nor the true import of the oath we have taken to administer the law equally and without fear or favor.

One sure remedy for the everyday racist and discriminatory class occurrences in our courts is to have more trial court judges who are Black and/or non-conformists and who are not afraid to use the authority of their office to end such practices.

A Black judge—if he is psychologically Black and not just physically dark of color; if he has been thrust forward by the convolutions of his Black society and is not ashamed of the route by which he arrived; if he is still a man (or woman) of the people and not blinded by the prestige, power and affluence accorded his position—this kind of Black judge will recognize racism and classism when he sees it; he will identify with the victims and be mindful that there, but for the grace of God, stand I; and he will proceed to invent legally approved ways and means of balancing the scales. This really is not difficult to do. Our white fellow judges have created so many exceptions to serve their purposes that we can always find an exception to support our judgment.[28]

The Judicial Council was designed as a critical forum for action in this new field of freedom:

The historical function of the judge is to insure adherence in practice to the guarantees of the constitution and the law. The paramount aim of the N.B.A. Judicial Council will be to assist our judges in doing just that. Our role is illustrated by the drawing on the cover of our program. Justice is supposed to be blind. It treats all individuals alike—rich or poor, black or white, male or female. Well, it's time to remove the blindfold that gives this illusion of fair treatment. We want to expose to the full glare of reality the inequities super-imposed in that great but unrealized objective. We want justice to see its errors, to identify its prejudices and to expose those who would pervert just laws with unjust penalties.

The meaning and the purpose of this conference of the N.B.A. Judicial Council is not to point out, analyze and explore the varied racist practices of our judicial system. Our purpose is to do what no other judicial council or legal gathering has had the courage to do—to engage in a meaningful exchange of experiences that will equip us individually to fashion new judicial approaches and remedies for old racial and class grievances; to consciously plan the re-examination and the eventual overruling of old outmoded legal theories and precedents which no longer serve the legitimate needs and aspirations of our new majorities; and finally, to assist judicially in returning America to her true constitutional moorings, to the end that we shall have a Nation united and a World at peace.[29]

As promised, the Judicial Council's first action was an effort to expand the number of Black federal judges. In Crockett's capacity as chairman, he sent a telegram to President Nixon asking him to seek the advice and counsel not just of the American Bar Association but of the NBA as well: "If you are to respond to the needs of the entire American Community, these important selections must embody the equally significant recommendations of the Black members of the legal profession, the vast majority of whom are not members of the American Bar Association."[30] Indeed, the NBA was formed in response to the racially exclusive practices of the ABA.

Despite Crockett's major accomplishment of being the first chairman of the Judicial Council, the summer of 1971 had other stresses. Crockett was frequently the victim of racial threats and attacks. One such incident was recorded in his scrapbook of newspaper clippings. The front page of the July 4, 1971, Sunday edition of the *Bay City Times* featured two large photos with the caption, "Trial of Judge Crockett." This was a cruel, racist farce, not a trial. The caption continued, "At left a lanky blond haired youth, in a full [black] mask, was sentenced to hanging Saturday by a shouting audience of about 70 during a bizarre skit billed as 'an example of American Justice.'" The mask was a grotesque form of blackface. The caption continued, "In the picture on the right, two Klansmen, attired in ceremonial robes, carry 'the nigger' off to his fate, a dunking in a nearby stream, while the audience howled with delight."³¹ Judge Crockett seldom annotated or commented on the newspaper articles he collected. This was an exception. With a simple red pencil, he drew an arrow from the date at the very top of the newspaper near the masthead and wrote, "Independence Day."

As the year came to a close, attention focused on Crockett's likely 1972 reelection campaign. The Judge Crockett Testimonial Committee was established to prepare the way. The committee was cochaired by Jane Hart, the wife of Senator Philip Hart, and federal district court judge Damon J. Keith. The executive secretary was Crockett's former law partner and colleague in Mississippi Claudia Morcom. The invitation to the committee's "Testimonial Reception" was not shy about its political objectives: "Besides demonstrating our regard for Judge Crockett, we hope your support of this reception will encourage him to become a candidate for re-election to Recorder's Court in 1972."³²

The Testimonial Reception illustrated how quickly the times had changed. As the *Detroit Free Press* noted, many of the tributes in 1971 were made by those who had been ardent foes in 1966. "George W. Crockett Jr., Recorder's Court judge who has upset the establishment for years, has apparently won respect from those same corners. He will be honored Oct. 26 at a $25-a-plate testimonial dinner at the Roostertail. Among the supporters are Douglas Fraser, a vice-president of the UAW, from which Crockett was fired in the late 1940s, and Detroit establishment attorney William Gossett, former president of the American Bar Association."³³ The UAW had actively campaigned for Crockett's defeat in 1966. Crockett and the National Lawyers Guild targeted the ABA in the early 1960s for its failure to demand that its southern members represent Black clients in the civil rights struggle.

Governor William Milliken was another latecomer to the Crockett "bandwagon." Just two years earlier, Milliken called for the Judicial Tenure Commission to investigate Judge Crockett for impeachment over the New Bethel Incident. Although he was unable to attend the reception, he sent Judge Crockett a warm congratulatory letter:

Dear Judge Crockett,

I am extremely sorry that it is not possible for me to be with you this evening for what I am certain will be a most deserving and memorable occasion.

However, I am particularly pleased to be able to offer my personal best wishes and congratulations to you as a man in high office who has a clear view of duty and the courage to act on that belief.

Leadership in today's complex, sometimes strident, world calls for many strengths virtually every moment of the day. You have both strength and vision and I am especially glad to be able to join many others in saluting you tonight.

Sincerely,
William G. Milliken, Governor[34]

It was becoming impolitic in Democratic circles not to support Crockett.

The *Michigan Chronicle* provided extensive coverage of the event. "Recorder's Court Judge George W. Crockett was serenely elegant, despite some embarrassment that only close friends could detect, as he received one tribute after another." It was a capacity crowd. Crockett was "acknowledged as one of the country's leading authorities on Constitutional Law, was cited for 'scholarship, integrity and courage' and for adding 'new dimensions to the continuing struggle for equality and decency in America.'" This was not the way it had always been for Crockett: "Last week's affair held an atmosphere of homage for Judge Crockett that was a far cry from events in 1966 when he was campaigning for election to the bench."[35] It was not just attitudes about Crockett that were changing; seismic shifts were taking place in Detroit's politics and demography.

On the Road to Reelection

Not surprisingly, Crockett announced that he would run for reelection in 1972. Even in an election year, however, he did not shy away from controversy. The "numbers game" had always been the poor man's lottery in cities like Detroit. Even though the numbers players were notorious for paying off the police, every now and then, they would become particular targets for the police and prosecutors. Crockett understood how numbers games were treated differently from other vices and other forms of gambling. In January 1972, prosecutors brought seven defendants before him, charged with numbers racketeering. Crockett sentenced them to relatively light fines, without jail or probation. The *Free Press* reported, "Crockett called the prosecution of the seven black numbers operators an example of 'selective' laws against gambling which outlaw among poor people but largely ignore gambling in more affluent sectors of society." Moreover, the defendants in this case were at the bottom rung of the ladder. According to Crockett, "These are little men who go around and pick up 10 and 15 cent bets, largely in the ghetto area." He also understood the social context of the people playing the numbers: "Gambling is a human instinct, especially among people who are most affected by unemployment, recession, and other conditions of the times. They know the odds are stacked against them, but hope beats eternal. They say tonight at 6 o'clock I'll know the number, and maybe I'll have enough to pay my rent or catch up on the insurance policies."[36] He echoed themes he had talked about since his 1966 campaign. Too often, law enforcement was directed at the poor and marginalized, while police ignored wealthier people gambling in their homes or clubs.

Crockett's decision, once again, generated controversy, as reflected in the *Free Press*'s letters to the editor. For example, Morton Brody wrote, "The sentence handed down by Recorder's Court Judge George W. Crockett Jr. against the seven Detroit numbers racketeers is totally irresponsible. If this is the judgment that Judge Crockett normally metes out to known hoodlums and gangsters, then he should be impeached." Clarence Richard Clawson suggested racial motivations: "Once again, that pillar of justice, Judge Crockett, has given us a shining example of his inherent racism. Does anyone really believe that he would have let those poor black numbers people with alleged Mafia ties off so easily if they had been white?" V. M. Carter was more sympathetic: "No real justice can be served by jailing a few numbers carriers. In order to kill a dragon, one must cut off the head; if all seven of the defendants had been jailed they would have been immediately replaced by seven new errand boys."[37]

Crockett wrote a letter in his own defense: "It was not accidental that I declared these seven as 'little men.' After five years on this bench, I have yet to see brought before the bar of justice a big operator or a Mafia member or even an alleged representative of organized crime." He was most concerned about the ways laws were enforced disproportionately to target the poor and disadvantaged: "I cannot say that I am morally opposed to gambling. I do not think that most people today are. But they are opposed to a dual system of justice—one which applies one set of laws to the rich and the powerful and another to the poor and the underprivileged."[38]

Crockett was not one to back down. Instead, he upped the ante. Recorder's Court judges rotate in various roles. The next time Judge Crockett was the judge responsible for signing warrants, he declared that he would not sign any more felony warrants for people charged with "picking up numbers." The forum for the ruling was the now familiar writ of habeas corpus. Twenty-seven persons arrested in a raid of two alleged numbers gambling houses filed habeas petitions before Judge Crockett. According to the *Free Press*, the "judge said he was angry over what he called police efforts to 'get banner headlines' by arresting people involved in 'petty little numbers cases.'" Crockett retorted, "Now if you go to the suburbs and get the big shots who are getting all the numbers money, you'll get a warrant with no problem." His decision came after the prosecution asked for a thirty-day adjournment in the habeas proceeding "so it could complete its investigation and paperwork on the cases." In essence, this was another incident of "arrest to investigate." Crockett denied the request. "Judge Crockett said the only evidence police presented to him Friday was the testimony of a police officer who said he had observed one of the defendants go to a home daily with a brown bag in his hand. 'All that proves is that the man likes to go to that house with a brown bag,' Crockett said. 'In my opinion they didn't have any evidence in court today, period.'"[39]

Crockett continued his role on the national stage as chairman of the Judicial Council. School integration remained a central civil rights issue, but busing, as a remedy, was becoming increasingly controversial in conservative circles. Crockett came out forcefully against President Nixon's attack on court-ordered busing, stating that Nixon's statements were "disrespectful of the role of the Supreme Court in our constitutional system" and "undermines the faith that Americans, particularly black Americans, hold for the system of justice." Underlying the dispute were important issues of separation of powers: "This behavior on the part of American leadership can only erode the people's reliance on the law for their protection. Black Americans have traditionally looked to the Supreme Court as the guarantors of America's constitutional freedoms. Where now shall we look?" The focus on busing missed the larger question of ongoing segregation: "Bussing, Crockett said, is 'a method, albeit an imperfect one, to achieve the 14th Amendment promise to furnish equality of educational opportunity.'"[40]

In Detroit, a battle was brewing over Referendum E, which gave Detroit voters the chance to make positive changes in the Recorder's Court. The court had too few judges for its heavy caseload and, therefore, a large backlog of cases. Capacity problems were currently addressed by recruiting visiting judges from other jurisdictions on rotating bases. In 1969, the Michigan Supreme Court used this backlog as a pretext for its sham reorganization proposal that would have moved Crockett from the criminal docket and essentially eliminated the Recorder's Court, merging it into the Wayne County court system. If the cause of the backlog was a lack of capacity, then the answer to the problem was adding more Recorder's Court judges. This was the intention of Referendum E, which was on the August primary ballot and would add seven new judges to the existing thirteen-member bench. Crockett was a vocal advocate of the proposal. "Recorder's Court Judge George W. Crockett today called for the addition of new judges in Recorder's Court not only to improve the pace and quality of criminal justice but to restore to Detroiters the right to elect their own judges."[41] If the proposal passed, there would be no more need for the visiting judges.

Referendum E also opened the door for more Black judges. Crockett knew the statistics: "Blacks represent about eleven percent of Michigan's population and almost 50 percent of Detroit's population. But they constitute only two-tenths of one percent (0.23%) of Michigan judges." The numbers were stark. Michigan had 19 state appellate court judges, none Black; 105 probate judges, none Black; and 175 municipal and common pleas judges, only 2 of whom were Black. He concluded, "In short, of the approximately 500 state and federal judges in Michigan, only thirteen of them are black and half of Michigan's black judges sit on the Recorder's and Traffic Courts in the City of Detroit."[42]

For Crockett, the lack of Black judges was a threat to both justice and democracy: "The fear [of the establishment] is that Black judges will take literally and seriously the Constitution's guarantee of equal justice to all and will actually make the system work." In cities like Detroit, such actions were essential for social progress: "A more integrated Recorder's Court and Traffic Court is key to ending police brutality, to improving police community relations and getting more Blacks on the police force. It is the key to a more humane judicial approach to the problems of victimless offenses and to the issues of pre-trial detention, mass arrests and illegal searches and seizures." Crockett had been fighting a lonely battle on the bench. Referendum E held the promise of providing additional allies in the struggle. More progressive Recorder's Court judges were necessary to end business as usual on the part of the police and prosecutors: "I would hope that the judges of the new court, individually and collectively, would end the traditional subservience to the prosecutor's office and the Police Department, and that all of us would be more insistent in our demands that these two law enforcement agencies obey scrupulously, and at all times, each of our federal and state constitutional mandates with respect to warrantless arrests, searches, humane treatment of persons in custody and the use of fatal force."[43]

Judge Crockett was also on the August primary ballot. When the Detroit Bar Association judicial rating came out, "George W. Crockett Jr. was the only incumbent Recorder's Court judge who received an 'outstanding' rating."[44] Not surprisingly, Crockett also had a strong endorsement from Nadine Brown of the *Michigan Chronicle*, speaking directly to the issues of integrity. "Anyone who has been disgusted with the performance of politicians, who after elected forget about their campaign promises should find reason to be hopeful in the realization that there are some politicians who have integrity and the courage of their convictions. Recorder's Court Judge George W. Crockett has proved to be the possessor of both."[45]

In the wake of the primary, the Black community in Detroit had much to celebrate. Judge Crockett was the top vote getter among the Recorder's Court incumbents, receiving ten thousand more votes than the second-place finisher.[46] There was other good news. Referendum E passed by an almost two-to-one margin in most parts of the city.[47]

As suggested by the all-star members of the Crockett Testimonial Committee, Crockett's reelection campaign was undertaken from a position of strength. One of his campaign fliers featured an endorsement from Rosa Parks: "Our youth need models of courage, of integrity, of compassion and of faith in justice. George Crockett provides all of these." In a sign of changing times in a post-Reuther world, the flier also featured an endorsement from new UAW president Doug Fraser: "The courts are, after all, where workers, minorities, the poor and the underprivileged must look for justice—and they get that in Judge Crockett's court."[48] Whereas the UAW political arm spearheaded attacks against Crockett in 1966 and refused to endorse him, Crockett's former employer was now fully behind his candidacy.

Some things had not changed in six years. Once again, Crockett received the endorsement of the *Free Press,* and once again, the hostile *Detroit News* opposed his candidacy. One *Free Press* editorial stated, "George Crockett has often been a controversial figure. But usually, after the controversy has died down, Crockett has been exactly correct in his positions, and we admire his courage in sticking to his convictions. His knowledge of criminal law is impressive both for its depth and his ability to apply it effectively. The idea that Crockett is a 'soft' judge is a myth. Lawyers and other judges report that he is one of the sternest judges on the bench and, especially where crimes of violence are concerned, one of the toughest sentencers."[49] The *Detroit News,* on the other hand, curmudgeonly wrote that it was time for changes in Recorder's Court, but even the *Detroit News* saw the writing on the wall: "George W. Crockett Jr. may have moderated his capricious attitude somewhat and will likely be reelected by a large vote; but essentially he looks upon himself as an advocate of causes rather than as a detached judge of the law, hence we cannot support him."[50]

In the end, Crockett did not need the endorsement of the *Detroit News.* Just as in the primaries, the final vote tally showed him the clear winner. According to the official election returns for the 1972 election of Recorder's Court of the City of Detroit, George Crockett received 188,146 votes, while his closest competitor, Judge Donald S. Leonard, received 158,799 votes.[51] Judge Crockett would serve another six-year term on the bench.

While reelection was a tremendous professional accomplishment, Crockett had reasons to be happy in his personal life as well. He remained close with his old friends and mentors. In his scrapbook for 1972, Crockett kept a letter from Maurice Sugar describing the values that had guided both of them throughout their careers. In it, Sugar had written, "Not only do you possess the qualities of a jurist skilled in law, but you have shown it in human terms and with understanding and compassion for the poor, the underprivileged and the disadvantaged."[52] Prior to the election, Crockett had given an interview to the *Detroit Free Press* columnist Frank Angelo. In the column, Angelo wrote, "Crockett exudes the impression of a man totally at peace with himself, and for good reason. He speaks with affection of his family, a wife and three children who have distinguished themselves in their careers."[53] After many twists and turns, from prison and threatened disbarment to the scourge of the Red Scare following *Dennis*, Crockett was able to find, once again, a happy life in the law.

From a Second Term in Recorder's Court to Corporation Counsel to Congress

Police lawlessness and the resulting poor relations with the Black community lay at the center of Detroit's social problems dating from the nineteenth century and more recently from the 1943 race riot to the 1967 Rebellion to the 1969 New Bethel Incident. Even by these low standards, the police unit Stop the Robberies, Enjoy Safe Streets (STRESS) marked the beginning of a new and troubling epoch. Formed in January 1971, STRESS was founded by Police Commissioner John F. Nichols and quickly developed a reputation for extraordinary violence and unorthodox tactics.[54] STRESS was an undercover unit that used decoy tactics that soon devolved into episodes of entrapment, often ending in little more than state-sanctioned murder. "During the two and one-half years it operated, STRESS was responsible for twenty-two homicides and fourteen non-fatal shootings of mostly Black Detroiters."[55]

Detroit's Black communities faced the dual problems of police overenforcement and underenforcement. Units like STRESS terrorized and overenforced communities. At the same time, the police followed the policy of underenforcement when addressing many of the community's real problems, like drugs and crime. Underenforcement invited communities to find their own solutions to the problems. Three Detroit youths, Hayward Brown, Marcus Clyde Bethune, and John Percy Boyd, influenced by Malcolm X's antidrug messages, took it upon themselves to fight the heroin trade in their neighborhoods.[56] Brown was still in high school, while Boyd and

Bethune were students at Wayne State University. On December 4, 1972, the three's anticrime efforts put them on a collision course with STRESS, as both had staked out the same drug house. The drug dealer sped off in his car, chased by Brown, Bethune, and Boyd in their Volkswagen Beetle, as well as by the STRESS officers in plainclothes in their white Plymouth sedan. Thinking that the white sedan was full of the drug dealer's henchmen, Brown, Bethune, and Boyd exchanged gunfire with those in the sedan as the STRESS team tried to force them off the road. Some of the police officers were injured in the encounter. Brown, Bethune, and Boyd escaped but triggered a police manhunt.[57]

A few weeks later, on December 27, 1972, police were staking out an apartment building where the three young men were hiding. Another altercation and exchange of gunfire ensued, leaving one police officer dead and one with permanent injuries.[58] Remarkably, Brown, Bethune, and Boyd escaped again, unleashing an even larger and more brutal manhunt.[59] Bethune and Boyd were tracked down in Atlanta and were killed in a shootout with police. Brown was apprehended in Detroit by Wayne State University public safety officers.[60]

Hayward Brown was charged with seven counts of assault with intent to commit murder and one count of first-degree murder. The prosecutor refused to consolidate the charges, meaning that Brown would face three separate trials. Ironically, in a random draw, the first trial was assigned to Judge Crockett. The jury reforms triggered by New Bethel Two had already made substantial differences in the jury-selection process. In Brown's case, the jury consisted of seven Black women, three Black men, and two white women.[61] The lead defense attorney was none other than Ken Cockrel. More than a trial of Brown, Cockrel made the courtroom a public forum for the trial of STRESS and its violent history. On May 3, 1973, after ten hours of deliberations, the jury acquitted Brown on all charges.

The verdict outraged conservative factions in the city, but the outcome in the first trial was no fluke. Different juries in the second and third trials in courtrooms stewarded by different Recorder's Court judges reached the same conclusion. Brown was acquitted on all counts in all three trials.[62] Each trial was a media sensation, keeping the issue of STRESS and police brutality in the headlines from the first police encounter on the streets in December 1972 to the last verdict in July 1973. Indeed, since the New

Bethel Incident in 1969, the topic of police practices was hardly ever out of the headlines. While these court victories were exhilarating for Detroit's Black community, they were equally maddening for the city's conservative whites. Politics in Detroit and the region became more polarized, as the divide between whites and Blacks and between progressive whites and conservative whites increased.

The year 1973 was an election year for Detroit mayor. In 1969, Black candidate Richard Austin narrowly lost the mayoral election to Wayne County Sherriff Roman Gribbs. Emblematic of the growing political divide, Detroit police commissioner and STRESS founder John F. Nichols and Coleman A. Young emerged as the two finalists in the 1973 primary. As an attorney in the 1950s, Crockett defended Young before the House Un-American Activities Committee. Young's testimony was pressed into a record album and sold on the streets of Detroit, furthering his reputation as a streetfighter and unconventional leader. In return, as a state senator representing Detroit, Young defended Crockett in the state legislature when the senate tried to remove Crockett from the bench. Now, this outspoken leader of the Black community was facing off against a conservative representative of the Detroit Police Department.

Starting in the 1950s and accelerating before the 1967 Rebellion, white flight was reshaping the region and its politics. By 1973, the Black population in Detroit was inching closer and closer to the 50 percent mark. But numbers were not enough. Unity was just as important. The Black United Front (BUF), which was created to support Crockett in the wake of the New Bethel Incident, galvanized the Black community in a wave that continued through the 1973 mayoral campaign. The 1973 election was a watershed moment for the city. Young was able to marshal the unity of the Black community into a coalition with groups of white liberals to become Detroit's first Black mayor. He received more than 56 percent of the vote. For lifetime Detroiters, his election was almost unimaginable. For Crockett, who long advocated working within democratic processes but doing so in a focused and disciplined manner, a Black mayor of Detroit was a hallmark of electoral progress. Crockett later reflected that the "New Bethel incident gave 'a sense of political empowerment on the part of blacks in Detroit . . . From that point on, they realized the importance of going to the polls and electing candidates responsive to their needs and rights.... It really was the beginning of the movement' that led to Young's election as mayor."[63]

This political progress necessarily complemented the work that Crockett and others were performing on the bench. Without a doubt, judges rigorously enforcing constitutional principles can produce radical change. But it is also true that judges interpret the law; they do not make it. Many changes require executive and legislative power. Mayor Young, by executive order, abolished STRESS as one of his very first actions. He introduced residence requirements to ensure that police and firefighters lived in the city that employed them. He implemented aggressive affirmative-action programs in the police and fire departments to counteract lengthy histories of race discrimination. These policies began to attack the root causes of police brutality.

Another sign of the shifting power balance in the city was the fact that Crockett was elected chief judge of the Recorder's Court in 1974. For the first time, the top executive positions in the city and in the Recorder's Court were held by African Americans. Crockett served as chief judge from 1974 until his retirement at the end of his second judicial term in 1978. A hallmark of his time on the bench was a call for progressive reforms of the criminal justice system. Just at a time when the country was moving toward a renewed War on Crime, Crockett was urging an entirely different approach: "The criminal justice system will continue to stagger under its own inadequacies until equal opportunity and equal justice become the foundation of any attempts to reform the system.... Advocacy of speedier convictions and more severe sentences, of more and better equipped police, of more and tougher judges is not the answer.... We are not going to stem the tide of increasing crime until we come to understand and accept one simple truth—that punishment is no cure for poverty, nor for drug addiction, nor for ignorance, frustration or despair."[64]

In 1976, Crockett enjoyed a personal and professional joy that few can have. His son, George W. Crockett III, was elected to the Recorder's Court bench and served with his father. Sadly, not all of life's milestones are pleasant. In 1978, the same year Crockett stepped down from the bench, Dr. Ethelene Crockett, his wife of forty-four years, passed away. Crockett was sixty-nine years old.

Crockett did not stay retired for long. He served briefly as a visiting judge for the Michigan State Court of Appeals before Mayor Young recruited him to serve as acting corporation counsel, Detroit's top lawyer. At the age of seventy-one, Crockett had another unexpected opportunity. In 1954, Charles Diggs was elected Michigan's first Black congressman. The Thirteenth Congressional District, located entirely within the city of Detroit, was overwhelmingly Democratic. In June 1980, Diggs resigned, facing prison time for federal mail-fraud charges. Crockett ran in a crowded primary and prevailed with a plurality of 42 percent. He won the special election for the remainder of Congressman Diggs's term and won the general election for the coming full congressional term by an overwhelming 92 percent of the vote. Entering his seventh decade of life, George W. Crockett Jr. was going to Congress, the oldest Black person ever elected to the House of Representatives. He would not enter Congress alone. In the summer of 1980, he married Harriette Clark Chambliss, a Washington, DC, pediatrician.

10

Crockett in Congress

A Tall Tree Falls

When Crockett retired from Recorder's Court in 1978, he did so with his wife, Ethelene, who was ending an illustrious career as a physician and community leader. She knew she had cancer but did not know how seriously ill she really was. She passed away on December 29, 1978, leaving Crockett a retired widower. "If I would have known what I know now, I wouldn't have retired. . . . I'm disgustingly healthy and I feel disgustingly young and neither one goes along with retirement."[1] Later, as a member of the House Select Committee on Aging, he recalled, "I retired from active employment as a judge in Detroit when I reached retirement age. I got completely bored sitting around being ignored by everybody else and that was when I decided to go back to work. I would join those who have indicated that one way to shorten one's life is to be forced to become inactive when your health is such that you can remain active."[2]

Congress would open a new chapter in Crockett's life, but he would be no ordinary congressman. At his core, Crockett was not a political being. He was a man of principle, not politics. He had a deep set of values that had guided him his whole life. At the same time, paradoxically, next to Detroit mayor Coleman Young, he was probably the most popular political figure in Detroit. He was elected by an overwhelming majority and, therefore, held a "safe" seat. He was free to approach Congress on his own terms, more as a sage and a crusader for racial and economic justice. As time would demonstrate, however, his values were more those of the old Left, values that were being increasingly challenged by the new Right.

Crockett served on the Committee on Foreign Affairs, the Subcommittee on Africa, the Judiciary Committee, and the Select Committee on Aging and chaired the Subcommittee on Western Hemisphere Affairs.[3] But it was the fights over the most important issues of the day that would define his time in Congress—battles over increased militarism in the Western Hemisphere, over conservative budgets that attacked five decades of New Deal programs, and over the evils of apartheid in South Arica—as well as the continuation of his lifetime struggle for civil rights.

Battles in the Western Hemisphere: Crockett v. Reagan

The same election that brought Crockett to Congress also elected Ronald Reagan to the White House. It is difficult to imagine two men with more different life histories and principles. Reagan announced his bid for the presidency in Philadelphia, Mississippi, in a speech defending "states' rights."[4] Philadelphia was the town where the civil rights martyrs Goodman, Chaney, and Schwerner were brutally murdered in 1964 investigating a church burning shortly after speaking with Crockett. "States' rights" was a long-standing anti-civil-rights euphemism used to defend everything from slavery to Jim Crow segregation. It was inevitable that Crockett would vigorously oppose Reagan.

The men's first confrontation was over El Salvador. Reversing policies that had been implemented under President Jimmy Carter, the Reagan administration began sending military aid and equipment to El Salvador. It also sent fifty-six U.S. soldiers as "military advisers," a move that echoed how the conflict in Vietnam slowly escalated into a military catastrophe. In violation of the War Powers Resolution (WPR), Reagan failed to notify Congress of his actions within the designated sixty days. Crockett was livid about this clear violation of the law, but he responded to the crisis more like the civil rights lawyer of his past than as a congressman. He decided to sue the president.

Crockett contacted the Center for Constitutional Rights (CCR), which was founded by his friends Arthur Kinoy, Ben Smith, and William Kunstler in 1966 as an outgrowth of their collective work in Mississippi. Given his life's work, he was a hero to the younger CCR lawyers. Nevertheless, they were reluctant to take the case. The law was not good, and courts have historically been reluctant to get directly involved in foreign policy. But Crockett argued the facts forcefully, and CCR agreed to take the case.[5] *Crockett v. Reagan* was filed on May 1, 1981, the first major court challenge under the WPR.[6] One of the CCR lawyers later recalled that the "filing date was deliberately chosen for symbolic purposes: May 1 is Law Day, and the lawsuit argued that the president was not above the law. It is also International Workers Day, and the suit was an effort to express solidarity with the poor people of El Salvador."[7]

The case sought sweeping relief. The plaintiffs wanted court orders "directing that defendants immediately withdraw all United States Armed Forces, weapons, and military equipment and aid from El Salvador and prohibiting any further aid of any nature."[8] As civil rights lawyers, including Crockett, knew, you bring some cases to win; other cases are brought primarily to educate the public, catalyze a political campaign, or help build a social movement. *Crockett v. Reagan* was brought more for political than strictly legal purposes. Not surprisingly, the district court dismissed the case as presenting questions better addressed through the political process.[9] The court of appeals affirmed.[10]

Suing the president was a distinctively bold way for a freshman congressman to start his political career. *Crockett v. Reagan*, however, was the first of what would be many fights with the White House over increased militarism in the Western Hemisphere. In many ways, these conflicts were a reprise of the worst aspects of the Red Scare and McCarthyism: exaggerated fears of communism, misguided political judgments, and the false labeling of political opponents. Some thirty years earlier, Crockett was essentially powerless and at the mercy of Judge Medina, who had sentenced him to prison for contempt in *United States v. Dennis*. Now, he had the powers and prerogatives as a member of Congress.

Crockett used his powers on the House Committee on Foreign Affairs and particularly the Subcommittee on Western Hemisphere Affairs to do what he thought was right. He knew well from his own experiences that police officers lied in court. He was equally skeptical of official reports from the CIA and the State Department. He trusted his own judgment and would travel where needed to find facts. For example, he traveled as part of a U.S. congressional delegation to the Inter-Parliamentary Conference in Havana, Cuba, in 1981.[11] He opposed Reagan's invasion of the Caribbean island of Grenada, once again joining his House colleagues in a lawsuit against the president.[12] He was also a strong advocate for the rights of the Palestinian people.[13]

Crockett's stances drew substantial fire from the Right, particularly in 1987, when he became chairman of the Subcommittee on Western Hemisphere Affairs. A coalition of conservative groups called for Crockett's removal, labeling him "a left-wing extremist, who . . . represents a security risk to our nation."[14] The critics rehashed attacks that had been lobbed at him since the 1940s: "It's not like he's a liberal, or left wing; he's actually a [communist] collaborator." They attacked his long-standing membership in the National Lawyers Guild, a group his critics noted was "cited by the House Committee on Un-American Activities in 1950 as 'the foremost legal bulwark of the Communist Party, its front organizations, and controlled unions.'" Crockett did have his defenders: "'That's a lot of familiar crap,' said Rep. William D. Ford (D-Mich.), who claimed friendship with Crockett since 1951. 'It's commie-baiting. . . . In those days if HUAC called you, you were a communist, and if you took the Fifth (Amendment) they presumed you were pleading guilty. . . . These guys are trying to dust all that off now and that kind of conduct is what's really un-American.'"[15]

Crockett also found support from an unexpected source, Carl Parsell, the former president of the Detroit Police Officers Association, who had called repeatedly for his removal from the Recorder's Court. Parsell now admitted to using these same baseless allegations decades before. "Yeah, we were using those things in the 1960s to condemn George Crockett then." Parsell expressed contrition: "'We couldn't see straight at the time. . . . His fight for civil rights was no different than our (union's) fight for equality in the workplace.' [Parsell] used Crockett as a target, he said, to defuse police anger at a tense time. 'I hold nothing against him and hope he holds nothing against me. I know he's doing an excellent job in representing his district.'"[16]

Crockett used his power as chair to fight aggressively against military assistance to the "Contra" rebels in Nicaragua and to push for peace throughout Central America. Left-wing Sandinista rebels overthrew the repressive regime of Anastasio Somoza in 1979. The right-wing Contras formed in opposition in 1981 and received substantial aid from the Reagan administration. Congress passed three versions of the Boland Amendment between 1982 and 1984 prohibiting U.S. assistance to the Contras for the purpose of overthrowing the Nicaraguan government but permitting assistance for other purposes.[17] In response, in what would become known as the Iran-Contra scandal, the Reagan administration began illegally funneling aid to the Contras in defiance of Congress.

News of Iran-Contra broke in November 1986, after which Crockett led a small House delegation to Nicaragua for fact-finding. When he returned, he advocated for a complete moratorium on U.S. assistance to the Contras.[18] Crockett also criticized Reagan's efforts to avoid the jurisdiction of the World Court and the administration's efforts to impose restrictions on U.S. citizens traveling to Nicaragua.[19] He spoke in favor of the efforts of Costa Rica's president, Oscar Arias, for a regional peace plan.[20] Arias would go on to win a Nobel Prize for his efforts. Funding for the Contras became an issue with each passing year through fights over appropriation bills. Crockett's position was clear: "As my colleagues know, I do not favor any aid to the Contras. I do not think Contra aid has served U.S. interests or the interests of peace in Central America, and I believe Contra aid violates international law."[21] In response to Crockett's opposition, Contra supporters started devising ways of bypassing the jurisdiction of his subcommittee and the Committee on Foreign Affairs more generally.[22]

Crockett used his position as chair of the Subcommittee on the Western Hemisphere in other constructive ways. In the United States, race always matters, as does who holds power. Many Black Americans have a strong affinity for other members of the African Diaspora, about which most European Americans are oblivious. Crockett maintained a particular interest in and care for countries in the Caribbean. He sought special recognition for Jamaica in celebrating the twenty-fifth anniversary of its independence in 1987 and the following year advocated for relief measures in the wake of Hurricane Gilbert.[23]

Haiti has been a symbol of freedom and democracy since winning its independence from France in 1804. But it has had an often tumultuous history, largely due to externally imposed isolation. Early in his congressional career, Crockett advocated for the rights of Haitian refugees in the United States.[24] The repressive era of François Duvalier (known as "Papa Doc") and his son, Jean-Claude Duvalier (known as "Baby Doc"), came to an end in 1986, just as Crockett was assuming his chairmanship. Crockett was concerned principally with defending human rights and promoting Haitian democracy. He condemned the Reagan administration's human rights certifications and the release of military aid to the repressive Haitian government.[25] He warned that not enough was being done to safeguard democracy, noting the irony that the Republican administration was willing to spend hundreds of millions of dollars in military aid to undermine democracy in Nicaragua but unwilling to spend $20 million to ensure democracy in Haiti.[26] Along with many others, Crockett lamented that Haiti had suffered long enough.[27]

Crockett called for greater attention to the Caribbean generally: "The Caribbean region is extremely important to the United States—not only because of its strategic significance, but also because we are inextricably linked together by extensive patterns of migration. Yet this vital region remains the stepchild of the U.S. hemispheric policy, receiving a mere pittance compared to the aid we lavish on Central America. It is time for us to stop thinking of the Caribbean as our back door, and realize that it is in fact our front door. We neglect poverty and hopelessness in this region at our peril."[28]

Battles over Reagan's Budgets

Crockett was a child of the New Deal. One of his early political acts in 1936 was switching his affiliation from the Republican Party to the Democratic Party and joining Franklin Roosevelt's administration in the Department of Labor. Reagan's political agenda, consisting of deep cuts in federal spending, tax cuts, and dramatic increases in military spending, constituted a full-scale assault on New Deal programs.

Public values are often most dramatically embodied in public budgets. *Crockett v. Reagan* was filed on May 1, 1981. Crockett gave his first speech to Congress four days later. The speech was a principled attack on Reagan's first budget, with its seemingly endless cuts in social spending. Resonating in the remarks was his lifelong commitment to economic justice. He began by contrasting his work as a judge and his current role as a legislator:

Mr. Chairman and my colleagues, this is my first opportunity to address the Congress. I have sat here now for six months trying to understand the legislative process, and I find that I am far less comfortable than I was the thirteen years prior to that time when I presided over one of America's largest criminal courts. The big difference is that, as a judge one sees what justice requires and goes on and does it, without the necessity of convincing anyone else. Now, I find that it is necessary that I at least try to convince others why I am supporting the Fauntroy amendment to House Concurrent Resolution 115 [the Reagan budget]. I do so because I believe that that resolution is a callous piece of legislation. It takes the lives of millions of our citizens in its grip and throws them to the economic wolves in the name of "defense" and "less government."[29]

What followed was heartfelt critique of the values missing in the proposed budget and its devastating impact on ordinary people, particularly Crockett's constituents in Detroit:

The compassion and concern which led to the Federal Government's involvement in the well-being of every individual of this country were not temporary aberrations. They have given direction to American domestic policy for more than half a century. Now, in the wake of the Republican tide, that compassion seems to have faded; and the men, women, and children who will suffer are left with nothing more than platitudes about supply-side economics and strategic balances. Mr. Chairman, I invite each of my colleagues here in this Chamber to come with me to my district, in the heart of Detroit, and walk any street with me, and look into the faces of my constituents, and tell them you cut their food stamps because the Department of Defense needed another submarine, or you cut their education funding because Mr. Stockman thought it was expendable. When President Reagan talks about the "truly deserving needy," he is not talking about abstractions. He is talking about your constituents—and mine. My district contains a microcosm of the economic nightmare we face: Inflation and recession devouring the families, the workers, the small businesses. You have the same problems in each of your districts, but nowhere in this country is another district so devastated by our economic situation than the 13th District of Michigan. In my district, more than a quarter of the work force is unemployed today. Among blacks, unemployment is almost 50 percent. Among black young people, three out of four cannot find work. Unemployment benefits, meant to assist during times of economic downturn, are running out. And the automobile industry is in the biggest decline in its history. If the Federal Government turns its back now, where are we to go?[30]

Crockett brought a long historical view to the budget debate, as well as a consistent set of progressive values. He understood what was at stake: "This legislative body has chosen to adopt a framework for a national budget that effectively and painfully reverses fiscal and social policies that governed for more than half a century. Indeed, the new approach dredges up, in spirit and in fact, the discredited and self-defeating, trickle-down theories which led to the Great Depression of the 1930's. . . . We have now opted for a return to past injustices and a rejection of present and future promises."[31]

Deep cuts in domestic spending were only one pillar of the Reagan agenda. Tax cuts and sharp increases in military spending were the others. Crockett understood how interconnected these policies were and fought against every element. In fighting tax cuts, Crockett maintained a clear understanding of what his constituents needed: "Mr. Speaker, I find it inconceivable that any worker—employed or unemployed—or any poor person, or any senior citizen, or any minority group member would support any bill that calls for a reduction in Federal taxes at this time. And since the overwhelming majority of my constituents in Michigan's 13th Congressional District fall in one or the other of these categories, I, as their representative, will oppose and will vote against any bill that calls for a reduction in Federal revenues, and I urge my colleagues to do likewise."[32]

Crockett raised numerous objections to the proposed cuts. Those who were being hurt were the people he had fought for his whole life. He understood the plight of the poor and the working class and the stresses of unemployment. He cared not only about the extension of health care benefits for the unemployed but specifically for mental health benefits.[33] He feared that the conditions emerging in the 1980s were dangerously similar to those that produced the Detroit Rebellion in 1967.[34] He stood in the well of the House with a scroll containing more than fifteen hundred names of his constituents as a petition to stop the spending cuts to the needy.[35]

Social spending was being reduced and taxes were being cut largely to enable increases in military spending.[36] Crockett did not believe that military spending and militarism could bring anything but more violence and destruction. The entire enterprise was deeply misguided. The MX missile system, which Reagan dubbed the "Peacekeeper" missile, was a particular case in point: "It's an Alice-in-Wonderland concept that you build more weapons to promote peace. If that were truly the case, the billions of dollars of military equipment and training the U.S. exports every year would have brought peace to Lebanon, and to El Salvador, to Northern Ireland, and to South Africa. Obviously, weapons aren't the answer to the world's problems."[37] He firmly believed that military spending did not provide national security, particularly when it came at the expense of vital social problems: "These needed social programs undergird our free society and allow us to avoid the most serious threats to our national security—the twin evils of ignorance and want: both of which Mr. Reagan's budget would promote."[38]

Standing on principles and opposing militarization can be isolating experiences at times. Crockett was perhaps most alone in Congress in 1983 when he voted "present" rather in favor of a resolution condemning the Soviet Union for shooting down the civilian airliner Korean Airlines 007, which had wandered into Soviet airspace. The vote was 416 in "favor" and 2 "presents."[39] Crockett was joined in voting "present" by his friend and Detroit colleague John Conyers. His opponents viewed the vote as further evidence of his communist sympathies.[40] The truth was much more complicated. Three of Crockett's constituents were on that flight—Jessie Slaton, Margaret Zarif, and Joyce Chambers. Slaton was a fellow jurist and old friend. She was also a pioneer. She started her career in 1933 working as a secretary in Detroit City Hall. But she did not stop there; she moved higher. "At a time when blacks were rarely given public employment except as menials, she was one of the first in Detroit city government to occupy a white-collar position."[41] Finally, she became a judge on the Court of Common Pleas. Crockett said on the floor of the House, "I had known Jessie Slaton for many years, as one of the most conscientious and respected members of the bench."[42]

Crockett wrote about the tragedy: "We must not allow our foreign policy to be built on anger and frustration. We cannot allow ourselves to make this incident into the foundation of a new tower of weapons and military demagoguery."[43] He saw the clear relationship between the unthinking U.S. condemnations of the Soviets in response to the tragedy and the unthinking attitude that led Soviet officers to shoot down a civilian aircraft in the first place. More frightening still was that this same unthinking mentality was held by both sides in the Cold War and by those in direct control of nuclear weapons. New courses were necessary: "The growth of military arsenals and the insistence on military 'solutions' to problems will never bring peace to our world. They will only bring more death, and more accidents, and more civilian casualties."[44]

He refused to vote in favor of the resolution: "I would like to believe that these women, though, and the others on that ill-fated plane, would be as horrified as I am by the eye-for-an-eye attitude being espoused by many people, both in and out of our government, and by the use of this incident to try to increase our military arsenal. I think they would be sorry to see the frightening dimension of vengeance being uncovered by the incident, and would ask us to honor their memories in other ways."[45]

Battles for South Africa

Crockett long fought for civil rights for Blacks in the United States, culminating in the NLG Mississippi Summer Project of 1964 and his years on the Recorder's Court bench. Apartheid in South Africa was the leading human and civil rights struggle in the 1980s. Crockett gave his first speech to Congress concerning South Africa on June 25, 1981, laying down a marker on an issue that would become a defining aspect of his congressional career: "Mr. Speaker, the *Detroit Free Press*, one of my district's most respected newspapers, has recently taken an editorial stand in opposition to the Reagan administration's policies toward South Africa."[46] The editorial, "Africa: The U.S. Stands to Lose a Lot as It Cozies Up to Racist South Africa," spoke out against the changing direction of U.S. foreign policy.[47] Its analysis was based on leaked State Department documents obtained by the human rights lawyer Randall Robinson, director of TransAfrica, an anti-apartheid private research group based in Washington, and warned of the adverse international consequences if the United States improved relations with the pariah regime.

Crockett was back on the floor of the House the following spring opposing changes in U.S. trade policy toward South Africa: "Mr. Speaker, these events describe a South Africa that has embarked on an intensified campaign of terror, repression, and international blackmail, and bespeak a U.S. administration that has chosen to succumb to and collude with Pretoria's machinations. . . . There is nothing socially, economically, or politically redeeming in the administration's recent foreign policy gambit. The policy seriously compromises the ideals for which this country has stood. It exacerbates tensions in our foreign relations with the whole of the African continent."[48]

In 1983, Crockett shifted his attention from the oppressive nature of the South African regime to the integrity and dignity of Nelson Mandela and his long-standing imprisonment. He introduced legislation to make Nelson and Winnie Mandela honorary citizens of the United States and to urge the government of South Africa to free the Mandelas as political prisoners. He began the process of educating his colleagues about Mandela's plight: "Now 64, Nelson Mandela has spent the last twenty years of his life in a maximum-security prison on Robben Island and at Pollsmoor, South Africa. Yet despite the fact that he has been cut off from the liberation movement for twenty years, Nelson Mandela remains the leading symbol of resistance to oppression in South Africa, and the most widely recognized leader of that country's black population. Meanwhile, the South African Government has intensified its legally sanctioned oppression of the majority black population."[49]

February 7, 1984, became a historic day with Crockett's introduction of H.R. 430, the Mandela Freedom Resolution: "[The resolution] expresses the sense of the House of Representatives that the: (1) Republic of South Africa should release Nelson Mandela from prison and should revoke Winnie Mandela's banning order; (2) President should use his position to secure the release of Nelson and Winnie Mandela; and (3) Speaker of the House is requested to transmit a copy of this resolution to the President and to the Republic of South Africa." Crockett, the lead sponsor, was joined by Representatives Claude Pepper, Hamilton Fish, and James Leach. Crockett told his House colleagues,

Nelson and Winnie Mandela have endured serious hardship and many sacrifices as champions for human rights and fundamental political change in South Africa. . . . A dialog must be initiated between the white minority and black majority in South Africa if violence is to be avoided and peace achieved in that troubled country. The release of the Mandelas, in my opinion, is an essential element in the process of national reconciliation which is so long overdue. I urge our colleagues to join with us in support of the Mandela freedom resolution and to demonstrate their solidarity with the aspirations for self-determination of the oppressed majority population in South Africa.[50]

Crockett helped work H.R. 430 through the committee structure and brought it to the floor on September 18, 1984. He addressed the House:

The immediate release of Nelson and Winnie Mandela from their cruel and unjust imprisonment is critically important to domestic peace in South Africa and regional stability in the southern African region. For Nelson Mandela is widely acknowledged as the leader of black South Africa. He is the embodiment of the popular struggle against racism, repression, injustice, and domestic colonialism which contemporary South Africa represents. Nelson and Winnie Mandela, more than any other black South African leaders, [unite] and [inspire] the discriminated, the disenfranchised, and the downtrodden [people of] South Africa. By their example, the Mandelas have provided a shining beacon around which the brave and courageous will rally throughout the world.[51]

The resolution passed on a voice vote.

Crockett understood that Mandela was the key to a peaceful resolution of racism in South Africa: "Commonsense tells us that the only way to prevent a bloody racial struggle in South Africa is for the Government to talk—now and face-to-face with credible black leaders. Yet, the Pretoria regime, in its obstinacy, travels in the opposite direction." Nothing could happen without Mandela: "Mr. Mandela is key to any meaningful negotiations."[52] Speeches in Congress were not enough. In November 1984,

Crockett and many others were arrested in a "Free South Africa" protest in front of the South African embassy in Washington, DC.[53]

Crockett became the leading congressional watchdog calling out the South African government for its violence and human rights abuses.[54] He supported efforts for divestment and celebrated the appointment of Desmond Tutu to be archbishop of Cape Town.[55] Noting that South Africa was on the edge of Armageddon, he decried South Africa's declaration of a national emergency in June 1986 and its ensuing mass arrests of dissidents.[56]

With the dawning of 1987, greater attention turned to the importance of international sanctions against South Africa.[57] Once again, Crockett proposed legislation highlighting the plight of Nelson Mandela: "Mr. Speaker, I rise today, on behalf of myself and 30 of my colleagues, to introduce legislation designating June 26, 1988 as a national day of recognition for Nelson Mandela, South Africa's imprisoned, premier black leader."[58] While President Reagan remained largely unmoved, the rest of the world was rallying behind the cause of Nelson Mandela and ending apartheid in South Africa.

But not every institution was on the Mandela bandwagon. Crockett's alma mater was a case in point: "Last year, the University of Michigan chose not to honor Mandela, in spite of strong student and faculty support for the award, as a symbolic gesture to evidence a commitment to justice and freedom in South Africa."[59] Crockett wrote the Board of Trustees in protest and was the principal speaker in a countercommencement proceeding. The university reversed its position and voted to award Mandela an honorary degree the following year.[60]

It was only fitting that Crockett would see Nelson Mandela's release from prison before he left Congress. On February 22, 1990, he spoke from the floor of the House:

Mr. Speaker, a few short days ago, Nelson Mandela, the symbolic and real hope of justice and freedom in South Africa, left the confinements of the South African prisons where he has spent the last twenty-seven years. Like all freedom-loving peoples of the world, we rejoice in this step for Mandela, and for all the people of South Africa. His statesmanship, wisdom, and leadership will be crucial in the difficult negotiations that lie ahead. . . . But while he is no longer behind barbed wire gates, Nelson Mandela is not yet a free man. He and 23 million other black South Africans remain imprisoned by the racist system of apartheid.[61]

Dr. Charles H. Wright, founder of the Museum for African American History in Detroit that bears his name, assessed Crockett's impact: "Long before Nelson Mandela's release from life-time imprisonment became the popular movement of the late eighties, George Crockett was championing the cause of his liberation in the halls of the United States Congress and wherever else he happened to be." In 1986, Crockett was the first recipient of the Nelson Mandela Award from the Association of African Jurists.[62]

Battles for Human and Civil Rights

Crockett's core values changed very little during his life, from the time he won the speech contest at Stanton High School addressing the post–Civil War constitutional amendments to his entering Congress. Congress, however, gave him a broader national and international stage to advance his principles, in which race was always a central theme. In a speech to his NLG colleagues in 1986, Crockett addressed the "forces standing in the way of peace." He warned that present times were as fraught and dangerous as those of the McCarthy era: "Three of the most potent forces that stand in the way of peace in our world are pervasive racism in the formulation and implementation of policy, economic exploitation that undergirds United States foreign policy, and the lingering paranoia that continues to fuel anti-Soviet dogma and rhetoric. While these forces are certainly not new, they have come to dominate U.S. foreign policy in the last six years, more so than in any Administration since the 1950's."[63]

Crockett diagnosed the common cause for these pathologies as the perpetuation of white supremacy in the United States: "White Males at the Top: Look at the very top—the President, the Cabinet, and his closest advisors. The State Department's 'inner circle.' The National Security Council. Do you remember seeing any Blacks, any Hispanics, or more than one woman, in a really responsible foreign policy role? . . . What does this mean for the long-term chances for a peaceful, just, and non-racist world? It lowers the chances considerably."[64]

Just as he had advocated for greater roles for Black lawyers and judges, he recognized the importance of more diverse representation in U.S. foreign policy. Changing personnel would inevitably also change policy:

> There are many worthwhile causes to which we give our efforts— disarmament, anti-intervention, disinvestment in South Africa— but unless we address the real issue of who is making foreign policy, we are spinning our wheels and exhausting our efforts in losing causes. If we think such goals can be achieved in a country that is run almost exclusively by a group of rich white men, we are mistaken. Their worldview, and the way they have structured our social, political and economic order, often preclude the ideas of peace and justice. How can they understand and deal with a world predominantly non-white and poor—as our world certainly is—if they can't even accept non-whites in their own government? How can they support movements for justice in other countries when they can't see the injustice of race, color and class discrimination in their own country? We live in a multi-racial, unjust world. Its problems cannot be corrected by men who don't understand what it is to grow up powerless and oppressed. Until the status quo is changed to reflect and use the diversity as well as the knowledge we could have available to us, we won't solve anything.[65]

Sitting on the House Judiciary Committee, Crockett was in a good position to assess domestic civil rights issues as well. Given the entrenched obstinance of the Reagan administration, there was limited ability to instigate constructive change. Nevertheless, Crockett used his position to decry the injustices around him. He denounced Reagan administrative appointees and how they were dismantling the very infrastructure of governance and civil rights protections: "Mr. Reagan, true to his campaign pledges, has sought to reshape the executive branch in the image of corporate supremacy and racist ideology. He has gutted the agencies, departments, and other executive bodies charged with the protection of basic constitutional rights. He has dismantled antipoverty agencies and minority protection programs, enacted by Congress over decades of painstaking effort."[66]

Crockett spoke forcefully against Reagan's efforts to destroy the Legal Services Corporation: "Continued funding of the Legal Services Corporation . . . [is] absolutely crucial for the survival of these rights and services to the poor. It is clear from the historical record that states have been unwilling and the private bar is unable to meet these needs in a consistent, substantial way."[67] This was the same call Crockett had made about the absence of lawyers and bar associations doing civil rights work in the South in the 1950s and 1960s. State governments and state bar associations could not be trusted. Legal Services Corporation lawyers were needed to fight against states when appropriate. "Indeed, in some cases the legal problems of the poor involve disputes with public officials at the state and local levels who make decisions about their housing, their income, their health care, their children and other vital areas of their lives."[68]

Crockett supported a number of civil rights initiatives. After recounting his time in Mississippi in 1964 and the deaths of Michael Schwerner, Andrew Goodman, and James Chaney, he advocated for the extension of the Voting Rights Act.[69] He also backed the Equal Rights Amendment: "How long must women wait to gain equal entrance into the Constitution? The equal rights amendment says one simple thing: That the Constitution and Federal and State Governments shall not treat women differently than they treat men. It is a simple concept, a concept of justice."[70] Acknowledging that he was "the most senior black member of the Guild in terms of continuous service," he paid tribute to the NLG on the occasion of its fiftieth anniversary: "The times in which the Guild has operated have included some of the darkest days in our history, when the Constitution was under attack from the forces of McCarthyism, from racial and sexual bigotry, and from Reaganism. Yet it has endured these tests of time, and has remained one of the strongest advocates for justice and freedom in our country and around the world."[71]

Crockett worked from a deep moral center and continued to expand the scope of his human concern and his understanding of civil rights. This was exemplified in his approach to the AIDS crisis, calling for an end to antigay discrimination:

> The moral challenge that AIDS presents us with is this: To come out of this crisis not only with a better understanding of cancer and disease, but also with a greater understanding of and appreciation

for those around us. . . . The medical community is being challenged to find a cure. The challenge for the rest of us is not only to be as compassionate and helpful as we can, but also to seize this opportunity to examine our stereotypes and prejudices. None of these challenges are small orders. But each challenge must be met. The very outcome of lives, both now and in the future when AIDS has been conquered, depend[s] on it.[72]

Crockett was a pioneer on another important front as well. On the eve of his last year in Congress, he became the first congressman in history to advocate for the decriminalization of drugs. "Decriminalization is the only solution," Crockett told a *Detroit News* reporter: "'Our courts are burdened down with these drug cases and there is nothing they can do about it,' he said. Money now spent on drug enforcement should be shifted to job training for the urban poor, education, health care and day care."[73] Years before, he had sent Lloyd Tyler to rehabilitation for his addiction rather than to prison, seeing the issue as one of public health rather than criminal law. As a congressman, he applied the same principle as a matter of national policy.

Crockett Leaves Congress

After spending a decade in Congress, Crockett announced that he would retire—again and this time for real. Even at this moment of his career, he seemed to be haunted by the specter of Judge Medina:

Mr. Speaker, a few days ago the press carried the story of the death of the Honorable Harold Medina, who was the Judge who presided over the famous Communist trial in New York back in 1949 and 1950. In the course of that trial Judge Medina sentenced the five defense lawyers to prison. I am the only living survivor of those five defense lawyers. During the four months that I served in a federal prison it never occurred to me that one day I would also serve in the U.S. Congress and be a member of the committee having oversight jurisdiction over all federal judges and all federal prisons. Today, Mr. Speaker, I rise to inform my colleagues that I have decided to retire from the House at the conclusion of the 101st Congress.

After 68 years of working, championing unpopular causes, I am hoping to enjoy a little time off. Mr. Speaker, I will not miss running back and forth for the bells or the endless meetings this job entails, but I will miss the company of so many deeply committed men and women with whom I have had the pleasure to serve. . . . There is a time, however, when each man or woman must decide to leave the day-to-day struggles to others. When this Congress ends in January, I will go on to other less challenging challenges.[74]

While a man of strong principles, Crockett was also a man of grace and good nature. Representative Robert J. Lagomarsino, Crockett's Republican counterpart on the Subcommittee on Western Hemisphere Affairs, testified to this fact: "In the years that Judge Crockett has served as chairman of the subcommittee, and in spite of some deep philosophical differences we have had over some issues, he has always treated me and the other members of the minority on the subcommittee with the greatest respect and fairness. His approach has always been one of conciliation and consensus, and his gracious manner and gentlemanly nature have earned him the respect and admiration of his colleagues."[75] The pundits in the press debated Crockett's impact after five terms in Congress. Some made much of the fact that he did not introduce many bills. Crockett would respond with a wry quip. "We have enough legislation now to take care of just about every situation that arises, if we will just enforce it and apply it."[76] The truth is that any single congressman may have less impact on the law than an active trial court judge on the Recorder's Court bench does. But asking about legislation is the wrong question. Crockett's impact was of a distinctly different nature. Crockett spoke as the conscience of the House and admonished it from a distinctively Black perspective, understanding the long and difficult struggle for racial and economic justice.

Crockett's own assessment of his time in Congress was characteristically modest and self-effacing: "To be perfectly honest, I don't think I knocked myself out in this job in the way I did as a judge, for example. . . . I wish I had begun my congressional career about ten years earlier. I would have had more vim and vitality to give to the job." He told a *Detroit News* reporter that he left Congress more disillusioned than when he entered. The reporter wrote, "When he retired from the Court in 1979, Crockett still believed that 'our country and humanity generally is moving toward a more perfect world.'" But as to Congress, he said, "More frequently, I'm amazed at the shortsightedness of some of it and the selfishness of some of it. I'm not as starry-eyed as I was before I came.... Frankly, I had a higher opinion of the institution."[77]

Throughout Crockett's life, true to the inspiration of his mentor Maurice Sugar, he spoke, wrote, and defended those who were in need. With an uncommon devotion to the U.S. Constitution, Crockett refused to accept discrimination and government oppression. As a result, his enduring legacies are the immense courage he displayed and singular personal sacrifices he endured in challenging injustices and fighting for equality under law. For his devotion to civil rights and civil liberties and his belief that the law can protect even the least among us, he was, indeed, a tall tree.

When a tall tree falls, it makes a thund'rous sound
To tell the forest that a giant is dead,
And now there seems an empty spot of ground
Where once a stalwart presence raised its head.

But if we look, the ground on which it stood
Brings forth green seedlings, reaching for the sun
To find their place as stalwarts in the wood
Beginning as their parent had begun.

And so, the great soul whom we mourn
Has not left us without a legacy.
A host of fledglings studied 'neath his sway,
Each one may someday be a mighty tree.
Thus God, his will inexorable ordains
To make us mortals know that he still reigns.[78]

In the last irony of Crockett's life, in 1996, he was awarded the State Bar of Michigan's Champion of Justice Award.[79] He died on September 7, 1997, in a hospice near his Washington, DC, home at age eighty-eight. Bringing the story full circle, he is buried in Laurel, Delaware, with his parents and earlier generations of Crocketts who moved north to escape slavery.

Notes

Introduction

1 George W. Crockett Jr., "Racism in the Courts," *Howard Law Journal* 17 (1972): 296.

2 George W. Crockett Jr., "A Black Judge Speaks," *Judicature* 53 (1970): 361.

3 George W. Crockett Jr., "Racism in American Law," *Guild Practitioner* 48 (1991): 122.

4 Crockett, "Racism in the Courts," 296.

5 Crockett, "Black Judge Speaks," 361.

6 Ibid.

7 Crockett, "Racism in American Law," 124.

8 George W. Crockett Jr., "The Summer of '64: When Young American Men and Women Fought and Smiled, Struggled and Died. And Won, in America" (Special Report: The Civil Rights Movement Today), *Human Rights* 15 (Fall 1988): 15.

9 George W. Crockett Jr., "Forces Standing in the Way of Peace," *Guild Practitioner* 43 (1986): 69.

10 Crockett, "Racism in American Law," 122.

11 Warner Smith, "George W. Crockett: The Opener," *Black Law Journal* 1, no. 3 (1971): 247.

12 The legal case was ultimately resolved in the Supreme Court in *Dennis v. United States*, 341 U.S. 494 (1951).

13 Senator Joseph McCarthy waged an anticommunist campaign from 1950 to 1954. His name has become associated with the anticommunist mood that seized the nation during the late 1940s and early 1950s.

14 343 U.S. 1 (1953).

15 George W. Crockett to Members of the Michigan Bar, September 16, 1950, Edward Littlejohn Collection, Walter P. Reuther Library, Detroit, MI (hereafter ELC).

16 From the law firm's inception, its members were very active in the National Lawyers Guild. The firm's status as the first integrated partnership was

327

often discussed at NLG meetings. George Bedrosian, a member of the firm since 1963, stated, "[If] we were not the first, we certainly would have heard about it as Guild members were the most knowledgeable lawyers in America about such things." Bedrosian, interview by Edward Littlejohn, February 27, 1991. The authors' research has not disclosed a formal integrated law partnership that preceded Goodman, Crockett, Eden & Robb. The firm's partnership agreement was effective January 1, 1951.

17 See Edward Littlejohn and Donald Hobson, "Black Lawyers, Law Practice, and Bar Associations, 1844 to 1970: A Michigan History," *Wayne Law Review* 33 (1987): 1625–92.

Chapter 1. The Early Years

1 The following details are taken primarily from "Family History of Alzeda Crockett Hacker, of Pittsburgh, Pennsylvania; George William Crockett Jr., of Detroit, Michigan; and John Frazier Crockett, of Jacksonville, Florida, Compiled by George W. Crockett Jr. with Joan Willoughby," Washington, DC, Summer 1993. The full dedication reads, "This Family History is dedicated to all who came before us, whose courage and experiences we celebrate. It is also dedicated to Alzeda Crockett Hacker, the first-born of our generation and the family's eldest surviving member; and to my brother John. Finally, it is dedicated to those who come after us, with the hope that they may draw strength from the wisdom and knowledge of their heritage." The version of the history we are working from was also dedicated in a handwritten note: "For my Daughter, Ethelene with Pride, Admiration and Love from Dad. 8/6/93." The "Family History" is part of the ELC.

2 Ibid., 1.

3 Ibid., 3.

4 Ibid., 2.

5 Ibid., 10.

6 Barbara Jeanne Fields, *Slavery and Freedom on the Middle Ground: Maryland during the Nineteenth Century* (New Haven, CT: Yale University Press, 1985), 118.

7 "Family History," 1, reproducing William Scheller, "Maryland's Eastern Shore: Tracing the Underground Railroad," *Washington Post Magazine*, n.d.

8 We may never know why the Crockett family history contains this sleight of hand. Our intuition is that the secret of Charles Crockett's real means of escape served an important original purpose, perhaps protecting those who made their escape possible. Secrets in all families can become entrenched.

9 "Family History," 10.

10 Ibid., 16.

11 Ibid.

12 Ibid., 20.

13 Peg Dow, "Children Should Be Ahead of Their Parents, Should Climb a Step Higher and Make a Contribution to the Family and to Society," The Senior Years, *(Jacksonville) Florida Times-Union*, November 23, 1969, 28–29.

14 Ibid., 29.

15 Ibid.

16 Ibid.

17 Ibid.

18 George Crockett, interview by Tom Lonergan, transcripts, May 15, 1987, 3. Tom Lonergan produced a video documentary about Crockett. All of the Lonergan interviews are part of the ELC but have yet to be processed.

19 "Family History," 16.

20 Ibid., 16, 32.

21 Dow, "Children," 36.

22 "Family History," 32.

23 Ibid., 36.

24 Ibid., 40.

25 Ibid., 20.

26 The "Family History" probably mistakes either the year or the cause of death. The national influenza epidemic occurred during 1918–19. Ibid., 10.

27 Ibid.

28 Dow, "Children," 29.

29 Ibid.

30 Richard Willing, "Detroit's Crusader Moves On," *Detroit News*, October 21, 1990, B1, col. 1.

31 Dr. Ethelene Jones, interview by Peter Hammer, transcript, July 27, 2017, 2.

32 Ibid.

33 Ibid., 3.

34 Ibid., 45.

35 Crockett/Lonergan interview, January 19, 1986, 13.

36 Ibid., 3–4.

37 Isabel Wilkerson, *The Warmth of Other Suns: The Epic Story of America's Great Migration* (New York: Vintage Books, 2010), 47.

38 Robert Cassanello, *To Render Invisible: Jim Crow and Public Life in New South Jacksonville* (Gainesville: University of Florida Press, 2013).

39 Ibid., 139.

40 Jacksonville Historical Society, "Old Stanton High School," http://www.jaxhistory.org/portfolio-items/old-stanton-high-school/#lightbox/0/.

41 Ibid.

42 James Weldon Johnson, *Along This Way: The Autobiography of James Weldon Johnson* (New York: De Capo, 2000), 45.

43 Paul Ortiz, *Emancipation Betrayed: The Hidden History of Black Organizing and White Violence in Florida from Reconstruction to the Bloody Election of 1920* (Berkeley: University of California Press, 2005), 87.

44 Crockett/Lonergan interview, May 15, 1987, 10.

45 Crockett/Lonergan interview, December 1, 1988, 2. While at Morehouse, Crockett was his class president during his first, second, and third years, associate editor of the student newspaper, and a varsity cheerleader.

46 Crockett/Lonergan interview, May 15, 1987, 1.

47 Ibid.

48 Margaret Leary, *Giving It All Away: The Story of William W. Cook and His Michigan Law Quadrangle* (Ann Arbor, MI: Newport Research Press, 2014).

49 "Family History," 11.

50 Jones interview, 44.

51 Crockett/Lonergan interview, May 15, 1987, 3.

52 Paul A. Leidy, Office of the Secretary, University of Michigan Law School, to Mr. George W. Crockett Jr., July 28, 1931, ELC.

53 Crockett/Lonergan interview, May 15, 1987, 7.

54 Ibid.

55 Ibid., 8.

56 Ibid., 8–9. Crockett did teach one semester of labor law at Howard Law School while he was a lawyer for the Department of Labor in Washington.

57 Ethelene became Michigan's first Black obstetrician-gynecologist and the first woman president of the American Lung Association in 1978 and was inducted into Michigan's Women's Hall of Fame in 1988. Michigan Women's Hall of Fame, "Ethelene Crockett," http://www.michiganwomenshalloffame .org/Images/Crockett,%20Ethelene.pdf.

Chapter 2. Toward a Radical Law Practice

1 Smith, "George W. Crockett," 248.

2 Ibid.

3 Crockett/Lonergan interview, December 1, 1988, 2. He was admitted to the West Virginia bar in 1935.

4 "Equity and Fair Play," *New National Black Monitor*, Family Editorial Supplement, April 1977, 5, 6, Folder 11, Box 6, Morris Gleicher Papers, Walter Reuther Library, Detroit, MI.

5 "The Crockett Legacy: Lessons Learned, Dreams Inspired," program, Crockett Testimonial Dinner, Detroit, February 15, 1991.

6 "Equity and Fair Play," 6.

7 Ibid.

8 George W. Crockett Jr. to Edward J. Littlejohn, audiotape, June 2, 1991 (hereafter Crockett/Littlejohn audiotape).

9 "George Crockett Will Seek Place on GOP County Executive Group," undated and unsourced news clipping in ELC.

10 Ibid.

11 "Democratic Party Best for Negros—Crockett: Local Attorney Changes Registration, Gives Reasons for Action," *Fairmont (WV) Times*, July 29, 1938.

12 Ibid.

13 Ibid.

14 Ibid.

15 Ibid.

16 "Equity and Fair Play," 6.

17 Ibid.

18 Crockett/Lonergan interview, December 1, 1988, 13.

19 Ibid. Elizabeth, who became a schoolteacher, was born June 25, 1936, in Fairmont, West Virginia; George III, who became a judge of the Recorder's Court in Detroit, was born December 23, 1938, in Fairmont; and Ethelene, who became a physician, was born February 14, 1941, in Washington, DC. "Family History," 54.

20 "Equity and Fair Play," 6.

21 George W. Crockett Jr., "Jurisdiction of Employee Suits under the Fair Labor Standards Act," *Michigan Law Review* 39, no. 3 (1941): 419–29; Crockett, "Reinstatement of Employees under the Fair Labor Standards Act," *Michigan Law Review* 42, no. 1 (1944): 25–50.

22 Articles by Crockett include the following: "Black Judge Speaks"; "Commentary: Black Judges and the Black Judicial Experience," *Wayne Law Review* 19 (1972): 61–71; "Comments on *Mitchell v. United States*," *National Bar Journal* 1, no. 2 (1941–44): 157–61; "The Employee Remedy under the Fair Labor Standards Act," *National Bar Journal* 1, no. 1 (1941–44): 16–29; "Racism in American Law," *Guild Practitioner* 27, no. 4 (Fall 1968): 176–84; "Summer of '64"; "Forces Standing in the Way of Peace"; "Reforming Foreign Policy: We Must Live Together on This Planet" (Open Forum: Reforms in the Law), *Detroit College of Law Review* 1983, no. 4 (Winter 1984): 1157–61; "Results of the Federal Wage-Hour Law," *Crisis*, 1940; "Constitutionality of Federal Anti–Poll Tax Legislation," *National Bar*

Journal 2, no. 1 (1944): 46–64; "My Visit to the Soviet Union," *National Bar Journal and News* 2 (1961); "The United Nations, the American Negro and His Government," *Freedomways*, 2nd quarter 1965, 243–49; "Civil Rights in Michigan," *Michigan State Bar Journal* 45 (March 1966): 12–25; "Recorder's Court and the 1967 Civil Disturbance," *Journal of Urban Law* 45, nos. 3–4 (1968): 841–47; "Reflections of a Jurist on Civil Disobedience," *American Scholar* 40 (1971): 584; "Racism in the Courts"; "Racism in the Courts, Proceedings: Founding Convention of the Judicial Council of the National Bar Association," *Journal of Public Law* 20, no. 2 (1971): 385–90; "Criminal Justice in China," *Judicature* 59, no. 5 (1975): 241–47; "Judicial Selection and the Black Experience," *Judicature* 58, no. 9 (1975): 438–42; "Book Review: *Crisis in the Courts*, by Howard James," *California Law Review* 57, no. 2 (1969): 550–55.

23 Crockett/Littlejohn audiotape.

24 The first FEPC was advisory. It lacked authority to conduct hearings or to issue cease-and-desist orders. Crockett/Littlejohn audiotape. For additional discussions of the limitations of the structure and implementation of the FEPC, see Richard Rothstein, *The Color of Law: A Forgotten History of How Our Government Segregated America* (New York: Liveright, 2017), 162–67.

25 Exec. Order No. 9346, Further Amending Exec. Order No. 8802 by Establishing a New Committee on Fair Employment Practice and Defining the Powers and Duties (1943).

26 Eventually, Congress created a permanent FEPC, which became the forerunner of the Civil Rights Commission. Crockett/Lonergan interview, January 19, 1986, 5.

27 Crockett/Lonergan interview, January 19, 1986, 4–5.

28 Smith, "George W. Crockett," 250.

29 "A Man of Accomplishments," *Inner City Builder*, March 14, 1972, 5.

30 Crockett/Littlejohn audiotape.

31 Ibid.

32 See generally Leonard Gordon, *A City in Racial Crisis: The Case of Detroit Pre- and Post- the 1967 Riot* (Detroit: W. C. Brown, 1971); David M. Katzman, *Before the Ghetto: Black Detroit in the Nineteenth Century* (Urbana: University of Illinois Press, 1973); Alfred McClung Lee, *Race Riot* (New York: Dryden, 1943); B. J. Widick, *Detroit: A City of Race and Class Violence* (Chicago: Quadrangle Books, 1972).

33 Maurice Sugar, "The Good Old Days," speech at the Lawyers Guild Banquet, Detroit, September 16, 1960 (transcript by Maurice Sugar), *National Lawyers Guild Review* 37, no. 2 (Spring 1980): 52.

34 Christopher H. Johnson, *Maurice Sugar: Law, Labor, and the Left in Detroit, 1912–1950* (Detroit: Wayne State University Press, 1988), 274. In 1942, there were 55,000 Black workers out of the total UAW membership of 450,000. For comparison, Blacks employed in the auto industry represented 5.5 percent of total auto workers in May 1942. August Meier and Elliott Rudwick, *Black Detroit and the Rise of the UAW* (New York: Oxford University Press, 1979), 213. Historically, Black participation in the labor movement was low due to the skepticism of large Black organizations, such as the NAACP and the Urban League. Crockett's explanation for this skepticism is that it was based on economics: "The NAACP and the Urban League were concerned about getting support from the white community, which meant getting support from the corporate community. Therefore, the best that blacks in the trade union movement could hope for from those two organizations was that they would remain neutral and not try to discourage blacks from joining unions. Unfortunately, in many communities they did not remain neutral. And they actively sought to caution or to warn blacks against 'getting mixed up' with all these radicals in the trade union movement." Crockett/Lonergan interview, January 19, 1986, 3–4.

35 Maurice Sugar, UAW general counsel from 1939 to 1947, was never a member of the Communist Party within the UAW. Johnson, *Maurice Sugar*, 13. Apparently, he adhered to its principles and believed that Marxism and union democracy were intrinsically linked. "The essentials of the union constitution under which such democracy was possible was developed by Maurice Sugar and George Addes, secretary-treasurer of the UAW, who also remained the ongoing watchdogs of the constitutions" (15). Both white and Black leftists in Detroit sought to mitigate Black suspicions of unions and to eliminate prejudice against Blacks by emphasizing the universal destiny of workers. Sugar's view was that "the emancipation of black people and the emancipation of labor were the same thing" (277).

36 UAW-CIO, *To Stamp Out Discrimination, A Handbook, International Union, United Automobile, Aircraft & Agricultural Implement Workers of America,* Publication No. 25 (Detroit: UAW-CIO, 1943), 4.

37 External pressures came from various groups including federal FEPC, the local Citizens Committee for Jobs in War and Industry (organized by the local activist Reverend Charles Hill), and the leftist Michigan division of the National Negro Congress (Coleman A. Young, later mayor of the city of Detroit, was its secretary). Johnson, *Maurice Sugar*, 275.

38 Significant changes occurred in both the number and kind of jobs held. In the auto industry, the percentage of Blacks employed rose to 8.8 percent

in May 1943 and later to 15 percent by 1945. Meier and Rudwick, *Black Detroit and the Rise of the UAW*, 213.

39 Ibid., 214.

40 Ibid.

41 Crockett/Lonergan interview, January 19, 1986, 2. The Addes plan was widely supported by Black delegates and contributed to Addes's narrow margin of victory over Reuther at the 1943 annual convention. Johnson, *Maurice Sugar*, 277–78.

42 In addition to Crockett, membership on the committee included the four top UAW officers. The committee's office was located in the Cadillac Tower; Crockett was the first Black tenant there. Crockett/Lonergan interview, January 19, 1986, 6–7.

43 Crockett/Lonergan interview, January 19, 1986, 1–2. Most of the early Black UAW staff organizers were members or ex-members of the Communist Party. Meier and Rudwick, *Black Detroit and the Rise of the UAW*, 212.

44 Crockett described his early impressions of racial tensions in Detroit:

> There was a ferment on the part of blacks and their participation in UAW affairs, but it was a growing ferment. It really didn't have too much of a substantial base other than Local 600, Ford Rouge plant. And the other locals here and there had a black who had been elected a trustee or who was a shop steward. But there was no bringing this group together to suggest UAW policy....
>
> My natural colleagues . . . would be the blacks on the international union staff [John Conyers Sr., Horace Sheffield, Leon Bates, Oscar Noble, Walter Harding].

Crockett/Lonergan interview, January 19, 1986, 1.

45 Meier and Rudwick, *Black Detroit and the Rise of the UAW*, 214–15, 83; Crockett/Lonergan interview, March 27, 1987, 4.

46 The UAW-CIO International Executive Board approved the following clause for inclusion in all collective bargaining agreements: "The Company agrees that it will not discriminate in the hiring of employees or in their training, upgrading, promotion, transfer, lay-off, discipline, discharge, or otherwise, because of race, creed, color, national origin, political affiliation, sex or marital status." UAW-CIO, "Internal Correspondence to All Presidents of Local Unions Affiliated with the International Union, UAW-CIO, from George F. Addes, International Secretary Treasurer and Chairman, UAW-CIO Fair Practices Committee," March 12, 1945.

47 Meier and Rudwick, *Black Detroit and the Rise of the UAW*, 214.
48 Crockett/Lonergan interview, January 19, 1986, 6.
49 Ibid., 7.
50 Ibid., 12.
51 Crockett's opinion about the FPC is shared by others. See, e.g., Meir and Rudwick, *Black Detroit and the Rise of the UAW*, 213–15.
52 Crockett/Lonergan interview, January 19, 1986, 11. At the 1946 Atlantic City UAW-CIO convention, Crockett, with Maurice Sugar's assistance, worked to make the FPC permanent within the union. The UAW constitution was amended to establish the Fair Practices and Anti-Discrimination Department as successor to the FPC. William Oliver, a Black unionist, was named its head. The new department was financed by 1 percent of total annual dues payments. See Meir and Rudwick, *Black Detroit and the Rise of the UAW*, 213.
53 Johnson, *Maurice Sugar*, 291.
54 Ibid.
55 Ibid., 292. For discussion of a communist's view that Reuther used red-baiting to disrupt the nation's leftist coalition and to seize power, see John Swift, "Reuther's Seizure of the Ford Local: Its Lesson for Labor," *Political Affairs*, July 1952.
56 Johnson, *Maurice Sugar*, 292.
57 Patricia Edmonds, "Crockett Donates His Notes of Congressional Struggles," *Detroit Free Press*, February 14, 1991, 3A.
58 Steve Babson, Dave Riddle, and David Elsila, *The Color of Law: Ernie Goodman, Detroit, and the Struggle for Labor and Civil Rights* (Detroit: Wayne State University Press, 2010), 158.
59 Ibid., 159.
60 Crockett/Lonergan interview, March 28, 1987, 4.
61 Ibid., 4–5. Notwithstanding Sugar's prior interest in hiring Crockett, he desperately needed Crockett's expertise now. His office was deluged with labor cases. Many were so-called portal-to-portal suits filed by union locals under the federal wage and hour law, claiming that workers were entitled to compensation for the entire period they were on the work premises, including wash-up time. Because of Crockett's earlier service with the Wage and Hour Division in Washington, Sugar particularly wanted him to represent the locals. Ibid., 5.
62 Ernest Goodman, "An Unofficial, Incomplete Biographical Sketch and a Few Personal Recollections of Congressman George W. Crockett, Jr., by His Former Partner Ernie Goodman," National Lawyers Guild, Detroit Chapter, 48th Anniversary Annual Dinner, October 5, 1985, 2, Folder 12, Box 88, Part 2, Ernest Goodman Collection, Walter Reuther Library, Detroit, MI.

63 Littlejohn and Hobson, "Black Lawyers, Law Practice, and Bar Associations," 1664–65.

64 Ibid.

65 Ibid., 1663.

66 Ibid., citing interview with Goodman, April 14, 1987. The Lucy Thurman YWCA was the Black women's branch in Detroit. Its cafeteria was open to whites. Ibid., 1663n133.

67 Crockett/Lonergan interview, March 28, 1987, 7.

68 Littlejohn and Hobson, "Black Lawyers, Law Practice, and Bar Associations," 1663n133.

69 For discussion, see Johnson, *Maurice Sugar*, 296–97.

70 Johnson describes an eight-hour debate on November 29, 1947, over Sugar's firing, citing the meeting minutes. The attack on the legal staff was attributed to Emil Mazey, UAW executive secretary. Johnson, *Maurice Sugar*, 296–97.

71 Ibid., 297.

72 Ibid.

73 Babson, Riddle, and Elsila, *Color of Law*, 168 (quoting Goodman).

74 Ibid., 169.

75 Sugar and his wife, a Detroit schoolteacher, retired to their Michigan home on the shores of Black Lake, where Sugar lived quietly until his death in 1974. Johnson, *Maurice Sugar*, 298.

76 Smith, "George W. Crockett," 251.

77 Ibid.

78 Chip Gibbons, "Obstructing Justice," *Jacobin*, September 2018, 7.

79 341 U.S. 494 (1951).

Chapter 3. The Great Communist Conspiracy Trial

It is not our intention to reprise the massive record of the Foley Square trial or its lengthy appellate history. While we provide sufficient context for the reader to understand the legal context and national significance of the trial, our primary focus is on Crockett's role and recollections of the case.

1 "Communist Trial Ends with 11 Guilty," *Life*, October 24, 1949, 34.

2 Ibid.

3 Ibid. The bill, which passed the House in August 1949, did not receive action by the U.S. Senate before the trial ended. Most of the organized pickets were supporters of the defendants protesting the trial. See, e.g., "Thousands Head for Capital in Defense of '12," *The Worker*, January 16, 1949, 1; Edwin Lahey, "Heavy Trial Guard Hit by Reds," *New York Post*, January 17, 1949, 1;

"Top Reds Go on Trial: Defense Protests Guard of 400," *New York Herald-American*, January 17, 1949, 1; "Reds on Trial Shout 'Terror': Court Denies Defense Plea to Ban Police," *New York World-Telegram*, January 17, 1949, 1.

4 David Maraniss, *A Good American Family: The Red Scare and My Father* (New York: Simon and Schuster, 2019), 227–28.

5 "Communist Trial Ends with 11 Guilty," 31.

6 Ibid, 34.

7 See National Non-Partisan Committee to Defend the 12 Communist Leaders, *Due Process in a Political Trial: The Record vs. the Press, in the Foley Square Trial of the 12 Communist Leaders* (New York, 1950). This publication discusses the putative charges of bias during the trial and includes many representative citations from the trial record that support the allegations. As we will see, this publication, produced in support of the defense of the lawyers facing contempt charges, will play an important role in Crockett's fight over disbarment. It is also one of the most helpful extant guides to the trial transcript. See also George Marion, *The Communist Trial: An American Crossroads*, 2nd ed. (New York: Fairplay, 1950). This publication also raises and discusses the bias issue but is written as an obvious pro-defendant polemic. See also Hawthorne Daniel, *Judge Medina: A Biography* (New York: Wilfred Funk, 1952), 235–316, for discussion of the trial from the judge's perspective; Stanley I. Kutler, *The American Inquisition: Justice and Injustice in the Cold War* (New York: Hill and Wang, 1982), 152–82, which concentrates primarily on the defense lawyers' contempt portion of the case; and Scott Martelle, *The Fear Within: Spies, Commies, and American Democracy on Trial* (New Brunswick, NJ: Rutgers University Press, 2011).

8 Kutler, *American Inquisition*, 153.

9 For discussion, see Marion, *Communist Trial*, 126–28.

10 Tom C. Clark, "Why the Reds Won't Scare Us Any More," *Look*, August 30, 1949, 50.

11 Ibid.

12 The text of Clark's June 21, 1946, speech was published in Clark, "Civil Rights: The Boundless Responsibility of Lawyers," *American Bar Association Journal* 32, no. 8 (1946): 453–57 (quote on 457).

13 Smith Act, 54 Stat. 671, §§ 3–5 (1940) (codified as amended at 18 U.S.C. § 10–11 [1948]). Sections pertinent to the case were the following:

> Sec. 10 [Subversive activities]: advocating overthrow of government by force.
> (a) it shall be unlawful for any person—
> (1) to knowingly or wilfully advocate, abet, advise, or teach the duty, necessity, desirability, or propriety of overthrowing or destroying

any government in the United States by force or violence, or by the assassination of any officer of any such government;

(2) with the intent to cause the overthrow or destruction of any government in the United States, to print, publish, edit, issue, circulate, sell, distribute, or publicly display any written or printed matter advocating, advising, or teaching the duty, necessity, desirability, or propriety of overthrowing or destroying any government in the United States by force or violence;

(3) to organize or help to organize any society, group, or assembly of persons who teach, advocate, or encourage the overthrow or destruction of any government in the United States by force or violence; or to be or become a member of, or affiliated with, any such society, group, or assembly of person, knowing the purposes thereof. . . .

Sec. 11. Attempting or conspiring to commit [the above] prohibited acts.

It shall be unlawful for any person to attempt to commit, or to conspire to commit, any of the acts prohibited by the provisions [above].

Sec. 13. Any person who violates any of the provisions [above] shall, upon conviction thereof, be fined not more than $10,000 or imprisoned for not more than ten years, or both.

14 Excerpts from conspiracy indictment:

The Grand Jury charges:

1. That from on or about April 1, 1945, and continuously thereafter up to and including the date of the filing of this indictment, in the Southern District of New York, and elsewhere, WILLIAM Z. FOSTER, EUGENE DENNIS, also known as Francis X. Waldron, Jr., JOHN B. WILLIAMSON, JACOB STACHEL, ROBERT G. THOMPSON, BENJAMIN J. DAVIS, JR., HENRY WINSTON, JOHN GATES, also known as Israel Regenstreif, IRVING POTASH, GILBERT GREEN, CARL WINTER, and GUS HALL, also known as Arno Gust Halberg, the defendants herein, unlawfully, wilfully and knowingly, did conspire with each other, and with diverse other persons to the Grand Jury unknown, to organize as the Communist Party of the United States of America a society, group, and assembly of persons who teach and advocate the overthrow and destruction of the Government of the United States by force and violence, and knowingly and wilfully to advocate and teach the duty and necessity of overthrowing and destroying the Government of the United States by force and violence, which said acts are prohibited by Section 2 of the Act of

June 28, 1940 (Section 10, Title 18, United States Code), commonly known as the Smith Act.

2. It was part of said conspiracy that said defendants would convene . . . a meeting of the National Board of the Communist Political Association . . . to adopt a draft resolution . . . for the purpose of organizing as the Communist Party of the United States of America. . . .

3. It was further a part of said conspiracy that said defendants would thereafter convene . . . a meeting of the National Committee of the Communist Political Association . . . to amend and adopt said draft resolution. . . .

4. Said defendants would thereafter cause to be convened . . . a special National Convention . . . for the purpose of considering and acting upon said resolution. . . .

5. Said conspiracy that said defendants would induce the delegates to . . . dissolve the Communist Political Association. . . .

6. Said defendants would bring about the organization of the Communist Party of the United States of America . . . to teach and advocate the overthrow and destruction of the Government of the United States by force and violence, and . . . adopt a Constitution basing said Party upon the principles of Marxism-Leninism. . . .

7. Said defendants would bring about the election of officers and the election of a National Committee of said Party, and would become members of said Party, and be elected as officers and as members of said National Committee . . . and would meet from time to time to formulate, supervise, and carry out the policies and activities of said Party. . . .

8. Said defendants would . . . organize . . . units of said Party, and would recruit . . . members of said Party. . . .

9. Said defendants would publish and circulate . . . books, articles, magazines, and newspapers advocating the principles of Marxism-Leninism. . . .

10. Said defendants would conduct, and cause to be conducted, schools and classes for the study of the principles of Marxism-Leninism, in which would be taught and advocated the duty and necessity of overthrowing and destroying the Government of the United States by force and violence.

In violation of sections 3 and 5 of the Act of June 28, 1940 (Sections 11 and 13, Title 18, United States Code), commonly known as the Smith Act.

Marion, *Communist Trial*, 189–90.

15 The membership indictment:

> The Grand Jury charges:
> 1. That from on or about July 26, 1945, and continuously there-
> after up to and including the date of the filing of this indictment,
> the Communist Party of the United States of America has been a
> society, group, and assembly of persons who teach and advocate the
> overthrow and destruction of the Government of the United States
> by force and violence.
> 2. That from on or about July 26, 1945, and continuously there-
> after up to and including the date of the filing of this indictment, in
> the Southern District of New York, ... the defendant herein, has been
> a member of said Communist Party of the United States of America,
> the defendant well knowing during all said period that said Com-
> munist Party of the United States of America was and is a society,
> group and assembly of persons who teach and advocate the overthrow
> and destruction of the Government of the United States by force and
> violence.
> In violation of Sections 10 and 13, Title 18, United States Code.

Marion, *Communist Trial*, 191.

16 Maraniss, *Good American Family*, 229.

17 See Daniel, *Judge Medina*, 3–200, for discussions of Medina's personal history and professional work before his appointment to the federal bench
in 1947. See also "Communists: The Presence of Evil," *Time*, October 24,
1949 (with Judge Medina on the cover of the magazine).

18 Kutler, *American Inquisition*, 155. Justice Felix Frankfurter apparently
shared the opinion that Medina was the most "insufferable egoist" to
appear before the Court and also described him as a "messianic" character
and a "super-egoist." Ibid., 267n27 and references therein.

19 See Daniel, *Judge Medina*, 218–19, for discussion.

20 Ibid., 225–26.

21 Kutler, *American Inquisition*, 155.

22 Daniel, *Judge Medina*, 226.

23 Dennis, a prolific publisher of pamphlets about the Communist Party,
wrote several articles on the trial and his involvement acting as his own
lawyer. See, e.g., "'Dangerous Thoughts': The Case of the Indicted Twelve"
(1948); "The Case for the Communist Party" (1949) (his opening statement to the jury); "In Defense of Your Freedom" (1949) (his summation

to the jury); "Ideas They Cannot Jail, Part V" (1950) (his summation); all articles are in the ELC.

24 See Daniel, *Judge Medina*, 221–24; "Communist Trial Ends with 11 Guilty," 32–33.

25 Kutler, *American Inquisition*, 155; Daniel, *Judge Medina*, 224.

26 Kutler, *American Inquisition*, 155.

27 Ibid., 155–56.

28 Daniel, *Judge Medina*, 224. Dennis was out on bail from the contempt conviction during the trial.

29 Johnson, *Maurice Sugar*, 73, 98–99.

30 Kutler, *American Inquisition*, 156.

31 George Crockett Jr., interview by Edward Littlejohn, Washington, DC, March 28, 1993.

32 Ibid.

33 Ibid.

34 Ibid.

35 Maraniss, *Good American Family*, 227.

36 Crockett/Littlejohn interview, March 28, 1993.

37 Charles L. Sanders, "Detroit's Rebel Judge Crockett: Champion of Justice for Blacks Sparks Mini-Revolution in Court," *Ebony*, August 1969, 114, 120.

38 Jones interview, 7.

39 Robert A. Popa, "Judge Crockett: Lightning Rod for Controversy," *Detroit News*, April 6, 1969.

40 Crockett/Littlejohn interview, March 28, 1993.

41 Ibid.

42 Ibid. Crockett's entry into the case was reported in *The Worker*, Michigan ed.: "Crockett, Noted Attorney, Joins Civil Rights Fight," January 16, 1949, 1.

43 Crockett/Littlejohn interview, March 29, 1993.

44 Ibid.

45 Ibid.

46 Ibid.

47 Ibid.

48 Following the Foley Square trial, Judge Medina was a much-celebrated and sought-after speaker. Collections of his speeches may be found in Harold R. Medina and Maxine B. Virtue, *Judge Medina Speaks: A Group of Addresses* (Albany, NY: M. Bender, 1954); Harold R. Medina, *The Anatomy of Freedom* (New York: Holt, 1959). See also Daniel, *Judge Medina*.

49 The defense's pretrial motions were reported in the press primarily as delaying tactics. See, e.g., "Defense Retards Communist Trial," *New York Sun*, January 17, 1949, 1; "Reds' Lawyers Resume Trial Delay Tactics," *New*

York World-Telegram, January 18, 1949; Russell Porter, "11 Communists Fail to Halt Trial Here, Court Area Quiet," *New York Times*, January 18, 1949, 1; Norma Abrams and Henry Lee, "Reds Squawk in Vain as Trial of 12 Opens," *Daily News*, January 18, 1949, 1.

50 The jury challenge received extensive press coverage. See, e.g., "Medina Insists upon Deciding Red Jury Issue: Judge Denies Motion to Disqualify Himself during Challenge—System Held Wall St. Tool," *New York Sun*, January 19, 1949, 1; "'12' Win Right to Call Witnesses on Illegal Juries," *Daily Worker*, January 21, 1949, 2; "Judge Belittles Attack by Reds on Jury System," *Detroit Free Press*, February 2, 1949; Russell Porter, "4 'Colored' Lists for Juries Shown," *New York Times*, February 8, 1949, 1; Harry Raymond, "Bare Jim Crow Jury Lists," *Daily Worker*, February 16, 1949, 1; Russell Porter, "Communists Lose Challenge to Jury: Trial Monday Set," *New York Times*, March 5, 1949, 1; Russell Porter, "Jury Is Completed at Trial of 11 Reds: 7 Women and 5 Men Include 3 Negroes, 2 Jobless, 2 Toilers—4 Alternates to Be Picked," *New York Times*, March 17, 1949, 2.

51 Crockett/Littlejohn interview, March 29, 1993.

52 Ibid.

53 Ibid.

54 Ibid.

55 Ibid.

56 Ibid.

57 Ibid.

58 Ibid.

59 The jurors and alternates who were eventually impaneled included three Black jurors (one being the forewoman). "Communist Trial Ends with 11 Guilty," 32–33.

60 Mary Hornaday, "'Communist Cry of Bias' Refuted by Jury List," *Christian Science Monitor*, March 10, 1949.

61 Kutler, *American Inquisition*, 156.

62 Yesol Han, "Defining American Freedoms: Jurists Respond to the American Communist Party Trial, 1948–1952" (master's thesis, Columbia University, 2011), citing the historian Ellen Schrecker, who recounted her encounter with Judge Medina at a dinner party in the 1960s. Schrecker, *Many Are the Crimes: McCarthyism in America* (New York: Greenwood, 1998), 198.

63 *United States v. Dennis*, trial transcript (S.D.N.Y. 1949), 1186–87, 1190–91. Ultimately, the trial consumed 21,157 pages of text covering twenty-eight volumes of transcripts. A complete set of the trial transcripts are in ELC.

64 Harry Raymond, "McGohey Offers Stool Pigeon as First Witness," *Daily Worker*, March 24, 1949, 1; Russell Porter, "Budenz Testifies of Oath to

Stalin," *New York Times*, March 24, 1949; Russell Porter, "Budenz See Reds Politburo Puppets," *New York Times*, April 5, 1949.

65 Michal R. Belknap, *Cold War Political Justice: The Smith Act, the Communist Party, and American Civil Liberties* (New York: Praeger, 1977), 85.

66 For discussion, see Marion, *Communist Trial*, 93–106; National Non-Partisan Committee to Defend the 12 Communist Leaders, *Due Process in a Political Trial*, 28–30.

67 National Non-Partisan Committee to Defend the 12 Communist Leaders, *Due Process in a Political Trial*, 28–29. See ibid., 37–39, for references by Judge Medina to the defendants' use of language.

68 Crockett/Littlejohn interview, March 29, 1993.

69 320 U.S. 118 (1943).

70 320 U.S. at 157.

71 Crockett/Littlejohn interview, March 29, 1993.

72 National Non-Partisan Committee to Defend the 12 Communist Leaders, *Due Process in a Political Trial*, 35–36; page references are to the trial transcript.

73 Ibid., 36–37.

74 For example, the prosecution witness and FBI "contact" man in the Communist Party Herbert A. Philbeck "named" an MIT professor as a communist during his trial testimony. "Professor at M.I.T. Named as Teacher of Red Revolution," *New York Times*, April 9, 1949, 1.

75 Crockett/Littlejohn interview, March 29, 1993.

76 See National Non-Partisan Committee to Defend the 12 Communist Leaders, *Due Process in a Political Trial*, 27–28; page references are to the trial transcript.

77 Crockett/Littlejohn interview, March 29, 1993.

78 See National Non-Partisan Committee to Defend the 12 Communist Leaders, *Due Process in a Political Trial*, 10–12, for references to the trial transcript in this regard.

79 Ibid., 6–7.

80 Ibid., 39–40.

81 See ibid., 44–46, for examples from the trial record.

82 Ibid., 6–7, citing the trial record at 2340–41.

83 Crockett/Littlejohn interview, March 29, 1993.

84 Russell Porter, "U.S. Rest Case in Red Trial: Judge Limits Dismiss Moves," *New York Times*, May 20, 1949.

85 Crockett/Littlejohn interview, March 29, 1993.

86 Ibid.

87 Ibid.

88 National Non-Partisan Committee to Defend the 12 Communist Leaders, *Due Process in a Political Trial*, 3.

89 Clark, "Why the Reds Won't Scare Us Any More," 50.

90 Crockett maintained a scrapbook that contains over six hundred newspaper articles about the Foley Square trial. The authors reviewed these articles and, with the exception of the decidedly pro-defense *Daily Worker*, they, in the aggregate, clearly support the claims of media bias.

91 See "Communist Trial Ends with 11 Guilty." Photographs were not allowed in the courtroom. This article contains excellent sketches of the trial's principals, including the jurors, and was described by *Life* as the "most comprehensive pictorial record made of the trial."

92 Ibid., 31, 35, 33.

93 Crockett/Littlejohn interview, March 29, 1993.

94 Ibid.

95 David King Dunaway, *How Can I Keep from Singing: The Ballad of Pete Seeger* (New York: McGraw-Hill, 1982), 11.

96 See Daniel, *Judge Medina*, 274–76; Medina, *Anatomy of Freedom*, 89–90.

97 Kutler, *American Inquisition*, 156, 165. See also 266n6 for a description of documents that indicated the FBI's knowledge of defense strategies.

98 Ibid., 266n6.

99 Ibid. Crockett and his partner, Ernest Goodman, remained surveillance targets through the 1970s. See Kenneth O'Reilly, *Racial Matters: The FBI's Secret File on Black America, 1960–1972* (New York: Free Press, 1989), 180–81 (the FBI monitored Crockett's and Goodman's activities as leaders in the National Lawyers Guild's Committee for Legal Assistance in the South), 182 (both men were placed on the counterintelligence list). Later, the FBI worked with right-wing extremist groups in Detroit to discredit Crockett and his political campaigns for city council and judge.

100 Crockett/Littlejohn interview, March 29, 1993.

101 Ibid.

102 Ibid.

103 Ibid.

104 *Dennis v. U.S.*, 339 U.S. 162, 162–63 (1950). Dennis was convicted of willfully failing to appear before the House Un-American Activities Committee in compliance with a subpoena. At trial, Dennis had challenged the qualifications of federal government employees to sit as jurors because their employment required a loyalty oath (Executive Order 9835, popularly known as the "Loyalty Order") that would make them hesitant to vote for an acquittal. The Supreme Court affirmed Dennis's conviction on the basis that government employees could not be held biased as a matter of law

solely by reason of their employment. The defendant, the Court held, had to show actual bias. Justices Black and Frankfurter dissented.

105 Crockett/Littlejohn interview, March 29, 1993.

106 Ibid.

107 Ibid.

108 Ibid.

109 Ibid.

110 National Non-Partisan Committee to Defend the 12 Communist Leaders, *Due Process in a Political Trial*, 65–67. Page references are to the court transcript.

111 Daniel, *Judge Medina*, 225.

112 Ibid., 230–31.

113 See ibid., 235–83, for Judge Medina's views and versions of many aspects of the trial discussed in this chapter, which, not surprisingly, differ substantially from those expressed by Crockett and others associated with the defense. Included are Medina's observations of the protracted jury challenge, the defense attorney tactics that he regarded as intentionally calculated to disrupt and delay the trial, and his basis for the contempt citations against the defendants and the defense lawyers. Regrettably, this biography contains neither a bibliography nor note source references.

114 See *U.S. v. Dennis*, 171 F.2d 986 (D.C. Cir. 1948), Joint Appendix, vol. XVI, pp. 12264–327 [Trial Testimony] (hereafter Joint Appendix). See also George W. Crockett, "Freedom Is Everybody's Job: The Crime of the Government against the Negro People," n.d. This pamphlet is devoted primarily to the portions of Crockett's summation concerned with the Communist Party's support of fundamental rights for Blacks.

115 Crockett, "Freedom Is Everybody's Job," 2–3; Joint Appendix, 12264–65, ELC.

116 Joint Appendix, 12270.

117 Both witnesses, William O'Dell Nowell and William Cummings, were Black.

118 Crockett, "Freedom Is Everybody's Job," 5–7, 9; Joint Appendix, 12272–73, 12276.

119 Crockett, "Freedom Is Everybody's Job," 13, 14–15; Joint Appendix, 12280, 12281–82.

120 Kutler, *American Inquisition*, 157.

Chapter 4. Aftermath of United States v. Dennis

1 Trial transcript, 12522–28.

2 Judge Crockett's views and recollections of the contempt proceedings are drawn primarily from his interviews with Edward Littlejohn on March 29, 1993, in Washington, DC. Three audiotapes were made.

3 See Daniel, *Judge Medina*, 225–26.

4 Trial transcript, 12523. The adjudications of contempt appear in the trial transcript at 12522–27. The certificate was titled "Contempt Certificate Pursuant to Rule 42(a), Federal Rules of Criminal Procedure" and consisted of sixty pages that contained forty specifications of contempt for acts that occurred between January 27 and October 4, 1949. Nine of the specifications applied to Crockett. See *Report of Investigation of Summary Contempt Citation against George W. Crockett, Jr. of the Michigan Bar*, 4–5 (prepared by National Lawyers Guild, Detroit Chapter and Wolverine Bar Association, January 6, 1950); see 4–10 for a discussion of the appropriateness of summary contempt proceedings, without notice or hearing, when the trial judge fails to act "instantaneously" to preserve the court's dignity and authority.

5 Trial transcript, 12523–24.

6 Trial transcript, 12523.

7 The judge listed thirteen broad categories of conduct that he claimed completed the conspiracy. Trial transcript, 12525–26.

8 Rule 42(a) of the then extant Federal Rules of Criminal Procedure required the judge to certify that he "saw or heard" the contemptuous conduct, that it occurred in the "presence" of the court, and that the judge recite the facts on which the contempt was based. In addition to the obvious problem of how the judge could have seen or heard a conspiracy allegedly formed outside of court, there was no hearing and, therefore, no record for appellate review as required by Rule 42(a). Judge Medina simply made the entire trial record, thousands of pages of transcript, a part of the contempt proceedings. See *Report of Investigation of Summary Contempt Citation*, 10–12, for discussion.

9 Trial transcript, 12526–27.

10 Crockett/Littlejohn interview, March 29, 1993.

11 Trial transcript, 12535.

12 Crockett/Littlejohn interview, March 29, 1993. The actual contempt citation, Specification 27, accuses Crockett of standing, in addition to failing "to assist the Court in restoring order." Crockett's version from memory, of course, is somewhat different but is substantially accurate. See also *Report of Investigation Summary Contempt Citation*, 22.

13 Crockett/Littlejohn interview, March 29, 1993. For a verbatim record of this contempt citation, see Specification 38, which is contained in *Report of Investigation Summary Contempt Citation*, 27–28.

14 *Report of Investigation Summary Contempt Citation*, 17–18.

15 All nine specifications alleging contemptuous conduct by Crockett are discussed and analyzed in *Report of Investigation Summary Contempt Citation*,

12–30. The report concluded that Crockett's conduct, considering an atmosphere of public inflammation and an unsympathetic judge, was no more "than is to be expected from a lawyer obedient to the responsibilities of his profession and the interests of his clients" (30). The report also concluded that the severity of the punishment imposed on Crockett "was unjustified by even the least charitable view of what he said and did" (30).

16 Crockett/Littlejohn interview, March 29, 1993.

17 See, e.g., "Reds Get 5 Yrs.: Carl Winter Given Term, $10,000 Fine," *Detroit Times*, October 21, 1949, 1; "From Paris to Peking, They Rap Jailing of 11," *Daily Worker*, October 24, 1949, 1; "Sentence for Contempt No Surprise: Lawyer for Accused Rey Says No Price Too Dear for Cause," *Pittsburgh Courier*, October 24, 1949.

18 Telegram, Ernest Goodman to George Crockett, October 15, 1949, Ernest Goodman files, ELC.

19 George Crockett Jr. to Ernest Goodman, October 17, 1949, ELC.

20 "It was prepared by a group of New York attorneys who examined more than 13,000 pages of the record, with a view to determining whether the press reports of the proceedings were substantiated by the record. Our Committee is of the opinion that the contents of this document deserve the consideration of members of the Bar." National Non-Partisan Committee to Defend the 12 Communist Leaders, *Due Process in a Political Trial*, 1.

21 Ernest Goodman to George Crockett Jr., October 26, 1949, Goodman files.

22 Telegram, George Crockett Jr. to Ernest Goodman, October 27, 1949, Crockett files, ELC.

23 Kutler, *American Inquisition*, 159.

24 Ibid.

25 See, e.g., "Lawyers Blast Jail Term for Crockett," *Daily Worker*, December 2, 1949; "The Story of George Crockett: A Latter-Day Darrow," *Daily Worker*, December 5, 1949, 4.

26 See, e.g., "Civic Leaders Defend Convicted Lawyer: Medina's Action Called Threat to Fair Trial System," *Pittsburgh Courier*, December 2, 1949, 12; "Ford Local 600 Supports Appeal by City Lawyer," *Michigan Chronicle*, December 31, 1949.

27 Ernest Goodman, interview by Edward Littlejohn, November 26, 1995.

28 Babson, Riddle, and Elsila, *Color of Law*, 179.

29 *Sacher v. U.S.*, 182 F.2d 416 (2d. Cir. 1950).

30 Ibid., at 466.

31 Ibid., at 465. Clark noted that twenty-nine of the thirty-nine acts charged occurred in the first five months of the nine-month trial, twelve before the

trial proper. Ten acts cited during the last four months, he found, were less serious than the earlier ones. Ibid., at 465n4.

32 Ibid., at 420.

33 Ibid.

34 Ibid., at 429.

35 Ibid., at 423–53.

36 Ibid., at 454.

37 For discussion of the view that Supreme Court decisions reflect public opinion, see C. Pritchett, *Civil Liberties and the Vinson Court*, 3rd ed. (Chicago: University of Chicago Press, 1964), 233–42. Pritchett's thesis is that the Vinson Court, when confronted with McCarthyism and the Smith Act prosecutions, tended to legitimate the government's action. Many commentators have asserted that Supreme Court decisions often reflect public opinion. See, e.g., William Mishler and Reginald S. Sheehan, "Public Opinion and the Supreme Court as Countermajoritarian Institution? The Impact of Public Opinion on Supreme Court Decisions," *American Political Science Review* 87, no. 1 (1993): 87, 90–91; Ronald A. Dahl, "Decision Making in a Democracy: The Supreme Court as a National Policymaker," *Journal of Public Law* 6 (1957): 279–95; Belknap, *Cold War Political Justice*.

38 Kutler, *American Inquisition*, 160, citing communication from Clark to Black, March 15, 1952, Hugo L. Black Papers, Library of Congress. Kutler's chapter on the Foley Square trial contains excellent and detailed analyses of the contempt appeals, including the decisions of the U.S. Supreme Court. Also discussed and well documented are the attorney disbarment proceedings that followed.

39 Robert J. Glennon, *The Iconoclast as Reformer: Jerome Frank's Impact on American Law* (Ithaca, NY: Cornell University Press, 1985), 163, 36. Glennon also cites *Sacher* as an example of Frank's influence on the Supreme Court that actually retarded the course the law ultimately took, contrary to his customary challenges for the Court to extend civil liberties.

40 Ibid., 36.

41 Mich. Const. amend. sec. 22 (1951).

42 The text of Goodman's recollections appears in his papers, undated and titled "Michigan State Bar." This version was edited and shortened by Edward Littlejohn.

43 Ibid.

44 "Police Guard Judge Medina: Lawyer He Sentenced Spotted in Audience," *Detroit News*, September 29, 1950.

45 Ibid.

46 E. Blythe Stason, "Disciplining Subversive Members of the Bar," *Michigan State Bar Journal* 30 (1951): 16.

47 Crockett/Littlejohn interview, March 29, 1993.

48 Goodman states that he was never extended a similar invitation. Goodman/ Littlejohn interview, November 26, 1995.

49 Crockett/Littlejohn interview, March 29, 1995. The *Detroit News* did publish a correction: "News Error Is Corrected: Lawyer Crockett Not a Communist Member," April 21, 1950. Other press coverage failed to make this important distinction. "U.S. Upholds Red Lawyer Sentences," *Detroit Free Press*, March 11, 1952. A similar error was made two years later after the state bar's disciplinary hearings ended. "State Bar Hits Red Lawyer," *Detroit Times*, October 21, 1954, 1.

50 Babson, Riddle, and Elsila, *Color of Law*, 181.

51 Ibid.

52 Ibid., 185.

53 Memorandum of Partnership Agreement Between Ernest Goodman, George W. Crockett Jr., Morton A. Eden, and Dean Robb, n.d., ELC.

54 Babson, Riddle, and Elsila, *Color of Law*, 203–6.

55 William L. Patterson to George W. Crockett, November 5, 1951, ELC (Patterson's letter refers to and quotes from a letter from Crockett dated November 2, 1951).

56 George W. Crockett to William L. Patterson, November 6, 1951, ELC.

57 Hittle Act (1951), 1956 Mason Mich. Sup., Sec. 750, 545a–d.

58 Kutler, *American Inquisition*, 161.

59 341 U.S. 494 (1951). Justices Black and Douglas dissented. Crockett, Isserman, and Sacher argued the case for the petitioners. *Dennis* took the "clear and present danger" test in a new, more restrictive direction, making it more manipulative than ever. As a result, speech could be suppressed, considering the gravity of a danger, e.g., sedition, even if the probability of such a result was small and remote. Of the pre-*Dennis* cases, the most notable is *Schenck v. U.S.*, 249 U.S. 47 (1919). In *Schenck*, Justice Holmes's famous opinion articulated the "clear and present danger" test that focused on the "circumstances" and the "nature" of speech rather than the "immediacy" of the danger it posed. Shortly after *Schenck*, in *Abrams v. U.S.*, 250 U.S. 616 (1919), Holmes himself dissented from the Court's application of the "clear and present danger" test. He and Justice Brandeis would have modified the test to regulate speech that posed a "clear and *imminent* danger" rather than the *likelihood* that dangerous results would follow. Ten years later, in *Whitney v. California*, 274 U.S. 357 (1927), which upheld a criminal syndicalism conviction on the strength of membership in a communist organization and assisting to organize it, Justice Brandeis, joined by Holmes, argued that speech should be protected unless "immediate serious violence was to be expected or was advocated." Ten years after *Whitney*, *De Jonge v. Oregon*, 299 U.S. 353 (1937), held that mere participation in a Communist Party meeting could not be made a crime.

60 *Dennis*, 341 U.S. at 501.

61 Ibid., at 502.

62 Ibid., at 579 (Black, J., dissenting).

63 Ibid., at 583 (Douglas, J., dissenting).

64 Ibid., at 581 (Black, J., dissenting).

65 341 U.S. 952 (1951).

66 Kutler, *American Inquisition*, 161.

67 Ibid. In 1948, Wallace ran for president of the United States on the Progressive Party ticket.

68 Crockett/Littlejohn interview, March 29, 1993.

69 See *Communism in the Detroit Area—Parts I and II: Hearings Before the House Un-American Activities Committee*, 82nd Cong., 2nd sess. (February 25–29, March 10, and April 29–30, 1952) (hereafter Detroit Hearings).

70 Philbrick infiltrated the party during the 1940s and surfaced as a surprise witness during the Foley Square trial. His 1952 autobiography, *I Lead Three Lives*, was adapted into a popular television series that chronicled his life as an advertising executive, communist, and anticommunist informant. Philbrick died on August 16, 1993, at age seventy-eight.

71 Detroit Hearings, 2712.

72 Ibid.

73 See, e.g., Jack Crellin, "Calls Pastor 'Tool' of Reds: Probers of Reds Threaten to Expel Noisy Attorney [Crockett]," *Detroit Times*, February 27, 1952, 1; Fred Tew, "Probers Denounce Rev. Hill as Traitor for Aiding Reds," *Detroit Free Press*, February 28, 1952, 23, contains a photograph of Crockett with the caption, "Roused Committee's anger."

74 See Fred Tew, "Committee Loosens Reins, Defiant Witness Runs Wild: Fight over Terminology Bitterest of Hearing," *Detroit Free Press*, February 29, 1952, 8. Young was called as the national executive secretary of the National Negro Labor Council, an interracial group that fought employment discrimination.

75 See, e.g., "Rev. Hill 'Too Hot': Militant Pastor Blasts Negro's Status," *Courier* (Detroit ed.), March 1, 1952, 1; "Ministers Back Hill! But Man and Woman on Street Say: 'Young Stole Show,'" *Courier* (Detroit ed.), March 8, 1952, 1.

76 Babson, Riddle, and Elsila, *Color of Law*, 212 (citing HCUA, *Communism in the Detroit Area*, 2820–22).

77 Maraniss, *Good American Family*, 62.
78 Ibid.
79 Bill McGraw, "Reunion Notes Young's Stand against Communist-Hunters," *Detroit Free Press*, June 4, 1993, 15.
80 Detroit Hearings, 2879–92.
81 Ibid., 3103. Watts was appointed director of Detroit's Department of Public Works after Coleman A. Young was elected mayor in 1973.
82 Ibid., 3259.
83 Goodman/Littlejohn interview, November 26, 1995.
84 See, e.g., "List of Persons Identified as Reds at Hearing in Detroit," *Detroit Free Press*, December 28, 1952, B10.
85 Ibid.
86 *Sacher v. U.S.*, 343 U.S. 1 (1952).
87 Ibid., at 11.
88 Ibid.
89 Ibid., at 89 (Douglas, J., dissenting).
90 Kutler, *American Inquisition*, 163.
91 *Sacher*, 343 U.S. at 17.
92 Ibid., at 18–23 (Black, J., dissenting).
93 Ibid., at 42–89 (Frankfurter, J., dissenting).
94 Kutler, *American Inquisition*, 163–64, for discussion.
95 "U.S. Upholds Red Lawyer Sentences," *Detroit Free Press*, March 11, 1952.
96 Lorraine Hansberry, "Noted Lawyer Goes to Jail: Says Negros' Fight for Rights Menaced," *Freedom*, May 1952.
97 Maraniss, *Good American Family*, 284.
98 George W. Crockett Jr. to the State Bar of Michigan, March 14, 1952, ELC.
99 George W. Crockett Jr. to Dr. Benjamin Mays, March 24, 1952, ELC.
100 "Hearst Red Smear Hits 7 Negro College Presidents," *Chicago Tribune*, November 25, 1995, 3. The article identified the Hearst Newspaper Syndicate papers, including the *New York Journal-American* and the *Chicago American*, as sources of the "smear."
101 George W. Crockett to Dr. Benjamin Mays, December 6, 1955, ELC.
102 Dr. Benjamin Mays to George W. Crockett Jr., December 8, 1955, ELC. Mays became president of Morehouse in 1940, long after Crockett had left, and remained president for twenty-seven years. In his autobiography, *Born to Rebel* (New York: Charles Scribner's Sons, 1971), he wrote about being "smeared" and vigorously denied any association with communism or the Communist Party (229–31). In recounting the accomplishments of Morehouse graduates, Mays noted that one graduate was a judge of Detroit's Recorder's Court. Crockett, however, is not mentioned by name (186).

103 Kenneth McCormick, "State Police Ready to Grab Reds," *Detroit Free Press*, April 20, 1952; "Appeals Legality of Anti-Red Law," *Detroit Times*, July 31, 1952 (the *Detroit Times* reported that State Police Commissioner Donald S. Leonard was ready to arrest five hundred known communists at the time of the law's enactment); "Governor Will Seek Fund to Curb Reds," *Detroit News*, April 1, 1952; "State Advised about Reds: Detroit Police Confer with Attorney General," *Detroit News*, April 2, 1952.

104 "Dondineau to Fire Red Teachers," *Detroit Free Press*, April 22, 1952, 1. The *Free Press* reported the Detroit school superintendent planned to dismiss any teacher proved to be a communist: "the Trucks Law requiring Communists to register will give us an avenue through which facts can be proved."

105 Don Honeshell, "2 Parties Lose Place on Ballot: Plan Red Roundup," *Detroit News*, April 18, 1952, quoted the state civil service director as saying, "There are about 12 we suspect now. . . . Others have resigned for various reasons. The entire 22,000 workers are under close observation." The two parties affected by the new act were the Michigan Communist Party and the Socialist Workers Party. The Socialist Workers Party, not officially recognized by the U.S. Communist Party, was deemed to fall within the Trucks Act's definition of organizations seeking "to alter the form of government of the United States by unconstitutional means." The day Governor Williams signed the Trucks Bill, April 17, 1952, the Socialist Workers Party was notified by a letter from the Michigan Secretary of State that it had been declared subversive under the meanings of the new law. F. M. Alger Jr., Michigan Secretary of State, to Howard Lerner, Socialist Workers Party, April 17, 1952, ELC. The action was rescinded after Goodman obtained an injunction in federal court. F. M. Alger Jr., Michigan Secretary of State, to Howard Lerner, Chairman, Socialist Workers Party, June 4, 1952, ELC.

106 1952 Mich. Pub. Acts 117, emphasis added.

107 Goodman/Littlejohn interview, November 26, 1995.

108 Brown was a member of Detroit's prominent Black law firm Lewis, Rowlette, Brown, Wanzo & Bell. See Littlejohn and Hobson, "Black Lawyers, Law Practice, and Bar Associations," 1625.

109 Goodman/Littlejohn interview, November 26, 1995.

110 Ibid.

111 Telegram, Myles J. Lane to George W. Crockett Jr., April 21, 1952, ELC.

112 George Crockett, interview by Dr. Charles Wright, March 27, 1987, transcript, 1–2; Crockett/Littlejohn interview, March 29, 1993.

113 Goodman/Littlejohn interview, November 26, 1995.

114 "Suit Delays Red Arrests," *Detroit News*, April 23, 1952; "Reds Get Order against New Law," *Detroit Times*, April 24, 1952; "Red Listing Delayed by

U.S. Court," *Detroit News*, April 23, 1952. The order was entered by Chief District Judge Arthur F. Lederle.
115 *Albertson v. Millard*, 106 F. Supp. 635 (E.D. Mich. 1952). The majority was Chief Judge Charles C. Simons of the Circuit Court of Appeals and District Judge Frank A. Picard. Judge Theodore Levin dissented and agreed with Goodman's arguments that the Trucks Act was preempted by the federal Internal Security Act, 50 U.S.C.A., Sec. 781 (15), known as the McCarran Act, and that it violated the Fourteenth Amendment as its definitions of "Communist" and "Communist Party" were vague (647–51). The decision received favorable editorial treatment in the Detroit press. See, e.g., "Court Denies Traitor Haven," *Detroit Times*, July 31, 1952, in which communists are called "weasel[s]" and "subversives" whom the Trucks law will drag "from the darkness—where they work best—and expose them to the glare of public scrutiny—beneath which Communists wilt and shrivel."
116 Goodman/Littlejohn interview, November 26, 1995.

Chapter 5. "I Wasn't Alone"

1 Crockett/Littlejohn interview, March 28, 1993.
2 The descriptions of the Foley Square lawyers being taken into custody are taken from: Crockett/Littlejohn interview, March 29, 1993; Lonergan/ Crockett interview, March 27, 1987; and George W. Crockett Jr., speech notes, n.d., ELC.
3 Lonergan and Crockett, interview transcripts, March 27, 1987.
4 Crockett speech notes.
5 Crockett/Lonergan interview, March 27, 1987.
6 Crockett speech notes.
7 George W. Crockett Jr. to Ethelene Crockett, April 24, 1952, ELC.
8 On June 18, 1952, Crockett's partner Dean Robb wrote to Maurice Sugar after Robb, his wife, Barbara, and Ethelene had driven to Kentucky for a prison visit: "I wasn't sure Geo. was happy to see us. He said something about the fact that visitors disturb the mental processes that have been developed to acclimate one to prison life & now that's disturbed." Dean Robb to Maurice Sugar, June 18, 1952, ELC.
9 George W. Crockett Jr. to Ethelene Crockett, April 28, 1952, ELC.
10 George W. Crockett Jr. to George W. Crockett III, May 1, 1952, ELC.
11 Crockett speech notes, 6–7.
12 Ibid.

13 Crockett/Littlejohn interview, March 29, 1993.
14 In February 1955, Crockett executed an affidavit that described the segregated conditions at Ashland, Kentucky, prison. His affidavit was filed in a lawsuit brought by Benjamin J. Davis, one of the Foley Square defendants seeking to enjoin segregation in federal prisons on the basis of race or color.
15 Crockett/Littlejohn interview, March 29, 1993.
16 Crockett speech notes, March 29, 1993.
17 Crockett/Littlejohn interview, March 29, 1993.
18 Crockett speech notes, March 29, 1993.
19 Crockett/Littlejohn interview, March 29, 1993.
20 George W. Crockett Jr. to Ernie Goodman, May 22, 1952, ELC.
21 Jones interview, 5.
22 Ibid., 6.
23 Ibid., 17.
24 Crockett to the State Bar of Michigan, March 14, 1952.
25 Crockett Defense Committee to "Dear Friends," March 21, 1952, ELC. The letter was signed by the attorney Daniel P. O'Brien and Reverend Wesley O. Barnett, cochairmen, and attorney C. Lebron Simmons, executive secretary. The letter stated that the committee consisted of "outstanding laymen and lawyers."
26 George W. Crockett Jr. to Ethelene Crockett, May 18, 1952, ELC.
27 George W. Crockett Jr. to Ethelene Crockett, June 10, 1952, ELC.
28 George W. Crockett Jr. to Ethelene Crockett, August 16, 1952, ELC.
29 At the time, there were no "good behavior" reductions for sentences of six months or less.
30 Maraniss, *Good American Family*, 308.
31 Ibid.
32 George W. Crockett Jr. to Maurice Sugar, October 14, 1952, in which Crockett reports on the status of disciplinary proceedings against the Foley Square lawyers, including his own.
33 See Kutler, *American Inquisition*, 164–82, for detailed discussions of the Foley Square lawyers' disciplinary actions. See also National Lawyers Guild, New York City Chapter, "Memorandum on the Implications of Sacher, et al. v. U.S., and of the Decision Ordering the Disbarment of Harry Sacher and the Suspension for Two Years of Abraham J. Isserman from Practice in the Southern District of New York," April 30, 1952, ELC. The memorandum concluded about the order against Sacher and Isserman, "[It] cannot fail to have a profound effect, adverse we believe, on the careers of trial lawyers and the conduct of trials in the future" (11).
34 Kutler, *American Inquisition*, 166.

35 Jerold S. Auerbach, *Unequal Justice: Lawyers and Social Change in Modern America* (London: Oxford University Press, 1976), 246; "The Nature and Consequences of Forensic Misconduct in the Prosecution of a Criminal Case," *Columbia Law Review* 54, no. 6 (June 1954): 946–83. Auerbach also discusses other lawyers who were subjected to disciplinary actions for representing accused communist and other unpopular clients after the Foley Square trial (*Unequal Justice*, 232–62).

36 *In re* Disbarment of Isserman, 345 U.S. 286 (1953).

37 *In re* Isserman, 9 N.J. 269 (1952). See Kutler, *American Inquisition*, 168–72, for discussion of the personal, and apparently vindictive, role of Chief Justice Arthur Vanderbilt in Isserman's New Jersey disbarment cases.

38 *In re* Disbarment of Isserman, 348 U.S. 1 (1954).

39 See *In re* Isserman, 35 N.J. 198 (1961). In 1961, an entirely new court reexamined the facts and decided that events after Isserman's disbarment caused the court to "seriously question the justice of it" (200). After Isserman had carried the stigma of disbarment for nine years, the court decided that "this is more than enough" (200). Isserman was ordered reinstated, with the caveat that he had to retake the bar examination.

40 *Sacher v. Association of the Bar of New York*, 206 F. 2d 358 2d Cir. (1953).

41 *Sacher v. Association of the Bar of New York*, 347 U.S. 388, 389 (1954) (Reed, J., dissenting).

42 See Kutler, *American Inquisition*, 168.

43 See *Gladstein v. McLaughlin*, 230 F. 2d 762 (9th Cir. 1955). Gladstein had applied for a writ of mandamus seeking to disqualify Federal District Judge Frank McLaughlin on the basis of bias and prejudice against him. The Ninth Circuit Court of Appeals ordered Judge McLaughlin to refrain from continuing the disbarment proceedings.

44 Kutler, *American Inquisition*, 172.

45 The "Request for Investigation of George W. Crockett Jr." and formal complaint, dated March 12, 1952, were made by Ernest Wunsch, Secretary of Grievances for the Third Judicial Circuit, ELC.

46 See the thirty-three-page pamphlet "Report of Investigation of Summary Contempt Citation against George W. Crockett Jr. of the Michigan Bar" (1950), which was prepared by a joint committee of the Wolverine Bar Association and the Detroit Chapter of the National Lawyers Guild. It thoroughly analyzed each of the contempt specifications against Crockett. The report concluded that he had been wrongly cited and unjustly punished. In August 1950, an eight-page supplement to the report was published and distributed after the 2–1 decision of the U.S. Court of Appeals for the Second Circuit was announced.

47 Crockett's records contain several draft copies of the petition, each with a different "Partial List of Signers." The longest list has 171 signers.

48 For discussion, see Littlejohn and Hobson, "Black Lawyers, Law Practice, and Bar Associations," 1680–82.

49 Crockett/Littlejohn interview, March 29, 1997.

50 George W. Crockett Jr. to George W. Crocket III, New York, January 14, 1952, ELC.

51 Ibid.

52 George W. Crockett Jr. to Maurice Sugar, September 29, 1952, ELC.

53 George W. Crockett Jr. to Maurice Sugar, October 14, 1952, ELC. Stevenson was the Democratic nominee for president in 1952.

54 Graves was a past president of the Wolverine Bar Association and frequently represented the local chapter of the NAACP. He and the Black lawyer Francis M. Dent became well known for their work in attacking racially restrictive deed covenants in Michigan. In 1948, their case *Sipes v. McGee*, 316 Mich. 614 (1947), was decided as a companion case with the U.S. Supreme Court's landmark decision *Shelly v. Kraemer*, 334 U.S. 1 (1948). See Littlejohn and Hobson, "Black Lawyers, Law Practice, and Bar Associations," 36–37.

55 Sugar attended some meetings of the committee. Crockett Defense Committee, "Summary of Minutes of Meetings Re: Crockett Disbarment, June 10, 1952," ELC. Crockett's records contain letters to Sugar from himself and Dean Robb, the committee's executive secretary, advising him of developments and seeking advice.

56 "Memorandum to Smith Act Defendants Subject: Staff," December 11, 1952, 1, Goodman Collection.

57 Ibid., 4.

58 Ibid.

59 Ibid., 2.

60 Ibid.

61 Ibid., 3, 4.

62 "On U.S. History," n.d., Goodman Collection.

63 Ibid., 4.

64 Ibid.

65 Ibid.

66 Ibid., 1.

67 Ibid., 2.

68 Babson, Riddle, and Elsila, *Color of Law*, 253–54.

69 Ibid., 254.

70 "Memo on the Memos," December 1952, 2, Goodman Collection.

71 Babson, Riddle, and Elsila, *Color of Law*, 265.

72 Goodman/Littlejohn interview, December 4, 1995. This version of the original interview was edited and revised by Littlejohn and Goodman. Goodman's main argument was that the Michigan statute's definitions of *communist* and *Communist Party* were void because of their vagueness. Because Goodman had filed suit in federal court five days after the law became effective, there had been no state court interpretation of it. The Supreme Court remanded the case for construction of the statute by the Michigan courts. *Albertson v. Millard*, 345 U.S. 242 (1952).

73 See Littlejohn and Hobson, "Black Lawyers, Law Practice, and Bar Associations," 42.

74 Davenport was appointed assistant prosecutor in 1945; he remained there until 1956, when he was appointed to the Detroit Common Pleas Court. In 1957, he was appointed judge of Detroit Recorder's Court, where he remained until 1976. Ibid., 28–29.

75 Jones was an assistant Wayne County prosecutor from 1935 to 1944. He was appointed to an unexpired term on the Recorder's Court bench in 1950 and became Michigan's first Black judge. Later, he was unsuccessful in a bid to be elected to the post. Ibid.

76 Crockett/Littlejohn interview (telephone), May 7, 1997.

77 Harry Sacher to George Crockett, May 4, 1953, ELC.

78 Babson, Riddle, and Elsila, *Color of Law*, 255.

79 Ibid.

80 Ibid., 257.

81 Ibid., 258.

82 Ibid., 259.

83 Ibid., 258.

84 Ibid., 261.

85 Ibid., 264.

86 Maurice Sugar to Osmond K. Frankel, March 8, 1954, ELC.

87 George Crockett to Harold Medina, March 8, 1954, ELC.

88 Sugar to Frankel, March 8, 1954.

89 Transcript, *U.S. v. Foster*, C 128–87, March 19, 1954, 4.

90 Crockett/Lonergan interview, March 27, 1987.

91 State Bar of Michigan Grievance Committee No. 8, "Findings and Recommendations of the Committee, in the Matter of George W. Crockett Jr.," March 23, 1954. An Order to Show Cause based on the report was by Wayne County Circuit Judge Chester P. O'Hara, Case No. 80579, October 11, 1954.

92 The judges were Herman Dehnke, presiding; Archie D. McDonald; and Edward T. Kane. See Opinion, *In re* George W. Crockett Jr., Circuit Court for County of Wayne, No. 80579, October 11, 1954.

93 Crockett's records contain the prepared statement he read and filed with the court on November 12, 1954, ELC.

94 See Opinion, *In re* George W. Crockett Jr.

95 Ibid.

96 Crockett/Littlejohn interview, March 29, 1993.

97 *Offutt v. U.S.*, 348 U.S. 11, 14 (1954). The *Offutt* opinion was written by Justice Frankfurter. It relied on *Cooke v. U.S.*, 267 U.S. 517 (1925), which was based on the Court's supervisory authority over the federal courts. Justices Black and Douglas concurred but would have given the petitioner a jury trial, as they argued in their *Sacher* dissents (*Offutt*, 348 U.S. at 18).

98 *Codispoti v. Pennsylvania*, 418 U.S. 506, 529 (1974).

99 418 U.S. 488 (1974). *Taylor* amounted to a *sub silentio* overruling of *Sacher*. See also *Codispoti*, 418 U.S. 506, which was decided the same day as the *Taylor* case.

100 *Bloom v. Illinois*, 391 U.S. 194 (1968).

101 *Taylor*, 348 U.S. at 501–2. The *Taylor* case was argued by Professor Robert A. Sedler, the authors' colleague at the Wayne State University Law School. Unlike *Offutt*, *Taylor* was a state court case. Accordingly, the rights guaranteed in *Taylor* were based on the Due Process Clause of the Fourteenth Amendment. See Robert A. Sedler, "The Summary Contempt Power and the Constitution: The View from Without and Within," *New York University Law Review* 51, no. 1 (1976): 34–93; Melvin B. Lewis, "Judicial Forging of a Political Weapon: The Impact of the Cold War on the Law of Contempt," *John Marshall Law Review* 27, no. 1 (1993): 3–24; Note, "The Modem Status of the Rules Permitting a Judge to Punish Direct Contempt Summarily," *William & Mary Law Review* 28, no. 3 (1987): 553–82.

102 Babson, Riddle, and Elsila, *Color of Law*, 265, 271.

103 *Wellman v. U.S.*, 227 F.2d 757 (6th Cir. 1955).

104 *Nowak v. U.S.*, 238 F.2d 282 (6th Cir. 1956).

105 For a detailed discussion, see Belknap, *Cold War Political Justice*, 132–45.

106 350 U.S. 497 (1956).

107 *Albertson v. Attorney General*, 345 Mich. 519 (1956).

108 354 U.S. 298 (1957).

109 Chief Justice Fred Vinson died in 1953 and was replaced by Earl Warren, who led the Court in a constitutional law revolution that began with *Brown v. Board of Education*, 347 U.S. 483 (1954). In 1954, Justice Robert Jackson died and was replaced by Justice John Marshall Harlan, the namesake and grandson of the famous justice who dissented powerfully in *Plessy v. Ferguson*, the Court's notorious "separate but equal" decision.

Justice William Brennan was appointed to the Court as a replacement for Justice Sherman Minton. All three were appointed by President Eisenhower and were regarded as opponents of the Smith Act. In the *Yates* case, only Justice Clark dissented. For discussion of changes in the justices and their roles in *Yates,* see Belknap, *Cold War Political Justice,* 236–48.

110 *Yates,* 354 U.S. at 321.

111 367 U.S. 290, 297 (1961). This case involved a prosecution under the "membership clause" of the Smith Act, 18 U.S.C.A., § 2385, which the government attempted to avoid the rigorous evidentiary requirements established by *Yates.* See also *Scales v. U.S.,* 367 U.S. 203, which was decided the same day as *Noto* and affirmed a "membership clause" conviction. For discussion of *Scales,* see Lucius J. Barker and Twiley W. Barker Jr., *Freedoms, Courts, Politics: Studies in Civil Liberties* (New York: Prentice-Hall, 1965), 95–125.

112 By 1956, the attorney general reported that after *Dennis* there had been 18 trials and 108 convictions, including the *Dennis* defendants under the Smith Act's conspiracy and advocacy clauses. The act's membership clause was less "fertile" for the government. By 1960, there had been only seven indictments and five convictions. Only the *Scales* conviction was sustained by the Supreme Court. See Belknap, *Cold War Political Justice,* 157–95, for additional case results data. In *Brandenburg v. Ohio,* 395 U.S. 444 (1961), the Court "thoroughly discredited its holding in *Whitney v. California,* 274 U.S. 357 (1927) that advocating violent means for change could be outlawed merely because it involved" danger to the security of the state (395 U.S. at 447). Justice Douglas's concurring opinion made specific reference to *Dennis*: "I see no place in the regime of the First Amendment for any 'clear and present danger' test, whether strict and tight as some would make it, or free-wheeling as the Court in Dennis rephrased it" (395 U.S. at 454). The proper distinction, Douglas wrote, "is the line between ideas and overt acts" (395 U.S. at 456). The modern or Brandenburg Test for illegal speech requires advocacy that (1) is directed to inciting or producing imminent lawless action and (2) is likely to incite or produce such action (395 U.S. at 447).

113 *Wellman v. U.S.,* 354 U.S. 931 (1957).

114 Babson, Riddle, and Elsila, *Color of Law,* 273.

115 *Maisenberg v. U.S.,* 356 U.S. 670 (1958).

116 Goodman/Littlejohn interview, December 4, 1995. This version of the original interview was edited and revised by Littlejohn and Goodman.

117 Crockett speech notes, March 29, 1993.

118 Crockett/Littlejohn interview, March 29, 1993.

Chapter 6. Early 1960s

1 Committee on Un-American Activities, U.S. House of Representatives, *Guide to Subversive Organizations and Publications* (revised and published December 1, 1961, to supersede *Guide* published January 2, 1957), 121, ELC.

2 Babson, Riddle, and Elsila, *Color of Law*, 274.

3 Victor Rabinowitz, *Unrepentant Leftist: A Lawyer's Memoir* (Urbana: University of Illinois Press, 1996), 174.

4 Jack Greenberg, *Crusader in the Courts: Legal Battles of the Civil Rights Movement* (New York: Twelve Tables, 2004), 377.

5 Ibid.

6 Ibid.

7 See, e.g., "Judge Crockett: Lightning Rod for Controversy," *Detroit News*, April 6, 1969; S. Huck, "When the Reds Run a City," *Review of the News*, June 26, 1974, largely a right-wing diatribe aimed primarily at Crockett and Coleman A. Young (elected Detroit mayor in 1973).

8 W. E. B. Du Bois, *Darkwater: Voices from Within the Veil* (1920; repr., New York: Cosimo Classics, 2007), 8.

9 Crockett/Lonergan interview, March 27, 1987, 5.

10 Crockett/Lonergan interview, December 1, 1988, 18.

11 Ibid., 19.

12 Ibid., 10.

13 Goodman/Littlejohn interview, March 14, 1991.

14 Goodman/Littlejohn interview, November 26, 1995, 3.

15 Ibid., 10.

16 Babson, Riddle, and Elsila, *Color of Law*, 281, 282, 283 (quoting the Goodmans' letters).

17 Littlejohn and Hobson, "Black Lawyers, Law Practice, and the Bar Associations," 55.

18 Ibid., 55–56.

19 Ibid., 56–57.

20 George W. Crockett Jr. to the editor of the *New York Times*, April 22, 1963, 2, ELC.

21 Crockett, "Racism in American Law" (1991). "The legal profession has had very little attraction for Negro youth. Black lawyers constitute the lowest percentage of Negroes in any professional group. There are two primary reasons for this. First, because for a hundred years, we were excluded from a fair opportunity to obtain a legal training. Secondly, because the national image of the Negro lawyer has afforded black youth very little prospect of financial success" (128).

22 George W. Crockett Jr. to William L. Patterson, November 6, 1951, ELC.
23 Babson, Riddle, and Elsila, *Color of Law*, 293.
24 Robert F. Williams, *Negroes with Guns* (New York: Marzani and Nunsell, 1962).
25 Babson, Riddle, and Elsila, *Color of Law*, 293.
26 Interim Report of the Committee to Assist Southern Lawyers, Approved by the Executive Board of the National Lawyers Guild, June 9, 1962, submitted by Co-Chairmen George W. Crockett, Jr. and Ernest Goodman and Co-Secretaries Len Holt and Benjamin Smith, 1, ELC.
27 Rabinowitz, *Unrepentant Leftist*, 175.
28 Ernest Goodman, "The NLG, the FBI and the Civil Rights Movement: 1964—A Year of Decision at 3" (unpublished manuscript, n.d.), ELC.
29 Address by Ernest Goodman at the First Baptist Church, Petersburg, Virginia, March 28, 1962, under the auspices of the Southern Christian Leadership Conference, ELC.
30 Interim Report of the Committee to Assist Southern Lawyers, 4.
31 Ibid., 3.
32 Morton Lesson, letter following appearance in federal court on behalf of Sam Mitchell in June 1962, n.d., ELC.
33 Irving Rosenfeld, "Report on Guild Committee Participation at Two Conferences in the South," n.d., 1, ELC.
34 George W. Crockett, "Report on the Conference with the American Bar Association—Committee on Civil Rights, May 26, 1962," 1, ELC.
35 Ibid., 2.
36 "A Workshop Seminar for Lawyers on Civil Rights and Negligence Law" (conference brochure, 1962), ELC.
37 Ibid.
38 Greenberg, *Crusader in the Courts*, 374.
39 Ibid.
40 Ibid., 360–65.
41 Arthur Kinoy, *Rights on Trial: The Odyssey of a People's Lawyer* (Cambridge, MA: Harvard University Press, 1983), 181–82.
42 Ibid., 184.
43 Ibid., 189; William M. Kunstler, *Deep in My Heart: The First Person Story of a "Freedom Lawyer" and His Battles in Countless Dixie Courtrooms* (New York: William Morrow, 1966), 215.
44 Kinoy, *Rights on Trial*, 181 (quoting Holt).
45 Ibid., 185.
46 Ibid., 186.
47 Ibid., 187.

48 Ibid., 188.

49 Ibid.; for other accounts of the meeting, see Len Holt, *Act of Conscience* (Boston: Beacon, 1965), 108–10; and Babson, Riddle, and Elsila, *Color of Law*, 310–11. Jack Greenberg uncharitably asserted that Holt "wasn't a very good lawyer or reliable" (*Crusader in the Courts*, 380). "Reliability" is an interesting notion. Holt was reliable to the Black citizens of Danville. He had the trust and faith of his clients and was a very effective bottom-up movement lawyer. Conversely, Greenberg was a very effective top-down movement lawyer. While it can be tempting to want to choose sides, the world is more complicated than that. Tensions are rife in complex problems like the United States' history of racial oppression. In retrospect, it is sometimes more constructive to acknowledge and understand the competing tensions rather than to pass judgment or try to artificially resolve them.

50 Holt, *Act of Conscience*, 136.

51 Kinoy, *Rights on Trial*, 190–91.

52 Ibid., 190.

53 Babson, Riddle, and Elsila, *Color of Law*, 313 (quoting interview with Nate Conyers, August 22, 2007).

54 Kinoy, *Rights on Trial*, 177–208; Kunstler, *Deep in My Heart*, 211–32; Babson, Riddle, and Elsila, *Color of Law*, 308–20; Holt, *Act of Conscience*, 132–59.

55 Babson, Riddle, and Elsila, *Color of Law*, 312.

56 Ibid. (quoting interview with Nate Conyers, August 22, 2007).

57 Ibid., 307.

58 Kinoy, *Rights on Trial*, 213.

59 Ibid., 215.

60 Babson, Riddle, and Elsila, *Color of Law*, 318.

61 Kinoy, *Rights on Trial*, 215.

62 Ibid., 218.

63 At first, no one suspected the depth of the government conspiracy. It appeared that this was an action of state and local police officials, but there was a darker hand at play. The raid on the NLG and SCEF was planned and coordinated with U.S. Senator James Eastland of Mississippi, arguably the most powerful member of the southern white power structure, in conjunction with the Internal Security Subcommittee of the Senate Judiciary Committee. J. G. Sourwine, counsel to the Senate Subcommittee, "had actually been in New Orleans the day of the raid, fully equipped with blank subpoenas signed by Eastland." The seized documents, technically under control of the U.S. Senate, were subsequently transported across state lines to Mississippi. Ibid., 220.

64 Ibid., 219.
65 380 U.S. 479 (1965).
66 Babson, Riddle, and Elsila, *Color of Law*, 327.
67 Ibid.
68 Rabinowitz, *Unrepentant Leftist*, 178.
69 Babson, Riddle, and Elsila, *Color of Law*, 327–30.
70 Ernest Goodman and George W. Crockett Jr., "Convention Report of the National Lawyers Guild's Committee to Assist Southern Lawyers (CASL)," n.d. [1964], 2–3, ELC.
71 Ibid., 3–4.
72 Ibid., 4–5.
73 Ibid., 5.
74 Ibid., 7–8.
75 Ibid., 10.
76 National Lawyers Guild, "Project Mississippi: An Account of the National Lawyers Guild Program of Legal Assistance to Civil Rights Workers in Mississippi: Summer 1964," n.d., 5, compiled by David P. Welsh, ELC.
77 "Convention Charts New Guild Course," *National Lawyers Guild Newsletter*, no. 1 (May 15, 1964): 1, ELC.
78 Ibid.
79 Babson, Riddle, and Elsila, *Color of Law*, 331–32.
80 Ibid., 332.
81 Ibid., 334.
82 "What Is COFO? Mississippi: Structure of the Movement and Present Operation" (COFO Publication #6, n.d.), ELC.
83 Len Holt, *The Summer That Didn't End: The Story of the Mississippi Civil Rights Project of 1964* (1965; repr., New York: Da Capo, 1992), 32.
84 Ibid.
85 Babson, Riddle, and Elsila, *Color of Law*, 334.
86 Holt, *Summer That Didn't End*, 32.
87 Ibid., 90.
88 Ibid.
89 James Forman, *The Making of Black Revolutionaries* (Seattle: University of Washington Press, 2000), 380–81.
90 Greenberg, *Crusader in the Courts*, 378.
91 Forman, *Making of Black Revolutionaries*, 381.
92 Memorandum to National Lawyers Guild Executive Board, from George W. Crockett Jr. and Benjamin Smith, Co-Chairs Committee for Legal Assistance in the South, concerning Mississippi Summer Program, n.d., 1, ELC.
93 Ibid. (emphasis in original).

94 Ibid.

95 Ibid., 2.

96 National Lawyers Guild Committee for Legal Assistance in the South, Orientation Conference Program, June 5–6, 1964, ELC.

97 Babson, Riddle, and Elsila, *Color of Law*, 338–39.

98 "Guild Establishes Field Office in Jackson, Mississippi," n.d., ELC.

99 Ibid.

100 Crockett and Smith, "Mississippi Summer Program," 2.

101 Holt, *Summer That Didn't End*, 38.

102 Memorandum from Ernest Goodman, President, to All Members of the National Lawyers Guild, concerning Mississippi, and the Guild Committee for Legal Assistance to the South, April 15, 1964, 2, ELC.

103 Affidavit of Eli Hochstedler, April 21, 1964, 1, ELC.

104 Ibid.

105 "Instruction Sheet, From George W. Crockett, Jr., Program Director, To: All Attorneys Participating in the Guild's Mississippi Project," 1–2, in Attorney Brochure on Mississippi Law relating to Civil Rights and Constitutional Guarantees, June 6, 1964, ELC.

106 Ibid., 2.

107 NLG, "Project Mississippi," 12.

108 Babson, Riddle, and Elsila, *Color of Law*, 339 (quoting Crockett/Lonergan interview, May 15, 1987).

109 Ibid.

110 NLG, "Project Mississippi," 10.

111 Ibid., 10–12.

112 Louis E. Lomax, "The Road to Mississippi," in *Mississippi Eyewitness: The Three Civil Rights Workers—How They Were Murdered* (Menlo Park, CA: E. M. Keating, 1964), 11.

113 Ibid., 12.

114 NLG, "Project Mississippi," 12.

115 Quoted in Lomax, "Road to Mississippi," 8.

116 William M. Kunstler, "Mississippi Violence and Federal Power," in *Mississippi Eyewitness*, 26.

117 Lomax, "Road to Mississippi," 12.

118 Babson, Riddle, and Elsila, *Color of Law*, 342 (quoting Crockett/Lonergan interview, May 15, 1987, 6–7).

119 Ibid., 333.

120 Holt, *Summer That Didn't End*, 20.

121 Lomax, "Road to Mississippi," 14–19.

122 NLG, "Project Mississippi," 14.

123 Ibid.

124 Ibid., 15.

125 "George W. Crockett, Jr.," *Encyclopedia.com*, https://www.encyclopedia.com/education/news-wires-white-papers-and-books/crockett-george-w-jr.

126 Anna Johnson Diggs to President Lyndon Baines Johnson, June 23, 1964, ELC.

127 "NLG Press Release: For Immediate Release," June 25, 1964, ELC.

128 NLG, "Project Mississippi," 9.

129 Rabinowitz, *Unrepentant Leftist*, 179.

130 NLG, "Project Mississippi," 15.

131 Ibid., 7.

132 Ibid., 8 (ellipsis in original).

133 Ibid., 18.

134 George W. Crockett Jr. to Mr. W. L. Sims, Lowndes County Bar Association, July 2, 1964, 2, ELC.

135 Ibid., 2–3.

136 George W. Crockett Jr. to Samuel Koenigsberg, July 13, 1964, 1, ELC.

137 Ernest Goodman, National Lawyers Guild President, and Herman B. Gerringer, National Lawyers Guild Secretary, to Honorable Lyndon B. Johnson, President of the United States, July 14, 1964, 1, ELC.

138 Kunstler, *Deep in My Heart*, 319.

139 Ibid.

140 *Jet* 26 (1964), cover. See accompanying story, which includes references to Crockett and his photograph (16–19).

141 Claudia Morcom, interview by Tom Lonergan, transcript, November 5, 1988, 8–9, 12, ELC.

142 NLG, "Project Mississippi," 23.

143 Ibid., 24.

144 Ibid., 25.

145 Babson, Riddle, and Elsila, *Color of Law*, 352.

146 George W. Crockett Jr. to Ernest Goodman, August 12, 1964, 3, ELC.

147 Ibid.

148 Ibid., 1.

149 Ibid., 2.

150 "Remembering Mississippi, 1964–65: Interview with Claudia Morcom," *Solidarity*, May–June 2014, https://solidarity-us.org/site01/atc/170/p4159/.

151 Memorandum from Claudia [Morcom] to Jim, n.d., 1, ELC.

152 Ibid., 2.

153 Ibid.

154 Kinoy, *Rights on Trial*, 260.

155 Kunstler, *Deep in My Heart*, 326.

156 Ibid., 330–31.

157 Ibid., 333.

158 Ibid., 337.

159 Kinoy, *Rights on Trial*, 281.

160 Memorandum from Ernest Goodman, President, to All Members of the National Lawyers Guild, concerning the 1965 Guild Program in South for Desegregation of Public Facilities, 1965, 1, ELC.

161 Ibid.

162 Ibid., 2.

163 Ibid., 3.

164 Ibid., 4.

165 News Release by Mississippi Freedom Democratic Party, 507½ N. Farish Street, Jackson, Mississippi, 2, n.d., ELC.

166 Charles R. Markels to Ernest Goodman, April 27, 1965, 1, ELC.

167 David G. Lubell to Ernest Goodman, April 30, 1965, 1, ELC.

168 Hugh R. Manes to Ernest Goodman, May 6, 1965, 1, ELC.

169 Memorandum from Ernest Goodman, President, to All Members of the National Lawyers Guild, concerning the 1965 Guild Program in South for Desegregation of Public Facilities, 1965, 1, ELC.

170 Ibid.

171 National Lawyers Guild, Seminar Workshop on Enforcement of Title III of the Civil Rights Act of 1964, Program Brochure, June 12, 1964, ELC.

172 Ibid., 2.

173 Ibid., 3.

174 Babson, Riddle, and Elsila, *Color of Law*, 359.

175 Claudia [Morcom] to Ernest Goodman, June 16, 1965, 1, ELC.

176 Ibid.

177 Ibid.

178 Ibid.

179 Babson, Riddle, and Elsila, *Color of Law*, 359.

180 Goodman, "NLG, the FBI and the Civil Rights Movement," 15.

181 Babson, Riddle, and Elsila, *Color of Law*, 361.

182 Memorandum from Claudia H. Morcom concerning Guild Programs Present and Future, n.d., 1, ELC.

183 Ibid.

184 Babson, Riddle, and Elsila, *Color of Law*, 363.

185 Claudia H. Morcom, Memorandum on Future Guild Operations in the South and Mississippi, n.d., 1, ELC.

186 Ibid., 2.

187 Goodman, "NLG, the FBI and the Civil Rights Movement," 16, 17.
188 Ibid., 16.

Chapter 7. Election to Detroit Recorder's Court, the 1967 Rebellion, and the L. K. Tyler Case

1 Edward J. Littlejohn, "Law and Police Misconduct," *University of Detroit Journal of Urban Law* 58, no. 2 (1981): 173–220.
2 Robert Shogan and Tom Craig, *The Detroit Race Riot: A Study in Violence* (Philadelphia: Chilton Books, 1964), 87.
3 B. J. Widick, *Detroit: City of Race and Class Violence* (Chicago: Quadrangle Books, 1972), 73.
4 Civil Rights Congress of Michigan, "The Leon Mosely Shooting: Fact Sheet," n.d., ELC.
5 Ibid.
6 "Toy Suspends Two Police in Slaying of Boy: Witnesses Say Victim Was Beaten and Shot," *Detroit Free Press*, June 12, 1948, 1.
7 "Open Mosely Case Inquest: Doctor Details Injury to Boy Shot by Police," *Detroit News*, June 21, 1948, 2.
8 "Witnesses Say Mosely Slugged by Policeman," *Michigan Chronicle*, June 1948, 1.
9 "Police Killing Stories Differ: Witnesses Tell Jury Boy Was Beaten," *Detroit News*, June 24, 1948 32.
10 "Police Beat Youth, 4 More Witnesses Say," *Detroit Free Press*, June 24, 1948, 28; "Police Beat Gun Victim, Inquest Told," *Detroit Free Press*, June 22, 1948; "Three Say Mosely Wasn't Warned," *Detroit Times*, June 23, 1948.
11 "Slaying Held Unjustified: Jury Ruling Fails to Fix Criminal Blame," *Michigan Chronicle*, June 28, 1948.
12 The verdict was a banner headline and front-page story in the *Detroit News*: "Patrolman Justified, Court Says: NAACP's Actions 'Assailed as Pink,'" December 20, 1948, 1. See also "Court Blasts Communists, Lauds Melasi," *Detroit Times*, December 20, 1948, 1.
13 "Judge Frees Slayer of Mosely: Policeman Restored to Job at Once," *Detroit Free Press*, December 20, 1948.
14 Uncaptioned judicial opinion by Judge Arthur E. Gordon in *People v. Melasi*, n.d., 1–2, ELC.
15 Ibid., 3.
16 Ernest Goodman to Honorable Arthur E. Gordon, Detroit Recorder's Court, December 29, 1948, 1, ELC.
17 Ibid., 7.

18 Maurice Sugar, letter addressed to Dear Sirs, December 29, 1948, ELC.

19 "13th's Favorite Son: Official Launch Crockett Campaign," March 26, 1966 (no source identified), ELC.

20 Ibid.

21 William Sudomier, "Rights Panel Told to Use Big Stick on Erring Police," *Detroit Free Press*, April 28, 1966, 3B.

22 Ibid. For additional discussions of how police processed civilian complaints in Detroit before and after the adoption of an elected Detroit Board of Police Commissioners, see Edward J. Littlejohn, "The Civilian Police Commission: A Deterrent of Police Misconduct," *University of Detroit Journal of Urban Law* 59, no. 1 (1981): 5–62, 23–31, 42–44.

23 Campaign flier, 1966 Campaign for George W. Crockett Jr., n.d., ELC.

24 Ibid.

25 "Poindexter, Crockett in Court Race," *Detroit News*, June 9, 1966.

26 "4 Negroes Win Boost for Judge," n.d., no source identified, Scrapbook Recorder's Court 1966–72, ELC.

27 Crockett campaign advertisement, *Michigan Chronicle*, n.d., Scrapbook Recorder's Court 1966–72.

28 Morgan O'Leary, "Hectic '49 Trial Haunts Crockett's Bid for Bench," *Detroit News*, October 17, 1966.

29 Ibid.

30 Ibid.

31 Ibid.

32 Colin Moynihan, "Papers Detail Decades of FBI Surveillance," *New York Times*, June 25, 2007, https://www.nytimes.com/2007/06/25/world/americas/25iht-fbi.1.6309392.html. See also Ruth Martin, "'They Feel the Beams Resting upon Their Necks': George W. Crockett and the Development of Equal Justice under Law, 1948–1969," *Michigan Historical Review* 39, no. 2 (Fall 2013): 51–75, 66; and Chip Gibbons, "Obstructing Justice," *Jacobin*, September 2018, 4.

33 Moynihan, "Papers Detail Decades of FBI Surveillance."

34 Anti-Crockett flier, 1966, Scrapbook Recorder's Court 1966–72, 4–5.

35 Ibid.

36 Moynihan, "Papers Detail Decades of FBI Surveillance."

37 Crockett flier, "Solidarity House Must Not Control the Negro Community," n.d., Scrapbook Recorder's Court 1966–72.

38 Ibid.

39 "As We See It: Recorder's Court Needs 11 New, Astute Judges," *Detroit Free Press*, July 28, 1966, 6A.

40 "Thirteen Endorsed for Recorder's Court," *Detroit Free Press*, November 4, 1966.

41 Goodman, Crockett, Eden, Robb & Millender announcement of departure of George W. Crockett Jr., January 1, 1967, Scrapbook Recorder's Court 1966–72.

42 Crockett, "Racism in the Courts," 297.

43 367 U.S. 643 (1961).

44 384 U.S. 436 (1966).

45 Smith, "George W. Crockett," 254.

46 "As We See It: Justice Was Thwarted by Being Taken Lightly," *Detroit Free Press*, May, 27, 1967, 4A.

47 Ibid.

48 John Griffith, "Police Keep Secret File on Judge Crockett," *Detroit Free Press*, May 28, 1967.

49 "Judge Crockett Upheld," *Detroit Free Press*, June 2, 1967 (letter from Louis F. Simmons Jr.).

50 Ibid. (letter from Milton Henry).

51 Crockett, "Black Judge Speaks," 362.

52 "The Administration of Justice in the Wake of the Detroit Civil Disorder of July 1967," *Michigan Law Review* 66, no. 7 (1967): 1554–66 (footnotes omitted).

53 Ibid., 1549.

54 Ibid., 1549–50 (quoting letter from Judge Crockett to the Recorder's Court) (brackets and ellipsis in original).

55 Crockett, "Black Judge Speaks," 362.

56 "Administration of Justice," 1550n30.

57 Crockett, "Black Judge Speaks," 362.

58 "Administration of Justice," 1555 (footnotes omitted).

59 Ibid.

60 Ibid., 1577n148.

61 "As We See It, U-M's Court Study Shows Value of Keeping Cool," *Detroit Free Press*, October 7, 1968, 8A. See also Chester Bulgier, "U-M Study Lashes '67 Riot Justice," *Detroit News*, September 22, 1968, 1.

62 Crockett, "Recorder's Court and the 1967 Civil Disturbance," 842.

63 Crockett, "Black Judge Speaks," 363.

64 Crockett, "Recorder's Court and the 1967 Civil Disturbance," 846.

65 Ibid., 847.

66 "Prosecutor Files Appeal to Crockett Riot Ruling," *Michigan Chronicle*, March 9, 1968, 1.

67 Ibid.

68 Ibid., 11.

69 Babson, Riddle, and Elsila, *Color of Law*, 389.

70 "Judge Crockett Attends Maids Meeting," *Hotel Bar and Restaurant Review*, October 1967, 1, Scrapbook Recorder's Court 1966–72.

71 Babson, Riddle, and Elsila, *Color of Law*, 392 (quoting letter from George Crockett to Victor Rabinowitz).

72 Ibid., 393 (quoting Resolution on Separate Black Nation).

73 Ibid. (quoting letter from Crockett to Rabinowitz).

74 "By Doc Green: The Judge Tells It," *Detroit Free Press*, n.d., Scrapbook Recorder's Court 1966–72.

75 Smith, "George W. Crockett," 254–55.

76 Ibid., 255.

77 Douglas Glazier, "2nd Addict Gets Probation," *Detroit News*, February 20, 1969, 1, 18A.

78 Smith, "George W. Crockett," 253.

79 "Judge Crockett Attends Maids Meeting," 3.

80 Smith, "George W. Crockett," 255.

81 Ibid., 256.

82 "Judd Arnett Says: Day of Reckoning's Here," *Detroit Free Press*, March 2, 1969.

83 "Readers Rap Judge for Felon's Release," The Public Letter Box, *Detroit News*, February 26, 1969.

84 "George W. Crockett Jr.: A Communist Agent in Judge's Robes," *Harper Woods Herald*, March 6, 1969.

85 Political cartoon, *Detroit News*, February 20, 1969, Scrapbook Recorder's Court 1966–72.

86 Al Blanchard, "The New Law," *Detroit News*, n.d., Scrapbook Recorder's Court 1966–72 (ellipses in original).

87 Joseph E. Wolff, "Brennan Lashes Crockett Leniency," *Detroit News*, February 26, 1969.

88 Will Muller, "A Job for the New Judicial Commission," *Detroit News*, February 21, 1969.

89 "As Our Readers See It: Did Judge Crockett Make Right Decision?," *Detroit Free Press*, February 27, 1969.

90 "Guild Backs Crockett: Police Brutality Scored," *Legal Chronicle*, February 28, 1969.

91 Telegram, Fred G. Burton, Chairman, to Judge George W. Crockett Jr., February 28, 1969, Scrapbook Recorder's Court 1966–72.

92 Clark Hallas, "Entry, Cure Hard to Get at Dope Hospital," *Detroit News*, February 27, 1969.

93 Smith, "George W. Crockett," 255.

94 Ibid.
95 Chester Bulgier, "Judge Failed to Inform Police of Brutality Charge—Spreen," *Detroit News*, February 1969, Scrapbook Recorder's Court 1966–72.
96 "By Doc Greene: The Judge Tells It," *Detroit Free Press*, n.d., Scrapbook Recorder's Court 1966–72.
97 Smith, "George W. Crockett," 255.
98 Ibid.
99 Ibid., 256.
100 "Crockett Is Blasted by Parsell," *Detroit News*, March 28, 1969.

Chapter 8. The New Bethel Baptist Church Incident

1 There are two recent resources for readers interested in further investigation of the New Bethel Incident: Say Burgin, "'The Shame of Our Whole Judicial System': George Crockett Jr., New Bethel Shoot-In, and the Nation's Jim Crow Judiciary," in *The Strange Careers of the Jim Crow North: Segregation and Struggle Outside the South*, ed. Brian Purnell, Jeanne Theoharis, and Komozi Woodward (New York: New York University Press, 2019), 235; Matthew D. Lassiter and the Policing and Social Justice HistoryLab, "New Bethel Incident," in *Detroit under Fire: Police Violence, Crime Politics, and the Struggle for Racial Justice in the Civil Rights Era* (University of Michigan Carceral State Project, 2021), https://policing.umhistorylabs.lsa.umich .edu/s/detroitunderfire/page/republic-new-africa.
2 Richard T. Cooper, "Is City Dying of Fear? Racially Distressed Detroit Anxiously Awaits Its Future," *Los Angeles Times*, May 31, 1969, 6.
3 Ibid., 7.
4 Christian Davenport, *How Social Movements Die: Repression and Demobilization of the Republic of New Africa* (New York: Cambridge University Press, 2015), 223.
5 Roger Allaway, "How Police Responded," *Detroit Free Press*, n.d., Scrapbook New Bethel Church Incident, ELC.
6 Crockett/Lonergan interview, May 13, 1989, 1.
7 Lassiter and the Policing and Social Justice HistoryLab, "New Bethel Incident." This intense surveillance leads to an important question that was never examined in the public record. What were officers Czapski and Worobec doing at the church in the first place? It is doubtful that they had any awareness of what was happening with the RNA or the actions of other law enforcement officials. It is very possible that the entire New Bethel tragedy was the product of poor communication and coordination on the part of law enforcement.

8 "Timetable of Events in Shooting," *Detroit Free Press*, March 30, 1969.

9 Ibid.

10 Herbert W. Boldt and Robert M. Pavich, "Two Charged after Gunfight in Church: Ambush Slayers of Policeman Hunted," *Detroit News*, March 31, 1969.

11 Associated Press, "Judge Frees All but 2 Blacks after Duel with Detroit Cops," *Detroit News*, April 1969, Scrapbook New Bethel Church Incident, ELC.

12 William Serrin, "How Did It Begin?" *Detroit Free Press*, March 31, 1969.

13 Ibid.

14 "Black Legislators Decry New Bethel Damage," *Michigan Chronicle*, April 12, 1969.

15 "Two Are Jailed after Slaying of Police in Shootout," *Detroit Free Press*, n.d., Scrapbook New Bethel Church Incident.

16 "Judge Frees All but 2 Blacks."

17 Boldt and Pavich, "Two Charged after Gunfight in Church," 4a.

18 "Two Are Jailed after Slaying of Policeman in Shootout."

19 Boldt and Pavich, "Two Charged after Gunfight in Church."

20 "Crockett: Just Justice," *Argus*, April 14–28, 4.

21 "Timetable of Events in Shooting."

22 Crockett/Lonergan interview, June 15, 1987, 1.

23 *In re* Habeas Corpus Hearing Held at First Precinct, Detroit Police Department, 1300 Beaubien Street, Detroit, Michigan, on March 30th, 1969, in Connection with the Arrest of Certain Persons at the New Bethel Baptist Church, 8540 Linwood, Avenue, Detroit, Michigan, Certificate on Habeas Hearing at 1 (March 30, 1969) (hereafter Certificate on Habeas Hearing).

24 Ibid.

25 "Timetable of Events in Shooting."

26 Standard form for Writ of Habeas Corpus, filled out by Judge Crockett on March 30, 1969, filed in Recorder's Court, March 31, 1969, ELC.

27 Certificate on Habeas Hearing, 5–6.

28 Ibid., 6–8.

29 Ibid., 8.

30 Ibid., 11.

31 Ibid., 12.

32 Ibid., 18.

33 Ibid., 21–27.

34 Ibid., 28–29.

35 Ibid., 31.

36 Ibid., 33–34.

37 Ibid., 46, 47.

38 Ibid., 48, 49–50.

39 Ibid., 51.

40 Boldt and Pavich, "2 Charged after Gunfight in Church."

41 Certificate on Habeas Hearing, 62.

42 Ibid., 65.

43 Boldt and Pavich, "2 Charged after Gunfight in Church."

44 Certificate on Habeas Hearing, 66.

45 Ibid., 53, 60, 69, 73, 77.

46 "Timetable of Events in Shooting."

47 "Two Are Jailed after Slaying of Police in Shooting."

48 Jerry M. Flint, "Controversial Judge: George W. Crockett Jr.," *New York Times*, April 1, 1969.

49 "Judges: Fallout from a Shootout," *Time*, April 11, 1969.

50 "Police Group President Assails Judge Crockett," *Detroit News*, March 31, 1969, 4A.

51 Ibid. (ellipsis in original).

52 Ibid.

53 S. Res. 44, 75th Leg., "A resolution to invoke action by the Judicial Tenure Commission of Michigan" (Mich. April 1, 1969), ELC.

54 Ibid.

55 Al Sandner, "Milliken Joins Call for Crockett Inquiry," *Detroit News*, April 2, 1969.

56 John Peterson, "The Shoot-Out—Step by Step: A Quiet Patrol . . . and Death," *Detroit News*, April 6, 1969.

57 Herbert M. Boldt, "Police Fear Crockett Ruined Search for Officer's Killer," *Detroit News*, April 1, 1969.

58 Leonard Levitt and Charles Manos, "Police, Wives Pickett Crockett," *Detroit News*, April 1969, Scrapbook New Bethel Church Incident.

59 "Milliken Asks Probe of Crockett," *Detroit Free Press*, April 3, 1969.

60 Ibid.

61 Ibid.

62 Ibid.

63 Levitt and Manos, "Police, Wives Pickett Crockett."

64 Ibid.

65 Morrie Gleicher, interview by Tom Lonergan, transcript, October 22, 1988, 1, 2.

66 Ibid.

67 Ibid.

68 Ibid., 3.

69 Ibid.

70 Statement by George C. [*sic*] Crockett, April 3, 1969, ELC.
71 Gleicher/Lonergan interview.
72 Ibid.
73 "Judge Defends Shootout Decision," *Miami Herald*, April 4, 1969.
74 "Judge Crockett Charges Racism: Says Actions Legal," *Jet*, April 24, 1969.
75 Statement by George C. [*sic*] Crockett, 1–2.
76 Ibid., 2.
77 Ibid., 5.
78 Ibid., 6.
79 Ibid.
80 Ibid., 6–7.
81 Ibid., 7.
82 Ibid., 8 (ellipsis in original).
83 "Crockett, Just Justice," 4, 5.
84 "Crockett Raps Press for 'Distortions' of Truth," *Michigan Chronicle*, April 12, 1969, 4.
85 Gleicher/Lonergan interview.
86 Detroit UPI, "Crockett Defends Action as 'Legal, Proper, Moral,'" n.d., Scrapbook New Bethel Church Incident.
87 William Serrin, "Fisher Agrees: Crockett Says He Acted Properly," *Detroit Free Press*, April 1969, 1, Scrapbook New Bethel Church Incident.
88 Ibid., 2.
89 Gleicher/Lonergan interview.
90 "Bar Groups Support Crockett: Urge Restraint by the Public," *Detroit Free Press*, April 5, 1969.
91 "Chief Justice Comes Out in Defense of Crockett," *Detroit Free Press*, April 9, 1969.
92 Allen Phillips, "Against Backdrop of Bethel Case: Brennan Criticizes Arrest Rules," *Detroit News*, April 9, 1969.
93 Rev. Albert B. Cleage Jr., "Message to the Black Nation: Crockett Brings Law and Order to Our City," *Michigan Chronicle*, April 4, 1969.
94 Ibid.
95 "Milliken Blasted on Probe Call: Crockett Support Growing," *Michigan Chronicle*, n.d., Scrapbook New Bethel Church Incident.
96 Amos A. Wilder, "With Our Schools: Crockett Stands High as Symbol of Hope," *Michigan Chronicle*, April 4, 1969.
97 C. C. Douglas, "People, Places and Situations," *Michigan Chronicle*, April 1969, Scrapbook New Bethel Church Incident.
98 Ibid.
99 *Detroit News*, April 15, 1969 (paid DPOA advertisement).

100 "Crockett Ad Defended by DPOA," *Detroit Free Press*, April 19, 1969.

101 "Judge Crockett Tells His Side," *Jackson Blaze*, April 26, 1969.

102 "As We See It: Detroit Cannot Afford to Follow DPOA Lead," *Detroit Free Press*, April 16, 1969.

103 William Serrin, "Crockett Checkup Called Illegal: Police Phone 'Survey' Halts," *Detroit Free Press*, April 1969, 16A, Scrapbook New Bethel Church Incident.

104 WILX TV Channel 10, Commentary, Crockett Removal Campaign, Thursday, April 17, 1969, ELC.

105 "Crockett Ad Defended by DPOA."

106 "Crockett Calls Ruling 'Vindication,'" *Detroit Free Press*, April 23, 1969.

107 *Detroit Police Officers Association v. Honorable George W. Crockett, Jr.*, Michigan Judicial Tenure Commission, Motion to Dismiss Complaint, 1 (1969), ELC.

108 "DPOA Takes Crockett Case to Tenure Commission," *Detroit Free Press*, May 1, 1969.

109 William Serrin, "Crockett Decision Not Reported Out," *Detroit Free Press*, April 26, 1969.

110 Clark Hoyt, "State Judicial Unit Drops Charges against Crockett," *Detroit Free Press*, November 29, 1969.

111 Serrin, "Crockett Decision Not Reported Out."

112 Ibid.

113 William Serrin, "New Detroit May Back Crockett," *Detroit Free Press*, April 25, 1969.

114 Ibid.

115 Law Committee, New Detroit, Inc., "The New Bethel Report: 'The Law on Trial,'" April 1969, introduction, ELC.

116 Ibid., 25.

117 Ibid., 22.

118 Ibid., 22–23.

119 Ibid.

120 Burgin, "Shame of Our Whole Judicial System," 247.

121 Ibid., 254.

122 Law Committee, New Detroit, "New Bethel Report," 26.

123 Serrin, "New Detroit May Back Crockett."

124 Law Committee, New Detroit, "New Bethel Report," 27.

125 "DPOA Raps Report Backing Crockett," *Detroit Free Press*, April 26, 1969.

126 Ibid.

127 "Letters to the Editor: Justice Led to Hostility, Charges Goodman of ACLU [*sic*]," *Michigan Chronicle*, April 26, 1969.

128 "HEAR! The Honorable George W. Crockett Jr. Speak on 'Crime and Punishment in the Black Ghetto,' Saturday, April 26, 1969 at 6:00 p.m.," invitation, ELC.

129 Lee Winfrey, "2,000 Supporters Pay $2 to Hail Crockett at Brunch," *Detroit Free Press*, May 4, 1969 (ellipsis in original).

130 "Academy Award for Human Rights Goes to Judge George Crockett," *Michigan Chronicle*, May 24, 1969, 10.

131 "Prayer Delivered at the Tribute Dinner Honoring Judge George W. Crockett Jr.," May 13, 1969, Scrapbook New Bethel Church Incident.

132 "Remarks by Congressman Charles C. Diggs Jr. at Testimonial for Recorder's Court Judge George Crockett," May 13, 1969, Latin Quarter, Detroit, Scrapbook New Bethel Church Incident (ellipsis in original).

133 "Academy Award for Human Rights."

134 "Judge Crockett Jr. Accepts Invitation to U. of Calif. Law Graduates," *Legal Chronicle*, May 8, 1969.

135 Walker Lundy, "Crockett Gets Support from New Detroit," *Detroit Free Press*, May 21, 1969.

136 *Detroit Free Press* supplement, no title, November 1969, Scrapbook New Bethel Church Incident.

137 Andrew Mollison, "CCR Rips Bethel Case Handling," *Detroit Free Press*, April 1969, Scrapbook New Bethel Church Incident.

138 Susan Holmes, "Officer's Death Condemned: Police Hit in Church Shootings," *Detroit Free Press*, May 21, 1969, 4A.

139 "Who's Polarizing the Community? CCR Should Recant," *Detroit News*, May 23, 1969.

140 Berl Falbaum, "CCR Chief under Fire in Bethel Controversy," *Detroit News*, May 23, 1969, 10A.

141 "DPOA Takes Crockett Case to Tenure Commission," *Detroit Free Press*, May 1, 1969.

142 "200,000 Sign Attack on Crockett," *Detroit Free Press*, May 20, 1969.

143 Hoyt, "State Judicial Unit Drops Charges," 2A.

144 "Racism Is Cited as Cause of Crime," *National Bar Bulletin*, n.d., Scrapbook Recorder's Court 1966–72.

145 Kenneth E. Banks, "Class Justice Gone, Detroit Jurist Avers," *Cleveland Plain Dealer*, August 11, 1969.

146 "Racism Is Cited as Cause of Crime."

147 Banks, "Class Justice Gone."

148 Len Schafer, "Crockett Endorses Austin, Spreen," *Southend*, September 1969, Scrapbook Recorder's Court 1966–72.

149 Ibid.

150 Ibid.

151 John Oppendahl, "Big Court Shakeup Asked to End 4,000-Case Back-log," *Detroit Free Press*, November 20, 1969.

152 John Oppendahl, "Judges Ask Top-Level Talks on Planned Court Shakeup," *Detroit Free Press*, November 21, 1969.

153 "A Devious Ploy: We Can't Buy Court Reorganization Plan," *Michigan Chronicle*, November 1969, Scrapbook Recorder's Court 1966–72, ELC.

154 Glen Engle, "Compromise Offered on Court Shuffle," *Detroit Free Press*, November 29, 1969.

155 Steven Golob, "State Judicial Panel Clears Judge Crockett," *Detroit News*, November 27, 1969.

156 Hoyt, "State Judicial Unit Drops Charges."

157 John H. Gillis, Chairman of the Judicial Tenure Commission, to Chief Justice Thomas E. Brennan, September 25, 1969, Scrapbook New Bethel Church Incident.

158 Hoyt, "State Judicial Unit Drops Charges."

159 "The Judge Is Denied Justice," *Detroit Free Press*, December 4, 1969.

160 William Schmidt, "Court Plan to Transfer Crockett Devised by State Ten-ure Board," *Detroit Free Press*, December 13, 1969.

161 Associate Justice Eugene F. Black to the Editors of the *Detroit News* and *Detroit Free Press*, December 10, 1969, 2, 3, Scrapbook New Bethel Church Incident.

162 John Oppendahl, "Crockett Explains Why He Freed 2 Robbery Suspects," *Detroit Free Press*, December 8, 1969.

163 "But Where Was the Evidence?" *Detroit Free Press*, December 9, 1969.

164 Senate Resolution No. 166, "A Resolution to invoke action by the Judi-cial Tenure Commission of Michigan," December 9, 1969, Scrapbook New Bethel Church Incident.

165 Roger Lane, "Crockett Ruling Spurs Angry Senate Debate," *Detroit Free Press*, December 12, 1969.

166 Senate Resolution No. 166.

167 Senate Resolution No. 163, "A Resolution commending the State Judicial Tenure Commission and expressing public acknowledgement of the pro-priety of the action and fitness for office of Judge George W. Crockett," December 3, 1969, Scrapbook New Bethel Church Incident.

168 Chief Justice Thomas E. Brennan to Mr. Ernest Goodman, December 16, 1969, ELC.

169 "Crockett: Voters to Decide," no source, n.d., Scrapbook New Bethel Church Incident.

Chapter 9. The Struggles in Recorder's Court, 1970–78

1 Heather Ann Thompson, *Whose Detroit? Politics, Labor and Race in a Modern American City* (Ithaca, NY: Cornell University Press, 2001), 128.

2 Ibid., 129.

3 Robert A. Popa, "Judge Crockett: Lightning Rod for Controversy," *Detroit News*, April 6, 1969.

4 Thompson, *Whose Detroit?*, 156 (quoting Ken Cockrel, "Speech at the Repression Conference," January 1970).

5 Ibid., 130.

6 Ibid., 130–31.

7 Ibid., 132.

8 Ibid.

9 Ibid.

10 Lassiter and the Policing and Social Justice HistoryLab, "New Bethel Incident."

11 Thompson, *Whose Detroit?*, 133, 134.

12 Ibid.

13 Ibid., 135.

14 Ibid., 136.

15 John Oppendahl, "Jury Bias Claim Frees Convict," *Detroit Free Press*, n.d., Scrapbook Recorder's Court 1966–72.

16 George Cantor, "Crockett Bail Ruled Invalid: Convict Stays," *Detroit Free Press*, June 21, 1970.

17 "Crockett Ruling Upset by State High Court," *Detroit Free Press*, June 25, 1970.

18 Carol Schmidt, "Crockett Criticizes Chicago Riot Trials," *Macomb Daily*, February 28, 1970.

19 "Detroit Cases Cited: Hoover Assails Lenient Judges," *Detroit News*, May 9, 1970.

20 Chip Gibbon, "Obstructing Justice," *Jacobin*, September 2018, 3.

21 "Detroit Cases Cited."

22 Telegram to Judge George W. Crockett, Recorder's Court, May 9, 1970, Scrapbook Recorder's Court 1966–72.

23 Earl Caldwell, "Black Judge Set Goals at Parley: They Form Their Own Unit at Lawyers' Conference," *New York Times*, August 8, 1971.

24 Ibid.

25 "Black Federal Judge in South Is New Goal," *Detroit News*, August 5, 1971.

26 Crockett, "Racism in the Courts," 296.

27 Ibid., 296–97.

28 Ibid., 297–98.

29 Ibid., 299.

30 "Black Lawyers Demand Voice in Naming Jurists," *Pittsburgh Courier*, October 23, 1971.

31 "Trial of Judge Crockett," *Bay City Times*, July 4, 1971, 1, ELC.

32 Invitation Letter from Judge Crockett Testimonial Committee, signed by Jane Hart and Honorable Damon J. Keith, n.d., Scrapbook Recorder's Court 1966–72.

33 "Crockett to Be Honored," *Detroit Free Press*, October 3, 1971.

34 Governor William G. Milliken to Judge George Crockett, October 26, 1971, Scrapbook Recorder's Court 1966–72.

35 Nadine Brown, "Cite George Crockett, 'Legend in Our Time,'" *Michigan Chronicle*, November 3, 1971.

36 Jim Schutze, "Judge Goes Easy on 7 Gamblers: Calls Law Unfair," *Detroit Free Press*, January 29, 1972.

37 "Crockett Has No Right to Make Own Laws," *Detroit Free Press*, February 5, 1972 (letters to the editor).

38 Judge George Crockett, "Judge Must Weigh Demands of Justice," *Detroit Free Press*, February 11, 1972.

39 Tom Ricke, "Crockett Won't Sign Warrants in Numbers Cases," *Detroit Free Press*, February 26, 1972.

40 "Nixon Bussing Stand Assailed by Crockett," *Detroit News*, February 16, 1972.

41 "Judge Crockett: Vote Yes on Referendum 'E,'" *Michigan Chronicle*, August 5, 1972.

42 Nadine Brown, "We Can Change Courts: Crockett," *Michigan Chronicle*, August 5, 1972.

43 Ibid.

44 Judy Diebolt, "Bar Association Reveals Its Ratings of Judgeship Candidates," *Detroit Free Press*, July 23, 1972.

45 Brown, "We Can Change Courts."

46 Official canvas of votes cast at the primary and special election held in the city of Detroit, August 8, 1972, Scrapbook Recorder's Court 1966–72.

47 John Oppendahl, "Voters OK Adding 7 Judges," *Detroit Free Press*, August 9, 1972.

48 "What They Say about Judge Crockett," George W. Crockett reelection campaign flier, Scrapbook Recorder's Court 1966–72.

49 "As We See It: Voters Have a Good Chance to Better Recorder's Court," *Detroit Free Press*, October 24, 1972.

50 "The Nov. 7 Election: Time for Changes in Recorder's Court," *Detroit News*, October 25, 1972.

51 "Official Election Returns for the 1972 Election of Recorder's Court of the City of Detroit," Scrapbook Recorder's Court 1966–72.

52 Maurice Sugar to George Crockett, June 18, 1972, Scrapbook Recorder's Court 1966–72.

53 Frank Angelo, "He Hunts for Answers: A Judge Bemoans Our Hasty Justice," *Detroit Free Press*, March 20, 1972.

54 Thompson, *Whose Detroit?*, 81–82.

55 Edward Littlejohn, Geneva Smitherman, and Alida Quick, "Deadly Force and Its Effects on Police-Community Relations," *Howard Law Journal* 27, no. 4 (1984): 1133n5. For additional information on STRESS, see Edward J. Littlejohn, "Law and Police Misconduct," *University of Detroit Journal of Urban Law* 58, no. 2 (1981): 208–18; and Edward J. Littlejohn, "The Civilian Police Commission: A Deterrent of Police Misconduct," *University of Detroit Journal of Urban Law* 59, no. 1 (1981): 11–13.

56 Thompson, *Whose Detroit?*, 147. Brown would later tell a *Detroit Free Press* reporter, "The community was being drowned by drugs and the authorized parties [police] ... weren't doing anything. ... We took it upon ourselves to do something about it." Thomas Fox, "STRESS Suspect Says He Fought Pushers," *Detroit Free Press*, April 29, 1973, 3A.

57 Thompson, *Whose Detroit?*, 147–48.

58 Ibid., 148.

59 Melba Joyce Boyd, *Wrestling with the Muse: Dudley Randall and the Broadside Press* (New York: Columbia University Press, 2004), 23–29.

60 Thompson, *Whose Detroit?*, 149.

61 Ibid., 150.

62 Ibid., 152–53.

63 Marty Hair, "1969 Church Arrests Spawned Political Power Change in City," *Detroit Free Press*, March 28, 1989, 14A (ellipses in original).

64 Norman Sinclair, "Toughness Won't Help, Crockett Says: Crime-Poverty Link Outlined," *Detroit News*, May 12, 1976, 22A.

Chapter 10. Crockett in Congress

1 Susan Brown, "A Reformer Judge Retires," *Detroit Free Press*, January 15, 1979, 3A.

2 *New Business Perspectives on the Older Worker: Hearing before the Select Committee on Aging*, House of Representatives, 97th Cong., 1st sess., October 28, 1981.

3 He was active in the Congressional Black Caucus, the Democratic Study Group, the Congressional Caucus on Women's Issues, the Congressional Arts Caucus, and the Northeast-Midwest Congressional Coalition.

4 Jon Schwartz, "Seven Things about Ronald Reagan You Won't Hear at the Reagan Library GOP Debate," *Intercept*, September 16, 2015, https://theintercept.com/2015/09/16/seven-things-reagan-wont-mentioned-tonight-gops-debate/.

5 Jules Lobel, *Success without Victory: Lost Legal Battles and the Long Road to Justice in America* (New York: New York University Press, 2004), 190–91.

6 *Crockett v. Reagan*, 558 F. Supp. 893 (D.D.C. 1982). The lawsuit contained two principal causes of action. First was a violation of Congress's constitutional prerogative to declare war and a failure to comply with the reporting requirement of the WPR. The second cause of action alleged a violation of the Foreign Assistance Act—prohibiting security assistance to governments with gross human rights abuses.

7 Lobel, *Success without Victory*, 192.

8 *Crockett*, 558 F. Supp. at 896.

9 *Crockett*, 558 F. Supp. at 898–99.

10 *Crockett v. Reagan*, 720 F.2d 1355, 1357 (D.C. Cir. 1983).

11 Office of History and Preservation, Office of the Clerk, U.S. House of Representatives, *George William Crockett, Jr.: 1909–1997, Black Americans in Congress, 1870–2007* (Washington, DC: U.S. GPO, 2008), 508 (prepared under the direction of the Committee on House Administration of the U.S. House of Representatives).

12 Ibid.

13 *Congressional Record* 127 (1981): 23861 ("Stabilization and true peace in the Middle East will only come when the United States and all other parties involved seek serious negotiations between Israel and the PLO. Pouring more arms and military equipment into the area will not stabilize anything until the essential problems are addressed."); *Congressional Record* 133 (1987): 34777 ("I believe that closing the PLO offices creates but another obstacle to a peaceful solution of the Middle East conflict. There can be no Middle East peace without the participation of the Palestinian people. I am convinced that the only way a comprehensive peace settlement will be achieved is through an international conference, involving all parties, including the PLO."); *Congressional Record* 135 (1989): 24812 ("There can be no Middle East peace without the participation of the Palestinian people. That undeniably means that the PLO can no longer be excluded. It is ample time for the United States to realize that it must open a full dialog with the PLO and encourage the Israeli Government to do the same.").

14 "Washington Talk Briefing: Crockett under Attack," *New York Times*, February 1, 1987, 50 (quoting J. Michael Waller from the Council for

Inter-American Security, acting as chief spokesman for the American Security Council).

15 Joanne Omang, "Rep. Crockett and the Volley from the Right," _Washington Post_, February 10, 1987 (quoting J. Michael Waller from the Council for Inter-American Security).

16 Ibid.

17 Brown University, "Understanding the Iran-Contra Affair," accessed May 20, 2020, https://www.brown.edu/Research/Understanding_the_Iran_Contra_Affair/n-contrasus.php.

18 _Congressional Record_ 133 (1987): 5402–95.

19 _Congressional Record_ 133 (1987): 15656–16084, 17049–104.

20 _Congressional Record_ 133 (1987): 31694–727.

21 _Congressional Record_ 134 (1988): 3196–3277.

22 _Congressional Record_ 134 (1988): 18430 ("I object to the manner in which this resolution is being brought to the floor today. It by-passes the Foreign Affairs Committee. The Foreign Affairs Committee—and more specifically, the Subcommittee on Western Hemisphere Affairs, which I have the honor to chair—has oversight jurisdiction over United States policy toward Nicaragua."). Instead of increased militarization, Crockett favored peaceful elections and cease-fires. _Congressional Record_ 135 (1989): 28940–60; _Congressional Record_ 135 (1989): 26904–63. National elections did take place in Nicaragua on February 25, 1990, with the (non-Contra) opposition candidate winning. Crockett praised the election's role in finding a peaceful resolution of conflict. "The February 25 election in Nicaragua—pronounced as free and fair by the more than 3,000 international observers—has validated the position that an internal political solution, rather than war, was the answer in Nicaragua." _Congressional Record_ 136 (1990): 2882. This, it was hoped, would be a lesson for others: "We hope that the example that Nicaraguans on both sides of this campaign in settling their differences peacefully and democratically will bode well for El Salvador." _Congressional Record_ 136 (1990): 2883. For Nicaragua, the next steps needed to be toward national reconciliation.

23 _Congressional Record_ 133 (1987): 22759 ("As chairman of the Subcommittee on Western Hemisphere Affairs, I believe the people of Jamaica share with us common ideals of democracy and freedom. Jamaica has always been and will continue to be a bulwark of stability in the vitally important Caribbean region."); _Congressional Record_ 134 (1988): 25069–171.

24 _Congressional Record_ 128 (1982): 10437–541; _Congressional Record_ 130 (1984): 16993–17068.

25 *Congressional Record* 133 (1987): 27720–46 ("The administration has recently certified that the human rights situation in Haiti has improved enough to warrant the release of additional military assistance to the Haitian Government. The facts, however, indicate otherwise.").

26 *Congressional Record* 133 (1987): 32935 ("Mr. Speaker, today, along with my colleagues Mr. Gilman and Mr. Fauntroy, I will introduce a resolution expressing the sense of the Congress in support of the electoral process now taking place in Haiti. His resolution also urges the United States, international and regional organizations, and countries throughout the world to support that process with all the resources at their command. This resolution is a product of our growing concern that not enough is being done to stem the violence that now plagues Haiti."); *Congressional Record* 136 (1990): 9420 ("The tragic irony is that it would only take a small amount of money to make a difference in Haiti. The $20 million authorized by the House Foreign Affairs Committee would have gone a long way toward assisting the Haitian people with critical imports and their elections. I am saddened by the fact that instead of $20 million, the appropriations committees will probably settle for $3 million in new money. Meanwhile, they appropriated over $700 million for Panama and Nicaragua.").

27 *Congressional Record* 134 (1988): 1658–89.

28 *Congressional Record* 134 (1988): 16515. Crockett's lasting contribution to the Caribbean was as a thoughtful critic of the shortcomings of U.S. economic and foreign policy and as a proponent for new approaches. He led efforts examining the Caribbean Basin Initiative (CBI), which gave voice to often excluded groups—community organizations, farmers, church groups, and labor unions. These perspectives helped inform one of the few pieces of legislation Crockett would introduce, the Caribbean Regional Development Act of 1988. This was "a bill to promote equitable and participatory development, national and regional economic integration, and food security and self-reliance in the Caribbean through responsive aid and development policies and programs." *Congressional Record* 134 (1988): 16515. When historically excluded voices are listened to, policies change: "What we heard in those consultations was that our aid is not getting to and benefiting the people who need it. Our consultations produced a series of guidelines for U.S. aid policy that would more effectively promote equitable and just development in the Caribbean" (16515).

29 *Congressional Record* 127 (1981): 8515.

30 Ibid.

31 *Congressional Record* 127 (1981): 18978. Crockett was proud of his progressivism. "My election to Congress gives testimony to what I believe is

an important and abiding sentiment in Detroit and in other parts of the country, that the liberal/progressive tradition is not dead. On the contrary, I believe that in the end the people of this country will not give in to simplistic answers now offered by the conservative platform. The liberal/ progressive tradition will not be cast aside in the name of military 'superiority' or budget-balancing." *Congressional Record* 127 (1981): 16081 (quoting from George W. Crockett Jr., "Michigan Blitzed: A Reagan Budget Case Study," *Freedomways* 21, no. 2 [1981]: 87–92). Crockett was also willing to criticize fellow Democrats over Reagan's 1982 budget: "After the debacle of last year's budget battle, I had hoped that the Democratic leadership would find its way back to the true philosophical strength of the Democratic Party, and stop chasing after the Republican bandwagon which is heading toward the nearest cliff. In my opinion, the leadership has bent over backwards to accommodate those members who, while elected as Democrats, have been voting as Republicans. In the meantime, those of us who were elected as Democrats and vote as Democrats, and the millions of Americans we represent, are left out in the cold." *Congressional Record* 128 (1982): 11757.

32 *Congressional Record* 127 (1981): 17641.

33 *Congressional Record* 129 (1983): 22,628 ("Put another way, unemployment as a major source of stress has consequences for physical health, mental health, and family functioning. Specific examples of the consequences of unemployment can be found not only in the headlines of the daily papers, where the stresses of unemployment are mirrored in the increases in violence, depression, and unhealthy conditions, but also in scientific studies of unemployed individuals.").

34 *Congressional Record* 128 (1982): 30039 ("And the question is: How long will their patience last? I served as a Judge of the criminal court in Detroit in 1967 when the first of our great national riots broke out. It was not one single incident that brought on that manifestation of despair. Instead, it was the accumulation of events, such as the accumulation that is taking place now and that has caused my district to have an unemployment rate the highest in the Nation, 24.9 percent. And many of you are expressing concern about an unemployment rate of 10.9 percent.").

35 *Congressional Record* 128 (1982): 22098 ("Mr. Speaker, I only wish there were time in this body to read to you the names of each of the individuals who signed this petition. Perhaps then my colleagues would have some understanding of the depth of feeling in my district, and in others around this country, for the damage being done.").

36 *Congressional Record* 128 (1982): 18679 ("I cannot believe that Members of this body believe they can justify spending almost $180 billion this year

for so-called national defense, while they can callously deny food stamps to tens of thousands of families; while they can cut health and nutrition programs to millions of children and elderly; while they can reduce education funding so that the next generation will suffer permanent damage; and while they sit back and watch as whole cities are devastated by unemployment, inflation, and industrial malaise.").

37 *Congressional Record* 131 (1985): 6304.

38 *Congressional Record* 131 (1985): 3508.

39 Helen Dewar, "House Acts as One on Soviet Deed," *Washington Post*, September 15, 1983.

40 David Horowitz, "McCarthyism: The Last Refuge of the Left," *Commentary*, January 1988, https://www.commentarymagazine.com/articles/david -horowitz/mccarthyism-the-last-refuge-of-the-left/.

41 Historic Elmwood Cemetery & Foundation, "Jessie Slaton (1908–1983)," accessed May 24, 2020, https://www.elmwoodhistoriccemetery.org/biographies/ jessie-slaton/.

42 *Congressional Record* 129 (1983): 24171.

43 Crockett, "Reforming Foreign Policy," 1157.

44 Ibid., 1158.

45 *Congressional Record* 129 (1983): 24172.

46 *Congressional Record* 127 (1981): 14341.

47 "Africa: The U.S. Stands to Lose a Lot as It Cozies Up to Racist South Africa," *Detroit Free Press*, June 14, 1981.

48 *Congressional Record* 128 (1982): 3528.

49 *Congressional Record* 129 (1983): 9397.

50 *Congressional Record* 130 (1984): 2286.

51 *Congressional Record* 130 (1984): 25884 ("Let there be no misunderstanding of what this resolution represents. With its approval, the U.S. House of Representatives is declaring its abhorrence of the dangerously misguided policies of South Africa with regard to the black, colored, and Asian peoples who comprise the overwhelming majority of that country's population. With its approval of this resolution, the U.S. House of Representatives is calling upon the South African authorities to halt their blind march to tragedy, bloodshed, and violence and to begin a serious attempt at national reconciliation and dialog with all the people of South Africa. Through its approval of this resolution, the U.S. House of Representatives admonishes the Government of South Africa that it is only through discussions and compromise, through hard bargaining and negotiations that a violent revolutionary change can be avoided in the present South African political system, with all the implications that such violence would have for international peace and security.").

52 *Congressional Record* 131 (1985): 22520.

53 Karlyn Barker and Ed Bruske, "Charges against 11 Arrested in Embassy Sit-In Dropped," *Washington Post*, December 1, 1984.

54 *Congressional Record* 131 (1985): 3344 ("Mr. Speaker, the recent governmental actions in South Africa—18 persons killed in the black crossroads squatter camp outside of Capetown and the arrest on charges of treason of six leaders of the United Democratic Front, an alliance seeking nonviolent change—once again highlights South Africa's determination to maintain its repressive apartheid system at all costs.").

55 *Congressional Record* 131 (1985): 14267–389; *Congressional Record* 132 (1986): 7830–93.

56 *Congressional Record* 132 (1986): 13433–527, 16236–315. In 1986, Crockett introduced H.R. 373, in which the government of South Africa was urged to indicate its willingness to engage in meaningful political negotiations with that country's Black majority. In addition to renewing the call to free Nelson Mandela, the resolution called for the formal recognition of the African National Congress. Ibid., 1746–80. Representative Newt Gingrich, a consistent Crockett opponent, opposed the resolution, labeling the ANC a "communist front organization." Ibid., 21142 ("There is strong evidence that the African National Congress is, in effect, a popular front, that at least 19 of its 30 members of its executive committee are members of the Communist Party."). Unlike H.R. 430, this resolution failed to get the two-thirds vote needed to suspend the rules for a vote and, therefore, failed to pass, despite having majority support. "All Actions H. Res.373—99th Congress (1985–1096)," Congress.gov, accessed May 20, 2020, https://www.congress.gov/bill/99th-congress/house-resolution/373/all-actions?overview=closed&KWICView=false.

57 *Congressional Record* 133 (1987): 3492–3590.

58 *Congressional Record* 133 (1987): 28453.

59 *Congressional Record* 133 (1987): 6620.

60 Crockett was always willing to prod an institution to do the right thing. "I would like to believe that the decision by the board to change its stance shows a willingness on the part of the university to recognize and respond to the legitimate concerns of minority students at the University of Michigan—concerns which have been expressed and reported recently in the national news media. I hope it is only one step in a process whereby the university and its minority students can work together to strengthen the university and uphold its commitment to justice and equality—both in Ann Arbor and Johannesburg—and, indeed, throughout the world." Ibid.

61 *Congressional Record* 136 (1990): 2486–87.

62 Charles H. Wright, George Crockett, and Nelson Mandela, program for "The Crockett Legacy: Lessons Learned and Dreams Inspired," 7, International Marketplace, Detroit, MI, February 15, 1991.

63 George W. Crockett Jr., "Forces Standing in the Way of Peace," *Guild Practitioner* 43 (1986): 67.

64 Ibid., 68–69.

65 Ibid., 69. Crockett made similar objections about the lack of people of color in foreign-policy positions on the House floor. *Congressional Record* 127 (1981): 14050–310.

66 *Congressional Record* 127 (1981): 28247.

67 *Congressional Record* 127 (1981): 12997.

68 Ibid.

69 *Congressional Record* 127 (1981): 22859–996.

70 *Congressional Record* 129 (1983): 32674.

71 *Congressional Record* 133 (1987): 13426.

72 *Congressional Record* 129 (1983): 10811–12.

73 "Nation in Brief: Michigan: Lawmaker Calls for Legalizing Drugs," *Los Angeles Times*, December 18, 1989.

74 *Congressional Record* 136 (1990): 5699.

75 *Congressional Record* 136 (1990): 11479.

76 Omang, "Rep. Crockett and the Volley from the Right."

77 Richard Willing, "Detroit's Crusader Moves On," *Detroit News*, October 21, 1990, B1.

78 Written by Judge Wade H. McCree Jr. in tribute to the attorney Harold E. Bledsoe (ca. 1974).

79 "Crockett Gets His Just Reward," *Metro Times*, September 25–October 1, 1996, 9.

Index

Printed in the USA
CPSIA information can be obtained
at www.ICGtesting.com
LVHW040808221023
761614LV00007B/29